Cliometrics as Economics Imperialism: Across the Watershed

Studies in Critical Social Sciences

VOLUME 273

The titles published in this series are listed at *brill.com/scss*

Cliometrics as Economics Imperialism: Across the Watershed

Critical Reconstructions of Political Economy

VOLUME 3

By

Ben Fine

BRILL

LEIDEN | BOSTON

Library of Congress Cataloging-in-Publication Data

Names: Fine, Ben, author.
Title: Cliometrics as economics imperialism : across the watershed :
  critical reconstructions of political economy, volume 3 / by Ben Fine.
Description: Leiden ; Boston : Brill, [2024] | Series: Studies in critical
  social sciences, 1573-4234 ; 273 | Includes bibliographical references
  and index. | Summary: "In Cliometrics as Economics Imperialism, Ben Fine
  traces the cliometric revolution, from before its emergence through
  three phases of the new, the newer and the newest economic history.
  These phases are shown to correspond to those of "economics
  imperialism", the colonisation of topics and fields by mainstream
  economics, moving successively through as if they are perfectly working
  markets imperfectly working markets, and these combined plus arbitrary
  inclusion of other variables"– Provided by publisher.
Identifiers: LCCN 2023042621 | ISBN 9789004689268 (hardback) |
  ISBN 9789004689275 (ebook)
Subjects: LCSH: Economic history. | Imperialism--Economic aspects. |
  Economics–Philosophy. | Economic policy.
Classification: LCC HC59.3 .F528 2024 | DDC 330.9–dc23/eng/20231019
LC record available at https://lccn.loc.gov/2023042621

Typeface for the Latin, Greek, and Cyrillic scripts: "Brill". See and download: brill.com/brill-typeface.

ISSN 1573-4234
ISBN 978-90-04-68926-8 (hardback)
ISBN 978-90-04-68927-5 (e-book)
DOI 10.1163/9789004689275

Printed by Printforce, United Kingdom

Contents

Preface   IX
List of Figures and Tables   XI

1   Economic History as Economics Imperialism: a Retrospective   1
    1   The Personal Background   1
    2   Cliometrics across the Watershed, from General Principles ...   6
    3   ... to Practice   9
    4   Concluding Remarks   28

2   Consumerism and the Industrial Revolution   36
         Postscript as Personal Preamble   36
    1   Introduction   37
    2   Economic History through Which Looking Glass?   39
    3   Is There a Supply and Demand for Industrial Revolution?   42
    4   Economic Theory and the Consumerist Approach   45
    5   Is Emphasis on Demand and Supply the Answer?   50
    6   The Demand for Fashion in Clothes   55
    7   Missing Markets   56
    8   Production of Clothing   63
    9   Persistence of Luxury Goods in Clothing   65
    10   Concluding Remarks   66

3   Economies of Scale and a Featherbedding Cartel? A Reconsideration of
    the Interwar British Coal Industry   71
         Postscript as Personal Preamble   71
    1   Introduction   74
    2   Neither Economies of Scale ...   75
    3   ... nor Featherbedding Cartel   78
    4   Royalties: the Unobserved Barking Dog   84

4   Coal, Diamonds and Oil: towards a Comparative Theory of Mining?   91
         Postscript as Personal Preamble   91
    1   Introduction   92
    2   Minerals and Landed Property   95
    3   Cartels and Minerals   104
    4   Concluding Remarks   114

5 Reflections on and from the Cliometric Revolution   116
        Postscript as Personal Preamble   116
   1   Introduction   117
   2   Cliometrics as Economics Imperialism   119
   3   Discarding Dissent   126
   4   Concluding Remarks   137

6 From Principle of Pricing to Pricing of Principle: Rationality and
   Irrationality in the Economic History of Douglass North   139
        Postscript as Personal Preamble   139
   1   Introduction   140
   2   From New to Newer Economic History   144
   3   Shifting Vision of the Historian of the Western World   149
   4   From Principle of Pricing to Pricing of Principle   156
   5   Concluding Remarks   165

7 Douglass North's Remaking of Economic History: a Critical
   Appraisal   169
        Postscript as Personal Preamble   169
   1   Introduction   170
   2   Theoretical Considerations   172
   3   Making Economic History   177
   4   Theoretical Considerations: a Critique   182
   5   North's Journey from Theory to History: a Critique   190
   6   Transaction Costs in History: a Critique   197
   7   Concluding Remarks   204

8 From New to Newer Economic History   206
        Postscript as Personal Preamble   206
   1   Introduction   207
   2   New and Improved: from as if Perfect to Imperfect Markets   209
   3   Testing the New Product   215
   4   Concluding Remarks   231

9 From QWERTY to Microsoft and Beyond   234
        Postscript as Personal Preamble   234
   1   Introduction   235
   2   David and the Two Goliaths – Economics and History   237
   3   Hayekian Revenge on Path Dependence   250
   4   Culture, Institutions, Narrative and All That Jazz   256

5   Crafting the Newer Economic History   258
6   Finance before Financialisation   261
7   Concluding Remarks   265

References   267
Index   297

Preface

This is the third volume in a series of edited pieces (co-)authored by me. The first two volumes (Fine, 2024a and b) covered general features of economics imperialism from its pre-history, beginning with the marginalist revolution, through to its current phase in which market imperfections alongside other variables to suit are deemed sufficient to address not only the economic but also more or less any other topic or field across the social sciences (and even the humanities). At most, case studies, some in depth and some in passing with references to other work, were illustrative as opposed to central.

This volume is different, offering a detailed encounter between economics imperialism and a particular discipline, economic history, although the focus is primarily upon the cliometric revolution (indicative of the first phase of economics imperialism) and its immediate aftermath – what I call the newer as opposed to the new economic history. The current, newest phase of economic history is only anticipated and touched upon, other than in the introduction in which a retrospective account is given of how its emergence and prosperity reflects both the triumph of economics imperialism as far as economic history is concerned, and its convergence with, or incorporation within, mainstream economics.

Initially, it was intended that the material covered here would appear as case studies in the earlier volumes on economics imperialism. But, to my surprise, as I am no economic historian as such, I found that I had contributed more than enough on economic history, and its relationship to economics imperialism, for it all to warrant a volume of its own. This has also meant that the contents of this volume on economic history, and material from it that might have been assigned to other volumes, has been brought forward relative to initial intentions.

Future volumes are proposed on development economics/studies, mainstream economics, heterodox economics, Marxist political economy, neoliberalism, South Africa, and policy, each of which touches upon economics imperialism to a greater or lesser extent without its being the main business. But to quote, reluctantly in light of repetition avoidance, here is what I had to say about the series as a whole in the preface to the second volume:

> The motivation for these volumes, and the others to follow – is covered in the Preface to the first volume and will not be reproduced here. Suffice it to say that the exercise of revisiting my published work, and placing it in the context not only of scholarship but also more general engagements,

has been extremely rewarding for me personally and, hopefully, will prove so for the reader, especially if interested in both the contemporary scene and its history, not least as a means by which to engage critically with what has been, is, and will be.

I go on to say that bringing economics imperialism up to date gave rise to a surprise. For, whilst economics imperialism has proceeded apace without a break from the time that I first identified it explicitly in Fine (1997a) there is a watershed, around the end of the noughties, in which explicit reference to economics imperialism has moved in the opposite direction to economics imperialism itself – neglect that is characteristic alike of both proponents and critics of mainstream economics. In this respect, economic history is something of an exception, but not because its increasingly extreme subordination to economics imperialism is closely observed post-watershed. On the contrary, it is overlooked but, where it does breach with the more general pattern is that economics imperialism is scarcely explicitly acknowledged for economic history in the pre-watershed period as well. Reasons for this are to be found in the pre-history of economic history itself as economics imperialism, the location of economic history in economics departments in the USA, and the relative absence from the cliometric revolution of the leading pioneers and promoters of economics imperialism, those from the University of Chicago. For details, see Chapter 1.

Otherwise, "One part of the previous preface, I am pleased and obliged to reproduce. For, last, and by no means least, I cannot begin to thank enough those who have supported me throughout my career, particularly co-authors and collaborators but ranging beyond this to family and friends. Appreciation must also go to David Fasenfest and Brill for making the venture possible, and for encouraging and supporting its coming to fruition".

Figures and Tables

Figures

1   Diagram of claim ownership, Kimberley mine, 1877   102
2   Spindletop, the astounding southeast texas gusher which changed the history of America and the world on January 10, 1901   105
3   1903. Horses and carts travel down the plank road called boiler avenue which provided access to Spindletop's boiler locations   106

Tables

1   Amalgamations in the coal industry, 1927–1938   80

Economic History as Economics Imperialism: a Retrospective

1 The Personal Background

I am not an economic historian – I have never taken a single course in economic history, although I did teach on one at graduate level over a number of years, in part as a partial replacement for the retired Eric Hobsbawm.[1] However, if I were to try and claim to be an economic historian, I could muster together a fair bit of evidential dabbling over and above teaching it or, more exactly, an MSc option on modern British economic history – it was so long ago that coverage used to stop at the beginning of the Second World War.[2] Like any serious Marxist political economist, though, I have studied *Capital* in detail, from which the confrontation with economic history is unavoidable, not least the journey through the industrial revolution and capitalism's subsequent history (with Britain as leading case study) as well as the transition from feudalism to capitalism.[3]

Such beginnings offered a number of lessons: the division of (economic) history into distinct periods (modes of production for Marxism, and the different stages within them); the need to limit concepts and theory to specific social and historical contexts from which they should both be drawn and applied; and, for capitalism, attention to its particular relations, structures, processes, agencies and contradictory dynamics in which the imperatives of the accumulation of capital, and the forms that it takes, are paramount. In this vein, work on contemporary developments on the British economy prompted interest in the historical origins of state intervention (and the leading role played by finance and multinational corporations of British origin) (Fine and

---

1 With prominent economic historian, Roderick Floud, and, for one year, with Deidre, then Donald, McCloskey, and Jonathan Zeitlin also involved at a later stage (with severe clashes over the validity of flec-spec).

2 As my daughter said, "Dad you lived in history" and she does not mean in the making but in the past, like dinosaurs. The same applies to historians who are now interviewing me about things that happened in the UK going back to the 1970s and on South Africa in the 1990s.

3 For an overview of Marx's *Capital*, see Fine and Saad Filho (2016) now in its sixth edition and almost its fiftieth year. For value-theoretic contributions on the transition, see Fine (1978) and Fine (1980a).

Harris, 1975, 1976 and, ultimately, 1985). The economic history of the British coal industry became a major focus for research in its own right (Fine, 1990a and b and 1993, and Fine et al. 1985a and b) leading through political connections to work on the South African economy, and its history (especially Fine and Rustomjee, 1992, 1995, 1997 and 1998). Engagement with South Africa, and move to SOAS with corresponding teaching responsibilities, placed development economics and studies on the agenda with its affinities with economic history (of the developed world) with some attention to the developmental state literature (especially and most recently Fine and Pollen, 2018; also Fine et al. eds, 2013).

On an almost entirely separate track from this trajectory, I was drawn into a longstanding study of consumption, especially around consumer durables and food with, once again, considerable attention to its historical aspects. I got into researching the ownership of consumer durables accidentally – a job applicant, whose work I read as an interviewer, had contributed to the topic. I came to the conclusion that the work done on it, even in the narrowest of statistical terms, was flawed.[4] I put forward an alternative method for statistical research drawn from my purely mathematical Phd on social choice theory.[5] This in turn led to a research project on ownership of consumer durables and their relationship to female labour market participation, and to labour markets more generally. Such endeavours both dovetailed with Marxist value theory and the domestic labour debate. Interest in consumption both led to historical studies, and the critique of the notion of an eighteenth-century consumer revolution around

---

4 The problem with the approach to the so-called order of acquisition of consumer durables is that more people could acquire a durable but this could lead it to become lower in the calculated order of acquisition, a violation of the condition of monotonicity! The reason is that its chances of moving to second from third may go up but not sufficiently to beat the durable occupying second, whereas its loss of third positions means it gets beaten there and has to move down to fourth as a result! So now you know. See Fine (1983) initially and Fine and Simister (1995) by when much empirical work had been done, and movement onto food, the nation's diet, was in full swing using the same methods. For a rounded and fuller account in the context of the evolution of the system of provision approach to consumption, see Bayliss and Fine (2021).

5 Although social choice offered considerable pleasures to me as a mathematician in posing and solving varieties of technical issues, and it also got me a job with tenure through publishing in leading journals, I had been inclined to give up the topic as a waste of time. I have reaped the professional rewards of not doing so. However, I have returned to the topics involved over the intervening years to reap their simple pleasures but it has also offered some broader rewards, most recently in addressing how to measure inequality, and in how to understand the complexities of identity, quite apart from informing (empirical) work on the nature of (consumption) norms. See Fine and Mendes Loureiro (2020 and 2021), Fine (2009b) and Fine et al. (1996).

Wedgwood's pottery, and the development of the system of provision approach to consumption, not least through its application to food.[6] The influence of postmodernism and, therefore, the historically and socially specific, remained unavoidable in addressing the economic and historical cultures of provisioning. Another leitmotif was the influence of neoliberalism both in and of itself as an intellectual influence and in setting the agenda for alternatives. This was very different in economics (where it meant perfectly working markets to which the response was imperfectly working markets) than other disciplines (where it meant realms of freedom as opposed to more or less authoritarian forms of induced self-control). Indeed, from the 1990s, developments across the social sciences are marked by what I have termed a dual retreat from the extremes of neoliberalism and postmodernism (Fine and Milonakis, 2003) especially with regard to the understanding of material culture – how, for example, provisioning itself and the cultures of provisioning are intimately and variously intertwined and shifting over time, place, product and person.

It is also worth mentioning that my major assault on social capital, and, indeed, any contribution across any topic, was always open to consideration not only for its relationship to economic history but to interdisciplinarity and the history of (economic) thought more generally.[7] But, undoubtedly, what drew these separate elements together and combined them to some degree into a single purpose was the hypothesis put forward of a revolution taking place within and out of economics, associated with a corresponding second phase of economics imperialism (Fine, 1997a).[8] The first phase, or old economics imperialism, most closely associated with Gary Becker, sought to extend as if perfect market economic principles to the non-market. The second (new) phase, though, especially with Joe Stiglitz to the fore, offered a reaction against the principles of the first by emphasising market imperfections (especially those around informational asymmetries across optimising agents for Stiglitz but also incorporating increasing returns and externalities for others, each more or less precluded by perfect market economics and its antipathy to state intervention). A third phase has followed in which the other two, and especially the second, are complemented by the inclusion of whatever explanatory factor is considered relevant or of interest for whatever reason (and irrespective

---

6   Apart from those already mentioned, my engagements with economic history, led to more or less occasional, but always beneficial, interactions, amongst others, with Barry Supple, Roy Church, Martin Daunton and Frank Trentmann.

7   See Fine (2001b, 2010a and, most recently, 2023a) for social capital, plus Fine (1998a) on labour markets and Fine (2002a) on consumption for example.

8   See Fine (2024a and b) for a full account rather than the drastic summaries that follow.

of consistency and coherence with core economic principles, for example we have utility maximisation but add other behavioural motivations to suit).

Across the three phases of economics imperialism, there are some common aspects that are worth highlighting. First, in establishing its economic principles, much was taken out of economic and social theory (to be taken as fixed or irrelevant) over and above a narrow form of methodological individualism (profit and/or utility maximisation subject to constraints) – given preferences, technologies, endowments, non-market relations and efficiency and equilibrium through perfect competition as the norm from which there might be deviation as a concession to realities.[9]

Second, the colonising of other subject matters, disciplines and fields on this basis, beyond its own dependence upon free-floating markets allowing market supply and demand, necessarily involves bringing back in, BBI, all of those considerations that had to be excluded to establish the original principles in the first place. There can be no individual optimisation subject to constraints if the constraints and goals are variable (and especially if subject to social and historical determinants as opposed to aggregation over otherwise disconnected individuals).

Third, on this basis alone, there are considerable tensions involved for economics imperialism across a number of aspects, both for economists themselves and especially for social scientists, and historians, more generally who are subject to its predations. Quite apart from the legitimate scope of application of economic principles to the economic let alone the non-economic, these concern what is the scope of application of so-called rationality in its dualism with irrationality? How valid is methodological individualism in general, and the corresponding reductionisms associated with mainstream economics, let alone in its given preferences/optimising form, as opposed to attention to the historical, social, structural, cultural and relational? Are formal models appropriate given that they are deterministic (subject to stochastic variation) and, therefore, at most allow for a limited level of scope of application and outcome?

Fourth, for these and other reasons, the incidence and impact of economics imperialism are variegated, contingent upon both how these various tensions, and others, are accommodated, however uneasily, alongside the inherited and continuing traditions of colonised disciplines and topics. There are also non-academic and external factors to consider – whether these be economic or

---

9   The glib characterisation of the differences between economics and sociology – as one being optimal choice subject to constraints, and the other why there are so few choices and so many constraints – is apt as far as it goes.

non-economic or some combination of the two. Can anyone doubt that US hegemony exerts its own influence materially, culturally and academically both in and of itself and by way of the nature of counter-reactions?

Be all this as it may be as a way of framing our understanding of economics imperialism in practice, and further aspects will reveal themselves later, my own confrontation with economic history as economics imperialism falls into two phases of its own. The first phase rests on my contributions to economic history which precede my explicit reference to (the second phase of) economics imperialism but which, implicitly at least, do engage with the issues associated with economics imperialism. Some of these contributions appear in earlier volumes on economics imperialism (Fine, 2024a and b) either as examples of economics imperialism as such or as illustrations of how the reductionisms of mainstream economics after the marginalist revolution have always strayed beyond the economic as understood on its own narrow terms, not least to deal with political and policy issues of the day (Fine, 1980d and1982b). Others appear here (Fine and Leopold, 1990; Fine, 1990b, 1993a and 1994).

The second phase of my work on economic history and economics imperialism, then, follows upon acknowledgement of the latter's own second phase, the new as opposed to the old economics imperialism, beginning with Fine (1997a) as previously indicated. Given that the new economics imperialism is heavily grounded upon the microeconomics of informational and market imperfections, it is hardly surprising that attention was drawn to what started out as the application of the new economic history to business history, with the work of Naomi Lamoreaux and her colleagues to the fore. This is covered in Chapter 8.

But, before any of this could be published, with some minor exceptions, it became part and parcel of much grander ambitions. Initially, economic history more generally was to serve as a case study of economics imperialism, itself to be set in a longer account of the evolving and shifting relations between economic theory (and political economy) and the other social sciences. This also involved a longstanding collaboration with Dimitris Milonakis. As we began work on this project, what was initially a single book became two, and plans were made for one then two further separate books on the evolving relations between economics (and political economy) and economic history. The two books on economics imperialism in general, with passing reference to economic history, eventually appeared as Milonakis and Fine (2009) and Fine and Milonakis (2009). But the two projected volumes on economic history were never finished.

Nonetheless, some of our work for the two volumes was completed, and even published in article form (Fine and Milonakis, 2003; Milonakis and Fine,

2007) appearing here as Chapters 6 and 7. Other work was completed but not published and so can also appear here, not least on Lamoreaux and others, especially Paul David and debate around path dependence, as well as reflections at the time on the cliometric revolution, Chapters 9 and 5, respectively.[10] These offer what remain relevant insights into the shifting relationships between economics and economic history, both in and of themselves as well as what could be identified and understood at the time of writing, however imperfectly.

2   Cliometrics across the Watershed, from General Principles ...

In summary of our position on the new economic history or cliometrics in the noughties, it offered an exemplary case study of economics imperialism as the second, newer phase of cliometrics was gathering momentum and as its third, and newest, phase was noticeably prospective if not acknowledged as such at the time. For reasons already given, it attracted our dedicated attention, not only as it progressed but also for its first phase.[11] More specifically, a comprehensive account was given of the evolving position of Douglass North, acknowledged to be one of the founders of cliometrics, and a major influence on new institutional economics (another classic example of economics imperialism) (Fine and Milonakis, 2003; Milonakis and Fine, 2007). Associated with him, more than for anyone else, the bywords became institutions matter, as does history, or should we say histories.

One glaring absence in our work at the time was an equally close attention to the work of Robert Fogel, acknowledged at the time as being as influential as North in promoting cliometrics, and sharing the 1993 Nobel Prize in Economics with him for having done so. There were a number of reasons for this neglect. First, and probably foremost, is that North served our purposes of specifying the nature and dynamics of economics imperialism more readily than Fogel. Second, such an assessment would have required a full review of *Time on the Cross*, and the huge controversy and literature that it generated around the economics of US slavery and its abolition. We would almost certainly have addressed this before completing our books on economics and economic history but, as indicated, that never happened.

---

10   See also Milonakis (2006).

11   And the "old" economic history of before, against which the cliometric revolution was
      reacting, in drafts by Dimitris that were more or less complete, including my comments.

The purpose here is not to correct this lacuna and offer a full retrospective assessment of Fogel and his contributions to, and influence upon, cliometrics. Nor, unlike our earlier work which tended to project forward on the basis of cliometric's forward march, will this approach be brought up to date – what happened next in more detail. Each of these tasks is too formidable and a major research project in its own right, especially the latter which, to a large extent, includes the former. Bear in mind, as will be apparent and is universally acknowledged, the literature on cliometrics is heavily self-regarding for criticism and shortcomings. Rather, the opportunity will be taken to offer a backward, rather than a forward look, at the evolution of cliometrics by assessing where it is now, and how it got there. In this broader context, some assessment will be offered later on the position of Fogel although, like much else that follows, alternative views will arise out of different perspectives (and be contested) and the gathering of more evidence on who said what and why.

To look back upon the evolution of economic history/cliometrics and its relationship to economics imperialism, I will draw upon two very different sources, one general and the other specific. The general is the overall account of economics imperialism itself from the same backwards perspective, as laid out in the first two chapters of Fine (2024b). Here, a number of key features are identified over and above those already presented in terms of the three phases of economics imperialism, BBI and variegated outcomes across disciplines, fields and topics. Specifically, first, a watershed is identified in the literature on economics imperialism, timed (coincidentally or not) around when our two books appeared and the debates they inspired. Prior to the watershed, there was considerable debate, explicit or otherwise, around economics imperialism, less over whether it was happening and more over whether it was a good thing or not. After the watershed, it is as if economics imperialism does not exist as part of the debate. The issues involved are still discussed but with scarcely a reference to economics imperialism as such. In other words, economics imperialism, although proceeding apace, especially through its second and third phases, is overlooked as a general phenomenon across the social sciences and is treated as primarily an intradisciplinary issue without regard to broader intellectual developments (and their origins and causes).

Second, a major reason for the post-watershed demise of (reference to) "economics imperialism" is that its new (and newer) phase sees itself as absolutely breaking with the old, with the introduction of market imperfections and that history and institutions, and many other things, matter for economic outcomes and for addressing the non-economic. In other words, in what became a popular terminology to some degree, economics imperialism had given way to reverse imperialism, with heavy influence of the other social sciences on economics rather than the latter colonising them. In a nutshell, we are not economics imperialists because we are neither neoliberal nor Chicago, see below. By the same token, unlike the proud promotion of economics imperialism by its proponents in the first phase, not least by Gary Becker and his ardent followers, the new(er) phase of economics imperialism did not recognise let alone promote itself as such. So why would its opponents do so?

Third, the point, then, is not that economics imperialism was in decline, quite the opposite. Nor was opposition as such necessarily in decline, other than in name and it has tended to remain vigorous, especially, in intradisciplinary or topic critique, whether as minority sport or otherwise. Rather, whether it would have been otherwise or not, the silence over economics imperialism allowed it to proceed by at least simplistic reductionism or simple neglect of alternative approaches – treated, often dismissively for lacking theoretical rigour and/or empirical evidence, their varieties of methodologies, methods, theories and conceptualisations as a more or less undifferentiated OTHER, although drawn upon for the purposes of colonisation for variables to include and propositions to examine. By the same token, the mainstream economics' own (admittedly developing) principles and practices become privileged, especially those involving models and econometrics with a prior if wavering commitment to framing around equilibrium, efficiency, optimisation and individualism (but with willingness to suspend these as considered necessary).

There is also a separate, but related, OTHER in the forward march of economics imperialism, deriving from BBI what has been left out by core economic principles. The omitted is the OTHER, not least as it traditionally "belongs" to other social sciences and its principles, etc. As mainstream economics, and economics imperialism, perceive themselves as failing in analytical and empirical terms, the OTHER is called upon as remedy. The most obvious example is institutions as it becomes a proxy for all that is not immediately supply and demand. But the same, to a greater or lesser extent, applies to ideology, culture, norms, customs, trust, social capital, the state, etc, etc, and, not least, history itself. Such OTHERS can, if rarely, overlap with the concerns of other analytical OTHERS, those associated with class, power and conflict. Anything goes in principle if not in practice, especially with the newer phase of economics imperialism.

Fourth, reinforcing the idea of economics imperialism as variegated, interdisciplinary outcomes have been mixed. Economics imperialism can establish itself as a field within another discipline. It can lead to a new discipline or field. It can establish itself within economics. Or it can straddle the boundaries between disciplines. To some degree, which outcome occurs depends upon continuing traditions across the disciplines concerned, the nature of the topic, and the external environment. What economics imperialism cannot do is to engage in meaningful intra-and inter-disciplinary debate, other than marginally and by way of exception as, from the postures of other social sciences, its positions are (correctly seen as) simply extreme and fundamentally flawed.

Fifth, nonetheless, where there is engagement, even where critical, it tends to be around striking a right balance, between theory and evidence, rationality and irrationality, the economic and the cultural, the individual and the social, the inductive and the deductive, and so on. But there is no prospect of balance, of reverse imperialism, other than on the terms dictated by economics imperialism however much it might appear or promise otherwise.

Sixth, echoing the third point above, much of the response to economics imperialism by those critical of it has been to view it primarily from the point of view of scholarship and their own perspectives and, as such, as bordering on the ridiculous and not worthy of critical attention. There may also have been intimidation by the technical requirements in mathematical and statistical terms, dovetailing with what is seen as an undeserved arrogance and (policy) prestige of economics as a discipline.

3 ... to Practice

So much for economics imperialism in general – and looking back at what it has become after the watershed, as the means to locate a corresponding evolution of economic history. The specific source by which I do this is by reference to the cliometric literature itself. But this has become too voluminous to survey as is apparent from, for example, the recent Handbook of Cliometrics which runs to well over 1700 pages (Diebolt and Haupert, eds, 2019). Apart from ploughing through this volume, and casually keeping a watching brief on cliometrics since I last studied it in some depth more than a decade previously, I have now drawn upon another handbook, The Handbook of Historical Economics (Bisin and Federico, eds, 2021) which itself runs to almost one thousand pages.

Much more reference will be made to this latter volume, admittedly as it offers a sharper means than the other Handbook by which to gauge the trajectory of cliometrics, in part because of agreements as well as disagreements, subject to how evidence is sifted and interpreted. Initially, observe, especially given both handbooks, how successful has been the cliometric revolution in its scale and scope, something I suspect is uncontroversial. Interestingly, through bibliographic analysis of journal articles and the like, a judgement is offered that the cliometric revolution was slower than is usually thought, especially given measurement by use of econometrics in economic history contributions.[12] This is explained in part by an intergenerational lag as new methods are learned and diffused but also by resistance to over-reliance upon such formal methods by economic historians themselves, see below. Despite this slowness, and allowing that conceptualisation will have been ahead of technical implementation, there seems little dispute over just how successful (and fast) has been the spread of cliometrics. Indeed, slowness is a hard pill to swallow, given how fast cliometrics has spread geographically (Cioni et al. 2021, p. 24):

> Even if our conservative measure may not capture all true 'Cliometric' articles, one might conclude that by the turn of the 20th century, the Cliometric Revolution had won, at least in the most advanced countries. The approach was dominant in economics departments in the USA and, with some exception, in the United Kingdom and other Anglo-Saxon countries and had made huge inroads in (Western) Continental Europe.

In addition, if now usually taken for granted, the cliometric revolution first and foremost originated in the USA, something that has done much to influence its evolution, character and impact, see below.

Even so, such bibliometric analyses did not, although they could, distinguish the different phases of economics imperialism and the corresponding new, newer and newest economic history. Indeed, Cioni et al. (2021) tend to confine the cliometric revolution to what I have termed its first phase. And, instead of seeing it as passing into a second phase, they argue that there was a second revolution in economic history with two separate elements, leading to a break with the original cliometric revolution. One, originating with Paul David and path dependence, see Chapter 9, is seen by Margo (2021) as deriving from the contributions of Acemoglu and his colleagues,[13] and is renamed Persistence Studies, with acronym, PS. Thus (Cioni et al. 2021, p. 17):[14]

---

12   See Margo (2021, p. 10) and Cioni et al. (2021).

13   Who also contribute to the Historical Economics Handbook (Acemoglu et al. 2021).

14   Note a slightly different take is offered by Margo (2021, p. 3–4) in part to explain the slow diffusion of cliometrics, with two schools, one gung-ho to apply formal economics (associated with Fogel) and the other, eventually, associated with North. Thus: "One school argued that traditional economic history was insufficiently scientific and needed the mathematical and statistical tools of post-war economics to make it more rigorous. Here, the idea was not so much to create new questions for inquiry but, instead, to reinterpret conventional wisdom in light of new data and new methods … The second school of thought was quite different. It viewed economic history as a bulwark against narrow theorizing in economics about the underlying sources of long run growth and development.

> First, scholars have started to look for the historical origins of current outcomes, hence persistence studies (henceforth PS). The idea of path dependency had first been put forward in a famous paper by David (1985) on the QWERTY keyboard, but arguably the Second Revolution was started by the publication of the seminal paper by Acemoglu et al. (2001) on the effect of colonial institutions on levels of development in 1995.

The other involves not so much PS but the incorporation of the non-economic and is seen to derive from Gary Becker and, as a result, continuing from above:

> Second, economists have extended to historical issues their interest in 'non-economic outcomes studies' (henceforth NEOS) which dates back at least to the seminal work by Becker.

Whilst it is claimed that "the overlap between PS and NEOS is minimal", p. 29, this is scarcely credible now given the scope of variables that fall under PS, not least colonial institutions and the like, unless the distinction is being drawn by use of explanatory outcomes as opposed to explanatory variables. Indeed, there is absolutely no reason why persistence and the non-economic should not be jointly applied. From my perspective, both PS and NEOS share more in common as newer forms of economics imperialism than they differ with one another and, as such, also conform to later phases of cliometrics rather than a second revolution at its expense (as amply confirmed by the Handbook devoted to cliometrics). Nonetheless, there are logical (or definitional) and historical conundrums to be addressed in interrogating the forms and content of cliometrics over time, and whether the hypothesis of economics imperialism does rough justice to these or not.

Against this backdrop, I will take a look at the cliometric revolution and its aftermath through the prism of the more general account of economics imperialism offered in the previous section. First, is there a watershed in the acknowledgement of economics imperialism in the trajectory of the cliometric revolution? Certainly, following the watershed, there is hardly any reference in the economics history literature to economics imperialism as discussed more generally in Fine (2024b, Chapters 1 and 2). In the Historical Handbook, I identified just one reference on a more or less casual reading across the entire collection. It is in the overall introduction in which, remarkably, Bisin and

---

... The second school I associate with Douglass North – although, again, there were many others who made similar arguments (and still do)".

Federico (2021, p. xv) suggest that, "We think of Cliometrics as an acquisition of economics by history in the sense that historians trained in economics started to use formal economic reasoning and statistical testing to tackle big issues". Nonetheless, what I have termed an example of the old economics imperialism, rather than as reverse imperialism as they imply, is soon reversed in their account. They observe, "one other perhaps less prominent but nevertheless essential feature of [sic or?] important aspect of recent work in Historical Economics is the expansion of the boundaries of the discipline beyond economic themes as traditionally intended", to which a footnote is added, "This is also consistent with a trend in economics – which is at times accused of an 'imperialist attitude' towards social sciences in general", p. xvi.[15]

So, after the watershed, the trajectories of newer and newest economic history are not explicitly conscious of economics imperialism. But what about before the watershed for the cliometric revolution itself, and the new economic history as it first emerged as an instance of the old economics imperialism in its first phase. Here, there is an anomaly since the overt acknowledgement of economics imperialism is notable, but for its absence. There are a number of reasons for this, each of wider significance for the continuing relations across economic history, economics imperialism and economics itself. As is generally acknowledged as an important factor in the emergence of the new economic history, one more or less unique to the USA, economic history had traditionally been located in economics not history departments, and had been a compulsory course for students. As a result, as the first phase of economics imperialism was emerging in the post-war period more generally, it was inevitable that there would be those trained in both economics and economic history who would be to the fore in promoting the new economic history.

This is why cliometrics could experience a rapid rise, irrespective of the degree to which it was or was not promoted as economics imperialism as such. However, the "old" economic history had a long history of debate over the relative merits of economic theory as the foundation of economic history, running back to the methodenstreit of the 1880s, just after the marginalist revolution, which primarily concerned the relative merits of induction and deduction. In addition, the old institutional economics of the 1930s still exerted continuing influence, especially as it captured major empirical developments in the US economy, around the rise of corporatism, trade unionism, welfarism, technological change, and the impact of the Great Depression.

---

15   Note imperialism does not warrant any sort of mention in the index to the Handbook, and the colonial only four entries, indicating the slant of the contributions. The other Handbook is no less negligent of the imperial but more generous to the colonial.

In this light, it is hardly surprising that prospective cliometricians should be sensitive to the issues involved in promoting the new economic history as an example of economics imperialism. Indeed, many leading neoclassical economists themselves, such as Arrow and Solow, expressed concern over the undue extension of the economic principles they themselves had developed, or were developing, beyond a narrow scope of application. As Solow (1986, p. 21) neatly puts it on behalf even of traditional neoclassicals, there is:[16]

> the sinking feeling that a lot of it ... gives back to the theorist the same routine gruel that the economic theorist gives to the historian. Why should I believe, when it is applied to thin eighteenth-century data, something that carries no conviction when it is done with more ample twentieth-century data?

In retrospect, and observed by others on many previous occasions from its origins onwards as already mentioned, cliometrics was not only popular amongst its proponents, but also subject to intensive critical self-examination, Diebolt and Haupert (2022, p. 15) muse:

> How did cliometrics, in particular, and economic history, in general, arrive at this crossroads, where it is at once considered to be a dying discipline and one that is spreading through the economics discipline as a whole?

With economic history both successful within economics and losing itself in one discipline at the expense of the other, a corresponding identity crisis persists. Unsurprisingly, cliometrics gave rise, and continues to do so in its later phases, to a tripartite division between those who support it gung ho (never

---

16 This is echoed over thirty years later by Fenoaltea (2019, p. 11) in the opening contribution to a special issue continuing to bemoan the deficiencies of cliometrics, or to praise its achievements in response: "We have become no more than economists who deal with yesterday's numbers rather than today's: economists without an independent contribution to the field, necessary perhaps to staff some undergraduate courses, but of very low priority in filling senior positions. To our shame and cost we cliometricians have totally neglected the most important contribution we could have made to economics: we have failed as economists". Comments on Fenoaltea, biased against cliometrics in my selection, are telling. For de la Escosura (2019) cliometrics has been too accepting of economics; Baffigi (2019, p. 44) suggests, "On all three facets of cliometricians' activity – economics, history, and economic history – we can spot the sign of a failure". The major achievement is seen as the creation of new data bases.

mind the limitations) those who oppose it as unduly narrow and reductionist in all respects, and those seeking a balance between the two, see below.

As a result of these factors, the lack of "economics imperialism" before the watershed for the cliometric revolution might be sufficiently explained by how longstanding were the issues for economic history involved within the discipline of economics, its home within the USA, and sensitivity to these issues both analytically and strategically. But there is one further, possibly decisive factor that tends to be overlooked in this context – pure and simple, it is the relative absence of Chicago, the home and springboard (especially through Becker, with Stigler not far behind) for the first phase of economics imperialism. For, if Chicago had taken the lead in cliometrics, it would almost certainly have been promoted as part of a broader, and overt, strategy of economics imperialism.

It is a moot point whether this would have made it more or less successful given the sensibilities of those trained in economic history, and those trained in economics, who were now well-embedded in Keynesian as opposed to monetarist perspectives.[17] Whilst microeconomics might have been more acceptable as a more or less neutral technical apparatus for the purposes of historical analysis, it would have been much less acceptable if the historical were also to be rounded up within a monetarist macroeconomic framework, with the corresponding neglect of so many factors considered decisive in addressing transformational or revolutionary change in institutions, culture, technology, demography, etc (although hardly part of the Keynesian framework either). It should also be borne in mind that Becker was particularly unworldly when it comes to the historical – both in the work that he did do, as well as what he did not. His extension of economic principles to education, discrimination, the family, crime, etc, was always met with considerable dissent from other social sciences, and even within economics itself; and, throughout his voluminous work, it is as if unemployment and money and finance simply do not exist (Fine, 1998c).

I suspect that the relative absence of Chicago from the cliometric revolution is uncontroversial, and it has been explained by the ability of less prominent institutions to jump the bandwagon and take the lead (Coats, 1990). But there may well have been more to it than this of some relevance. Chicago, as elsewhere, was caught in a dilemma. With economic history within economics as a compulsory course, requiring presence of corresponding academics, there was

---

17   Ironically, Milton Friedman's work on monetary policy in the Great Depression can be
       cited as an early cliometric study (Friedman and Schwartz, 1963).

the opportunity for it to take the lead in the cliometric revolution as in the first phase of economics imperialism more generally. To do so, though, would be to embrace the particularly sharp and longstanding tensions between promoting the first phase of economics imperialism and incorporating all the qualifying, even undermining, traditional concerns of the economic historian. In short, do you take over economic history or do you marginalise it for the good of economics (imperialism) especially in light of the lingering influence of old institutional economics and the hegemony of Keynesianism, progressive neo-classicals, and their more open stance towards limiting the scope of economic principles and their more favourable stance to acknowledging the role of the non-economic, and the privilege of other social sciences in assessing it and its impact?

Whether and how these conundrums played out in Chicago needs to be the subject of detailed archival research. In his account, Mitch (2011, p. 263) observes the decline of economic history in Chicago economics:

> Since 1980, however, economic history has declined at Chicago. This is evidenced concretely in the elimination of the economic history require-ment for the PhD in the early 1980s, in the decline in the percentage of doctoral dissertations written in the field after 1990, in the shift of the two remaining economic historians into other fields, and in the termination of the economic history workshop, with material of historical interest shifted to Fogel's workshop on biodemography.

Significantly, though, he does not find, correctly, that this is explained by the rise of formalism, etc, within economics, not least as this has prospered else-where within cliometrics and at Chicago itself, unavoidable in light of its New Classical Economics. For he continues:

> The most obvious explanation for this trend is the rise of formalism and the emphasis on mathematical technique in the economics profession. However, this explanation is not fully satisfactory. Formalism and tech-nical skills do not preclude an interest in historical developments, as evi-denced, for example, by the John Bates Clark medalist Daron Acemoglu's interest in economic history at the Massachusetts Institute of Technology or the MacArthur Award winner Avner Greif's use of game theory to study medieval and early modern institutions at Stanford University. Indeed, at Chicago in the 1980s and 1990s the theorist Robert Lucas became interested in problems of growth and development and has even writ-ten on the Industrial Revolution, while James J. Heckman has applied his

formidable empirical skills to studying the economic history of African American economic prospects in the twentieth-century U.S. South.

What seems a more likely explanation, for which I can provide at most anecdotal evidence, is that, consciously or otherwise, a strategic decision was made to marginalise, and to discard, economic history rather than to promote it. Here is what Deidre, then Don, McCloskey, a leading participant as economic historian in cliometrics, reveals, cited in Kafka (2016):[18]

> Though tenured in both economics and history and just a few years away from a full professorship, she left the University of Chicago in 1980 because among the couple dozen faculty members in the econ department there, she says, "there are the barons and the help", the barons being Nobel winners and their protégés, the help being those carrying heavy teaching loads and administrative tasks. "I could see that they were putting me in the help category", she says.

But McCloskey was not the only cliometrician at Chicago. James Heckman, Nobel Prize Winner for econometrics, was there from 1973, often seen as a contributor and major support to cliometrics. He, however, is no neoliberal and his work on econometrics is orthogonal to that of the New Classical Economics, as well as being located in a separate centre dedicated to interventionist public policy.

Yet the major exception that proves the rule is Robert Fogel, generally acknowledged to be a founding parent of the cliometric revolution, having joined Chicago in 1964 and, as observed, joint Nobel Laureate with Douglass North for cliometrics. Once again, though, without going into details, he hardly qualifies as a neoliberal, he pursued his continuing interests by leaving Chicago

---

18   I seem to recall from the time that McCloskey's departure from Chicago also involved a further factor, that can be interpreted along similar lines, that he left in a huff because of delay in promoting him to full professor, something well-deserved in light of his prominence as an economic historian. Nor is this ideological, other than in relation to the value of economic history as such, with McCloskey heavily committed to the neoclassical paradigm. Of course, without dumping her neoclassicism, she has later embraced rhetoric and narrative and, to her credit, engaged with all strands of heterodoxy, with aplomb and recognisable success. But, upon the ideological front, it is worth noting, possibly as a surprise to her heterodox admirers other than of a neo-Austrian persuasion, as late as 2013, she is reported as a new member of the Mont Pèlerin Society, and a speaker in 2017, https://www.desmog.com/mont-pelerin-society/.

in 1975, only returning in 1981 to the Business School to set up a centre to study demography.

So Fogel is another exception that proves the Chicago rule. But it is worth dwelling on his case for other reasons that shed light on the economics imperialism dog that did not bark before the watershed. There is no doubt that he played a major role in promoting cliometrics through the use of economic theory, reliance upon (statistical evidence) and the construction of data sets. Here is what he has to say in some retrospect about his endeavours (Fogel, 1983, p. 24) "cliometricians ... apply the quantitative methods of behavioral models of the social sciences to the study of history". I would observe, in contrast to the early Douglass North, this is not a manifesto for applying as if perfect market principles to economic history. Fogel is more rounded and historically minded and does not restrict himself to neoclassical economics. He goes on to highlight six differences between the new and the old economic history. First is subject matter, "'scientific' historians tend to focus on collectivities of people and recurring events, while traditional historians tend to focus on particular individuals and particular events", p. 42. Second is preferred types of evidence – quantitative versus literary, for example. Third is standards of proof and verification – empirical-scientific model as opposed to legal discourses or the like. Fourth is the role of controversy – estimating procedures versus quality of interpretation. Fifth is that the traditional involves more loners and is less collaborative. And sixth is that the traditional is more communicative to the general public. And he concludes that, p. 69/70:

> The genuine differences between "scientific" and traditional historians over subject matter, methods, and style should not obscure their more numerous and more fundamental affinities and complementarities ... each mode has a comparative advantage in certain domains of research, they supplement and enrich each other.

In short, Fogel is far from being a head-banging market-perfection, neoclassical economist. Further, the two classical, and highly controversial studies (especially the first) with which he is so closely associated, on slavery and US railways, also do not conform to such narrow theoretical perspectives. By the same token, despite their prominence within the literature and in the continuing debates over the merits of cliometrics, these two studies are unrepresentative of the first phase of cliometrics, even though often taken to be so.

This account dovetails neatly with Fogel's (1970, p. 129) often observed commitment to, even the unavoidability of, counterfactuals. What if Fogel had not pioneered the cliometric revolution alongside Douglass North?[19] Would things have turned out differently in pace, rhythm and outcome? As with all counterfactuals, the answer is necessarily shrouded in the mysteries of identifying causal and conditional factors and how they interact with one another and are mutually determining. But it is arguable that, paradoxically, despite being more rounded than many of those promoting the cliometric revolution in its initial phases, and despite the controversies generated by his major initiating case studies, Fogel's role was extremely facilitating to the development and acceptance of the new, newer and newest economic history, precisely because he was more rounded and accommodating in his approach to the old. In this sense, he was ahead of the game, unlike North who is better seen as moving through it. So, through Fogel, this both allowed for acceptance for those sympathetically inclined during the first phase despite sensibilities attached to the historical aspects of economic history that were being discarded by cliometrics, and it paved and smoothed the way for the later, more rounded phases.

In short, this lengthy discourse on cliometrics and the watershed can close with the following observations (and will allow discussion of the other general aspects of economics imperialism as applied to economic history to be that much shorter). For, whilst as discussed in Fine and Milonakis (2003) and Milonakis and Fine (2007) through close scrutiny of Douglass North, cliometrics followed a typical pattern of economics imperialism through its three phases (subject both to North's influence and idiosyncrasies) the first phase of application of as if perfect market principles was already overladen with the sorts of considerations that would arise in the later phases. This is a simple consequence of the longstanding presence of debates over the merits of economic theory for economic history (unavoidable even in the locale of economics departments), the relative absence in the new economic history of Chicago heavyweights or others in promoting economics imperialism as the way forward for social science in general, dissatisfaction with the level of theory and evidence within traditional economic history and its over-reliance on the non-economic, and the more rounded framings associated with economic historians (and economists) themselves. In a sense, wherever it might have led, cliometrics was part of the business of economic history as usual but with more theory and evidence. It was not conceived as, nor promoted as, economics imperialism.

This assessment is both supported and sheds light on the second general aspect of economics imperialism, how its second phase is posed in terms of

---

19   See Diebolt and Haupert (2018).

the first. For this, in part explaining the watershed and demise of "economics imperialism" in the literature other than for economic history, the as if perfectly working markets phase is strongly rejected for being imperialistic as opposed to the market imperfections phase. Exactly the same applies to economic history except, as brought out in detail in Chapters 7 to 9, little or no reference is made to economics imperialism in the rejection. It is simply the economics that is too reductionist and unrealistic especially for the historical issues of the long run and major economic and social change and market imperfections, itself to be augmented by other variables in the third phase of economics imperialism.

Interestingly, because of opposition to it, there is a view that economics imperialism is confined to its first phase alone after which it was rejected by more rounded economists. This only follows if we confine economics imperialism to its first phase and do not allow it to move through further phases, as dictated by developments within economics itself as it departs from its Chicago versions. Thus, Nik-Khah and Van Horn (2012), through archival research, show the importance of the Chicago for the first phase of economics imperialism, something that is hardly controversial, but then consider economics imperialism declined in importance and so was at most momentary (Fine, 2024b, Chapter 8, for a critique). This, however, seems to overlook that non-Chicago economics can also be, has been and still is, imperialistic, quite apart from the implications for the weak representation of Chicago in the cliometric revolution because of its inability or unwillingness to finesse the greater sensitivity to the limitations of Chicago-style economics for economic history as its cliometric revolution is engaged. As indicated in the general account of economics imperialism's three phases summarised above, the second, market imperfection, new phase of (newer) cliometrics presents itself as both critical of, and breaking with, its first phase of Chicago-like, perfect market economics imperialism. The only twist in the tale of economic history as economics imperialism is the latter's overt absence across what has been a watershed in the prominence of economics imperialism for many other fields and topics as its second phase takes the old as critical point of departure and, at least implicitly, denies it is itself imperialistic as a result.

The third is how does economics imperialism as applied to economic history treat the OTHER. This, in turn, does itself have two aspects. One is in its relations to other disciplines. Here, the backward view is imperative. For it indicates that, at least by its newest phase, economic history has been totally absorbed within economics. Evidence for this comes in a strong form from the Handbook of Historical Economics despite, or ironically because of, a lingering belief that it is otherwise, and an enduring desire that it be so. Thus, for the latter, the very use of the term historical economics is indicative of the wish to see a synthesis of history and economics which is subordinate to neither, exploiting the comparative advantage of each in combination. It goes hand in hand with the mistaken belief, other than by an extremely narrow, self-serving definition, that cliometrics came and went with the rise and fall of what I have termed its first phase – so that the market imperfection and plus substance of the newer and newest economic history can be seen as historical economics rather than simply economics (imperialism) applied to history.

More specifically, in their introduction to the Handbook, appropriately titled, "Merger or Acquisition?", Bisin and Federico (2021, p. xvi) suggest:

> In the end, the specific comparative advantages of history and economics which in our opinion the chapters distill and identify provide a forceful argument in favor of a merger between the disciplines along these lines.

Yet, what exactly are the advantages that each bring? We are told, p. xxxi:[20]

> Historical Economics is a very promising and important field. As all interdisciplinary endeavors, it differs from its parent-fields. It differs from economic history for the breadth of research questions, which include political and social issues, and above all for its statistical methods, which rely heavily on causal inference and at times on structural modeling. Historical Economics differs also from economics in that the availability of data is a serious constraint. Economists have showed remarkable ingenuity in overcoming the constraint, but they could be more aware of the fundamental trade-off: dealing with 'large' issues with weak (to say the least) data vs limiting oneself to 'small' issues with accurate and reliable data.

There is nothing here that has not become standard fare for the economist in the latest phase of economics imperialism, with the inclusion of political and social issues not distinctive for economic history given for example the new (newer and newest) political economy, economic sociology, institutional

---

20   See also Diebolt and Haupert (2020, p. 27) who conclude, possibly unwittingly, how limited is the historical content of economic history: "So in the end, what is cliometrics and what is its place in the history and lexicon of economic history? Is it history with an economic (technical) approach? Or is it economics with a long run view of the world? Or has cliometrics become a subset of economic theory? The answer, not surprisingly, is all of the above".

economics, etc. The appropriation of economic history is just more of the same. And, as much, is the explicit stance of the first contribution to the Handbook, "The Economic History of Economic History: The Evolution of a *Field in Economics*", emphasis added. For, Margo (2021, p. 10):

> economic history became incorporated into economics with latter's principles and methods applied to historical evidence and topics, eroding its potential to be a separate field – other than as fields in economics applied to history.

Indeed, p. 13:

> However, to a significant extent, papers being written today in economic history routinely follow the logic of modern empirical economics especially the emphasis on identification of causal parameters. This is true whether or not the paper is written originally for an economic history journal, or finds its way to an economic history journal after being submitted to a mainstream journal or a field journal outside of economic history.

Ironically, those working in economic history have been keen to have their work published in the main mainstream economics journals for prestige purposes, as they are going to be judged as economists not as historians nor even as economic historians.[21] In general, they have failed, indicating that it is the economics rather than the history that is of interest to the hegemonic, appropriating discipline.

Such assessments, in general, are more than supported by the specific case studies that follow in the Handbook, recalling that these are intended to demonstrate the presence of the historical over and above the economic. What stands out is the absence of the historical, and the ahistorical nature of the theory. This is true of the way in which evolution and persistence are conceived, as at most stochastic mechanical models (Voth, 2021). There is "Dynamic General Equilibrium Modeling of Long and Short-Run Historical Events", involving quantitative general equilibrium analyses of the Industrial Revolution and the period of 1889–1929 in the United States (Hansen et al. 2021, p. 331). For Nunn (2021) social is analogous with biological evolution, with potential for

---

21   Nor is it surprising that economic history should seek outlets in economics given its US location within economics.

mismatches and cumulative change. Culture is perceived as the means to embody whatever gains are achieved. And, for Acemoglu et al. (2021, p. 366):[22]

> Our framework is a simple dynamic game-theoretic model, with society consisting of a number of groups of individuals who have preferences over policy and over institutional arrangements (which determine what types of economic relations are possible, for example).

And they report that to explain institutional stasis or path dependence with change, p. 386:[23]

> We developed a dynamic game-theoretic model to organize these ideas. Different groups care both about current policies and institutions and future policies, which are themselves determined by current institutional choices. The discount rate of different groups is a measure of how forward-looking they are and how much they care about the future. Equilibria in this game take the form of (stochastic or deterministic) paths of institutions. Institutional change can happen because of internal dynamics or because of shocks to the economic environment or political power of different groups.

Along with others, they use a median voter to decide balance on collective actions taken even though there may be no voting system, nor democracy, in place.[24]

More of the same comes from Bowles et al. (2021) drawing upon complex individual agent models (i.e. optimisation plus) p. 428:

> Our model, while retaining the focus on class and other forms of group conflict of the political economy approach, is based on three departures. First, we have integrated within-and between-population conflicts and institutional transitions into a common model. Second, our explicit dynamical system allows us to study (albeit in a rudimentary manner) the out-of-equilibrium movements of a system, that is, the process of institutional change itself. Third, our actors are not fictive representatives of unitary groups, but instead individuals whose substantially

---

22   With Acemoglu being seen as having provided the classic study of the new historical economics along its PS strand.

23   See also Persson and Tabellini (2021).

24   See Appendix to this chapter for some elementary game theory.

uncoordinated actions are based (realistically) on sparse information, limited cognitive capacities, and (for the most part) local rather than global objectives.

The presence and/or role of "the state" is explained by the universal choice between using surplus resources for conflict or otherwise (Levine and Modica, 2021) or even by "one standard deviation increase in suitability for cereals, as opposed to roots and tubers, is associated with a twelve percentage point increase in the probability of a state being present" (Stasavage, 2021, p. 883). More generally for institutions and culture, referencing McCloskey (1991), Bisin and Verdier (2021, p. 509) suggest:

> systems of differential/difference equations are interesting frames useful to identify and organize historical narratives by means of simple phase diagrams between relevant historical state variables. In the context of the joint interactions of culture and institutions, this approach provides a simple and easily applicable analysis uncovering the nature and source of important feedback effects between these variables.

Productivity is understood by the degree of diversity (new ideas to share) and homogeneity of populations (scale effects) and the impact of contraception through a marital search model (Greenwood et al. 2021).

What is striking about these vignettes is how closely they conform to contemporary economics in its third phase of economics imperialism, not their application to history as such. Equally marked is the increasing dependence and prodigious sophistication of the statistical methods and data sets deployed. And the same applies to the longstanding disregard for criticism, fallacies even, in what is involved, not least dependence upon (ahistorical) core theory but its increasing displacement as the theoretical source for reduced form estimation. Instead, sophisticated statistical estimation becomes the model with loosest connection, as opposed to guilt by association across variables, to underlying theory. Only occasionally is this acknowledged and then it is a matter of moving on. Thus, Caicedo (2021) refers to what I will call the Deaton criticism (as he has been in the forefront of making it, especially in the context of RCT, randomised control trials)[25] – how discovered empirical relations are suspect until a mechanism underpinning them is demonstrated. Indeed, Bisin and Moro (2021, p. 270) observe:

---

25   See Deaton and Cartwright (2018).

While the identification of causal effects in Persistence studies has produced significant first-order results, it has also highlighted how little we know about the mechanisms driving these effects.

More generally, in the context of addressing Africa's supposed poverty, Frankema (2021, p. 559) acknowledges with fulsome references (omitted here) that:

> The persistence studies as such have been criticized from many sides – and not just by professional historians. Comments have been made on the reliability, validity, and uncritical use of historical data, ... on estimation methods and, ... on conceptual issues related to the 'compression of history', and euro-centric bias ... Voices have also been raised against the historical determinism inherent to persistence studies and their neglect of fundamental patterns of change in Africa and beyond.

But his response, "I will keep most of these cans of worms closed", is even more telling and symptomatic.

In brief, precisely because it has become incorporated within economics, economic history has become at most distinguished from within it merely by its subject matter, the past. From the point of view of the disciplinary OTHER, this means first and foremost that other forms of economic history, those that are incompatible with mainstream economics, even for the newer economics imperialism, become homogenised and set aside. This is far from new and became a consequence of cliometrics in its first phase, for which so-called social history did not set aside the economic but dealt with it entirely differently than the new kid on the block. Here it is vital to reject the common stance amongst the new, newer and newest economic historians that the old were atheoretical and unconcerned with the (quantitative) evidence. These are simply untrue as a generalisation. It is just that different theory (not least political economy,[26] and for Adam Smith and Karl Marx, for example) and

---

26   Of course, I do not mean the new political economy, described by Koyama (2019, p. 752) for historical economics as follows: "Political economy also involves the application of economic models to nonstandard settings. In its modern form, it also stresses the importance of using economic theory to guide the empirical analysis of political questions. Its practitioners likewise need to have command over both economic theory and econometric techniques and knowledge of institutional details and particularities. Cliometrics and modern political economy can thus be viewed as two closely related and complementary fields within economics".

other evidence besides the empirical are deployed (as well as the empirical if not understandably to the degree and in the form of cliometrics). Tellingly, in defence of, and in characterising, cliometrics, Diebolt and Haupert (2019a, p. 63) suggest, "New Economic History, or Cliometrics, represents a move from the historical, descriptive approach of describing a historical event, toward the use of economic theory to analyze an event" and this leads them to conclude, "Cliometricians make use of *the whole gamut of economic theory*", emphasis added, p. 65. Both statements are false or misleading in implying the old economic history was universally descriptive and atheoretical, and that a full range of economic theory has been deployed by cliometrics. Instead, what is striking is how much theory has been used in the old economic history, and how little in the new – itself reflecting a major feature of cliometrics and mainstream economics, profound ignorance of the history of economic thought. Unsurprisingly, then, economic history tends to eschew the historical as the basis for theory construction, and the sorts of questions it asks, what is capital(ism) for example, although the (British) industrial revolution has been intensively covered from a variety of perspectives (Haupert, 2019; Broadberry, 2021, for coverage of recent contributions).

Central for the latter, though, has been patterns and "causes" of growth for which reliance upon both old (to measure total factor productivity, TFP) and new (endogenous technical progress) have been prominent. Each is known to be fundamentally flawed (Fine, 2016; Fine and Dimakou, 2016, for accounts). Perversely, economic history tends to explain the rhythms of TFP by factors whose presence would invalidate its calculation – perfect competition for input and output markets, full employment and distribution determined by technology alone. For new growth theory, so-called Barro-type regressions at least implicitly depend upon market imperfections, increasing returns to scale, an absence of price/value theory (although markets deliver) and conflation of movements along or towards presumed steady-state (balanced growth at equilibrium rate) even though the empirics clearly demonstrate that none of these is characteristic of growth, as it is subject to surges, collapses and shifts, with considerable imbalance within and across sectors. Essentially, growth is ahistorically seen as a Cobb-Douglas production function with whatever factor inputs (which run into the hundreds) you care to include.[27]

---

27   Yet another issue is the construction, and use, of GDP as if unproblematic across time and place (there is a tension between a common standard for the empirics, and reflecting the nature of the economies under consideration). I return to this issue in the conclusion in the context of financialisation, see the Chapter's closing footnote before Appendix. For the moment, observe that in response to the renewal of interest in the nature of "GDP"

Against this lengthy discourse on the reduction of economic history to a reduced mainstream economics, how economic history has addressed the other OTHER can be relatively short. For, as should be apparent, the non-economic OTHER shifts from the rational/irrational divide with the new economic history, to the irrational as explicable as the rational response to market imperfections with the newer economic history, to the inclusion of whatever variables suit in the newest economic history – reflecting exactly the same trajectory as economics imperialism itself. Even so, by virtue of its subject matter and traditions, whilst the last stage can include more or less anything in principle, certain topics come to the fore in practice, although they tend to tail upon mainstream economics. The institutional as the other covers more or less everything from property relations, transaction costs, ideology and culture as decisive in the history of economic performance, with North taking a lead for institutions (and ideology and neuroeconomics although his take has not so much been followed for these).[28] Rhetoric and narrative have occupied a special, if not prominent, place as, in later if parallel paths as for North, both McCloskey and Mokyr, raise their profile in finding erstwhile economic history inadequate. For Mokyr (2021, p. 790):

> Attitudes (that is, cultural beliefs) and aptitudes (that is, technical competence) thus played central roles in the British Industrial Revolution and the origins of modern growth ... Both of these depended in turn on underlying institutions, often designed for very different purposes.

As often, it is worth quoting McCloskey (2019, p. 112) at length for her dissatisfaction for what she was, and to indicate what she has become:

---

since the Global Financial Crisis of 2007/8, Assa (2019, p. 81) reckons that most studies only stretch back to the 1930s, and a "longer and broader view reveals the exercise of estimating national income or wealth as a form of numerical rhetoric. Rather than a statistical measure, GDP is an indicator of power (for countries, classes and industries) as well as an instrument for advocating specific policies. Therefore, any critique must go beyond technical issues and fixes, and look at the political context and consequences of various historical versions of GDP, and any possible democratic reform of it".

28   For Diebolt and Haupert (2019b, p. vii): "To date, the main achievements of cliometrics have been to slowly but surely establish, in the Fogel tradition, a solid set of economic analyses of historical evolution by means of measurement and theory and, following the path blazed by Douglass North, to recognize the limits of neoclassical theory and bring into economic models the important role of institutions. Indeed, this latter focus ultimately spawned a new branch of economics altogether, the new institutional economics".

I hesitate to cast the first stone, because I am not without sin. True, as the men caught in the #MeToo movement nowadays often say in extenuation, the sinning was a long time ago. Still, by confessing my own sins here and now I can avoid the impoliteness of naming particular works by my beloved colleagues in economic history that routinely misuse analytic narratives – that is, existence theorems, weakly "consistent" with the data, and not comparative, either. It would be easy to name them. It would be even easier to name colleagues who use tests of statistical significance – also weakly "consistent" with the data, at low power, and anyway usually irrelevant to the economic and historical question at issue, which is almost always not fit, but coefficient size, substantive oomph. But I won't. So, bless me, father, for I have sinned. It has been half a century since my last confession.

But, more constructively, she concludes, p. 121:[29]

And so (the hypothesis goes) an economic history without meaning is incapable of understanding economic growth, business cycles, or many other of our mysteries. A humanomic economic history would extend but also to some degree call into question the techniques of modern economics, and the numerous other social sciences from law to sociology now influenced by an exclusively Max U theory. Economic history, that is, can embrace the humanities, without forsaking measurement, and become more, not less, scientific.

Despite this embracing of a wider perspective, late and limited by the standards of both postmodernism and material culture,[30] turning to the fourth general feature of economics imperialism, the outcome of the rise and trajectory of cliometrics has been to lead to a strengthening of the divisions between economics and history and between economic and social history, not least in light of the construction of the latter as a uniform OTHER alongside an intolerance to heterodox political economy that cannot itself be opportunistically incorporated. As Margo (2021, p. 14) puts it:

---

29   And, in review of McCloskey's (2021) turn to "humanomics", Paganelli (2023) summarises, "The explanatory power of this great enrichment [ie growth over the most recent centuries] is thus in the power of words, in the powers of ideas, not in material or institutional incentives, or scientific innovations, let alone in utility maximization".

30   See Shiller (2019) for mainstream emphasis on the new narrative economics.

Professional history lost interest in cliometrics many years ago and shows few signs of interest in the new strands of historical scholarship emerging in economics. However, it does not follow that historians have lost interest in economic history per se. Those historians who were displaced by cliometrics and who have little interest or incentive to follow developments in economics have long since migrated to greener pastures, such as the Business History Conference.

What is true of business history, and its varieties of approaches, is also true of other fields in social history.

As a result, as already seen, the venture of restoring historical economics is futile on the terms in which it is being promoted. There is the irony that the historical in the effort is entirely subordinate to the economic and, whilst the terminology is identical to the descriptor for (the some of the "old") economic history from prior to the marginalist revolution, the earlier historical economics is treated as if it, alongside political economy and heterodox economics, does not exist.

As a result, the fifth and sixth general aspects of economics imperialism are readily addressed. In terms of the assessed and targeted balance with the "economic", resolution is sought entirely on the terms of mainstream economics. And, as for opposition, it seems mostly to move in alternative universes, dialogues of the deaf, apart from when sinners repent but offer more of the same in the vein of the third phase of economics imperialism.

4   Concluding Remarks

I have given cliometrics a hard time, no more nor less than mainstream economics and economics imperialism. As a result, I am only too aware and experienced of being ignored or at most treated as if a defender of old economic history in its parodied forms of descriptive narrative without theory. Accusations against opponents are also liable to be made of critique being used as a veil for incompetence in (the technical aspects of) economic theory and econometrics, and as a hostility to hard empirical evidence. To guard against such possibilities, I address these two issues directly if simply, and that of data also.

First, I am not against models nor mathematical methods (Fine, 2023b, for discussion at length). I have deployed them myself on numerous occasions. But their limitations in principle and, possibly more important, in practice must be acknowledged. They are inevitably highly deterministic (subject to random variation and initial conditions) and ahistorical (conceptualisation imposed upon, rather than drawn from, the object of study). I tend towards the (Keynes') view that mathematical models are at most an aid to thinking. They bring out the full implications of assumptions (which may or may not be obvious) and this allows what is present and what is not to be discovered and critically addressed. In short (theoretical) models are a way of positing a particular view about how the world (an economy) functions. Paradoxically, without them, we would be unable to say what is wrong with mainstream economics (and its application to economic history) as with the flaws in measuring total factor productivity for example.

So models are ok as long as they know their limited place. Second, much the same applies to econometrics, for which I adopt a very simple view. Statistical methods, beginning with the simple average of a distribution all the way through to sophisticated estimations on large data sets, are merely the presentation of that data in a way that allows it to be interpreted. It may or may not be a helpful presentation but what it is not is a causal explanation (as is often taken to be the case, especially given the language of dependent and independent variables). It might be suggestive of causation but, primarily, econometric results offer more of what is to be explained than explanation itself – and the explanation can range over how the variables were conceived, theoretically situated, and how the data were generated and interpreted, over and above estimation itself.

Third, I have no problem with empirical evidence and positively welcome what is generally acknowledged to have been a major achievement of cliometrics, the generation and use of new data sets. This is, however, subject to some reservations which I only raise as issues but which should be subject to research. As Margo (2021, p. 12) observes, "Intellectual developments outside of economic history have dramatically raised the profile and acceptance of use of historical evidence in economic analysis" and a major factor has been technological, computing. And, for Haupert (2017, p. 1065):[31]

It is hard to overestimate the impact of technology on cliometric research. The gathering, codifying, and organizing of immense data sets

---

31   See also Diebolt and Haupert (2019a, p. 75): "It isn't that we don't value the construction of datasets anymore, it is that they have become commonplace. Digitization and technology have made the creation of new datasets for research more common, because they are more easily available in digital form. This reduces the cost in terms of time and money to travel to archives, transcribe data, codify it, and clean it. It is easier to share, manipulate, and analyse with modern technology. Hence, new data sets more frequently appear and provide fodder for new research".

is possible only with sophisticated computer software. The application of more advanced modeling and data analysis techniques is possible only with advanced computing technology. Technology by itself has not created the clio movement, but has certainly accelerated its influence and broadened the avenues of possible research. It has led to new frontiers of research methodology and topics and made new, cutting edge techniques possible.

This raises the question of to what extent the raised profile of data use in economic history is the consequence of the rise of cliometrics or simply a coincidence of its rise with the more general developments in computing power and the acceptability of using historical and empirical evidence. Even more important is it begs the question not of the greater use of data and statistical methods, but the uses to which they are put. A question of considerable interest to me, which remains unexamined, is how the greater availability and use of data has impacted upon theory development (rather than how theory has deployed the data). For cliometrics, it seems to have consolidated orthodoxy but is this the case more generally? What, as endlessly emphasised, is true is that cliometrics has entirely taken its cue from economics (imperialism) not only in the sorts of empirical methods deployed but also the theory with which they are underpinned. This is both reflected in, and consolidated by, the US location of economic history within economics departments, and the engagement with other social sciences on the terms dictated by economics imperialism. Had cliometrics taken sociology or political theory as a leading thrust in its interdisciplinarity, as opposed to an afterthought after its initial revolution, then the tensions for cliometrics for the historical as opposed to the economic would have been that much more intense, and the avoidance of class, capitalism and the meaning and specificity of categories of analysis impossible. Both cliometrics and mainstream economics (imperialism) were oblivious to postmodernism and its aftermath until the cultural and the like were ready to be incorporated in their third phases.

The contributions reproduced here, or presented for the first time, straddle these various concerns. Chapters 2 to 4 belong to what might be described as engaging with economics imperialism but not explicitly so. The first concerns consumption and the consumer revolution, and the other two focus on mining, one of them heavily reliant on relatively elementary econometrics to establish the importance of scale economies and mechanisation. In a sense, they can be interpreted as contributions to the new economic history although critique of mainstream economics in its application to economic history is heavily present.[32] The remaining chapters are primarily organised around the clio-metric revolution and its consequences, charting the roles played by Douglass North, market imperfections economics and path dependence and more.

Each of these chapters has been or can be assigned relevance for contempo-rary issues, something on which cliometrics tends to pride itself. Yet the three great prominent crises of the most recent period – the Global Financial Crisis of 2007/8, the pandemic, and the environment – might reasonably be said to have been untouched by the insights to be gleaned from cliometrics. Most notable, unlike every other social science, is the absence of financialisation as a key concept in both economics and economic history. It is symbolic of theo-retical narrowness and lack of contact with empirical realities.[33]

Appendix: Playing with Game Theory

Sen (1970) in the spirit laid down by Arrow, put forward a theorem in which it was impossible to find social choice that satisfied both the Pareto criterion and "liberalism".[34] To give a flavour of his result, suppose there are two individuals, A and B,[35] and three alternatives: both read a book; A reads it; or B reads it. A is illiberal and wants no one to read it but prefers to read it rather than B reading it (to protect B). B wants to read the book but would prefer even more for A to read it (to educate A). A reading it, alternative x say, dominates B reading it, y, by Pareto (each prefers A over B reading). B reading it, z, dominates nobody doing so by B's liberal dispensation. And nobody reading it dominates A read-ing it by A's liberal dispensation. It follows that x dominates y, which in turn

---

32   Of relevance is Margo's (2021, p. 10) observation that: "Indeed, when the first generation of cliometricians took a careful look at the economic history literature they realized there were intellectual holes, often profound, wherever they looked. The pickings were ripe, not slim".

33   See Mader et al. (eds) (2020) for overview of financialisation. There has, though, been close attention to finance, if not financialisation, across orthodoxy with the presumption that it is positive for development up to a point (a so-called threshold). This begs the question of why GDP should have been reinvented to include financial services as a con-tributing sector, previously being a transfer, as critically assessed by Christophers (2013) Assa (2017) and Itaman (2021). As I parody in the context of South Africa, it is as if finance does little – or offers more systemic dysfunction than function – takes 25% of GDP for doing so, and claims to have added 20% to GDP (Ashman et al. 2021).

34   For an overview of the literature on Sen's piece, and his responses, see Erasmo (2023). It is drawn to the conclusion that Sen's notion of liberal is illiberal.

35   The book is supposedly salacious, with A designated prude and B lascivious by Sen.

dominates z, and z dominates x – x>y>z>x – a cycle of choice indicative of impossibility of reconciling Pareto with liberalism.

Inevitably, I came across this result whilst engaged in social choice theory for my doctoral studies, supervised by Sen in the early 1970s. It puzzled me and led to my reinterpreting it in two different ways, each presented in Fine (1974 and 1975). The first was to suggest that the choices had been mis-specified since it was apparent that each had well-defined preferences over whether to read the book, and each might consider that the other should choose to read or not by the principles of liberalism. But it is transparent that the individuals have preferences over what preferences each would want the other to have (but do not) – better for other not to read or to read, for A and B, respectively. This is what I called interdependent preferences. They are clearly irksome for mainstream economics (and its commitment to Pareto) given they can be illiberal. I want you to make up your own mind but would prefer you to make it up as I would want you to – in a sense, this is shown to be illiberal even if not authoritarian other than indirectly.

For Sen's example, A would appear to be illiberal, at least for preferences over B's preferences. And B would appear to be liberal, if possibly patronising, over preferences over A's preferences. What if both are liberal over the other's preferences; each genuinely wants the other to make own choice without regard to what it is. Such preferences might even dominate their preferences over reading the book or not which may be a matter of no concern – there are plenty of books out there. Each of both reading or both not reading the book is a possible (equilibrium) outcome as choices and interdependent preferences (over other reading the book or not) are simultaneously determined. So what? Although not realised at the time in my own contribution, this is culture, institutions, history or whatever (preferences over others' preferences, and possibly even your own – I must become more liberal). And what this example shows is anything goes, or at least either an outcome or its opposite is possible as an equilibrium outcome. Such are the potential limitations of ahistorically and asocially starting from abstract preferences, and preferences over preferences, and deriving outcomes from them.

The second approach I adopted to Sen's conundrum was to suggest it was incomplete in another way; he had only specified three alternatives – this sufficed for his purpose – but there is a fourth alternative, both reading it. This suggests that the choices should be over a set of four ordered pairs – depending on one or the other reading the book or not. In this vein, the dilemma becomes a strategic game in which each chooses to read the book or not. Whatever A does, B can be better off reading the book. And, whatever B does, it is better for A not to read the book. So the outcome would appear to be A reads, and B does not. This is worse than A not reading and B reading which is preferred by both, and so is Pareto-inefficient.

As observed in my contributions, this is simply an example of the Prisoners' Dilemma,[36] in which each of two Prisoners has an incentive to accuse the other as guilty of a crime whatever the other does, but each is worse off if they both accuse the other than if they had both remained silent. As chance would have it, or not as I cannot remember, I had also been working on the Prisoners' Dilemma at this time (Fine, 1973). A common response was that the Dilemma's Pareto-inefficient outcome is due to lack of cooperation and trust between the two, and pursuit of individualistic self-interest. I showed the latter not to be so – by constructing a Brothers' Dilemma.[37] In this, slightly modifying the outcomes, each seeks to minimise the sentence of the other and take the hit by pleading guilty but, as a consequence, each is worse off than if each had pleaded innocent.

In short, the Prisoners' Dilemma, appropriately termed the Isolation Paradox (Sen, 1961) is not so much about conflict of interest nor selfishness but the need for both cooperation and enforcement. Cooperation is not enough without enforcement as each has an incentive to breach cooperation even if it is agreed (whether in self-or other-interest). Altruism can be as damaging as self-interest! Once again, this is all about culture (of cooperation) to which can be added institutions (as enforcement).

But all of this is usefully set against the Assurance Game, as dubbed by Sen (1969) although better known as the Stag Hunt, deriving from Rousseaux. For this, collectively hunting stags gives better average rewards than individually hunting the only alternative, hares. So, as long as each of two hunters is assured the other will join the stag hunt, there is no problem in the sense that none has an alternative to go after hares if both are hunting stags together (other than out of individualism itself or possibly as a threat to gain more than average share of the stag meat, see below). So, yet again, there are issues of institutions,

---

36   The most famous example of the Prisoners' Dilemma is MAD, mutually assured destruction in which, whatever the other does, each of the USA and USSR, has an incentive to accumulate a nuclear arsenal although each is worse off than if none had done so. This generated interest in game theory during the Cold War at the Rand Corporation, leading to Nobel Prize for John Nash and the Pentagon Papers for, erstwhile mainstream economist, Daniel Ellsberg. Other prominent applications are tragedy of the commons (over-exploitation through individual self-interest at the expense of all) and climate change – whatever anyone else does, each has an incentive to play their part in aggregate overall over-use.

37   Today, it would have to be the Siblings' Dilemma but I also suspect the Prisoners have always been male too.

culture and ideology but not, at least in the outcome as such, conflict of interest as there is no incentive to breach commitment to the optimum (subject
to reservations just expressed over ideology and shares of the spoils). The difference between the Isolation Paradox and the Assurance Game is that one
requires enforcement (and cooperation) through some mechanism (culture,
ideology, institutions) the other only cooperation and so a bit less or different
culture, ideology and the institutional.

What has this elementary lesson in game theory got to do with economic
history? Here there are six points to make. First (economic) history can be
interpreted in terms of such games – at one level, whether the necessary institutions, etc, have been in place for better or worse outcomes, or in suggesting
(I hesitate to say explain) why they may have come into place in retrospect
(because stealing from one another is worse for all than respecting property, so
let's have property laws through enforcement, culture, ideology or institutions,
even though each might be better off with stealing if negative sum for society).

Second, basically, our two games are more than enough to show what game
theory can do in principle. However, they can be extended more or less indefinitely by moving beyond two players, to have the games repeated with possibilities of strategising and learning by players over what is interpreted as time,[38]
by increasing the numbers not only of players but also of strategies and varieties of outcomes (so the outcomes and strategies are mutually determining,
as with collectivity arising over time out of individualism through the achievement of a collective solution to which there is commitment).

In short, there is a more or less unlimited capacity to "explain" whatever
outcomes, by whatever explanatory factors. Third, however, moving towards
the more critical, each game of whatever complexity in terms of the players,
the strategies and the outcomes is entirely defined by how these are specified.
However much endogeneity there may be within the game in terms of different equilibria and their properties, these are the consequence of, caused by,
the unexplained, exogenously given combination of players, strategies and

---

38   There are technical issues over whether games last indefinitely or have an endpoint.
      For the latter, solutions are found by asking what players would do at the death and
      then working backwards to the present. The problem is, for example for the Prisoners'
      Dilemma, self-interest cannot be punished by the other player (the game has ended) and
      so the same applies working backwards to the present. For this and other reasons, econ-
      omists generally need to rely upon individuals living indefinitely or some sort of what is
      called overlapping generations in which each has an incentive around what happens after
      death. This might be termed the Danny Dyer syndrome – we are all related to someone
      from the past with lingering effects.

outcomes. These cannot be changed. If they are, then they become part of a slightly more complex game, with its own exogenously given determinants.

Fourth, even putting this major issue of reliance upon exogeneity aside, it raises the question of why there should be change from one game to another, and, not least, changing meanings of the game to its participants, quite apart from their abilities to subvert the game or to (re)invent it (distinguishing features of humans in evolution as opposed to biological/evolutionary game theory). In short, how do we get a game changer?

Fifth, more specifically, precisely because players, strategies and outcomes are given for any game, how do we account for new players, new strategies and, correspondingly, new sets of outcomes. They can only be imposed from outside.

Sixth, and in summary, even on its own terms, game theory would appear to be unable to address major questions of (economic) history – who are the players, what are the strategies, what determines the outcomes, how do new games come about across these elements, and what are the meanings of the game to its participants? Recall, we are talking about major economic and historical change, with corresponding shifts in classes, cultures and institutions, not more or less petty resolution of problems of conflict and cooperation. On the one hand, and unsurprisingly, these conundrums around exogeneity/ endogeneity (and material cultures) are shared with mainstream economics, starting with its given utility and production functions, its individualistic optimisation, and its focus on equilibrium and efficiency. These have been moved but not resolved as the mainstream has moved through its phases of economics imperialism. The same applies to game theory in which ahistorical games draw upon history for their construction but cannot explain history as a result other than by unexplained exogenous factors.

CHAPTER 2

Consumerism and the Industrial Revolution

Postscript as Personal Preamble

It was a great experience for me to reread this piece over thirty years after it was published for a number of reasons. First and foremost, I really enjoyed it, and it gave me a sense of pride for something well done. At the time, it was also a source of pride to be published in a leading history journal. It was also extremely helpful that the journal allowed lengthy contributions so that all issues could be properly covered.

Second, it was one of the first pieces I had contributed on consumption, through invaluable collaboration with fellow researcher Ellen Leopold, that went far beyond the boundaries of economics. Even so, whilst economics imperialism as such is not mentioned, reference is made to the convergence of economic history upon mainstream economics, see later chapters in this volume.

Third, in particular, the article engaged not only in economic and social history, but also brought together considerations of culture alongside issues ranging from the nature of the industrial revolution to the role, or not, of trickle-down in economic and social development. This is of significance for understanding the tensions across economic and social history, as well as their relationships to economics and political economy.

Fourth, in looking back, quite apart from consolidating my commitment to interdisciplinarity, the piece straddles the tensions that had been fought out, were being fought out, and continue to be contested around the proper use of economics in the study of history. At one level, if in a peculiar and critical way, it can be seen as a contribution to cliometrics, deploying mainstream economics from time to time, if primarily in its imperfectly working market forms (with much methodological, theoretical, conceptual and empirical content even if without heavy reliance on models and statistical analysis). At another level, it can be seen as critical of such an approach. Much (use of) economics in the first decades of cliometrics was weak, thereby perversely undermining the potential for criticising it by way of break rather than by improvement as an alternative. This piece does both and for good reason.

For, last, and by no means least, I strongly recall that a strong motive for the piece was provided by the context, one dominated by what at the time was dubbed Reaganism/Thatcherism but is now known as neoliberalism. To contest the idea of industrial as consumer revolution was to challenge a thicket of new conventional wisdoms – not least the driving force of consumption in economic change alongside that of the market, entrepreneurship and the norms set down by elites. The point is not to dismiss the importance of all such factors (and, as was common, to be seen as a productivist, only focusing upon the industrial and the revolution) but to locate them coherently in an overall analytical framework and historical context. Otherwise, almost any factor can be seen as positive or negative according to your predilection, something that has been commonplace in economics, history and beyond as particular themes and causal factors have their one, or more days, of being famous.

1   Introduction[1]

J. H. Clapham wrote in 1910 that, "Even if ... the history of 'the' Industrial Revolution is a 'thrice squeezed orange', there remains an astonishing amount of juice in it" (cited in Hartwell, 1965, p. 164). With so many squeezes since then, it might be thought that the orange was now well and truly dry. But the period is so rich in economic and social change and so much new empirical evidence has emerged that there is still room at the table for new and competing assessments, some adding a degree of analytical novelty. One such view which has appeared recently suggests that the eighteenth century be (re)interpreted as a consumer revolution. The leading exponent of this view is McKendrick, and much of his writing in this area will be assessed in this chapter.

In Section 1, the discussion is set within the framework of Cannadine's (1984) hypothesis that studies of the Industrial Revolution are heavily influenced by contemporary events (thereby potentially explaining the repeated orange squeezings as times change). It is argued here that this view needs to be developed further, especially to take account of the changing input from economic theory. In this context, the 'consumerist approach' associated with McKendrick is understood as a reaction against the current orthodoxy, which increasingly embraces cliometrics. Revisionism occurs, partly as a switch of emphasis from supply to demand, partly as a reinterpretation of the Industrial Revolution as the birth pangs of modern consumer society, and partly as a means of retaining or opening up explanatory factors beyond those within the narrowing confines of orthodox economic analysis.

---

1   Originally appearing as Fine and Leopold (1990). The authors acknowledge support from a research grant endowed by the Leverhulme Trust. Helpful comments were given on an earlier and much lengthier draft by John Mason and by referees through the editors.

Three subsequent sections explore each of these three components separately. Section 2 suggests that because of a tradition within economic theory
that treats the long run as if it were always operating at full employment, the
question of demand has been set aside. But rather than embracing a Keynesian-
type analysis applied to the long run, the consumerist approach reaches beyond
the limited explanatory variables associated with economic theory. Instead, it
relies upon social variables to shift out demand curves, in particular through the
initiating expenditure of the wealthy which trickles down and is transformed
into mass production/consumption.

Section 3 assesses critically the support that orthodox economic theory is
able to offer the consumerist approach. The conclusion drawn is that the role of
demand cannot be understood as an independent economic force for change –
intuitively as a shift in the demand curve – and that, in combination with other
factors, it may prove an impediment to economic progress. In this perspective,
the economic content of the consumerist approach is considered in relation to
the more 'balanced' framework of analysis of the Industrial Revolution which
takes it as the product of shifts in both supply and demand. It is argued that
such 'shift' theories of change can at best provide an organised description
rather than an explanation of change.

Such factors do refocus the analysis away from the narrow confines of economic theory into broader social factors. But the effect analytically remains
limited – to treat social change as a series of shift variables, in this case for
demand curves. The shift in emphasis from supply to demand is accompanied
by a shift in narrative from production to consumption. This is taken as the
focus in Section 4, in which the theory of life-style, fashion, etc, is critically
assessed in the specific case of eighteenth-century clothing. Necessarily, the
early sections here are oriented towards a critical dialogue with economic
theory. Rightly, the reader might question the relevance of this for understanding the complex and dramatic changes that are summed up by the
term Industrial Revolution. The conclusion to be drawn is that the Industrial
Revolution must be understood by reference to a structured explanation of
change (rather than as exceptionally large shifts in supply and/or demand) –
one which unites social and economic forces together rather than reducing
the one to the other.

To offer such an alternative is beyond the scope of this essay – but these
are available, as in the Brenner and Dobb-Sweezy debates, Marx's theory of
primitive accumulation, and Lenin's discussion in many places of the domestic
market in the context of the development of capitalism in Russia (Hilton, ed.,

1978; Aston and Philpin, eds, 1985; and, especially, Lenin, 1899).[2] And Section 3 briefly illustrates how political economists as diverse as Adam Smith and Malthus have had a most complex understanding of economic progress, even while emphasising the role of the market.

This is not to suggest that the consumerists do not have a world view of what is constituted by the Industrial Revolution. The final section of this chapter, which serves as a conclusion, assesses the ideological content of the consumerist approach. It suggests that the effect of directing attention to consumption through the market is to rewrite history favourably in terms of the rich and powerful, who act as the leading edge of change and as subjects to be emulated. The result is to construct a rationale in favour of contemporary consumerist society, however understood, and the role of those most privileged within it.

2   Economic History through Which Looking Glass?

In a stimulating survey of the past century's literature covering the English Industrial Revolution, Cannadine (1984) has argued that there have been four distinct paradigm shifts. In each of these, the perspective within which the Industrial Revolution has been studied and interpreted has been heavily influenced by the contemporary state of the economy. Thus from 1870 to 1920, under the influence of Fabianism, the plight of the poor and the need for state intervention came to the fore. From 1920 to 1950, the aura of global pessimism and the theory of cycles became prominent. During the post-war boom, growth and the affinities with development economics were significant. From the 1970s onwards, the impact and extent of the Industrial Revolution has been played down in line with poorer recent growth performance.

Cannadine's chronological periodisation of the literature has to be pressed further, for it depends upon a rather crude and direct relation between material and intellectual life. To oversimplify, the latter cannot simply be read off as a sign of the times since other factors also influence the path of scholarship. More specifically, Cannadine's approach leaves unanswered what are the contemporary events that are chosen as the prism through which to view the past, which past events are appropriate for this retrospective, and how this subject matter is related to the existing character and direction of development of the

---

2 Subsequent literature has been extensive but see Fine (1978 and 1980d) for attempts to tie it to value theory.

(academic) disciplines involved. There is no reason to presume that subjects such as economics and economic history will respond in the same way to contemporary events. There is, for example, no necessary overlap between the theories that govern them which will inevitably condition the way each selects, filters and interprets current 'reality'.

These points are well illustrated by observing that major changes, such as growth slow-down, have very different impacts on the various social sciences, even if each of these is nudged into revisions by contemporary change. It might be argued, for example, that the oil crisis of the 1970s led to a consideration by economic history of whether there was an energy crisis in the eighteenth century.[3] The same stimulus, however, had an entirely different effect within economic theory, giving a new lease of life to an otherwise moribund growth theory in the context of exhaustible resources. In this, the external world was scarcely examined. Rather, the esoteric and axiomatic theory of neoclassical economics was given a new arena of application for its optimality conditions – one in which 'oil' became symbolic of 'scarce resource', 'OPEC' became a 'monopoly', etc.[4]

In particular, then, the response of each academic discipline to changed circumstances cannot be entirely determined by the 'shock' or ethos of contemporary events but is equally dependent on its own internal traditions and dynamics. To point to these problems in the Cannadine hypothesis is not, however, to reject the relevance of the contemporary. Rather, it is to insist that it be embedded in a richer analytical framework, one that includes both literature and theory falling outside his mainstream periodisation. This proves necessary with the theory of the consumer revolution of the eighteenth century that forms a major focus of this chapter. It elevates the role of consumption or demand to be both the precursor to, and of equal stature with, the revolution in production as a major source of change.

One of the consequences of emphasising demand in the eighteenth century is to shift the emphasis away from supply in a much broader sense. For, as this period is perceived as containing the origins of modern contemporary society, it is itself subject to an interpretative transformation away from its characterisation as an industrial society and towards its image as a consumer society. Putting this another way, a feature of the debate that does emerge from Cannadine's survey is that it is not only the explanation of the Industrial

---

3   As ultimately denied by von Tunzelmann (1978).

4   As discussed in Fine and Murfin (1984a and b) and Fine (1990a). See also Fine (1982b) for the (scholarly or otherwise) significance of, and debate over, the distinction between royalty and rent.

Revolution that is subject to change, together with the specification of different sets of causal factors and how they operate, but also the very definition of what constitutes the revolution itself.[5]

Clearly, at the core will be issues concerning the pace of growth of output, population and their compositions. But, as the mainstream literature has evolved, there has been a tendency to limit the scope of the Industrial Revolution, certainly within economic history, to issues surrounding this core, reflecting the convergence between a narrowly conceived economics and economic history. A consequence of this approach has been to create an artificial separation between the economy, on the one hand, and urbanisation, the class structure, local and central government and the simultaneous revolutions in the arts, politics and religion, on the other. It is as if all of these are the effects of the Industrial Revolution rather than part and parcel of it.

Paradoxically, although a further narrowing or shift of focus to the demand side might appear to be a recipe for an even greater degree of economic reductionism, it has the opposite effect in practice. This is because of the association of demand with culture, style, life-style, etc, which serve as the analytical counterpart to technological change. Consequently, the demand-side approach potentially has a wider compass than the orthodoxy.

No doubt this makes the consumerist approach more attractive. It has been most vigorously pursued by McKendrick, who has employed a full range of traditional historical techniques, from the anecdotal to detailed archival research, to highlight the role of consumption. Beginning in the 1960s, and extending over almost two decades, he has written a series of celebratory articles on the entrepreneurial talents of Sir Josiah Wedgwood (McKendrick, 1959/60, 1961, 1964, 1970, 1973 and 1982). [6] Many draw on the same pool of primary evidence. Each enjoys a high degree of scholarship but each is also concerned to situate itself in a distinct wider context.

5　Thus, in Cannadine's periodisation, industrialisation shifts between impoverishment, cyclical movement, third world development and exaggerated economic performance.

6　For McKendrick (1970, pp. 290/1), Wedgwood was to: "be the first potter to introduce steam power into the Potteries, be the first potter to introduce a clocking-in scheme into the Potteries, be the first potter accurately to cost his accounts, be the first potter to allow his customers to 'serve themselves', be the first potter to take a successful merchant into partnership, be the first potter to organise a training school for artists, be the first potter to introduce a satisfaction-or-money-back policy, be the first English potter to dominate the European market, be the first potter to employ famous artists on an industrial scale, be the first potter to introduce the substantial use of female labour into the potbank, be the first potter to gear his prices to the fluctuating nature of demand, be the first potter to harness the fashionable taste for antiquities to mass production, and so on to a whole series of innovative 'firsts'".

The same material underpinning an early article on salesmanship and marketing provides the basis for an argument twenty years later in support of an eighteenth-century consumer revolution (McKendrick, 1959/60 and 1982). In the light of Cannadine, it is interesting to speculate why McKendrick should have sought to revive his earlier scholarship on consumer demand or, perhaps more importantly, why it has been received with a degree of interest. It is not enough to read off McKendrick's revival of consumerism as a simple response to the pattern of contemporary economic events, though it is tempting to point to the change in the use of his material between the 'you have never had it so good' emergence from post-war privations in the 1960s, and the 'there is no alternative' of the 1980s. In the 1960s, McKendrick argued that the unique entrepreneurial talents of Wedgwood gave him a competitive advantage over his rivals, from which he gained market demand at their expense. The later article, employing predominantly the same empirical material, has shifted ground considerably by suggesting that Wedgwood's activities are now characteristic of those that would typically create additional demand, and hence provide an active motive force behind the consumer revolution.

The hostility to the dominance of supply, the wish to revive the idea of the making of history by the wealthy as the leading and progressive edge, and the rise of a supply and demand framework have all been reasons for the emergence of the consumerist approach. McKendrick follows Braudel (1974, pp. 123–4) in pointing to the impetus of luxury as the source of changes in material life although 'before the nineteenth century and its innovations, luxury was more like the action of an engine often running in neutral than an element of growth' (see also Sombart, 1967). It only needs, by McKendrick's account, Wedgwood's assault on the pottery industry to move the engine into gear a century earlier. The economic engineering of this mechanism is taken up in the next section.

3   Is There a Supply and Demand for Industrial Revolution?

Within economics there has always been an uneasy dichotomy between the long run and the short run. It has usually been accommodated by focusing attention exclusively on either one or the other at any particular time or shifting what each means to suit theoretical or empirical purposes (Fine and Dimakou, 2016). In the era of Keynesianism, the short-run movement of the economy has been central, with macroeconomics occupying its leading edge. While microeconomics has grown in both sophistication and scope, especially in serving the theory of general equilibrium, the subject has advanced conceptually little beyond the partial equilibrium foundations provided by Alfred Marshall – which were designed to explain the behaviour of the individual consumer and firm. Aggregating these individual units into the economy as a whole yields macroeconomics when the market coordination of supply and demand are potentially imperfect in the short run. In the long run, such market imperfections tend to be set aside, so that aggregation leads to a focus upon the changing contours of supply and technology. This leads in economic history to the increasingly familiar measurement of growth and total factor productivity, necessarily calculated in principle on the basis of full employment.[7]

Over the past decade or so, the balance between macro and micro has been disturbed. Keynesianism has given way somewhat to a revival of monetarism in the form of the New Classical Economics.[8] There has also been greater attention paid to the 'supply side' in the light of policies designed to strengthen market forces (privatisation and deregulation) and individual incentives (tax cuts). Nonetheless, there remains an uneasy compromise between the short and the long runs. While Say's Law, the idea that supply creates its own demand, is rejected in the short run, which is predominantly demand-side determined, the long run is still primarily perceived as given by unexamined supply-side conditions. Thus, in statistical work, the long run is usually netted out as the supply-side trend around which short-run demand-side fluctuations are to be estimated and explained.[9]

Not surprisingly, economic history has reproduced this analytical division between the short and long runs and between demand and supply, respectively, particularly as cliometrics has brought it analytically closer to the theoretical framework of orthodox economics. Different economic periods have been designated by reference to supply, and especially to technology – as in the ages of steam, railway and automobile. Traditional historiography has, in other words, been dominated by an interest in supply-side questions which have clearly claimed the high ground in the study of the British Industrial Revolution. How was it that so much more of so much that was new and different could have been produced over such a short period? Inevitably, the sheer

---

7 Even though, inconsistently, slower rates of growth may be explained, for example, by higher levels of unemployment or, indeed, factors or assumptions that are assumed away in calculating total factor productivity but which are used to explain it. For a critique, see Nicholas (1982) and Fine (1980a, Chapter 5) and, most recently, Fine (2016, Chapter 5).

8 For a critique of which, from a Keynesian standpoint, see Davies (1989) and, from a more radical perspective, Fine and Harris (1987).

9 For an empirical critique of netting out long-term growth trends, see Stock and Watson (1988).

scale of the changes that took place has created a logical asymmetry between awareness of, and interest in, supply and demand.

The latter has lagged far behind. Equally unsurprisingly, the imbalance in historical analysis has been redressed by a revisionist school which seeks to place emphasis on long-term change as the consequence of demand as well as of supply. Gilboy (1932, p. 121) is frequently cited as an early exception to supply-side hegemony, arguing that, "In the field of economic history as well as that of economic theory there has been a tendency to overemphasize the factor of supply". Later historians have reiterated Gilboy's lament, bringing the role of demand into greater prominence (for example, Breen, 1986; Jones, 1973; Weatherill, 1988).

McKendrick (1982) argues most forcibly that the birth of the Industrial Revolution owes as much to demand or, more exactly, to consumption, as to supply. What is more, demand may even have been the midwife of the shift in supply. With respect to consumption, he talks of a "revolution", p. 1; changes "of life-style", p. 3; "consumer boom", "men, and in particular women, bought as never before", p. 9; so that "the first of the world's consumer societies had unmistakably emerged by 1800 ... (if not) all the features of modern consumer society", p. 13. In sum, "The consumer revolution was the necessary analogue to the industrial revolution, the necessary convulsion on the demand side of the equation to match the convulsion on the supply side", p. 9.

For orthodox historians, especially those leaning to the right across the intellectual spectrum, this demand-side approach has certain attractions. First, it is an open invitation for detailed study of the changing patterns of consumption. As these expand, they are perceived as the motive force of economic progress – neatly combining the welfare theorems of static laissez-faire economics with consumer satisfaction as the source of growth. Second, as consumption is increasingly confined to those with direct or indirect access to income, so economic progress is associated with the history of the rich or nouveau riche. Accordingly, for McKendrick, an important ideological accompaniment of the consumer revolution of the eighteenth century is the overcoming of the puritan ethic against consumption. Unfortunately, this development has been seen too readily as a reaction against a blanket ban on all consumption/enjoyment rather than as a moral outrage at its unequal distribution.

Third, the preoccupation with consumption diverts attention away from supply, production and work, which all too readily carry a connotation of Marxist and class analysis. Consumption, by contrast, is primarily (limited to, other than through emulation and distinction) a private affair for the individual concerned.

Finally, and paradoxically, there are resonances between this approach and the revival of contemporary monetarism. Those that have reacted against Keynesian policy-making eschew state intervention to manipulate effective demand and, instead, rely upon supply-side factors to provide full employment in the short run. In doing so, they tend to embrace the role of demand in the long run. And that demand will come from the nouveau riche of the 1980s, a consumer revolution whose necessary analogue is the deindustrialisation revolution and the life-style of the 'yuppie' as the current twentieth-century maker of fashion. These connections should not, however, be forced and the ideological factors concerned will be examined in greater detail in the concluding remarks.

4 Economic Theory and the Consumerist Approach

The theoretical content of the consumerists is more problematic. The simplest underlying economic model employed is the notion that increases in demand represent a shift out of the demand curve and more output at a higher intersection with a given supply curve. This is entirely unacceptable. If this occurs within a particular sector of the economy, then the shifting demand curve must be compensated for by an equivalent but negative shift in some other sector (Mokyr, 1977; McCloskey, 1981). If the shift concerns the economy as a whole, then we enter Keynesian territory in which increases in output can only follow upon excess capacity for, otherwise, inflation is the commonly perceived outcome. In economic theory, a common, but not mainstream model for long-run growth in the context of excess capacity is associated with Kaldor-Pasinetti and the widow's cruse, a goblet from which the liquid that is drunk is always replenished. Here, Kaldor put forward the dictum that workers spend what they earn and capitalists earn what they spend. The latter proposition follows in the joint presence of excess capacity and deficient demand, for what one capitalist spends creates demand and hence profits for the class as a whole. The simple Keynesian multiplier applies to the profit economy alone and the lower the saving rate of capitalists the more profits they have to earn in order to attain the level of investment and other autonomous expenditure. In short, demand (out of profits) creates its own supply (Fine and Murfin, 1984a, Chapters 4 and 5).

There are a number of disturbing features of this model, as far as the consumerist approach is concerned. First, apart from depending upon excess capacity, any increases in profitability on the supply side have the effect of depressing the economy, since necessary savings are achieved at lower levels of economic activity. This means that the complementary supply-side Industrial Revolution would have been self-defeating. Second, the model takes the growth rate as given, and determines that the level of saving should adjust to the level of investment by compensating changes in the distribution of income should one or other class change its saving behaviour. In other words, if capitalists spend more then the distribution of income will adjust in their favour and the saving and growth rates will remain as before.

More generally, those that argue that a shift in demand gives rise to an industrial revolution rarely specify what the latter means, even in a narrow economic sense. After all, the theoretical apparatus involved is identical to that partial analysis of a single market, say, for umbrellas, experiencing a demand shift in view of a damp summer. To pursue the analogy, shifts in the climate do not usually lead in such models to a higher growth rate in the use and manufacture of umbrellas but to a higher equilibrium level of output and price.

To return to the Industrial Revolution, the consumerist approach has neglected to specify whether increased demand should lead to a once-and-for-all shift in the level of output or, as seems less likely from such a shift but reasonably required of a revolution, a once-and-for-all shift in the level of the rate of growth of output.

Last, and ironically, the use to which the demand-led model of growth has mainly been put in conjunction with a supply-side analysis is the model of monopolistic stagnation, deriving from the economics of Kalecki.[10] This suggests that monopolies invest too little in order to sustain prices and to restrict output, while workers' wages are forced down to sustain profitability and at too low a level to sustain demand. Obviously, this Marxist genre of underconsumptionism is far removed from the intentions of the consumerist school. But it does serve to illustrate the difficulty of sustaining the school theoretically on the basis of aggregate demand shifts.

Much more fruitful is the idea that shifts in demand effect shifts of the supply curve itself rather than shifts along it. Whether for individual sectors or for the economy as a whole, the idea depends upon the role of the extent of the market, a type of argument predominantly associated with Adam Smith's focus on the potential for the growing division of labour. Crudely, the larger the market, the greater is the scope for economies of scale with existing technology. In addition, larger markets will provide greater inducements to innovate, since the potential returns will be so much greater. Such an approach appears

---

10   See Sawyer (1982), Cowling (1982) and, in the same tradition, Baran and Sweezy (1968). For a critique, see Fine and Murfin (1984a and b).

to be the most favoured explanation of those who seriously consider the matter of the effect of demand in the long term.[11] It is a sort of infant industry argument, only to be applied in the absence of any grown-ups. But the effect of protection, or larger and more certain demand, is subject to dispute – does it lead to "featherbedding" and higher prices, or to dynamic accrual of scale economies? Quite clearly, this cannot be answered by reference to demand alone. Which of these two responses occurs depends upon other conditions for which the structure of supply is most important, as well as the level and distribution of income.

Probing this further reveals problems for the consumerist approach. For, to put it in extreme form, the idea of firms straining to revolutionise supply but held back by deficient demand presupposes either a monopoly having mopped up the available markets, or a fragmented industrial structure operating in the absence of competition. Otherwise, firms would compete with each other for the available demand and rationalise where scale economies warranted it. All of this appears highly improbable for the period of the Industrial Revolution, where large numbers of small firms in competition with each other seem to have been more the order of the day and for at least a further century. Of course, greater demand would help any firm or industry, but whether this leads to cushioning or to innovation is conditioned by factors surrounding supply – availability of finance, for example, or market restrictions – most of which are studiously ignored by those relying upon the direct or indirect impact of demand upon supply.

Interestingly, McKendrick implicitly rejects the demand-led theory of transforming supply. His emphasis, for pottery and clothing and fashion more generally, concerns the entrepreneurial and social creation of a differentiated demand in conformity with status enhancement. Accordingly, limitations upon demand, especially where they affect economies of scale, are irrelevant since capital itself is fragmenting demand as a marketing strategy – changing the design, colours and articles of the pottery manufactured to serve and to sustain changing fashion.

Unsurprisingly, McKendrick's analysis of the pottery industry has not been free of criticism (especially by Weatherill, 1986). She argues that Wedgwood was a far from typical representative of the industry, and not its leader, so that he cannot be taken to be the exemplar of its specific success, let alone exemplar for the economy as a whole. It is also important to draw a distinction between

---

11   See Gilboy (1932), Mokyr (1984), Ben-Schachar (1984) and Musson (ed.) (1972). It is also the source of a mono-causal explanation. See Gaski (1982) and, for a critique, Geary (1984), Inkster (1983) and Bruland (1985).

the different sectors of the industry both in terms of the clay employed and the markets served. It is far from clear, for example, why a decorative piece of Wedgwood display should give rise to a functional demand for coarse tea-drinking ware. Even so, after a period of rapid expansion, by 1800 the sector employed only one per cent of all industrial workers and just half of one per cent of all employment (Weatherill, 1986, p. 299).

This cuts even the putative leading entrepreneur down to size. But even if this is set aside, and Wedgwood is granted the status of leading entrepreneur, does the type of role he played in the creation of demand necessarily lead to an Industrial Revolution through a consumer revolution? The answer is ambiguous. For the Wedgwood characteristics that McKendrick describes are ones that are usually associated with inefficiency, even within orthodox economic analysis. By employing fashion to charge a high price on a new piece and then dropping the price to reach a wider market, Wedgwood is essentially operating as a discriminating monopolist for "he had accomplished, in fact, the most spectacular example of a successful policy of product differentiation in the history of British pottery" (McKendrick, 1982, p. 140; see also Weatherill, 1988, p. 40). Nor is charging prices well above marginal cost to give goods a snob value a recipe for economic efficiency. Indeed, modern consumerist society is more associated with lower prices initially to gain acceptance for mass produced goods.

These factors point to static inefficiencies in Wedgwood's activities which would have had the further effect of fragmenting the market for pottery, thereby potentially delaying, not hastening, the availability of the demand for, and the supply of, a less fashionable but cheaper and more generally available product to serve more of the 'lower orders'. It is at least as plausible to see the luxury market of the eighteenth century as a supply-side obstacle to the development of mass production for the lower classes in the nineteenth century as it is to view it as a stimulus to emulation on the demand side.

In short, on theoretical grounds, the argument that demand as such can play a significant role in long-run economic change is extremely weak, and the theoretical analysis presented here suggests that the conditions under which it could play a role are not typical of the period of the Industrial Revolution. The consumerist approach tends to presume that if the consumption of the lower classes chronologically follows that of the upper classes, then this is evidence of trickle-down (and of a sort of multiplier demand effect from a higher-level stimulus). There is a simple fallacy in this. Without necessarily presuming that the growth of consumption habits is naturally determined or that they are uniform across a population, exactly the same sort of observations could occur even if there were no emulative effects. This is so if consumption is simply expanding across the population in line with rising incomes – you eat beef once you can afford it!

For coal, for example, during the course of the eighteenth century, there was a substantial increase in domestic consumption. Flinn (1984, p. 252) estimates it as rising from between one and two million tons in 1700 to over five million tons in 1800. The distribution and marketing of the coal required a highly sophisticated and complex set of activities, especially in the run from the mines of Newcastle down to the hearths of London (Flinn, 1984; Nef, 1932; Smith 1961; Pollard, 1983; Dietz, 1986). Not surprisingly, the growth of the domestic consumption of coal during the whole of the eighteenth century has tended to be overshadowed by the dramatic rise in its use for the production of iron from the last quarter of the century onwards and for its presumed role as an energy source in the Industrial Revolution. As far as domestic consumption is concerned, however, there are considerable parallels with the economics of the pottery industry – even if the Wedgwoods of coal do not readily present themselves. Yet it would be farfetched to view the rise in coal consumption as rising out of the emulative behaviour of the lower classes (with fashion emanating from London as the major domestic market). More important was the availability and cost of transport, the price of coal and (lack of cheap) potential substitutes, and the level of income, together with overall population size and housing conditions (given the weather).

Two further differences between coal and pottery are relevant here. First, it was more important in quantitative terms, contributing about 60, 000 to employment in 1800 (Flinn, 1984, p. 365) as compared to little over 10,000 in the Potteries (Weatherill, 1988, p. 453). Second, its ability to expand demand had been heavily circumscribed both by monopoly and by taxation. Though the effects of monopoly control on final prices may have been small, taxation is estimated to have raised prices by at least twice the costs of production, especially in the London market (Hausmann, 1984a and b). This is evidence of the driving force of income even in the context of restricted demand.

The arguments around pottery and coal concern individual sectors of the economy. They also concentrate on the expansion of existing markets rather than on the chronologically earlier creation of these markets. Study of the earlier period involves a closer look at the displacement of earlier forms of production and consumption, thereby siting the development of the market economy within a specific historical framework and identifying it as just one of many forms of economic life.

5   Is Emphasis on Demand and Supply the Answer?

Do these arguments against the consumerist approach lead, then, to the restoration of the orthodox dichotomy in which Say's Law appears to rule in the
long run and effective demand in the short run? The answer is not necessarily – first of all because the orthodoxy is no longer quite so simplistic. It recognises that the Industrial Revolution is the product of a complex multiplicity
of factors. Only the impassioned researcher of one particular aspect will tend
towards a self-interested mono-causal explanation. Moreover, demand is and
always has been taken into account, even if in a subsidiary capacity. This is certainly true of attempts to assess the impact of growing exports as opposed to
the domestic market (Cole, 1983) (although serving the world market would be
unable to explain, of itself, why one country rather than another should experience industrial revolution). And, as cliometrics renders more analytically rigorous the orthodox economic analysis underlying historical change, demand
factors are a logical requirement. For Cole, "A substantial literature has begun
to appear on the subject, and the growth of demand is now widely regarded
as one of the essential elements in the transformation of the economy", p. 36.
Even McCloskey (1981, pp. 120–22) who generally denies the role of demand for
the economy as a whole, makes three exceptions – in the case of foreign trade,
high unemployment and demand-induced technical progress – each of which
he dismisses on empirical grounds.

   However, the orthodoxy not only takes account of demand; embracing it
within a multi-causal explanation is taken one distinct step further by incorporating the variety of explanatory factors into a system of demand and supply.
Crafts (1981, p. 3) argues:

> Levels of demand that push the economy towards full employment in
> the short run might elicit greater investment and productivity increase,
> thereby enhancing the growth rate of the productive potential ... the
> long-run rate is made up of a large number of these short-run spells, and
> so the economy's rate of growth will depend on levels of demand. The
> majority of recent English economic historians of the eighteenth century
> have (*possibly unconsciously*) written in this vein. (Emphasis added)

This probably exaggerates the extent to which long-run models have been
worked out with a strong component of effective demand in attendance, and
with the long run constructed as a sequence of short-run (unemployment)
equilibria. As previously observed, orthodox economics has considerable difficulties relating the long run to the short run in this way. More accurately, Crafts

is describing an analytical procedure whereby the variables that are considered important to short-run macroeconomic analysis – such as demand created by exports, autonomous expenditure in the simplest multiplier model – are incorporated into explanations of the long term. What is equally significant is the implicit appeal to a stark synthesis in which both demand and supply interact to yield economic change. Even those who do not intend to do this are interpreted as having no choice, inadvertently contributing to the analysis of the level of demand and/or to the level of supply.

In other words, there is a sort of analytical reductionism in operation, in which all authors and their suggested causal factors contribute to the specification of the shifting supply and demand curves. Individual causal factors can be examined in this context by reference to their effect on such curves. Because the framework accommodates this, it is hardly surprising that, while there has been muted praise for the consumerist approach, criticism has rarely reached beyond the level of questioning the empirical emphasis. Paradoxically, opposition is more likely to come from those such as McCloskey, whose rigour in orthodox economic analysis and prior commitment to Say's Law in the long term lead him to tend to reject the long-term role of demand. Otherwise, the supply and demand framework gives rise to an appealing commitment to a multi-causal explanation for the Industrial Revolution, but one that depends upon the simplest of causal analytical structures that is essentially eclectic.

This discussion raises a number of further problems. First, is it appropriate to treat major historical events such as the Industrial Revolution in the same analytical and empirical framework as is used for an individual sector over possibly a shorter and less dramatic period? The likely answer is that the more extensive the degree of change, if of a qualitative nature, the more variables must be included in order that the source of shifts in demand and supply are isolated and the ceteris paribus-type assumptions are justified or, more exactly, adjusted. In principle, almost any variable could enter as a factor in supply and demand.[12]

Second, though, a sequential relaxation of the boundaries of ceteris paribus leads to a hierarchical ordering of the causal factors between those in the short run, which are always included, and those in the long run which, for the shorter period, act as parameters. In narrow economic terms, employment and output tend to be treated as variable in the short run and the capital stock as

---

12   Thus, there is a counterpart in the ideological realm to be found in Campbell (1987), for
     example, who argues – to parody – that just as the Protestant ethic shifted out the sup-
     ply curve, so the romantic ethic shifted out the demand curve. No wonder the economy
     boomed!

variable in the long run. Technical progress tends to endure a schizophrenic existence. At some times it is incorporated continuously into the economy; at other times, it has to be positively sought over the longer term. As Musson (1972, p. 1) observes of the growth models that are still standard:

> The scientific and technical achievements of the past two centuries are so overwhelmingly obvious in their transformation of economic and social life that it seems almost incredible that, until very recently, most modern economists, building 'growth models', left them entirely out of account.

Third, the causal model involved is one of simultaneous determination, in parallel with, if not always formally equivalent to, the mathematical sense of the term. Supply and demand are equalised by whatever underlying causal factors are taken to influence them. These factors, as mentioned in the previous point, are structured chronologically rather than causally. There is a tendency to look first at the elements making up the measurement of growth and total factor productivity, then to move to explain a second level of variables, such as exports, and, finally, to incorporate a third level of qualitative factors usually associated with socio-economic change, like entrepreneurship, skills and business culture. Doubts have to be raised about the explanatory content of such an approach. Though it does provide a powerful, if at times obscure econometric means by which to structure the presentation of empirical material, there is a profound absence of theoretical content, even if the underlying approach is the soon-forgotten optimising behaviour of individuals. McCloskey (1981) reminds us of this by referring to the isolated, closed and atomised economy of Robinson Crusoe when arguing that aggregate demand cannot shift output. Indeed, it is far from clear how supply and demand analysis can do anything other than chart the change in economic and social relations (and the relation between the two) when discussing the Industrial Revolution.

This is not, then, simply or predominantly to press for a richer set of variables to be considered as influencing supply and demand – an attractive option for those who wish to take account of class conflict, redistribution of income, work intensity, i.e. for those who wish to reject the undoubtedly restrictive and conservative variables that are the common fare of the neo-Keynesian approach. Rather, a structured theory of economic and social change is essential, one which relates underlying tendencies and tensions to more specific developments and resolutions. This is, of course, easier to propose than to elaborate, and nothing more than hints can be offered within the confines of this chapter. The analytical point of departure is the focus upon underlying historical and social forces that give rise to supply and demand but which are not reducible to them. The classic example is given by Marxist theory, in which the specification of a capitalist mode of production and its tendential laws of production give rise to abstract propositions from which more complex categories and the historical process are derived and analysed. That such a method is not confined to Marxism can be illustrated by reference to classical economists, even those who are generally considered to be supportive of the consumerist approach.

For Adam Smith, for example, the stage of commerce is perceived as an articulation between the growing division of labour and the limited extent of the market, which in turn reflects more fundamental historical forces determining the ethical balance between altruism and the wish for self-regard, on the one hand, and self-interest in conjunction with the natural propensity to truck, barter and exchange, on the other (Fine, 1982a, Chapter 5).[13] For Smith, the Industrial Revolution as transition to the commercial stage of society required breaking down feudal barriers to the market so that the division of labour could develop – a similar view underpins the contemporary ideology of the 'single market' for the European Community of 1992. In contrast Malthus, as praised by Keynes, stressed the progressive role played by landlords' unproductive expenditure in maintaining demand. This too, however, was linked to an underlying conflict between the virtuous pursuit of happiness and its potential for generating. excesses (most notably in population growth in the lower orders). For Malthus, Winch (1987, pp. 38–9) suggests, "treated all universal passions, impulses and wants, when considered abstractly or generally as being natural or good ... The danger to happiness lay not in these impulses but in the 'fatal extravagances' to which they gave rise". Accordingly, Winch quotes from Malthus, "The science of political economy bears a nearer resemblance to the science of morals and politics than to that of mathematics", p. 76 These few remarks should guard against reducing either Malthus or Smith to proponents of simple supply and demand theory.[14]

---

13   See also Rosenberg (1968) for the importance in Smith of shifting tastes and income between different classes as a source of a growing market.

14   Interestingly, both support the progressive role of the market, but their differences over the role of landlords reflects the extent to which they are perceived to spend on commodities or not. For Malthus, in particular, Winch perceives 'embourgeoisement' as a political and economic goal for the mass of society, so that the working class elevates itself out of its population/poverty trap. This has strong affinities with the trickle-down theory, even if it is only in the consumption of goods that emulation takes place. For a discussion of the role of demand in Malthus (see especially Vatter, 1959; Sowell, 1963; Rashid, 1977). Note there is a dispute about whether his theory of gluts applies to the long or to the short run.

In short, whether dealing in grand theory or analysing a single sector over a shorter period, the use of supply and demand provides an unsatisfactory approach. These curves – and the functions they serve – are themselves the product of a structure of economic and social forces that has to be identified. While primarily intending to set aside the consumerist emphasis on demand as an independent agent of economic progress, a much more general critique has been offered here of the approach to economic history that operates as a more or less complex interaction of supply and demand. The consumerist approach does not then involve a fundamental break with the orthodoxy's dependence upon supply and demand, but merely lies at one extreme – in contrast to the more balanced approach of Crafts, say, or in contrast to the other extreme, represented by McCloskey (1981) and Mokyr (1984) for whom supply conditions are paramount in the long run.

However, the emphasis on demand does serve to shift attention away from changes in technology to changes in 'taste'. Thus, the mainstream emphasis on supply has an informal literature supportive of its models and statistics addressing the transformation of production – as in considering entrepreneurship. The consumerist approach, in the general absence of formal models, relies almost exclusively on informal discussion of the historical transformation of preferences which are perceived intuitively to shift out the demand curve. Its effectiveness is considered in the next section in the context of fashion and clothing. The discussion emphasises findings which support our more general argument. First, the trickle-down of demand through the market is seen to have been exaggerated empirically. Emulation through cast-offs, for example, creates no additional market demand. Second, it might, even where it does affect market demand, impede the growth of mass production/consumption. The presence of a large servant class dependent upon and emulating their 'superiors' is restricted from access both to wage labour and the market for consumer goods, which would otherwise fuel domestic consumption. Third, the focus on demand analyses the effects of changes whose causes are arguably more vividly perceived through the neglected lens of effect on supply – the breakdown of domestic production and the proletarianisation of the household is more than, and removed from, the shifting of domestic demand from hearth to market. In short, the causes and courses of shifts in demand have to be related to a structured and dynamic explanation of the Industrial Revolution as a whole.

6   The Demand for Fashion in Clothes

McKendrick's (1982) article on the "Commercialisation of Fashion" (in *The Birth of a Consumer Society*) illustrates some of the limitations of operating within the 'supply and demand' framework and, within that, of leaning too heavily on just one of its axes. In his article, social emulation, class composition and emulative spending in the second half of the eighteenth century become the prime movers behind the development of mass-based consumer demand fifty years later. Demand emerges as a necessary precondition and stimulant to the subsequent growth of mass production. In particular, the 'trickle-down' effects of the demand for luxury goods, i.e. the gradual percolation and diffusion of upper-class tastes through all strata of society, anticipate and expedite the arrival of mass markets. According to McKendrick, once the pursuit of luxury "was made possible for an ever-widening proportion of the population, then its potential was released and it became an engine for growth, a motive power for mass production", p. 66.

Demand, in this scheme, becomes an active transforming agent on its own, viewed independently of production; McKendrick's writing manages to attach a kind of dynamism to the force of demand by documenting the frenetic pace and manifestations of changes in taste. In the rapid displacement of one style, colour, eighteenth-century flavour-of-the-month by another, the course of fashion begins to acquire a self-sustained momentum of its own.

For McKendrick, this progressive emulation is manifested by the dress of the domestic servant which, in the second half of the eighteenth century, is often almost indistinguishable from that of the employer. Foreign fascination for the apparent blurring of social distinction that this implied is much quoted; the historian Von Archenolz "complained that he could 'not distinguish between guests and servants' when he visited the Duke of Newcastle, and was particularly thrown by the fact that the butler dressed like his master", p. 58.

How this mirroring of costume between upper and lower classes came about is not addressed by McKendrick. For him, the transmission of taste, like that of demand, is a disembodied process, not explicable by reference to prevailing social or economic relations. There is no attempt to link the surge in demand in the late eighteenth century with the production and distribution of goods, nor is there any reference to the source and distribution of consumers' incomes unless it be by a minimal lip service paid to the supply side of the extraordinary world of late eighteenth-century fashion in clothing. But his clear lack of interest in its dynamics leads him to make casual and misleading references to "the sales of mass-produced cheap clothes" in an eighteenth-century context, p. 53. It may not be apparent to all his readers that no mass markets for cheap clothes (as opposed to fabrics and accessories) existed until almost a hundred years later, well after the arrival of the sewing machine in 1851. Even the systematic use of measuring tapes in the manufacture of clothes by size did not influence the cutting of fabric until the nineteenth century (Tozer and Levitt, 1983). Giving the impression that the supply underpinning mass markets already lay in readiness and simply awaited the catalyst of demand for luxury goods to spring into action is highly misleading. First of all, it conflates the idea of differentiation operating at the luxury end of the market with the standardisation of goods that is the hallmark of mass production. The emphasis on the expansion of markets through rapid and continuous change in the products themselves cannot be used to explain the process by which goods are homogenised to meet the requirements of large-scale volume production. In fact, the former can be viewed as obstructing or at least delaying the arrival of the latter. Having resolutely turned his back on both the producers and distributors to give centre stage to the role of demand, McKendrick is left without any means of explaining the transformation of a bespoke market in luxuries to a mass market of essential goods. It is simply observed, almost by a natural progression, in that "luxuries" become "decencies", and "decencies" become "necessities", p. 1. At some stage, the frenzied proliferation and pace of fashion change just burns out, leaving "a greater social uniformity ... which of course suited those producing and selling fashion". He argues that, "demand could be controlled to suit their needs" but without postulating any mechanisms by which this might have been achieved, p. 56. The madness of compulsive differentiation in the consumption of hand-made luxury goods is presented as simply petering out, through some unexplained shift in the zeitgeist, transforming itself into a more even-keeled and sensible uniformity which could then be exploited by producers to consolidate and generalise the emerging features of modern-day consumer society.

7   Missing Markets

One of the central flaws embedded in McKendrick's argument is his assumption that the expansion and broadening of interest in fashionable clothing during the second half of the eighteenth century in itself signified an expansion and broadening of the market demand for these goods. This is to confound consumption of goods with their exchange, i.e. to assume that the diffusion of fashion within society, from mistress to maidservant, demonstrated a progressive broadening of purchasing power. Social emulation, it is assumed, in itself begets emulative spending.

The argument is really a recasting of the optimist's position in the debate over changes in the standard of living caused by the Industrial Revolution. In the absence of any reliable information on the distribution of incomes during the period, the hypothesis of a closely stratified society which encouraged the idea of social mobility between groups would allow for the progressive redistribution of income as of fashion from the top down. More specifically, McKendrick argues that, "The expansion in the market, revealed in the literary evidence, occurred first among the domestic-servant class, then among the industrial workers and finally among the agricultural workers", p. 60. Though the argument depends upon emulative behaviour triggering emulative spending, it offers neither documentary evidence chronicling such behaviour nor any discussion of the social relations which might have influenced it.

In fact, neither spending nor any act of exchange appears in McKendrick's scheme of things at all. In the discussion of clothing, at least, the market remains an altogether shadowy not to say invisible figure. The acquisition of goods – as opposed to their display – is never addressed. Who purchases what, from whom and for what prices? What are the incomes or wealth of those making such purchases and what is their source; to answer those queries would be to detract too much from McKendrick's central concern which rests squarely, if narrowly, with the growth of consumer demand induced by luxury consumption. In an earlier article, McKendrick does attempt to address these issues, hypothesising that the marked increase in the second half of the eighteenth century of the participation of women and children in wage labour explains the sudden surge in money wages that led to an expansion of demand (McKendrick, 1974). Curiously, no mention is made here of the role played by social emulation and emulative spending. Women and children as industrial wage-earners are seen as contributing directly to an increased demand for household necessities and particularly for those goods formerly made by the women themselves rather than for luxuries. It is their wage income that pushes demand. This at least grapples with the sources of income that are translated into effective demand for consumer goods. It also suggests that the process of transformation in demand and production occurred together over a much longer period than is suggested by McKendrick's later work. Moreover, it points to the contradiction between the entry of significant numbers of women and children into the labour force and the growth of unproductive domestic servants in the eighteenth and nineteenth centuries. On the other hand, it takes a positive view of this transition, arguing that the shift of women into wage labour represented a liberation from the oppression of "cottage" industry, rather than the coercive deprivation of the means of home livelihoods.

In short, there are problems of consistency across McKendrick's work. Either he sets aside the source of the income that provides for growing demand, simply relying upon the filtering down of tastes from the wealthy to the lower classes. Or, in a sideshow, wage income is generated by the proletarianisation of women and children. Here, however, he would need to paint a much grander canvas of economic and social change over a longer period. Arguably, the destruction of domestic industry involves causal factors and associated effects whose own direct influence on demand is liable to be greater, through the wage income generated, than the indirect effect of the impact of fashion.

McKendrick's later article emphasises the key role played by the unproductive domestic servant as a carrier rather than an active consumer of fashion – transmitting changes in taste both from the upper classes to the working classes and from London to the provinces. It makes no reference to the dampening role played by the servant class as a whole on the evolution of wage labour and its limiting effect on the extent of the market – of so much concern to Adam Smith. The perpetuation of almost feudal relations between servant and served could not be dismissed as insignificant when the number of men and women so employed was estimated at almost one million in 1806 – 800,000 females and 110,000 males, equivalent to about one in every eleven people in the population at large (Hecht, 1956, p. 34).

Servants are withdrawn from other potentially productive activity and are paid a variable combination of wages, tips and goods in kind. Their exclusion from wage labour must have had an inhibiting effect on the development of both large-scale demand and mass markets, both key features of modern consumer society. In addition, their absorption into households other than their own held down demand for all those consumer goods which depended on the growth of individual households (everything from housing itself to sets of furniture and pottery) as well as on the growth of cash wages. In other words, the perpetuation of this relationship and its later extension to the middle classes can in itself be seen as moderating the growth of industrial capitalism.

Nowhere in McKendrick's article is the huge disparity of income between master and servant ever commented upon. Yet the annual income of most housemaids in the second half of the eighteenth century would have been insufficient to pay for the material for a single dress made up for her mistress (Barbara Johnson paid £7 I5s 9d in the 1760s for material for a day dress, a 'negligee', at a time when her housemaid was probably earning a basic annual salary of about seven guineas) (Hecht, 1956; Johnson, 1987). Clearly, domestic servants were not in a position to purchase newly-made clothes in imitation of their employers. On their incomes, they could not possibly contribute to any growth in the effective demand for new fashion goods. Emulative spending emanating from below stairs appears highly improbable.

Those clothes worn by servants which echoed upper-class rather than working-class tastes came to them, for the most part, directly from their employers, unmediated by markets of any kind. No money changed hands. Most clothes were simply handed down from mistress to maid with increasing frequency as the turnover in fashion tastes increased (in an early demonstration of dynamic obsolescence). Extending the lifespan of still serviceable, though slightly outmoded garments could widen the general currency for fashion dress by raising its visibility and extending its use. In this, it functioned as a form of advertising. However, no discerning exercise of taste on the part of domestic servants was required.

In fact, the strength of emulation as a transforming mechanism can be even more comprehensively questioned. Employers often selected and purchased clothes for their servants to wear, in pursuit of a kind of 'vicarious consumption' which McKendrick mentions in connection with exotically dressed black page boys who adorned some eighteenth-century households. (There is much evidence of this practice, from Parson Woodforde to Anne Lister.) Lavish dress provided by the employer, which cut across accepted social distinctions, reflected his or her taste, not that of the servant. Furthermore, clothes purchased in this way often remained the property of the employer. Extravagant dress for female servants in lieu of uniforms served as a kind of livery comparable to the more formal outfits worn by coachmen. Though male servants wore livery from an early date, uniforms were not adopted for female servants until the second half of the nineteenth century. Until then, their dress had always echoed the style and taste of their mistresses. For both male and female servants, clothes were a highly visible sign of their employers' wealth and status – much more so than their living quarters or diets, which remained completely hidden from the visitor's gaze and hence were less extravagantly catered for, Hecht (1956, p. 120).

The more exposed the servant to the public life of the house, the more he or she contributed to setting the overall social tone of the establishment, forming an integral part of the domestic display. Upstairs maids were clearly better dressed than those working exclusively below stairs. The coachman's livery was often the most elaborate of all, because he carried the employer's reputation directly into the public realm. Even when servants purchased their own wardrobe, its contents would be carefully vetted by an existing or potential employer to guarantee that it was in acceptable taste. In this respect, emulation – whether reflecting genuine preference or not – might be perceived as enhancing job prospects.

Many servants were also bequeathed dresses upon the death of their mistresses. For instance, Sarah, Duchess of Marlborough stipulated in her will that her wardrobe be divided between her lady's maid and two other maidservants, Hecht (1956, p. 116). The acceptance of the bequest in no way signified a preference for whatever fashion might be reflected in the clothes passed on. As an alternative to extending a housemaid's own wardrobe, inherited dresses might be sold on to the second-hand clothing market, a substantial and lucrative trade in the eighteenth century. So established was the market in used, reconditioned or repaired clothes that many servants were granted the rights to their masters' cast-offs as an agreed condition of their contract of employment. The preference for cash (from selling hand-me-downs) over the pleasures to be had from keeping and wearing the master's old clothes suggests a definite limit to the allure of emulation.

The persistence of a strong second-hand market does lend weight to the influence of the trickle-down effects of fashion. But equally powerful would be the attraction of slightly used goods set at low prices, relative to their cost when new. If cost is the primary factor in making such a choice – as it must be where a pair of boots could account for more than a month's wage – the contribution made by fashion or style is liable to be negligible.

Perhaps the clearest evidence of servants' apparel as an accoutrement of the household is in their wearing of mourning dress upon the death of an employer's relative. Clothes for this purpose were supplied by the employer. Following the death of her uncle in 1817, Anne Lister (1988, p. 1988) noted in her diary:

> The mantua-maker came & bombasines & stuffs were sent over from Milne's & bombasines from Butters. Chose mourning for the 2 women servants from the former place, & from the latter, 50 yds (a whole piece) bombasine at 4/9 for ourselves. The servants had each 8 yds, 6/8 wide twilled stuff at 2/4, and 3½ yards of the same for a petticoat.

It is interesting to note that material for the servants' mourning dress was half the price of that worn by the mistress. Servants had no choice in the matter, any more than would children in the household. They were required to assume – literally – the mantle of a grief which they were unlikely to feel, particularly since mourning dress was worn in memory of relatives outside the immediate household as well as for those within it. Mourning dress is simply the sharpest example of the control exercised by the employer over a servant's attire. None of the other means by which servants acquired their masters' or mistresses' clothes – through loans for the duration of service, hand-me-downs, bequests – demonstrates any preference for their employers' taste.

The element of choice or preference expressed through monetary or any other form of exchange simply does not come into it.

McKendrick concentrates on the surge in demand for fashionable clothing in the late eighteenth century, i.e. before the advent of significant advances in the technology of clothes production (all clothing remained hand-made). This allows him to raise the importance of demand as a pre-condition of, and catalyst for, the revolution in production that was presumed to follow. But, as suggested above, the omission of any evidence relating to the development, source or exercise of purchasing power weakens credibility in this concept of demand, and the emulation on which it is founded is also unproven. Moreover, by the time capitalist production of clothing, as opposed to fabric, is finally under way – in the second half of the nineteenth century – the structure of purchasing power is very different from that prevailing fifty years earlier. By the middle of the nineteenth century, a distinct pattern of demand emerges reflecting the rising income, and numbers, of industrial workers.

This coincides with a significant shift of population growth away from the south to the Midlands and the north, where the new centres of industry were located. While in 1801 only five towns in England apart from London boasted populations of more than 50,000 (Liverpool, Manchester, Bristol, Birmingham and Leeds) by 1851, their number had risen to 24. The same period showed the proportion of the labour force engaged in manufacturing, mining and industry rising from 29.7 per cent to 42.9 per cent. This considerable growth in cash wages as a source of demand was, therefore, based on a completely different pattern of social relations governing consumption (as well as those governing production). The influence of London fashion and the importance of domestic servants were both much weaker in the industrial hinterlands and largely contained within the squirearchy maintaining active links with the capital. There is something more than a little absurd in reducing these regional patterns of, and stimuli to, industrialisation to the dictates of London fashion emanating from the London upper classes.

It seems highly probable that the emergence of demand, as of consumption norms among the industrial working class, took place outside McKendrick's social nexus altogether, i.e. that the influence of the dynamic he describes was both self-contained and historically specific. McKendrick has no way of bridging the gap between the luxury trade he describes and the evolution of mass markets, just as he supplies no connecting thread to link the bespoke fashion trade with the evolution of the machine-based clothing industry.

One of several more plausible explanations for the change in taste is the spread of the Protestant ethic in dress, Ribeiro (1984). This emphasised modesty and conformity in place of worldly showiness and individuality, and was indisputably a middle-class phenomenon. The growth of the professions also contributed to the increasing sobriety of middle-class dress – clergymen, doctors and lawyers all donned working clothes that were uniformly black and unadorned. The gradual adoption of these habits by the aristocracy is in part a reflection of the decline in the influence of the court within the economic and social life of the country and of a rise in the secular culture of work. Emulation upwards signifies the court's (and the aristocracy's) decline as an arbiter of taste and style. The wearing of court dress, with its expensive and impractical finery, became increasingly rare, limited to gala royal occasions and grand social events. As the influence of the rising bourgeoisie grew, so their taste's emphasis on working dress began to take hold across a wider spectrum of society.

Equally overlooked by McKendrick was a more naked emulation by the upper classes of the dress of labourers. The introduction of the workman's frock-coat into the higher reaches of society is a clear example of this countervailing trend (repeated in the twentieth century by the fashion history of jeans). According to the Cunningtons' history of costume, the "frock" had become the common wear of the urban man by 1700. Designed for comfort (and therefore loose-fitting) from cheap materials, its distinguishing characteristic was a flat turned-down collar. By the middle of the eighteenth century, the 'gentleman' had taken it up as a comfortable alternative to his traditional heavy stiff coat. In the following decades, it became established ordinary wear for gentlemen. By the end of the century, it annexed the classier word "coat", becoming the "frock-coat", "with a long career ahead as a symbol of Class; a truly remarkable garment to have climbed the whole social scale from the farmyard to the Royal Enclosure" (Cunnington and Cunnington, 1972, p. 18). Nor were those who took up the wearing of the frock-coat unmindful of its political implications. With its reputation as a more 'democratic' mode of dress, it became popular during the period of the French Revolution among those wishing to show their opposition to the Ancien Regime (Tozer and Levitt, 1983, p. 55).

Both the examples of the frock-coat and that of the puritan ethic suggest that the trend towards equality in dress emanated from below, pushing its way upwards towards the wealthier classes, as well as from above and trickling down. This two-way influence, however, deprives luxury spending of its progressive attributes. The lower orders are no longer simply passive beneficiaries and transforming multipliers of consuming habits imposed from above, and spending by the upper classes is no longer required to serve as a catalyst in the transformation of goods from luxuries into basic necessities. The diffusion of the frock-coat represents an opposing tendency – the mutation of a humble garment into an essential component of the upper-class wardrobe. It also demonstrates that emulation need not necessarily lead to a cheapening of the final product through either increases in productivity or cheapening of materials. In other words, the widening of demand, on its own, cannot provide an impetus for progressive technical change.

8   Production of Clothing

Conspicuous consumption of clothing in the eighteenth century (as also in the nineteenth) depended on the provision of goods by labour-intensive means. It was the display of tailor-made goods on the body designed to reflect the individual's personal taste – and measurements – that conveyed some measure of wealth. Increased demand for these goods did not reflect any change in their price, any cheapening in the process by which they were made nor any change in their utility. Nor did it necessarily imply any significant growth in the numbers of people who could afford to make such purchases. Instead, increased consumption was a response to the quickened turnover in style which overrode all considerations of usefulness and availability of income.

Increased demand for luxury goods simply extended the use of hand production techniques. Until the arrival of the sewing machine in the middle of the nineteenth century, all clothing was hand-made. Though there had been considerable changes in the relationship of producers to distributors and retailers which allowed for the development of some ready-to-wear goods, the persistence of a highly labour-intensive method of production kept prices up. The fashionable world of eighteenth-century London demanded an ever-growing number of tailors, seamstresses, milliners and haberdashers to accommodate the sudden expansion in demand for bespoke garments. The incomes of these artisans rose as a group because of a surge in their numbers in response to demand for their services rather than through any increase in their individual productivities. Looking more closely at the way clothes were actually made in the eighteenth century – particularly women's dresses – it becomes easier to understand how they lent themselves to the rapid changes in taste that fashion demanded. The most important and most expensive element in a woman's dress was its fabric. Because a fashionable dress could require more than twenty yards of material, the contribution of the fabric to the total cost of a dress remained remarkably high, swamping both the labour costs involved in its manufacture and the costs of trimmings. Mid-century, the cost of the labour involved in making up the material into a completed outfit could still be as low as five per cent of the cost of fabric (Ribeiro, 1984, p. 53). The central role played by the fabric was in part reflected by the greater status and wealth of the mercer, who supplied it, relative to the mantua-maker or tailor who worked on it. Such economics dictated a long life in use for any particular piece of quality dress fabrics, which would be passed on from one generation to the next.[15] The much-cited Parson Woodforde in 1790 gave his niece a green silk damask gown that had belonged to an aunt who had died in 1771 (Tozer and Levitt, 1983, p. 45).

The use of large running stitches combined with a minimum of complicated cutting in eighteenth-century dressmaking allowed the same piece of fabric to be altered and restyled several times without seriously damaging it. In the absence of fixed sizes, dress styles were achieved by the pleating and draping of basic shapes rather than by close tailoring to the body in tight and small stitches. This enabled dresses to be fairly easily unpicked and rearranged and, with the addition of new, relatively cheap trimmings, to re-emerge in a new guise with a minimum of fuss and expense, particularly if the work was carried out by the woman herself. The stimulus of changing fashions, therefore, intensified and perhaps prolonged home-based and non-marketed dressmaking while encouraging a greater production and consumption of the small but essential newly manufactured trimmings (buckles, ribbons, stays, lace, etc) (Eversley, 1967, p. 239).

It was these latter, essentially superficial goods, that constituted the necessary differentiation in fashion. If emulative spending did occur, it is most likely to have been in the market for these trinkets which would have been more easily within the reach of modest incomes. Dress fabric, by comparison, appears to have served more as a consumer durable. For men, the Great Coat, passed down from one generation to the next, played a similar role. The value placed on these garments is revealed by the frequency with which advertisements for the recovery of stolen clothing appeared in eighteenth-century newspapers.

The persistence of the second-hand market in clothes (facilitated by the lack of fixed sizes and the loose cut of women's dresses) also underlines the durability of clothes – and their expense relative to income. In the 1780s, a female domestic worker earning as little as 3s per week might be asked to pay over 6s for a common second-hand gown and 4s 6d for a second-hand linsey-woolsey petticoat (Ribeiro, 1984, p. 64). The second-hand market at least enabled such

---

15   The durability of the basic fashion fabric is illustrated in "Tale of a Puce Dress", *Costume*, vol VI, no 1 (1972, p.100) (cited in Lemire, 1984, p. 22) which features a dress altered almost yearly from 1781 to 1788, with the addition of steel buckles, a new gauze handkerchief and a new apron, all applied to the original dress to bring it – and keep it – up to date with the latest fashion craze.

clothes to be recycled, to outlive their role as fashion goods and pass into the world of basic necessities without impinging on the realm of production.

At the same time, the proliferation of bizarre and often excessive fashion trimmings and accessories (mouse-skin eyebrows, muffs for the wrists, artificial nosegays) which so transfixed foreign visitors, may itself have masked the slow pace at which genuine advances in the production of clothes (as opposed to fabric) proceeded. Dress fabric worn by the wealthy remained a luxury good. The flurry and intensity of interest in fashion and its increasing diffusion throughout society were not accompanied by any substantial growth in the market for new clothes construed as necessities. Those at the bottom end of the market remained as dependent as ever on hand sewing of inferior and sometimes reconstituted fabrics (like shoddy).

While the peripatetic Scottish pedlars in the provinces would not sell finished ladies dresses, they could and did carry on a roaring trade in the small change of fashion, as McKendrick demonstrates. This could be the link between the world of fashion centred on London and its diffusion throughout the country. When clothes could be transformed through the minimum application of effort and at minimum cost, it becomes more credible to consider the transmission of taste across income groups. But taste, in this context, remains grounded in the world of decoration and surfaces; it does not engineer more profound changes in production and society.

9   Persistence of Luxury Goods in Clothing

An 1845 government report estimated that, on average, the working man spent just 8 per cent of his income on clothes and 82 per cent on food. By 1904, the proportion of expenditure on clothing had increased to 12 per cent (Briggs, 1958, p. 128). The persistence of relatively low expenditure on finished goods reflected the continuing dependence on home dressmaking to make ends meet, facilitated to some extent by the availability of the sewing machine after 1850.

The production of luxury goods remained to a great extent untouched by the revolutionary changes in machine-made clothing, even in the second half of the nineteenth century and into the twentieth. Well after the adoption of the sewing machine, it was not unusual for men and women to continue to have a great deal of their wardrobe made by hand. (The demand for the bespoke product continues in the late twentieth century, in the market for machine-made goods which are designed to look hand-made.) A department store like the Bon Marché took pains to emphasise the individual craftsmanship of the clothing they sold. The arrival of these large-scale emporia in fact extended the market for the hand-made production of clothes and related goods. In 1880, Lewis's department store in Liverpool, with 300 working tailors, claimed to operate the largest tailoring establishment in England (Briggs, 1958, p. 130). In 1890, Bon Marché had more than 600 men and women workers employed in ateliers within the store, to work on hand-made or made-to-measure items like men's shirts, trousseaus, baby clothes and white goods. (Because they were not in factories, sweatshops in stores also escaped state supervision by health and safety inspectors.) Specialised workshops which supplied hand finishing to a wide variety of products catered to the demand for differentiation in consumer goods. In the machine age, the snob value of 'custom made' grew apace. Cards advertising Bon Marché showed "pictures of skilled artisans working at their trades ... on the reverse side, the history of the craft ... the Industrial Revolution, apparently, had never been heard of" (Miller, 1981, p. 218).

When demand and supply are reviewed in their joint relationship historically, the evidence points to the development of distinct working-class tastes emerging with, for example, the arrival of cheap, mass-produced printed fabrics. The consumption by working-class women of cheap printed calicoes for themselves constituted almost the entire home market for printed cottons by 1818 (Forty, 1986, p. 73). The wearing of ginghams, woven and printed, was also largely confined to the working class. These expressed preferences are themselves signs of the growth of incomes and markets which are so conspicuously absent in McKendrick's tale of twentieth-century London.

10   Concluding Remarks

The discussion of fashion (above) is an attempt to respond to McKendrick on his own ground. Like McKendrick, it marshalls empirical evidence and contemporary commentary to create historical narrative that clings fairly closely to the period under consideration. But even operating within these limits, it is possible to undermine the credibility of the transforming role of demand simply by fleshing out some of McKendrick's hypothesised links in the chain of transmission (looking, for example, at relative incomes between master and servant, at their social relations and prevailing conditions of employment). Bringing in evidence to remind the reader of the existence of other classes between those at the top and those at the bottom (the professions, commercial and trade interests) each contributing their own tastes and habits to changes in the dress code, reveals the extraordinary narrowness of McKendrick's field of interest, for all the exuberant detail of fashion he puts on parade.

The concept of emulation (source of the trickle-down effect) is central in this and serves many functions. It establishes a progressive role for the upper classes in the creation of consumer society. They are seen as the ultimate source of demand, introducing ideas for consumption goods which are passed down through all other strata in society, transformed as they go from luxuries to decencies to basic necessities. There is an implication that the state of idleness made possible by unearned incomes may be warranted by the inventiveness of those so under-occupied in dreaming up demands for new luxury goods (a kind of leisure class R & D hothouse!). This view reaches its peak in Plumb's (1982) contribution where, for example, the impact of Empire shows through more in the discovery and breeding of exotic species from the New Worlds for sport and for pets than for their potential economic use and exploitation.

The belief that wealth produces 'breeding', which is itself the source of taste and refinement, is therefore used to justify the existence of the social pyramid. But the inequalities of that pyramid are entirely glossed over. There is no mention of either the changing sources and diffusion of income, nor of changes in the overall pattern of its distribution. In their absence, there is neither getting nor spending. So, the radical transformations in both brought about by the Industrial Revolution disappear from view. In their place is substituted a cashless and almost arcadian view of early capitalist society in which harmonious relations do away with gross inequalities and replace class-based antagonism. What safer example to draw upon than the relation between master/mistress and servant, a relationship which remained largely untouched by the development of wage labour in factories and which depended on the maintenance of personal quasi-familial relations between employer and employee. In this context, emulation of the mistress by the maidservant could be seen as proof of continuous harmony running right through the social hierarchy, from top to bottom, casting a whiff of 'happy families' over British society as a whole.

In this story not only could those at the bottom benefit directly and almost immediately from the superior tastes of their employers (by taking on their outmoded clothes) but in so doing they were also contributing to economic progress by whipping up consumer demand. But because this demand prefigures the Industrial Revolution, it can emerge within a pattern of social relations which are untainted by the conflicts that grew out of factory employment. The closely stratified nature of British society (by comparison with other European countries) is presented as a measure of the higher level of democracy in Britain. It allowed fashion to percolate down with greater speed and effect just as it fostered (at least the illusion) of greater social mobility. In other words society, in its patterns of consumption, though based on inequality, was not only benign; it was also progressive.

To create the image of a forward-moving society fuelled by demand from above, consumerists have to jettison the interests and contributions of at least three-quarters of its members. The incomes and consumption habits of the labouring and middle classes are left out of the picture altogether, obviating the need to measure the relative impact of luxury spending on the economy as a whole. This is just one indication of the general absence of the economy and its transactions; there is no production and no exchange. The state also falls away, allowing the reader to forget its role in promoting or enhancing the interests of some in society at the expense of others, whether through direct intervention to increase or reduce inequality or through passive acquiescence with the status quo. The picture of apparently harmonious social relations exemplified by the master/servant relationship gives the impression that corrective state action would in any case be superfluous.

Notions of conspicuous consumption, dynamic obsolescence, product differentiation, etc, all lurk in the background of McKendrick's eighteenth-century society. The retrospective application of current habits of consumption and marketing – which was carried out to excellent effect in McKendrick's studies on the entrepreneurial genius of Josiah Wedgwood – cannot be so easily accommodated in a broader picture of society at large. The sheer complexity of factors determining economic activity in any particular period precludes this wholesale transfer. Nonetheless, McKendrick has achieved an ideological tour de force, both in transforming the categories of consumerism into progressive causal factors and in identifying the eighteenth century with consumer society, itself identified with contemporary capitalism.[16]

For the latter, for example, the almost exclusive concern with female fashion which has dominated much of consumerism this century is not so appropriate for the eighteenth-century context, where the market might well have been dominated by men and where women's participation and economic leverage were more restricted. This is a curious oversight by McKendrick, since his work on women's and children's employment in the early factory system is one of the few attempts by a male historian to bring women's contribution into sharper relief (McKendrick, 1974).[17] The shift is partly explained by the withdrawal of

---

16   In contrast, say, to the distaste for consumption shown in the works of Veblen, Galbraith, etc. A startling example of the presumed affinity between eighteenth-century pottery and twentieth-century consumerism is provided by Breen (1986, p. 496) "Without too much exaggeration, Staffordshire pottery might be seen as the Coca-Cola of the eighteenth century".

17   Some of the inevitable biases that have crept into a historical tradition long dominated by men have been pointed out by, among others (Thirsk, 1978, pp. 22–3): "The criteria by which some (projects) have been judged more important and others less have been laid

explicitly economic variables from the later work, which concentrates on a more idealised view of the world of fashion and is more concerned with the transmission of cultural values than with the transmission of economic power.

The two are not seen as directly linked. This makes it possible to view the upper classes as the repositories of what have come to be seen as 'superior' rather than simply 'dominant' cultural values. Rather like the British Museum, or other institutions which have selectively appropriated culture from a wide range of sources and recast them in a British mould, so the fashions of the British upper classes, also drawn from elsewhere (Europe, the Far East, etc), have been repackaged and reintroduced as British. In both cases, the results of such refining eclecticism acquire a certain inviolability because of the significance assigned to those who espouse them. They appear as unchallenged and hence universally approved sources of cultural definition and renewal rather than as choices of a particular social group granted certain privileges at a particular time in history. Since this assigns them an essential role at the top of the social order, they are the bearers of modernity. The proper mechanism for the dispersal of the values they embody throughout society remains the trickle-down from above, or emulation from below. In this spirit, Plumb (1982, p. 334) provides the final word in the McKendrick volume, by way of a non-communist manifesto for demand that parallels Rostow's stages theory for supply:

> As Marx realised, the revolutionaries in 1800 were the bourgeoisie and most of these believed, as they had to, in modernity. No consumer society can exist or expand without such a belief.

To the extent that the Cannadine hypothesis, as discussed in Section 2, is correct, the consumerists bear the responsibility for reflecting the contemporary belief that modernity in the eighteenth century, as today, flows from the cosseted, if not corseted, bodies and minds of the bourgeoisie.

There is, nevertheless, something that is positive about the consumerist approach. It attempts both to conceal and to compensate for the poor service provided by economic theory in finding a place for demand in the long run and in significant economic and social change. Rather than do this through a more

----

down by our menfolk. Starch, needles ... vinegar, stockings do not appear on their shopping lists, but they regularly appear on mine". The presentation of women as the primary consumers of impractical and often absurd luxury fashions which render them immobilised and incapable of serving any function other than adornment reinforces an image of female dependency which is completely at odds with McKendrick's earlier emphasis on women's active participation in the workforce and contribution to home demand.

or less formalistic model of shifting supply and demand curves, it focuses on the latter alone through the supposedly dynamic impact of changing patterns of (luxury) consumption. Such are the conclusions of Section 3. But the analysis there, brought to fruition in the discussion of clothing in later sections, reveals the necessity of breaking out of the confines of such narrowly conceived notions of the Industrial Revolution. The transformation in the mode of work, in the organisation of society more broadly (institutional, regional, rural and urban, etc) in the family – all have to be considered in locating and structuring the role of the changing mode of consumption, with the latter both as cause and effect, and as impediment and stimulus to the birth of modern capitalism.

Economies of Scale and a Featherbedding Cartel? A Reconsideration of the Interwar British Coal Industry

> It would be possible to say without exaggeration that the miners' leaders were the stupidest men in England if we had not frequent occasion to meet the owners.
>
> Statement of 1925 attributed to Lord Birkenhead[1] (as quoted in Mowat 1955, p. 300)

⋮

Postscript as Personal Preamble

My research on the British coal industry was motivated by the wish to understand the historical origins of, and precedents for, state economic intervention through a select case study. The role of the state was an important aspect in the studies of current developments in the British economy, co-authored with Laurence Harris (Fine and Harris, 1975 and 1976) with longer term perspectives coming together later (Fine and Harris, 1985). As a case study, the coal industry was deliberately chosen for its having been under private ownership, and failed, and to have been taken into state ownership in the nationalisations after the second world war, and to have succeeded. But, by the 1970s, it was also at the forefront of class struggles, if not on the scale of the General Strike of 1926, ultimately leading to the one-year strike of 1984/85 that was crucial in setting the prospects for British economy and society to a degree that is as extensive as it is underestimated. The consequences of the defeat of the miners were wide-ranging for them, for the trade union movement more generally, for British politics and for the forms taken by neoliberalism under Thatcher, Blair and subsequently.

---

1 Birkenhead was "a character", renowned for his humour – a close friend of Winston Churchill, he described him as spending much of his time preparing impromptu remarks.

© BEN FINE, 2024 | DOI:10.1163/9789004689275_004

As a researcher, and activist, I was heavily involved in the miners' struggles, some account of which as well as a summary of my research is to be found in Fine (1990a and 2019). The research reported on here preceded the miners strike, and concerned the failed interwar industry. In this respect, it pushes against the conventional wisdom of entrepreneurial failure as peddled by the industry's economic historians who have tended to excuse it as having been more or less efficient against the pressures of the Great Depression, and poor geological conditions and labour relations. My perspective is different in two major respects. The first is to point to the major failings in mechanising the industry and concentrating on fewer, larger-scale mines.

The second, then, was to explain rather than to overlook and excuse these failings and, here, a neglected factor is brought into play, the private ownership by the surface owner above ground of the coal royalties beneath, the minerals in the ground, for which payment had to be made by mineowners to landowners. Interestingly, that private royalties served as an obstacle to mining development was a persistent theme from the end of the nineteenth century until they were nationalised with handsome compensation in 1938, before the war and the post-war nationalisation of the industry, and by a Tory government hardly committed to public ownership. Despite such indicators from those involved in and around the industry at the time, future academic commentary persisted in being more or less oblivious to it.

I was different for one major and one minor reason in particular. For the first, I had undertaken a major study of Marx's theory of rent or, more exactly, rent as the economic form of surplus appropriation taken by virtue of ownership of landed property. The single most important conclusion from this study is that the impact of landed property can be either conducive or obstructive to accumulation of capital contingent upon the nature of landed property (who gets access and under what terms). This is far more significant than the traditional preoccupations of rent theory, concerned with how is it determined, how much is it, does it grow over time and is it parasitic (something for nothing other than ownership) or not.[2] And, if one thing stands out about the British coal industry, it is how successful it was until the turn from the nineteenth to the twentieth century and, then, how rapidly it became unsuccessful in many respects, not least productivity and labour relations.

---

2   For review over debates on rent theory, and the distinction or not between rent and royalty, in the context of early examples of (unacknowledged) economics imperialism, see Fine (2024a).

The more minor concern, in initiating motivation, pushed in exactly the same direction with, in orthodox terminology but dear to a proper understanding of Marx's value theory and political economy, the importance of the restructuring of industry into larger more productive units through mechanisation. This is exactly where the British coal industry failed during the interwar period (and, to a large degree, succeeded relative to its European counterparts after the second world war and nationalisation). In short, such restructuring – what promoted and what obstructed it – not least through state intervention formed the way of analysing the British economy in the previously mentioned contemporary economic analyses as well as past and longer-term considerations.

What this chapter sought to establish is how important were scale and mechanisation to the (mis)fortunes of the interwar British coal industry, with the role of the private ownership of royalties both significant and neglected, taking two papers in particular as critical point of departure, Buxton (1970) and Kirby (1973), with the latter focusing on cartels as a deadweight on progress induced by competition. I cannot remember who and in what circumstances but my work was described as the last word on the issues. I had hoped not as there was much more that could be done at local levels. And my contribution did solicit a response from Greasley (1993) to which I was allowed a rejoinder reproduced here as an Appendix.

There is, though, a mystery. Why should economic historians have been so wedded to the idea of limited economies of scale in mining, so inconsistent with the scholarly evidence if properly sought out with a modicum of rigour, and, to be blunt, common sense given the scale of fixed capital required both to create a mine and render it operative (beyond a pick and a shovel). I can only come up with two reasons suggesting we might substitute economists and economic historians for miners and mineowners in the opening quote to this chapter, or is it the other way around. One is the dull compulsion of economic ideas, with mainstream economics dependent upon the absence of increasing returns in order to allow for competitive equilibrium – so the world must be the way our theory needs it to be. The other reason is the policy imperative of competitiveness (and the presumed conditions necessary and able to bring it about) through the market and absence of state intervention (or, at most, light regulation) themes that are far from confined to the British coal industry and the interwar years ... but I would think policymakers the stupidest of humans if I had not frequent occasion to meet their academic economist advisers.

1   Introduction[3]

Two classic propositions have dominated the economic historiography of the
interwar British coal industry. One offered by Buxton (1970) claims that mechanisation of the industry was important and, to some extent, deficient but that
there were no economies of scale; the other, from Kirby (1973)[4] claims that the
formation of statutory cartels in the 1930s impeded amalgamations by featherbedding inefficient producers (and so, paradoxically, depends on rejecting the
Buxton hypothesis). In this chapter, by a more careful and fuller consideration
of the readily available evidence, I attempt to show that both of these propositions are in doubt. By doing so, I wish to question the standard historiography.
What has to be explained is the failure to reap economies of scale, but this cannot be done on the grounds of the stifling effect of the state-organised cartel.
There is no reason to take Buxton and/or Kirby as an analytical starting point.

This is especially true of studies undertaken at a more disaggregated level,
which have come increasingly to challenge the traditional approach.[5] For many
objections can be made to aggregate statistical exercises, including those to be
described in this chapter, although it can be argued that my own are superior
to those of Buxton and Kirby which are casual at best. Indeed, my intention is
not so much to provide robust cliometric estimates for the interwar industry as
to show that the statistical methods that have previously been employed yield
results that are reversed if they are slightly improved and generalised.

Consequently, the challenge posed to the orthodoxy of Buxton and Kirby is
not one that should be met by further sophistication in the construction of the
data or in the statistical tests to confirm or refute the traditional historiography.

---

3   This chapter, first published as Fine (1990b), is based on Evans and Fine (1980a and b) where
    full presentation of the statistical results is to be found, and on other research done with
    Steve Martin. See also Fine (1990a). At various times, research has been funded by the SSRC
    (renamed ESRC under Thatcher) the Nuffield Foundation, the Leverhulme Trust, and the
    Central Research Fund of the University of London. I wish to thank anonymous referees and
    the editors for many helpful suggestions.
4   Note that I do not enter into the debate over the meaning of amalgamation, rationalisation,
    etc, between Buxton, Kirby, and others in this journal in 1972. It is not clear that these distinc-
    tions can usefully be made in coalmining where, for example, so much uncertainty is asso-
    ciated with production that multiple ownership of mines allows faces or pits to be held in
    reserve according to the vagaries of either market demand or geological faulting. By "mech-
    anisation", I usually refer to coal cutting by machine although there are many other forms of
    mechanisation, especially underground transport of the coal (as opposed to reliance upon
    legendary pit ponies and women and children).
5   See the emphasis on cartels through finance in Boyns (1987), the attention to marketing in
    Dintenfass (1985) and, for an overall view, Supple (1987).

Such efforts would be doomed to remain inconclusive and would exhibit sharply diminishing returns to scholarly labour. Rather than devoting further attention to them, I hope to encourage a consideration of issues other than those of economies of scale and cartels and the use of a wider set of techniques than the formal estimation of aggregate models.

In section 2, I consider Buxton's arguments and show that his statistical analysis is faulty and undertaken on a narrow data base. When it is corrected and extended, it is found to be fallacious. This is confirmed by a separate calculation of economies of scale based on the estimation, in physical terms, of aggregate production functions. Section 3 assesses Kirby's arguments and shows that he has also used the data too selectively in charting amalgamations. Further, he appears to have overestimated the effectiveness of the state cartel for the period for which he examines amalgamations, from 1930 to 1936. For the next two years, when the cartel arguably did work, amalgamations increased. In a final section, I consider the implications of the chapter for what has been a neglected factor in the study of the interwar coal industry, the role of coal royalties.

2   Neither Economies of Scale...

Buxton's arguments concerning the explanation of productivity increase in the interwar coal industry are based on two sorts of correlation. The first shows a positive and significant relation between productivity and the degree of mechanisation; the second shows no significant relation between productivity and size of mine. These correlations are a selection from cross-section between districts and time series within districts. The results are used to conclude that mechanisation was important for the industry but that economies of scale were not. There is, however, a fallacy in this reasoning. If productivity were determined simultaneously by mechanisation and mine size and if small mines were more mechanised than large, then Buxton's correlations would be correct but his conclusions would not. Size would appear not to affect productivity simply because any advantage associated with size was offset by the low level of mechanisation in the larger mines.

Ironically, Buxton argues that Scottish mines prove his point. They were small-scale but enjoyed relatively high productivity because of their earlier and higher level of mechanisation. Rather than supporting his case, these observations suggest that economies of scale have been unfairly assessed. To correct Buxton's errors in statistical inference is simple in principle; productivity must be explained by a multiple regression on mechanisation and size of mine, not by separate simple regressions. To this end, for eighteen districts, Q/L was regressed on QM/Q and Q/N using time series annual data for 1921 to 1938, where Q is output, L employment, QM mechanically cut output, and N number of mines. A time series analysis by district was preferred to cross-section by years since it was felt that mining conditions within a district across a time period would be more uniform than across districts at a point in time.

The results are conclusive. In all but five out of the eighteen districts, both mechanisation and average mine size were significantly positive at the 95 per cent level in explaining productivity increase. Of the five exceptional districts, in three mine size was insignificant, in one mechanisation was insignificant, and in one both were insignificant. Testing Buxton's hypothesis properly leads to its rejection.

For the sake of completeness, however, Buxton's simple regressions were also calculated. When taken alone, mechanisation was found to be significant for productivity in all eighteen districts. Contrary to Buxton, in all but four districts mine size was significant. Nevertheless, Buxton's relative ranking of mechanisation and mine size was found to be correct in all but three districts. Finally, in eleven districts, the inclusion of mine size with mechanisation improved the goodness of fit in explaining productivity levels.[6]

In summary, using and correcting Buxton's own method, the evidence tends to support the importance of scale economies. In addition, it must be borne in mind that this statistical analysis is biased by taking the 'living' as representative of the 'dead'. Suppose that mine size was important and that this tended to eliminate small-scale producers, ceteris paribus. Then no correlation would be observed between productivity and mine size since the small mines would survive only through some other (unobserved) advantage, such as favourable geology or access to markets. Otherwise, one could as well take surviving buildings as representative of the general sturdiness of medieval construction.

A more common way of assessing sources of productivity is through the estimation of a production function. Ideally, I would like to investigate the difference in productivity by mine since levels of mechanisation, size, and other inputs vary while geological conditions remain the same. This is impossible for lack of data. What can be done at the level of each district is to estimate whether output would have been greater if the number of mines had been fewer after taking due account of the amount of capital and labour employed.

---

6   The eighteen districts were formed out of the twenty-five used in H.M. Inspectors' reports, since aggregation across districts is used in the official statistics for certain years.

With the obvious notation, let $Q = AK^rL^sN^t$. If t is negative then productivity would have been higher with fewer mines, evidence of economies of scale. Whether r + s is greater or less than unity concerns economies of scale in a more usual sense.[7]

Although it is traditional to estimate production functions by use of factor rewards to measure marginal products, it is also well known that this method is erroneous since potentially independent price and physical changes are measured by a single index (Fine, 1980b and 2016). In any case, the method depends on constant returns and full employment (to justify the marginal productivity measure by factor rewards). The first I wish to investigate, the second is inappropriate for the interwar coal industry.

Consequently, Evans and I constructed our own physical measure of the capital stock by using the number of cutting machines in use, taking full account of the different types of machines as well as their changing productivity over time.[8] We did not use the production function in the form given above – because periods of excess supply and short working would bias the estimates of productivity downwards, since all capital would not be fully used. Instead, we inverted the equation and estimated it as the labour demanded to produce a given level of output with the capital stock already in place. We also used the rate of growth of output as an index of capacity utilisation, with relatively less labour needed the greater the level of output and the fuller the utilisation of machinery. Hence, $L = AQ^aK^bN^cG^d$ where G is one plus the rate of growth and d is hypothesised to be negative if excess capacity is significant.

Estimates were made for each district by employing annual data from 1921 to 1938 and these confirmed the existence of economies of scale. Here I present only a weighted average of our results, a representative production function for Britain, which is, after inverting back from labour demand:[9]

$$Q = AL^{3.6} K^{0.6}N^{-2.5}G^{0.5}$$

---

7 Rhodes (1945) uses a similar method to the one proposed here but with less sophisticated techniques. He sets t = 0 and imposes constant returns to scale, r + s = 1. Ingeniously, he attempts to test for economies of scale, having already ruled them out, by comparing summer with winter output – on the presumption that fixed capital is more fully used in the short run in winter. He finds evidence of increasing returns.

8 For details of this measure of capital stock (Evans and Fine, 1980a, Appendix III).

9 The average across the districts is formed by using the inverse of the variance of the coefficients as a weight in order to give greater importance to those estimates that are held with greater confidence.

If anything, the returns to scale are surprisingly high, particularly the returns to labour. This is perhaps explained by the use of purely capital-augmenting technical progress, as embodied in the index for capital, whereas other forms of technical progress, tending to reduce labour inputs, would be ignored, biasing the exponent on L upwards. It proved impossible to estimate separately the effects of technical progress over time because of the time trend on the other variables concerned.

In this analysis, no account was taken of changes in the length of the maximum working day or of shifts in the number of days of the year and the number of hours of the day actually worked. Further refinements might require attention to the other types of capital employed apart from the mechanisation of coal cutting. Nevertheless, within the considerable limits of the exercise as a whole, it seems plausible to conclude that the coefficients indicating increasing returns to scale may be too large but not so much so that they are qualitatively incorrect and to be doubted as such. Certainly, there must be a predisposition towards rejecting the Buxton hypothesis and, as an alternative, either exploring the production function approach with more sophistication or, preferably, testing for the presence of, and exploring any obstacles to, such economies of scale at a level of detail that would appear to preclude such statistical techniques, especially when applied at an aggregate (district or even national) level.

3   ... nor Featherbedding Cartel

In the previous section, it has been shown that there is evidence of economies of scale in the industry in the interwar period. This naturally raises the question of why more advantage was not taken of them. The standard explanation put forward by Kirby concerns the supposedly inconsistent effects of the Coal Mines Act of 1930 and so applies only to retardation of the industry in the 1930s. Under Part II of the Act, the Coal Mines Reorganisation Commission (CMRC) was set up under the chairmanship of Sir Ernest Gowers.[10] It was charged with the task of reorganising the industry into a smaller number of larger units. It was given powers of compulsion, subject to the judgement of the court of the Railway and Canal Commission on whether the amalgamations would lower

---

10   See the CMRC's own reports of its functions and the resistance it experienced. See also Thomas (1937).

the cost of coal, be in the public interest, and accord with the financial inter-ests of those mineowners directly concerned.

In the event the CMRC proved powerless. Part I of the 1930 Act was to be used to set up a state-organised cartel for the industry. Statutory marketing schemes, which were to come into operation on 1st January 1931, were designed to mitigate the structural adjustment costs of a declining industry by discour-aging "cut-throat" competition. Kirby argues that these two parts of the Act were inconsistent with each other. While Part II was designed to bring about reorganisation, Part I frustrated this aim by maintaining profitability in the otherwise uneconomic pits. This is by no means a novel argument. It was even used by a commentator on the industry at the time (Neumann, 1934, p. 434):

> quota works in the majority of cases to swell the value of inefficient undertakings, and has the effect of retarding amalgamations.

I disagree fundamentally with this position. At the theoretical level, there is no reason to assume that a cartel will hinder amalgamation, for the objective of a cartel is to achieve higher prices for any given level of output. Whatever levels of profits this allows, they can be made higher in proportion to the increased efficiency or lower cost of the methods by which the output is produced. Indeed, cartels are often seen as the basis on which rationalisation of indus-trial structure can proceed, and the German coal industry of this very period provides a plausible example of this process. The point about a cartel is that it may diminish the pressure to bring about reorganisation, through monopoly-pricing sustaining profitability, but it certainly does not diminish the incentive to cost reduction which is a separate source of profitability.

In short, it is worth emphasising that cartels are often seen as the institu-tional form in which restructuring can best be effected. Their existence as such is not decisive either in discouraging or in facilitating reorganisation. Kirby's theoretical approach is, therefore, flawed. In addition, he adduces empirical arguments to support his position but, as will be seen, these are equally prob-lematical. He tries to show that prior to 1930 the pace of amalgamation was greater than afterwards, which he takes as evidence of the obstructive effect of Part 1 of the Act. Under the Mining Industry Act of 1926, until 1930 volun-tary amalgamations were sought. Conveniently for the present issue, the Act made provision for data to be collected by the Board of Trade on the amalga-mations effected throughout the remainder of the interwar period. The data are summarised in the Table 1, which includes the rather scanty evidence used by Kirby. He notes that there were 26 amalgamation schemes between 1926 and 1930 compared with 32 in the longer period from 1930 to 1936. The number of workers involved in aggregate was 212,260 and 164,200, respectively. This hardly represents a dramatic decline. Rather, it suggests how limited amalgamations were in both sub-periods.

TABLE 1   Amalgamations in the coal industry, 1927–1938

(1) Year(s)	(2) Schemes	(3) Pits	(4) Employment	(5) Employment per scheme[a]	(6) Percentage of pits involved[b]	(7) Total output (million tons)
1927–8	17	172	125,960	7,409	3.19	237
1929	6	61	39,800	6,633	2.52	258
1930[c]	3	88	46,520	15,507	3.78	244
1931	3	28	10,500	3,500	1.25	219
1932	4	27	12,390	3,096	1.25	209
1933	6	22	19,580	3,263	1.03	207
1934	2	28	12,600	6,300	1.32	221
1935	8	173	83,100	10,388	8.34	222
1936	7	43	22,750	3,250	2.07	228
1937[d]	18	95	83,253	4,625	4.48	240
1938	10	46	24,726	2,473	2.16	227

a   Col. 4 divided by col. 2.
b   Pits involved in amalgamations expressed as a percentage of the total number of working pits.
c   Dominated by a single entry in south Wales with 60 pits and 32,000 workers.
d   The number of pits and employment are understated.

Subtotals

1927–30	26	321	212,280	8,165
1931–36	30	321	160,942	5,365
1931–34	15	105	55,070	3,671
1935–38	43	357	213,829	4,973

Subtotals (Kirby[e])

1926–30	26	na	212,260
1931–36	32	na	164,200

e   Kirby (1973, p. 282). The minor discrepancies between Kirby's and my figures remain unexplained.
SOURCE: REPORTS BY THE BOARD OF TRADE UNDER MINING INDUSTRY ACT, 1930, ON THE WORKING OF THE COAL SELLING SCHEMES UNDER PART I OF THE ACT (1931–38)

But there are serious problems in Kirby's analysis apart from limitations of the evidence that he considers. First, it is important to recognise that an amalgamation is defined as the complete unification of ownership of two or more undertakings. A statement of the number of pits and workers associated with each merger can, therefore, prove misleading, because the number is obtained by adding together the number of pits and workers of each undertaking involved in a merger and this may lead to a degree of double counting over time. For example, if a dynamic enterprise absorbed new collieries each year, the number of pits and workers involved in this merger activity would increase steadily. On the other hand, the number of pits available for new mergers would tend to decline as they were absorbed, unless there was frequent entry of new pits into the industry.

The history of the Powell Duffryn Colliery Company illustrates this. Formed in south Wales in 1928, involving 26 pits and 25,100 workers, fewer pits and workers were available for subsequent amalgamations. Even so, in 1935, Welsh Associated Collieries was also absorbed, yielding a total involvement of 93 pits and 37,600 workers, many of which were already, measured in the first amalgamation mentioned. In short, it is by no means clear how well these figures measure the rhythm of amalgamation when they are aggregated in this manner.

Second, from an examination of the number of mergers occurring year to year it appears that initially this was relatively high, diminished, and eventually recovered, surpassing the initial levels. Three broad phases can be discerned. The years 1927–30 (26 amalgamations) represent the period before there was any effect from statutory cartel regulations. The second phase, covering the years 1931–34 (fifteen amalgamations) corresponds both to the introduction of statutory cartels and to the depths of the 1930s depression. Total production of coal fell to a low level during this sub-period, a fall occasioned, it should be noted, by demand deficiencies rather than by stringent output regulation. The final phase, covering the years 1935–8, was associated with a brief recovery in demand, during 1936–8. Significantly, the number of amalgamations jumped to 43 for the years 1935–38. Kirby stopped short his empirical analysis in 1936, just when the merger phase was rising to a peak, thereby avoiding a change inconvenient to his argument.

Third, it is revealing to examine the rhythm of merger activity in the separate districts. The argument used for the U.K. as a whole should also apply to individual mining regions.[11] But this was not the case. Only five districts

---

11   Tabulated data of merger activity by district are available on request. Nobody has ever asked for them, and this may no longer be true. If a request comes, I will make a search through my own remaining documentation or suggest doing so through data lodged with the ESRC archive.

were involved in merger activity in the first phase of 1926–30, namely, south Yorkshire, west Yorkshire, south Wales, Northumberland, and Lancashire and Cheshire. Subsequently, merger activity seems to have been more widely dispersed across the districts, during the period when, in Kirby's view, it should have been slackening off. His limited aggregate evidence may be a statistical artefact reflecting diverse movements in different districts for reasons unrelated to the rhythm of cartel formation.

Fourth, Kirby has treated the role of cartels too casually both before and after the 1930 Act. Before 1930 a number of voluntary cartels were formed. There were three principal regional cartels, located in south Wales, Scotland, and the Midlands; each was formed in 1927–28 and covered the bulk of the regional output. The combined output of the three areas comprised approximately 80 per cent of the national total. No inter-regional co-ordination was established.

No doubt this gave an enormous impetus to the support by mineowners for Part I of the Act, compared with their outright opposition to Part II. But it cannot be assumed that the provisions of Part I were immediately effective, as is implicit in Kirby's analysis of their impeding effect on amalgamation from 1930 onwards. As noted above, a principal object of the marketing schemes was to improve the finances of the industry. Given that the demand for coal continued to deteriorate (further undermining the revenues of the industry) the incentive to violate cartel regulations is hard to exaggerate. It is imperative to examine the available evidence about the performance of the statutory cartel to see to what extent it could have shielded the inefficient from competition by maintaining prices.

The performance of these marketing schemes is outlined in eleven reports of the Board of Trade between 1931 and 1938. Briefly, the schemes were administered using two tiers. The nation was divided into seventeen districts (each with its own regional Executive Board); these represented the lower tier. The upper tier was the Central Council of Colliery Owners. The regulation of output was nationally organised by the Central Council but the responsibility for minimum prices was left to each district's Executive Board. Hence, the control of prices was not coordinated between districts; further, there was no compulsion for Executive Boards to set economically meaningful minimum prices. Indeed, the Scottish Executive Board was the subject of many complaints from adjacent districts, for failing to set restrictive minimum prices and subsequently dumping their output in other districts. As for the regulation of output, each mine was assigned a standard tonnage, the allowed proportion of which was determined by the district quota, which in turn was set nationally by the Central Council.

It is possible to distinguish two phases of the statutory cartel, before and after the introduction of a nationally coordinated centralised selling (made operational during 1936). During the years 1931–36 the Central Council adopted two broad methods of determining quotas. Apart from attempting to control prices, there was also the setting of a quota for each mine, in advance, as some proportion of the allocation for the corresponding quarter of the previous year. As demand was in decline, actual production fell continually, so that it fell short of quota allocations by between 2 and 10 per cent of output on an annual basis (quotas being fixed quarterly).[12]

This might still, of course, leave some individual producers constrained by their quotas. But provision was made for supplementary allocations of 2 to 5 per cent to those in quota shortage. Yet another factor, not necessarily weakening the cartel, but preventing it from acting as a barrier to amalgamation, was the trading in quotas (Lucas, 1937). These could be bought and sold by colliery companies so that, in principle, there was no obstacle to an expansion of production by a particular colliery, as long as the cost of a unit of quota lay below the reduced costs of some form of rationalisation. The Board of Trade reported a considerable use of the system of quota transfers, with exchange at a few pence per ton. In south Wales, for example, in the last quarter of 1931, 700,000 tons of quota were transferred in 108 transactions out of a total allocation of 11.1 million tons and an actual production of 10.1 million tons. Only in Scotland do transfer prices appear to have been high, with complaints that they reached 1s. 6d. per ton.[13]

From 1936 onwards, measures were taken to strengthen the discipline of the cartel, although the improvement in effectiveness is difficult to judge since demand picked up and reduced the incentive to evade the quota system. By the second half of the decade, previous weaknesses in relation to inter-district dumping (especially because of collapsed export markets) and in the observance of minimum price levels had been addressed by greater national coordination. However, the Board of Trade itself, in its 1938 Report, suggested that any stabilisation of prices was due as much to improved demand as to its own efforts.

To summarise the empirical arguments that I have brought to bear against Kirby, there is no evidence to support the idea that the state-organised cartel of

---

12   Details of the quarterly discrepancies between allocations and actual output, together with supplementary allocations, discussed below, are available on request. Again, this is a moot point more than thirty years after publication!

13   One shilling and six pence, or eighteen pence in old money before UK decimalisation (with 240d in a pound).

the 1930s impeded amalgamations. Amalgamations may have slackened in the early 1930s but they increased a few years later. This seems to reflect the state of the demand for coal. Again, the rhythm of merger activity was not uniform across districts. Moreover, cartels existed prior to 1930 and were, in any case, at their weakest in the early 1930s when merger activity was lowest, and only strengthened, if at all, in the late 1930s when merger activity was at its height. In short, it is far from clear that Kirby's hypothesis can even be tested effectively because of the weakness of the cartels at all times, and, to the extent that it can be tested, it appears to be refuted.

In some respects, the conclusions of this section are supported by a recent paper by Henley (1988). He seeks to establish the existence of a greater mark-up on direct costs in the 1930s than previously as a consequence of the cartel. His estimate is that there was an increase in the mark-up of between 12 and 13 per cent. Whatever the validity of this result (and, as usual, it depends on a number of heroic assumptions)[14] it is motivated by the notion that mineowners did not pass on cost reductions obtained through mechanisation. In other words, the enhanced mark-up is explained by increased profitability, gained by cost reduction. This suggests that the cartel was a framework in which rationalisation could proceed, whether by amalgamation or mechanisation. It might be said that what remains to be explained is not so much why or whether the cartel sustained prices but why the establishment of a cartel was not accompanied by even greater structural change and even higher mark-ups.

4   Royalties: the Unobserved Barking Dog

In the two previous sections I have questioned both the view that economies of scale were unimportant and that they were unrealised because of a state-organised cartel. No doubt the calculations could be more refined, but research might be better directed at more disaggregated levels. This still leaves unanswered the problem of the industry's poor performance, as evidenced by the low pace of productivity increase and mechanisation and by failure to rationalise production in fewer mines and companies.

---

14   His use of direct (wage) costs when these were being reduced by mechanisation is a problem since capital costs were increasing. This is like measuring labour rather than total factor productivity. The increased mark-up may then simply reflect increased non-labour costs. Further, Henley finds demand factors to be important and these may bias the results, particularly in view of short working.

Over fifty years ago, Paull (1968) identified four possible reasons for the failure of the interwar coal industry. First, there was a failure to rationalise. The argument for this is similar to that put forward by Kirby which we have found to be wanting. Second, the labour movement is accused of having obstructed mechanisation and rationalisation in its attempts to preserve existing work patterns and levels of employment. But, following the defeat in the General Strike of 1926, the miners' union was hardly in a position of strength and was further weakened in the 1930s by large-scale unemployment. Even had the union possessed a policy of opposition to mechanisation and amalgamation, its ability effectively to sustain the policy must be doubted.

The lack of finance was a third factor, particularly given the low level of profitability. But finance was made available for new sinkings in south Yorkshire (and for the reorganisation of the south Wales coalfield under Powell Duffryn as discussed by Boyns, 1987). Moreover, the argument becomes circular, with low profitability and low access to capital both arising from the failure to rationalise. But such a cycle could be conducive equally to mechanisation and to concentration through the pooling of finance within the industry, thus further intensifying competition, as Paull illustrates for the US industry, when the rationalised producers put pressure on the inefficient.

Fourth, failure to rationalise can always be explained away by natural conditions, with either the coal seams or the machines (depending on the way you look at it) proving unsuitable. This does not appear to hold for the British case since pits were mechanised, if only slowly. Further, the seams worked might change, or be changed, over time. If some were unsuitable for mechanisation, why was production not concentrated upon those that were suitable?

In view of these considerations, Paull drew the conclusion that, as none of these explanations was sufficiently weighty, ultimate responsibility for the slowness of change must rest with the entrepreneurs of the industry. This is an instance of entrepreneurial failure being invoked as an explanation when no other explanation is forthcoming.

I have argued elsewhere (Fine et al. 1985; Fine, 1990a) that the royalty system was an impediment to rationalisation and mechanisation, and the argument may be briefly recapitulated by restating the main theoretical and empirical grounds for this view. First, we must be sceptical of the relevance of neoclassical theory – there appears to have been no correlation between geological conditions and royalties, with marginal product determining the latter. Second, from the time of the Royal Commission on royalties of the 1870s, landed property increasingly posed problems for the mineowners. Two Royal Commissions (Sankey, unanimously, and Samuel) found in favour of the nationalisation of royalties, as, did the CRMC and, in 1938, the government which purchased them for the nation at a price of £66 million. The theoretical reasons for considering royalties may have played an important role in impeding rationalisation follows from a theory of landed property which sees the landowner as capable of appropriating a share of the mineowner's increase in profitability, especially where this derives from increased investment for rationalisation and/or mechanisation. To some extent, in a static sense, this is recognised by neoclassical theory, since a royalty is identified with an output-restricting tax.[15] My research with others suggests that the royalty problem became more severe as mines were extended in size or through exhaustion of working areas, thereby multiplying the leases required and impeding a cooperative resolution, between landlord and tenant, of the gains from expansion. Clearly, these changes would occur unevenly across different mines and districts, but the situation would tend to worsen over time as the scale and reach of mines were extended by size and exhaustion of extracted reserves.

Three arguments have been used to set this view aside. It might be thought that as royalties were a small element in total costs, they were, therefore, relatively unimportant. This is not the point, however – the same is true of profits – if neoclassical theory is rejected since the role of landed property cannot be measured by its level of remuneration (as if, by analogy, the existence of slum landlords, charging low rents, had nothing to do with the quality of housing). Dintenfass's (1985, p. 369) invaluable work, in showing how marketing through coal preparation was a decisive advantage for certain collieries, suggests the existence of an industry in which competitiveness was not determined primarily by lowest cost of production. Why were highly productive, large-scale, mechanised mines not competing with each other, with or without coal preparation?

Second, it might be argued that if the separate ownership of royalties were an impediment, then the appropriate land could have been bought up by the mineowners. Although this process did occur to some extent, this is a fallacious argument since the price of land is simply the discounted present value of a future stream of (anticipated) royalties (and other potential non-coal rents). Thus, if the royalty system impedes rationalisation and mechanisation as landlords appropriate a share of the surplus profits of cost-cutting, this will have its counterpart in a correspondingly inflated price of land if mineowners attempt to purchase the necessary land. This suggests a conflict over who appropriates the 'development gains' of rationalisation and it is not necessarily resolved by turning the leaseholder into the landowner (moreover, finance would be

---

15   The nature of a (mining) royalty has been the subject of debate, (Fine, 1982b).

stretched for a mineowner who purchased the land both for its coal and for its other economic uses).

A third objection is to assert that the royalty effect was limited, given other factors. In his assessment of the role of royalties, Supple's (1987, p. 406) official history concludes:

> Given the other reasons for withholding investment, it seems doubtful whether the royalty system prevented amalgamations (and slowed down mechanisation) simply because mineowners feared that any improvement in productivity would be appropriated by the royalty owner. But the royalty system clearly helped explain the original fragmentation of the industry, presented numerous practical obstacles in structural change, and in 1933 was offered by the MAGB as the reason why the efforts of the CMRC to secure widespread mergers was doomed.

This, to the contrary, suggests an important role for the royalty system, especially in determining the industry's structure, even if only in conjunction with other factors. It surely follows that it would equally serve to obstruct the restructuring of the industry, although this effect might be masked and reinforced by the other problems. That the restructuring could have occurred without economic incentives is doubtful. It is to be hoped that this will be studied in greater detail in the future, alongside other key factors such as finance, industrial relations and marketing.[16]

Appendix

My original piece solicited a response from Greasley (1993) to which I was allowed a rejoinder that follows (Fine, 1993a).

Is Small Beautiful? Mine Size in the British Interwar Coal Industry

In seeking to deny economies of scale, Greasley concludes that, "The key to higher productivity in interwar coalmining was *the spatial concentration of production*, which required the integration of cutting, loading, and winding into an efficient overall system" (Greasley, 1993, pp. 158–9, my emphasis). I agree

---

16 Those undertaking such studies should be aware that data for compensation paid upon nationalisation of the royalties are held by the author who should be contacted by anybody interested in them. The data, on royalty ownership, by mine and individual, is available from the ESRC archive. See Brunskill et al. (1985) for an account and use in case of Scotland.

with this view; indeed, it is what I was attempting to demonstrate in the context of the debate over whether rationalisation of the industry into fewer larger pits would have been conducive to greater efficiency.[17] It is hard to understand how Greasley can simultaneously argue for a lack of economies of scale and for the need to concentrate production unless he is attacking the rather weak proposition that throwing more machines and miners down a given pit infrastructure will yield more than proportionate gains in production. That will surely depend on such factors as excess capacity within mine layout.[18]

Greasley reports on other studies, including his own, estimating production functions which yield constant returns to scale. There are sometimes problems with these, such as failure to take into account the number of mines and the degree of excess capacity, but the implication would be that the level of output for any one mine is indeterminate since output can be profitably expanded indefinitely as long as unit costs are below price. Surely it is also the case that if constant returns are to be found across a region or the country as a whole, this is liable to reflect a mix of those with increasing and decreasing returns? Why was output not concentrated on those mines with increasing returns, for which econometric estimates in retrospect would then have been completely different?

These are unduly polemical points, relying upon a theory of competition that is inappropriate to the industry under consideration. Greasley's main point, however, seems to be devastating – that the capital stock index that I constructed, out of machine-cutters in use, more than doubled while the actual capital stock remained more or less the same over the interwar period. He suggests that this has the effect, given declining output and labour, of biasing upwards the estimate of scale economies and of returns to labour.

Suppose, then, that the real (Cobb-Douglas) production function is given, with familiar notation, by:

$$lnQ = a + blnL + clnK$$

If K is incorrectly measured by double, say, k = 2K, then:

$$lnQ = a + blnL + clnk/2$$
$$= (a - cln2) + blnL + clnk$$

---

17   And also whether rationalisation was or was not impeded by cartelisation. See above.
18   This is why estimating economies of scale, however accurately, on the basis of seasonal
       or cyclical variation is far from satisfactory although, ideally, account should be taken of
       these factors in estimating more fundamental relationships.

This simply has the effect of shifting the intercept term, not of changing the estimate of scale economies, although this is only exactly so if the difference between the two, measured and actual, capital stocks remains in the same proportion.

Why then do I get scale economies where others, especially Greasley, do not? One way of examining this is to attempt to reconcile the different empirical estimates in terms of specification and data employed – as Greasley has attempted in terms of the capital stock measure. This is beyond the scope of this rejoinder, and such efforts are almost certainly subject to rapidly diminishing returns. It is perhaps more important to emphasise the differences in motivation.

For Greasley, it is one of assuming the industry is in or moving towards perfectly competitive equilibrium, in which entrepreneurs are rationally choosing technology on the basis of relative prices of hand-got and more machine-intensive methods of production. It does not follow, but neither is it surprising, that constant returns should be estimated on this basis.

My motivation has been different. Subject to data availability and manageability, the issue is to estimate the effect on output if more capital and labour had been concentrated on fewer mines. Hence the use of the Cobb-Douglas production function:[19]

$$lnQ = a + blnL + clnK + dlnN$$

where N is the number of mines, with d expected to be negative. In this light, the use of K as measured by (quality adjusted) cutting machines seems much more reasonable, since it is a proxy for the extent to which mechanisation has been introduced and concentrated. By contrast, if it is considered that the problem with the industry is too many pits, with too little capital (or mechanisation) thinly spread, then the aggregate measure of capital stock is entirely inappropriate. Consider an extreme example in which large numbers of simple mines are sunk at great capital expense but without any other equipment. Then, no doubt, we would measure constant or diminishing returns. In the interwar period, large numbers of small mines, constant overall capital stock, and increasing-albeit slow-mechanisation, suggest that this is at least part of the picture.

---

19   The production function was estimated as an inverse demand for labour and with a
      growth variable to allow for excess capacity.

Nonetheless, I confess that the capital stock measure is far from ideal.[20] It might also have included conveyors and horsepower. The problem here is that, while these might have been incorporated into an index of the capital stock, they tend to be highly correlated with machine-cutting and would have created estimation problems if included as separate independent variables. Interestingly, Greasley (1993, p. 156) reports that seam thickness and length of roadways are inversely correlated to one another, and that both are significant only when separately estimated. This begs the question of why output was not concentrated on those pits with more advantageous seams and underground transport.

At the end of the day, calculations such as these, whichever one is inclined to believe, are extremely rough and ready. At most, they should be seen as establishing a predisposition in research conducted at a more disaggregated level wherever this proves possible. In this context, there is comparative evidence to draw upon, both between the UK interwar industry and its contemporary competitors, and with UK performance after nationalisation. In each case, it is stretching the historical imagination to believe that geology and technology were sufficiently unique at that time and place to deny the presence of scale economies and the benefits that could have flowed from rationalisation, reorganisation, and mechanisation.

---

20   It might also have been worthwhile to have used underground rather than overall labour.

CHAPTER 4

Coal, Diamonds and Oil: towards a Comparative Theory of Mining?

Postscript as Personal Preamble

In terms of my own intellectual biography, the introduction to this piece already points to its origins in the bringing together of two different areas of research – consumption and landed property. The first motivated looking at the vertical integration of mining itself with the organisation of its distribution – most notable for diamonds because of De Beers, oil because of the seven sisters and, for coal, if less prominent in popular consciousness, because of coals from Newcastle (and the Vend) and state organised cartels if not state monopoly through ownership. The second focused attention on how the specific historical forms (and distribution) of landed property affected the accumulation of capital and, by implication of the first, interacted with other aspects of provisioning beyond production to give rise to mining development and performance.

Precisely because of the approach taken to landed property – that it intervenes, positively or negatively, in historically specific circumstances – I was extremely, if not absolutely, hesitant to put forward anything at all approaching a general theory of mining (even as an alternative to Ricardian or neoclassical theories organised around the marginal producer). As it is land-dependent, how mining develops depends crucially on relations between producers and landowners. However, this piece also depended upon the bringing together of other, otherwise separate, pieces of my research; on South Africa and the historical origins, in diamonds and gold, of its minerals-energy complex (Fine and Rustomjee, 1997); a case study of coal in looking at the origins of state interventionism in the British economy (Fine 1990a, for a fuller overview; and Fine and Harris, 1985); and a case study of oil for locating in part the historical origins of the role of multinational corporations in the British economy (Fine and Harris, 1985, Chapter 3).

Across these separate studies, a common pattern was discovered – namely, one of extreme fragmentation in production that is eventually overcome through restructuring into smaller number of companies and production units, beautifully and strikingly demonstrated by the illustrations reproduced within the article for diamonds and oil (but no less striking in case of British coal). My own predilection and, to a large extent the framing of the restructuring (or not) of the British economy was to look to industrialists, financiers and/ or the state to bring about this restructuring. But what is striking in the three case studies is that the leading role was played by those commanding distribution as opposed to production (with the exception to some degree of coal, given its ultimate, as opposed to its initial, dependence upon nationalisation, with the historical Vend organising a cartel over distribution).

Although, then, this piece hesitates from seeing itself as offering a general theory of mining, as indicated by the question mark in its title, it does point to a theoretical issue of some significance. It is that the way in which landed property intervenes in accumulation, and determines what surplus is available and who gets to appropriate it, may be removed from the immediate incidence of the rental/leasing relationship. For oil and diamonds most notably, it is the distributors who historically form the most active agency in restructuring. This may be of relevance to other historical (or contemporary) studies of mining if not for other roles played by landed property, not least housing where financialisation has brought about significant changes in the values of rents and how housing is, or is not, provided.

1   Introduction[1]

The purpose of this chapter is to bring together what were previously two entirely separate areas of research in order to shed light on yet a third topic. The first area of research is how to approach the analysis of the determinants of consumption. In Fine and Leopold (1993),[2] it is argued that it is essential to distinguish between what are termed systems of provision. Corresponding to each commodity group, distinct structures and processes connecting production to consumption form an integral unity, linked by the intermediate activities such as distribution, retailing, design, and preference formation through material culture. In common parlance, we are accustomed to refer to the food, energy, clothing or transport systems.

Analytically this is also appropriate and, in the corresponding focus upon vertical integration within such systems of provision, a sharp point of

---

1   Originally published as Fine (1994). The research for this chapter has been supported by a grant from the ESRC, number R000232411 to examine the South African minerals-energy complex. In revising an earlier draft, I have benefited considerably from discussions with Bernard Mommer.
2   See Fine (2002a) for a heavily revised edition but also Bayliss and Fine (2021).

departure is made from most of the theories to be found across the social sciences. These tend to seek general explanations of production or consumption, etc, which apply horizontally across a range of, if not all, sectors of the economy without recognizing how each is differentially attached to specific systems of production.

The second area of research is the theory of landed property. Outside of Ricardian, neoclassical and Marxist theories of rent as a monopoly charge, it has been argued in the dynamic context of capital accumulation that rent is a form in which surplus profitability can be appropriated by a landlord, thereby intervening within, and influencing the pace and patterns of, capital accumulation (rather than simply being a price-determined or determining appropriation on the basis of given production conditions).

The third topic is that of mining development and, in particular, whether it is appropriate and feasible to construct a general theory of mining. According to the approach based on systems of provision, it would be necessary to consider mining in the context of the upstream activities to which is it attached. Further, its necessary dependence upon landed property also makes it a candidate for an appropriate confrontation with rent theory. In this, it differs from other heavily land-dependent economic activity, especially agriculture, by the 'inorganic' nature of the product involved[3] (and not just the 'destructibility' associated with extraction which, as Ricardo recognised, could equally apply to agricultural activity such as forestry).

In a recent special issue of Business History devoted to mining history, Harvey and Press (1990) provided an introduction in which they discussed the major issues involved, such as big business, integration and cartelisation as a means of identifying common themes and differences across the papers in the collection and others that had been previously published. This raises the issue of whether there can be a general theory of mining (history) one that commands a range of applications across time, place and ore. For those, for example, who have attended the International Mining History Conference, there must be some doubts – as commonalities would have to be sought between the activities of Incas and those on oil rigs!

This chapter takes a more positive view by engaging in a comparative analysis of (UK) coal, (South African) diamonds, and (predominantly US) oil

---

3   Fine and Leopold (1993), and especially Fine (1993b), distinguish the food system by its high level of organic dependence throughout the whole process of provision. See also Fine et al. (1996). This issue became embroiled in the nature/social dualism policing, Actor-Network Theory (ANT), and beyond (Fine, 2002a, 2003a and b, 2004a and 2005) ultimately, shifting to the environment (Malm, 2019).

– although each of these is only cursorily examined for particular historical periods.[4]

In the next section, emphasis is placed upon the system of landed property under which mining takes place. Taking the UK as a model, because of the slow maturation of the contradictions involved, it is shown that each industry exhibited a strikingly similar problem, arising out of the specific confrontation between landed property and accumulation of capital as the latter necessarily broadened its spatial scope.

Section 3 is concerned with the formation and operation of cartels, with emphasis now more upon the problems associated with the arrival of new sources of supply. The experiences of the three industries are different but the comparison sheds light on the importance of the interaction between cartels and vertical and horizontal integration, with the pattern of these often taking precedence over productive efficiency in the jockeying for competitive advantage.

In the concluding remarks, it is suggested that the analysis here might be extended to other cases and take into account other factors. Perhaps the most important is the guarantee of a supply of labour, a factor that might be dependent upon, particularly at the early stages of mining development, control of landed property in such a way as to preclude labour from its own independent reproduction through, for example, self-sufficient farming, as proved important in supplying labour to the South African gold mines.[5]

In short, this chapter is narrow in scope if not in ambition. By examining three specific minerals in the context of landed property and monopolisation, certain regularities are identified for which more abstract theoretical analysis is perceived to be appropriate.[6] Hopefully, this will prove a useful exercise in suggesting the potential for further analyses along similar lines by extension to other minerals or other factors, such as technical change, marketing and finance.[7]

---

4   I am particularly conscious of the failure to provide a comparative account of supply/coercing labour in mining. In the case of diamonds in South Africa, for example, see Gerstenberger (2022, pp. 283–95).

5   See Atkins (1991) for this in the context of the Jamaican sugar plantations and bauxite mines.

6   Chandler (1990) provides an example of the interaction between comparative economic history and theoretical analysis in his discussion of economies of scale and scope and the development of US, UK and German big business.

7   The literature on mineral rights and mineral law (including rights of capture) is not addressed but might be reassessed in the light of this contribution.

2   Minerals and Landed Property

A distinguishing feature of mineral exploitation is its dependence upon the so-called destructible properties of the land. In principle, subject to the differing costs associated with transport of inputs and outputs and with differing conditions in local labour and financial markets, the vast majority of economic activity is not spatially fixed by nature. This cannot be true of mineral extraction and, unlike agriculture, the removal of the earth's bounty does not possibly leave it susceptible to restoration to its original, or even enhanced, powers of production.

Despite this, surprisingly, there has been relatively little attempt to develop a specific economic theory of mining. Of course, there has been the economic theory of exhaustible resources (Dasgupta and Heal, 1979, for example) and attention to particular aspects of mining such as exploration. But these have depended upon the simple application of the well-worn principles of neoclassical economics,[8] with the consequent two severe problems for economists and economic historians.

First, neoclassical economics seems particularly ill-suited to handle either the statics or the dynamics of mineral extraction. For the statics, the evidence, in any other than a tautologous sense, is far from convincing for the Ricardian propositions, which carry over to the neoclassical theory, that there is both progression from better to worse land as demand expands, and a competitive evening out of production conditions or fertility through rent payments taking up the differences between them (with worst land or, more exactly, worst capital in use commanding no rent at all).

For the dynamics, mineral production has often provided new industries (hence creating, or associated with, new items of consumption) experiencing explosive technological change and growth in the wake of industrial revolutions and the opening up of the world economy as a single market for trade, finance and investment. A theory of fixed production possibilities, or exogenously given technological change, and of given consumer preferences is hardly the most apposite. Even if such theory could be successfully massaged to allow for endogenous technical change, etc, scepticism must remain whether an appropriate and distinct theory of mining could emerge.

The second, and related, problem for the economic orthodoxy, is that it does not really have an explanation of rent other than as a corollary of price theory.

---

8   See Matthews (1990), for example, who seeks to develop a theory of mineral development by appeal to supply and demand curves, distinguishing mining by its relatively inelastic short-run supply conditions.

Particular pieces of land, which offer physical properties in terms of production or consumption (e.g. 'beauty') will command a scarcity price which is given the name 'rent' but, other than in the specific properties of land – of which much is usually made of non-extension of supply despite reclamation and exploration in practice – the price (and derived revenue) of any other good would be determined in exactly the same way. Symptomatic of this in a more general way is the tendency of neoclassical economics to reduce all sources of revenue to a single notion of initial, if potentially uncertain, assets – as in human capital theory, whereby 'labour', for example, becomes 'capital'. With a similar fate embracing land, it is hardly surprising that a specific theory of rent is ultimately a casualty of the marginalist revolution (Fine, 1982a and 1983).

By corollary, much the same applies to the theory of mining which ought to command a theory of rent of a special kind. Attempts have been made to do this in the past through assigning the term royalty to the value of the minerals extracted (in return for removing the destructible properties of the land, with a higher payment when it is less costly to do so). Whether this should be considered a rent of a special kind or something distinct from rent, there is no escaping from the dull logic of marginalist principles other than in the terminology employed (Fine, 1982b and 1990a).

Some confrontation with these difficulties might have been expected from Marxist economics, with its emphasis upon accumulation and the social relations of production. The results, however, have been disappointing. There has been a tendency to reduce Marxist rent theory to a (re)distributional analysis, often with some assertion, or rejection, of correspondence with Marx's claim that landed property has the potential effect of reducing the organic composition of capital (or capital-intensity) in agriculture with the further possibility of this leading to a higher price to accommodate an (absolute) rent over and above differential rent and price of production. In other words, whereas for Ricardo (differential) rent is a physical property of the land for which ownership merely bestows the right to revenue with no further effects, for Marxist distributional rent theory, agency in landownership depends upon asserting an individual and class monopoly over access to a particular item of the means of production.

Unfortunately, this sheds little light upon the dynamics of accumulation, although it can be associated with a stagnationist hypothesis in which monopolisation restricts investment and output in the attempt to sustain profits through a higher price level. In shifting to a focus on the balance of power in a distributional struggle, and away from the iron laws of physical conditions of production, very little specific to land alone emerges – again, other than in name – because monopoly control over an essential input is by no means unique to land. In moving from agricultural rent to mineral revenues, nothing novel is added. In particular, in the wake of oil price rises in the 1970s, and the notion of OPEC as a cartel, Roncaglia (1985) has, for example, developed a theory of trilateral monopoly.[9] In short, there has been a tendency to conflate monopolisation over the supply of a particular commodity with the ownership of the particular pieces of land from which it is produced, although the two sources of monopoly are conceptually and, often in practice, practically distinct.

A rather different approach results from the debate between Fine and Ball over Marx's theory of rent, in which there proved much common ground (Fine 1979 and 1980c; Ball, 1980). Whilst this embraces extremely complex theoretical issues, its main conclusions can be usefully summarised. First, a distinction is drawn between extensive and intensive development – the extension of existing methods of production on to new lands and the intensive application of capital to land already in use, respectively. Here, there is both a parallel and a break with Ricardo's theory of the extensive and intensive margins in so far as he considers the latter as essentially equivalent to further application of capital to a given piece of land. It is as if the land exists twice, or more times over, so that the theory of differential rent continues to apply to the capital applied to the land rather than on the piece of land itself.

This is not so, however, for Marx since the intensive application of capital is the normal imperative of accumulation, competitively reducing the value of commodities in pursuit of surplus profits. However, in the presence of landed property, such surplus profits may instead be appropriated in the form of rent and, consequently, dampen the incentive to invest. Thus, there is a tension between extension of production on to new lands, for which – whether they be better or worse than those in use – an absolute rent is charged, and intensive accumulation on existing lands in use for which a differential rent is charged.[10] Nor is this a harmonious tension, evening out fertility conditions and allocating capital efficiently. Rather, in the dynamic context of increasing productivity through larger scale methods of production, it is a conflict over who is to gain from the increased surplus that can be extracted.[11]

---

9   For an attempt to apply a more sophisticated version of Marx's theory of rent to the oil industry, see Bina (1985).

10   Fine shows that the relation between extensive and intensive development is given by differential rent of the second type, equalling the difference between value and price of production due to differences in organic composition of capital, and as the potential limit of absolute rent.

11   This is most readily recognised in orthodox theory in terms of the accrual of development gains (and who is to receive them).

Clearly, this theory moves beyond the redistributional focus of other Marxist interpretations of rent theory, but it has one property in common with them which distinguishes both from Ricardian theory. Each depends for its results upon historical contingency – the existence and strength of the monopoly ownership of land in the case of the redistributional focus. For emphasis on patterns of accumulation, however, the role of landed property is also perceived to be contingent. It depends upon the nature of ownership of landed property and how it relates to the accumulation process. In other words, it concerns the conditions under which capital has access to the land for the purposes of production and accumulation. This goes far beyond the payment of rent for differential fertility or for monopoly control. It potentially depends upon a whole host of factors over and above the distribution of ownership and (legal) control of land to incorporate access to credit, markets, labour, etc, any one of which may play a decisive role in mediating the rent relation. Often these factors, conflicts over them, and the balance of economic and political power, are reflected in the form taken by leases – what is their customary length, rights of renewal, arrangements over ownership of fixed capital or improvements in the event of non-renewal, etc.

In short, the stance adopted by Fine and Ball is one that focuses upon the abstract conflict over the production and appropriation of surplus as accumulation proceeds, and on which it has an effect, but that such outcomes are contingently dependent upon the particular form taken by landed property historically. This debate, often explicitly, was more concerned with agriculture than landed property in general so that its implications for mineral production are not immediate and have not been made explicit.[12] Marx's own abstract specification of mining was to liken it to the transport industry since, to employ his use of the term, it did not work primarily with raw materials, by which he meant constant capital, commodity inputs that had previously been produced and sold by other capitalists.[13] To some extent this renders his theory of technical change inappropriate for mining for he argues that pursuit of (relative) surplus value depends upon the working up of more and more raw materials into commodities by a given quantum of labour, with this itself resulting in an increase in the technical composition of capital (capital-labour ratio) and requiring, as a precondition, the use of greater quantities of fixed capital and machinery.

---

12   Interestingly, neither Fine's nor Ball's interest in Marx's rent theory was inspired by agriculture, but by the coal industry and the construction industry, respectively.

13   Alfred Marshall also likened mining to transport but for purely descriptive reasons as the movement of the ore out of the ground.

The former condition continues to apply to the raw materials employed in mining, most obviously in the use of power, explosives, etc, as does the latter condition in the creation of the fabric of the mine – in constructing the large-scale 'mineral factory'. But, unlike agriculture where, to some extent, the raw materials, such as seeds, to be worked upon can be intensively used without ever larger use of land, in mineral extraction, by necessity, the absence of a produced raw material as basic to production implies the spatial extension of capital's operations – whether in depth, width or, in the absence of these directly, by the scope of extraction, as in oil wells.

In a study of the British coal industry, Fine et al. (1985) and Fine (1990b) use this theoretical insight, although it was usually kept in the presentational background, to explore the evolution of the relationship between capital and land from the middle of the nineteenth century (see also Evans and Fine,1980a and b; Fine, 1990a and 1993). Emphasis was placed on the system of large landed property in Britain, in contrast to the rest of Europe. For the latter, in general, minerals had been taken into state ownership at least by the beginning of the nineteenth century in order that mining concessions of sufficient size could be worked. In Britain, coal belonged to the surface owner, although both Crown and Church were most heavily represented.[14] This meant that mining could develop easily within the confines of existing landed estates, or even across them with relatively few leases to negotiate. Indeed, landowners positively had an interest in encouraging as many mineowners as possible to apply their capital to their mineral resources, as is also the case for parcelled tenant farming, for example. Leases were even designed, as with certain or dead rents which had to be paid irrespective of output extracted, to guarantee that coal was worked.

Yet, the inevitable consequence of the accelerating mineral extraction was for mines to strain spatially against the bounds imposed by the system of landownership. Increasing difficulties were encountered at the borders of properties, in the leaving of coal barriers to demarcate lease boundaries and also, for example, in providing for pumping and draining and even right of access, or wayleaves, across properties, possibly underground through where coal had already been fully worked out. These problems rapidly intensified in the period leading up to the first world war and, immediately afterwards; the Sankey Commission in 1919, followed by the Samuel Commission in 1925,

---

14   In previous research, Fine has computerised the data for compensation paid upon nationalisation of the UK coal royalties in 1938. It should be of interest to those engaged in local, company or personal histories as well as those concerned with the coal industry or landed property. See Brunskill et al. (1985) for an application to Scotland.

recommended the taking of the coal royalties into public ownership such were the perceived nature of the practical difficulties involved. In the event, with frequent amendments to legislation to enhance mineowner access to coal, the nationalisation of the royalties was delayed until 1938. The result was to impede the rationalisation and mechanisation of the industry – Britain lagging notoriously behind its competitors during the interwar years (Fine et al. 1985; Fine, 1990a).

What is the relevance of this for other minerals? First, although emphasis has been placed on the social relations governing access to landed property, geological properties are also important in conjunction with them. In Britain, because of the early use of coal and its availability in large quantities, together with the peculiarly concentrated ownership of landed property, it is possible to witness the gradual unfolding of the confrontation between landed property and capital as accumulation proceeded.[15] In other contexts, with the greater rarity and spatial concentration of the minerals concerned, or the early adoption of large-scale methods of extraction, such conflicts and their effects are liable to emerge rapidly, and possibly equally quickly to be resolved, at least temporarily.

Secondly, at such times of conflict, the conventional wisdom tends to treat the associated problems as practical rather than as a matter for theoretical scrutiny. Thus, in Britain, whilst the coal industry was apparently expanding smoothly in the nineteenth century, it was believed to be subject to the Ricardian theory of rent. This analysis was totally forgotten once more mundane matters of reorganising the industry efficiently were at stake. This approach has tended to be carried over into other historical analyses, whereas emphasis should be placed upon the economic interests involved and their impact upon the industry through the command of royalties or rents. This is not to deny the pressures for change coming from the imperatives of practicality, only to insist that these both have an economic character and are resolved to the greater or lesser benefit of the interests involved.

Consider, then, the South African diamond industry.[16] Soon after its origins, the parallels with the British coal industry in some instances are remarkably striking. The stimulus to the industry began in 1867 with the discovery of its 'first' diamond. By 1871 there were four major mines established, at Kimberley,

---

15   For those countries outside Europe with private ownership of minerals, it was often the case that mining companies gained large land concessions.

16   What follows on the diamond industry depends especially upon Gregory (1962), Lenzen (1970), Newbury (1989), Turrell (1987) and Worger (1987). See also Innes (1984) and Marks (1985a and b) for some background.

De Beers, Dupoitspan and Bulfontein with, respectively, 470, 622, 1441 and 1067 working claims, each measuring at most 31 feet square, and some even subdivided one or more times. In addition, no miner was allowed more than two claims. The evolving consequences in working the ore contained within a vertical pipe are not difficult to imagine. As Newbury (1989, p. 29) quotes, for example, from an official report of 1872:

> For a space of about half-a-mile men are ascending and descending the deep chasms which have been excavated, passing on foot or driving carts along the narrow roads between the claims. There are twelve of these roads, each about one hundred and fifty yards long by twenty feet wide. On either side of each road are deep gullies, in many places one hundred feet deep, and some sixty feet wide. In these gullies the mining is carried on. The scene is perfectly dazzling. It looks and is a monster in danger. Weak ladders, the very picture of insecurity, are used for ascent and descent, sometimes only a rope and foot-holes in the sides of the gullies. The ground dug out from the bottom of the gullies is conveyed to the top in galvanised-iron buckets passed along ropes or stout wires worked with pullies ... accidents are frequent. Carts and mules have fallen from the roads into the pits. But the worst danger to be apprehended is a landslip from one of the roads.

By 1874, concessions were made to allow ten claims per person and the process of monopolisation of production within each mine had begun. The initial situation is well-illustrated by Figure 1. From this point of highly fragmented ownership, a process of amalgamation of claims proceeded extremely rapidly throughout the 1880s.[17] But it was soon intricately intertwined with proposals to amalgamate across the different mines; without this amalgamation there were dangers of oversupply in which only the most productive mine – whether through natural conditions, extent of efficient organisation or (wage) cost-cutting – would be best placed to prosper or merely survive. Thus, the competition to amalgamate within a mine was part and parcel of the competition to amalgamate across the mines. Obviously, the major source of productive efficiency would come from the rationalisation of the internal operations of the mines, although allocative efficiency of a given level of output across the

---

17   For a fascinating set of visuals of the process and the nature of diamond mining in the presence of fragmented claim ownership, see https://grahamlesliemccallum.wordpr ess.com/2014/07/03/a-chronological-pictorial-of-the-kimberley-mine/.

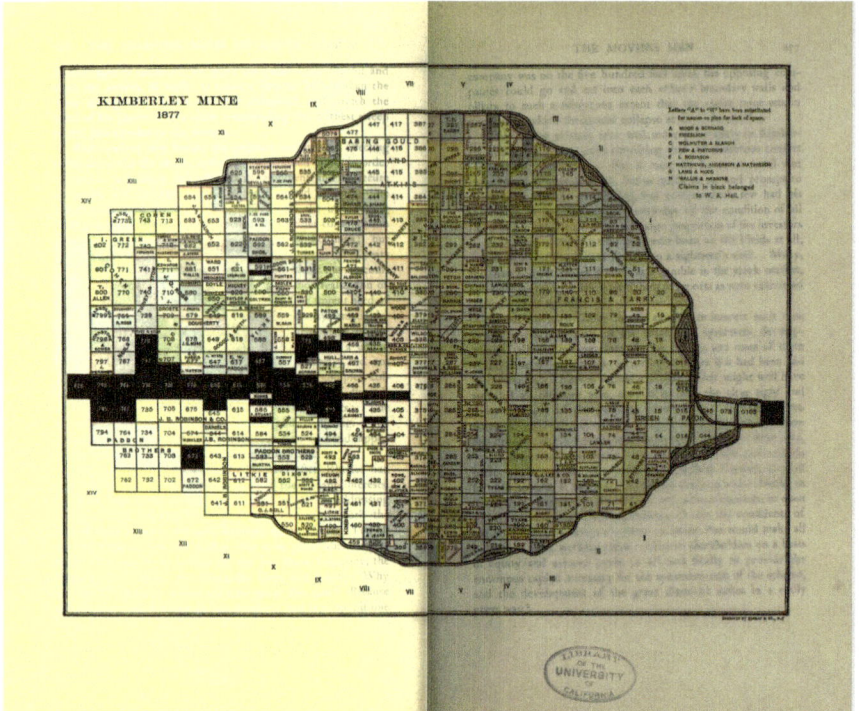

FIGURE 1   Diagram of claim ownership, Kimberley mine, 1877
            SOURCE: WILLIAMS, G F. (1905) *THE DIAMOND MINES OF SOUTH AFRICA*, VOL
            1 NEW YORK, NY: B F BUCK & CO. (INSERT BETWEEN PP. 276 AND 277)

mines is a further factor.[18] On the other hand, jockeying for ultimate control of the industry depended upon the extent of overall holdings across mines. As Worger (1987, p. 219) puts it:

> Throughout 1886 and 1887, therefore, the De Beers and Kimberley Central companies raced to amalgamate their adjacent mines.

Ultimately, these two companies engaged in a two-horse race, with De Beers for example, contracting to buy up the Compagnie Francaise, which held a part of the Kimberley mine, in order to forestall Central's control – although the situation was even more complicated by the complex cross-ownerships

---

18   Neoclassical economics would, of course, argue that marginal productivity should be equalised across mines.

by foreign financiers whose further support, in turn, was required to fund any final resolution of overall control. By the beginning of the next decade, the issue seemed to have been settled (Turrell, 1987, p. 225).[19]

> A practical monopoly of the four mines was only achieved in 1891 at a total cost of £14.5 million. De Beers Consolidated, the company that Rhodes predicted would be worth 'the balance of Africa', had asserted its control of the commanding heights of the Cape economy.

This might seem rapid enough both in the sweep of history and to compensate for the inefficiencies of fragmented production in the interim. But why was not a large-scale mine established earlier or even in the first instance? The traditional answer is to appeal to 'Diggers' Democracy', the idea that the original prospectors and claimants had sufficient political influence and militant resolve to sustain their own existence, at least temporarily, as against the inevitable logic of scale economies, negative externalities and the (re)definjtion and exercise of property rights as orthodox analysis might have it.

However, Turrell (1987, p. 74) persuasively argues rather differently:

> 1,200 small holders in a mine paid six to eight times the revenue of a monopoly company.

Further, against the orthodox view of the restriction of the number of claims an individual could hold as being motivated by commitment to diggers' democracy, he suggests the reason was to be found in the greater commitment to the interests of merchant capitalists, dealing in supplies to the miners, and to the expansion of indigenous farming, as against the interests of imperial-based mining capital and finance that would tend to import consumables from abroad. In the event, Southey, the Governor of Cape Town at the time, was swept aside for his apparent support for the diggers following the Black Flag Revolt of 1875, and property relations were amended so that monopolised and foreign capital came to the fore. However, whatever the forces behind and against amalgamation, the inefficiencies imposed by fragmentation of claims, intensified by production itself, provide a striking parallel with the more leisurely evolution of the same problems within the British coal industry.

---

19   Turrell (1987) points to much mythology surrounding the ultimate success of De Beers and Rhodes, highlighting the high cost that had to be paid as well as the use of illegal and dishonest practices, often a norm, it appears, in the early formation of mineral monopolies but one not subject to systematic theoretical analysis.

Developments in the US oil industry in the nineteenth century also exhibit some striking parallels.[20] Once again, a picture or two can better illustrate an argument than pages of theory, see Figures 2 and 3. Whether in Pennsylvania in the 1860s or Texas in the 1900s, the discovery of oil led to an extreme parcelisation of land for the purposes of production, even at the expense, in this case, of inefficiency through the rapid depletion of underground pressure that allowed the oil to gush as if released from a thousand pin pricks. By the end of 1901, 440 gushers graced the aptly named Spindletop (Knowles, 1983, p. 22):[21]

> Countless small owners, each with a few acres, provided the opportunity for the most insane speculators' boom the world had ever seen. Forty thousand fortune seekers, swindlers, gamblers, and prostitutes descended on Beaumont's 10000 residents. Millions of dollars changed hands in hours. Oil was so plentiful that it sold for three cents a barrel; drinking water was so scarce it sold for five cents a cup. When doctors announced it was safer to drink whisky than Beaumont water, the local Women's Civilian Temperance Union indignantly dispensed free boiled water.

Figure 2 shows America's Spindletop. Flowing 100000 barrels a day from a depth of 1020 feet, in a solid black stream 175 feet in the air, it proved that there was an abundance of oil in the earth. As shown in Figure 3, wells soon became drilled so close together that a man could walk from one rig floor to another without ever touching the ground. Every well was a gusher.

Such conditions, in oil as in diamonds, were highly conducive both to rapid expansion in supply and to unnecessarily high levels of costs of production, as the multiplicity of gushers dissipated underground pressure. It seems that tackling of excess supply through cartelisation was the route, as will be seen, to rationalisation of production.

3   Cartels and Minerals

The British coal industry organised a cartel at an extremely early stage with the legendary control over coals from Newcastle that served the London market. It lasted at least from the Elizabethan age until the mid-nineteenth century

---

20   For much of what follows on the oil industry, see Williamson and Daum (1959), Williamson et al. (1963), Koxhoorn (1977), Bina (1985), Hidy and Hidy (1955) and Yergin (1991).

21   See van Onselen (1982a and b) for social comparisons with the town life of the early Johannesburg.

FIGURE 2   Spindletop, the astounding southeast texas
            gusher which changed the history of America
            and the world on January 10, 1901
            SOURCE: *SPINDLETOP: THE GUSHER THAT*
            LAUNCHED THE OIL INDUSTRY HTTPS:
            //AWORKSTATION.COM/SPINDLETOP-THE
            -GUSHER-THAT-LAUNCHED-THE-OIL
            -INDUSTRY/

when the railway age stripped it of its advantage of coastal transport when
compared with the other inland coalfields. What lessons can be learnt more
generally for minerals?

First, in the discussion of the previous section, whilst the theory was concerned with both extensive and intensive development, the cases of oil and
diamonds at least were restricted to the intensive exploitation of a relatively
few sources of a particular mineral even if these were worked under conditions
of fragmented ownership. Clearly, to sustain a cartel, it is necessary to incorporate new sites of production as and when they emerge or, alternatively, to

FIGURE 3   1903. Horses and carts travel down the plank road called boiler avenue which
              provided access to Spindletop's boiler locations
              SOURCE: *DE SOTO TO SPINDLETOP: HOW OIL BIRTHED MODERN HOUSTON-*
              HOUSTON CHRONICLE HTTPS://S.HDNUX.COM/PHOTOS/46/43/14/10105663/3
              /RAWIMAGE.JPG

pre-empt their emergence. This observation, of course, is by no means unique
to minerals. But it does raise the issue of whether cartelisation is more easily
attainable and sustainable in mineral than in other sectors of the economy.

There appear to be two conflicting responses to this. On the one hand, the
dependence of mineral extraction upon suitably available land would appear
to restrict competitive entry to an extent that does not apply in other sectors for which, subject to scale economies and technological know-how, etc,
there are only 'artificial' barriers to entry. On the other hand, such entry barriers as are posed by the geological presence and discovery of minerals are far
from purely natural and, if relied upon, may prove uncertain and unreliable.
Moreover, the ability to impose obstacles to the access to mineral-bearing land
more heavily involves governments than in the case of manufacturing (given
the possible exercise of sovereignty over mineral-bearing land). Governments
may be unwilling to submit to a cartel from outside its natural frontiers, and
the greater freedom for capital to enter a sector for non-mineral sectors may

lead it to depend upon stronger forms of cartel organisation, with mineral producers more liable to breach discipline as a consequence of the geologically driven differences in costs of production which cannot be levelled by equal applications of capital.

With few exceptions, however, experience seems to suggest that control directly over mineral extraction and mineral-bearing land has not been the major source of cartelisation. This is borne out by the early British coal industry for which the 'Limitation of the Vend' derived from the control of the 'Company of Hostmen', those able to trade from the Tyne docks (Nef, 1932; Sweezy,1938). Further, a major threat to the cartel was posed by the alternative offered by the shipping and sourcing of alternative supplies through the nearby Wear. But with just two potential outlets, an accommodation, however stable, could easily be reached.

Similar considerations apply to the diamond industry. Whilst concentration of ownership in production in the late nineteenth century was important, the major source of cartelisation came through marketing agreements across the syndicates operating at the various mines, at least until the setting up of the Diamond Syndicate (from 1891) which depended primarily upon (temporary) monopolisation of South African supplies with De Beers. For, as Worger (1987, p. 21) observes:

> A diamond that might have fetched £5000 at the time of the first discoveries was worth only £200 or so by 1872 as prices continued to decline.

In addition, the demand for diamonds tended to exhibit pronounced cyclical movements, with corresponding effects on the industry and the welfare of Kimberley itself as a town, as miners and commerce flowed in and out with the fortunes of the industry. Consequently, a major development was the setting up of a reserve fund in 1892 to support demand in recession.

However, it should not be thought that cartelisation was simply, a possibly efficient, response to market uncertainty. The uncertainty was itself a product of the reorganisation of the industry. Fragmented production within the diamond mines, and lack of sufficient overall coordination often led to such major falls in the workings that operations had to be completely suspended until the earth could be cleared. In addition, the method of financing the industry – through speculative issues of shares for companies, many of which were certain to fail irrespective of whether the capital raised actually found its way into production – necessarily exaggerated the fluctuations even for those mines with sound finance and management and genuine productive returns.

For the oil industry, the lesser significance of monopolisation of production, as the means to a cartel, than through other mechanisms is transparent through the history of Standard Oil (McLean and Haigh, 1954). As Hidy and Hidy (1955, p. 169) report:

> In 1882 the Standard Oil group owned only four small producing properties acquired in the 1870's.

Even by 1891, it still only accounted for 26% of US output, its share peaking at around one third at the end of the century. At that time, however, it had control of nearly 90% of refining capacity. Its control of marketing was to be even greater. This had all been gained through a cumulative assault upon the upstream activities of the industry, with Rockefeller manipulating freight rates, undercutting or threatening to undercut rivals, building pipelines, buying up and closing refineries and generally forcing rivals to come to an accommodation or, more usually other than in production, a surrender to acquisition.

Ultimately, however, the monopoly established by Standard foundered on the twin obstacles of proliferating sources of oil and anti-trust actions. This raises the issue, not of how cartels are formed but how they can be maintained. Before turning to this, it is worth re-emphasising that the sequence of development in the cases of both oil and diamonds appears to begin with fragmented production with attendant inefficiencies in costs. The tendency to oversupply, however, serves merchant capital in its desire for highly competitive sources of cheap supplies but, thereby, creating problems through severe and amplified cyclical fluctuations. Next, a cartel is established through various levers in the chain of supply rather than in production itself. With cartelisation, larger-scale and more efficient organisation of production can ensue. Finally, this raises two further problems – how to organise the cartel and to protect it from the emergence of alternative sources of supply.

The British coal industry provides few lessons in response to these questions since it failed to provide a stable and effective cartel in the modern period until at least the state organised one in the 1930s, and fragmentation and inefficiency persisted until after nationalisation of the industry in 1947. With both diamonds and oil, it is easier to distinguish conceptually between the policing of the cartel, with the distribution of its benefits internally, and its protection from (potential) outside sources of supply, than it is to distinguish the mechanisms for doing so in practice. Both processes are associated with, and furthered by, vertical and horizontal integration[22] and, again, it follows that this is by no means the most efficient means for (re)organising the industry either in the allocation of supply or in the methods of production – since sustaining the cartel and jockeying for position within it would often take precedence over cost-efficiency.

For diamonds, by the 1890s, De Beers formed a cartel under the guidance of Cecil Rhodes in the interests of diamond merchants. Whilst output was restricted and producer prices rose by 50%, the price to the trade through De Beers rose by more than 200%. The Dutoitspan and Bulfontein mines were virtually closed, leading to high levels of unemployment in Kimberley as well as in the European cutting industry. But De Beers' control was far from secure. In the 1900s, new sources of supply emerged from the Premier Mine in South Africa and also from Namibia (1908) then under German control. Almost immediately, following Union in 1910, the South African state developed a keen interest in the industry, with a wish to see mines within its borders as fully employed as possible, being highly dependent itself upon diamond tax revenues.

With the development of alluvial diggings in South Africa, following the election in 1924 of a Pact Government at least nominally committed to the interests of white labour, a secure cartel only emerged following the Anglo American company's takeover of De Beers and an accommodation being reached with government. Ernest Oppenheimer's ability to achieve this depended upon his having made substantial inroads into both diamond production and marketing. By 1934, an agreement was cemented constituting the Diamond Producers Association, with adherence from both the South African Government and the Administrator of the then South West Africa. This was despite fierce conflict between the Government and Oppenheimer over the earlier closure of South African mines in response to the fall in demand for diamonds in the wake of the Great Depression. Clearly, supply adjustment had to take place through the mines under the diamond syndicate's control and, yet, this entailed a greater penalty to the South African Exchequeur and workforce, with the suspicion that Anglo could compensate itself on the sales of

---

22   For McLean and Haigh (1954, p. 57): "The record of the oil industry reveals that in the years before 1911 vertical integration was very definitely a two-edged sword. To the Standard Oil group, vertical integration was often used as a device to achieve, protect and extend a virtual monopoly of the refining segment of the oil business. To the independent companies, on the other hand, vertical integration was often a means of escaping the dominance of the Standard Oil group".

diamonds derived from others' or its own sources from outside South Africa (or from accumulated stocks). For Newbury (1989, p. 365):

> In effect, the industry climbed out of the crisis of the 1930s because South African diamond production was used as the regulator for a measure of control by the Diamond Corporation over total diamond purchases inside and outside the Union.

The account here is a breathtaking simplification of an intense and complex struggle over control both of and for the diamond industry. Apart from emphasising integration as a mechanism for exercising these, the role of the state has emerged as a new element of some importance. Essentially, it was caught between a number of competing objectives – as a beneficiary of the diamond industry seeking, like private capitalists, to pursue its own returns but recognising the need for stability of a cartel to this end, and as an agency representing wider interests whether these be of indigenous capitalists (wanting the support of markets and tax revenue from the foreign capital invested in mining) or of the white fraction of the workforce.

Consequently, it is hardly surprising that government flirted with the idea of taking the industry into its own hands. Although very few of these powers were ever used, Newbury (1989, p. 258) sums up the Diamond Control Bill of 1925:

> The government now had an instrument which it could use to determine quantities produced, set minimum prices, and call for returns of production. All sales agreements required ministerial approval. A 'Diamond Control Board' might be established to buy and sell, issue advances, and fund monopoly sales through its own officials.

Gregory (1962, p. 171) reports of the Precious Stones Act, No 44 of 1927, that:[23]

> "The main principle underlying this measure", said the Minister (of Mines) "is that alluvial diggings, subject to the interests of the State, and a fair participation of the State where necessary and desirable, should remain the reserve and preserve of the small man".

In the event, the lack of power that the South African state could exert over the sale of diamonds on world markets inevitably foreclosed its option of

---

23   The diggers were, however, disappearing by the end of the 1920s (Gregory, 1962, p. 190).

controlling the domestic industry. It was reduced to the role of supporting Anglo's organisation of the cartel, whilst grumbling over the levels of costs and benefits that this brought.

Clearly, the situation in the oil industry had been completely different. In this case, the interests of other participants prevailed over Standard Oil as they were aided by anti-trust legislation, leading in 1911 to the decree to break up Standard into a number of constituent companies. On the other hand, even with the massive expansion in demand, the industry remained monopolised if less so than before. In 1938, the largest ten companies controlled 58.6% of refining capacity and, in crude production, the largest twenty companies accounted for a little less than a quarter of all producing wells. Even so, under the perverse ideology of conservation, in which fear of shortage was used to rationalise a cartel to control against glut, some quota systems were used to maintain prices and profitability in US domestic markets. Conservation was also used by producers as the rationale for controlling undue release of pressure through the proliferation of gushers from separate parcels of land with access to the same underground wells.

However, the main developments were taking place on the world scene, where now the control of access to oil was as much a diplomatic and military relation as one of the economics of landed property – although the two are not entirely distinct (Bromley, 1991). The United States used its power to increase its share of cheap middle east oil from 15.7% in 1939 to 37% in 1945, and 71.3% in 1957, through a series of accommodations reached with other oil companies and governments. Whilst this compensated for the fall in the share of its own reserves over the latter period from 39.8% to 13.9%, a strict division was made between its own domestic and foreign markets, with imports restricted to around 20% of consumption into the 1960s despite a severe cost disadvantage in domestic production. Following Bina (1985) and Koxhoorn (1977), Fine and Harris (1985, p. 84) summarise the structure of the industry as it entered the second world war and as it emerged from it to support the post-war boom with cheap, if cartelised (oil) energy:

> The oil industry had two major divisions in its structure. On the one hand, there was the division between the US market and that of the rest of the world. Both were subject to cartel arrangements and the latter was protected from the former by tariffs. On the other hand, there was the division between the US majors (five of the Seven Sisters) and the other US producers. This division does not correspond to the previous one, since the US majors served both foreign and domestic markets through foreign and domestic production, respectively.

However, the condition to retain this structure was that the price level should be sufficiently high to allow profitability within the US domestic industry even as its cost disadvantage with external supplies increasingly widened. Not surprisingly, this structure began to erode and then collapse around the edges – like a fall of earth? – as oil imports into the United States grew to serve independent domestic refiners for whom a high oil price served only the interests of domestic crude producers. More important, independents were increasingly able to exploit oil through a variety of alternative sources around the world, not least because of the greater levels of state intervention in oil policy, including ownership of one or more of the integrated activities involved.

To cut a long and complex story short, the processes of vertical and horizontal integration within the industry were insufficient to hold the cartel within the majors. But, far from this leading to a collapse of the oil price, it was, in the oil crises of the early 1970s, associated with an increase in price sufficient to allow profitability for all agents concerned, including that of the US domestic industry. Subsequent developments lie outside the scope of this chapter. The purpose here is to point to the parallels with the diamond industry, even if, with the latter on a narrower global stage, the evolution of the industry depends upon a complex and contingent relation between intensive and extensive (including new) development of resources, the stability and relative advantage in cartelisation in association with vertical and horizontal integration, and the increasing significance of state intervention whether in supervising the cartel or in control of resources at a national and/or international level.

Finally, consider the use of the term monopoly capital(ism) which is often applied to the cartelisation of industry – as is so by Worger, for example (and also Innes, 1984). Elsewhere, Fine (1988) has argued that Sweezy employed the monopoly of the Vend as a model by which he was subsequently to understand the era of (the twentieth century) monopoly capitalism (see also Fine, 2009a). In short, output restriction for a sector is generalised to the economy as a whole to derive a theory of capitalism in its later stages as stagnating under the burden of unsold potential surplus and underconsumption.

There are a number of problems here. First, in classic Marxism, monopoly capitalism is conceived as an economic system of production, associated with generalised reduction in the value of labour power (or real cost of a given wage level) through the introduction of machinery (and, thus, the production of relative surplus value). It follows that monopoly capitalism cannot be associated with the developments in one sector alone, in the same way, by analogy, that a system of bourgeois democracy cannot be derived, indeed is denied by, the introduction of a limited electoral franchise. In addition, monopoly capitalism is defined neither by developments in a single sector, nor by cartelisation within it, nor, more generally, across a range of sectors by what is a feature of the commercial and not the productive system. Where the commodity concerned is diamonds, which do not enter into the consumption basket of the worker's normal living standards, even where it is a cartelised and capital-intensive industry, it is not definitive for signalling the presence of monopoly capitalism.[24]

The purpose of these remarks is to offer a word of caution against too readily associating cartels or monopoly with an undifferentiated stage of capitalism, potentially labelled monopoly capitalism, for which general theoretical propositions are then erroneously presumed – those propositions, paradoxically, are drawn from affinities with what are often pre-or early capitalist monopolies with an analytical priority on output restriction. Significantly, of course, the cartels of monopoly capitalism are less associated with stagnation than with the most rapid pace of growth and technical change, in part as competition is pursued through means other than markets, such as cost reduction and vertical and horizontal integration.[25]

For the mineral sector, the role of access to the landed property containing the resources, or the mechanisms for controlling such access along the chain of provision, is crucial. For example, for the British coal industry, when by the 1930s a cartel was at last organised under state initiative in response to drastic conditions of depression, it has been argued that this acted as an obstacle to rationalisation due to the featherbedding of small-scale, inefficient producers (Kirby, 1973 and 1977, and for greater background to the economic history of the British coal industry, Church, 1986; Supple, 1987). Yet, the general experience of cartels, including those in minerals, is that they positively encourage and make possible rationalisation and cost reduction, not least in the corresponding German industry at that time. Consequently, Fine (1990b) argues that the cartel was a (possibly contributory) response to, not the cause of, the low profitability of a fragmented industry, for which the equally fragmented and separated ownership of the coal measures played a significant, obstructive role to both mechanisation and rationalisation (see also Fine, 1990a). As

---

24 With the development of industrial diamonds for manufacturing (consumption goods) there is some potential for the industry to enter (indirectly) into the determination of, and reduction in, the value of labour power.

25 Insufficient emphasis upon this is one basis for the critique of the notion of monopoly capitalism employed by Cowling (1982) (Fine and Murfin, 1984a and b). For an explicit treatment of the periodisation of capitalism into stages, including that of (state) monopoly capitalism, see Fine and Harris (1979).

it were, the 'monopoly capitalism' as associated with a cartel proved the very antithesis of monopoly capitalism as the highest stage of capitalism.

4 Concluding Remarks

This chapter has sought to bring together the theory of landed property and an insistence upon analysis of vertically differentiated systems of economic activity in order to shed light upon a general theory or approach to mining. Whilst emphasis has been placed upon the complex, historically contingent and shifting relationship between landed property and accumulation of mining capital, and whilst the form of landed property has been different in each of the three case studies considered, there have been some remarkable parallels between them.

First, the fragmented system of landed property proved an obstacle to accumulation and productive efficiency, even if maturing extremely rapidly in the case of oil and diamonds, and over centuries in the case of British coal. Such impediments to greater extractive efficiency could not simply be overcome by amalgamation since the profits of doing so could be potentially appropriated by those in possession of the land.

Secondly, cartelisation developed out of upstream activity, for both oil and diamonds, prior to amalgamation in production itself. For British coal, in the absence of such effective cartelisation in the modern period, rationalisation of production was long delayed.

Thirdly, and not explicit in what has gone before, the cartelisation through distribution and/or marketing is associated with a vertical displacement of the rent relation – common, for example, in access to credit in some forms of agriculture. It is no longer the owners of land as such who are able to appropriate the surplus profitability associated with capital-intensive accumulation. Rather, this accrues to the cartel through its command over producers because of its exclusive access to markets.

There are other factors involved in mining systems. One of crucial importance is labour. This has been differently integrated in the three case studies considered here. For British coal, there is a long history of working class militancy on the basis of a rapidly growing waged workforce. It reached over a million by the first world war, having been formed out of the very same landed property relations that had previously foreclosed the option of small-scale farming and which were going to obstruct coalmining development in the interwar period. For diamonds, intense conflict over labour market conditions (and denial of genuine alternatives on the land for the vast majority of Africans, and many whites) was crucial in laying down the racially divided practices that were to prove so important to the subsequent goldmining industry and to the formation of South African society more generally. For oil, at least in the United States, industrial relations seem to have been less of a problem, although this has not always proved so in other countries (Nore and Turner, 1980, for example). Perhaps, this is due in part to the lower proportion of labour costs arising out of the differences in technology and geology involved.

Thus, consideration of labour and other factors warns against a general theory of mining as, indeed, does emphasis upon different forms of landed property and cartelisation. However, hopefully, it has been demonstrated that it is essential as a general approach to locate the conditions governing access to mineral land with the vertical integration of extraction to upstream activity.

CHAPTER 5

Reflections on and from the Cliometric Revolution

Postscript as Personal Preamble

This chapter has not been previously published although much of it was already drafted by March 2005. It formed part of a very much larger project, to be co-authored with Dimitris Milonakis, around an account of the evolving relationship between economic theory and economic history. That project, initially intended to be a case study and part of an account of the origins and trajectory of economics imperialism, eventually morphed into a proposed book of its own. This was substantially but never fully completed to publication (although it got far enough to be so long, it was divided into two projected volumes). In addition, especially but not exclusively around the close, critical account of the evolving economic history of Douglas North (Fine and Milonakis, 2009; Milonakis and Fine, 2009) much of our work was published in journals.[1]

The result is that I was confronted with large numbers of files of texts of overlapping material, ranging across drafts that had been published, and those that had not. This made it extremely difficult to put this chapter together in a way that avoided overlap with the other chapters drawn from published articles. This has been not just a matter of avoiding self-plagiarism, with different texts having benefitted from copy and paste, but also of selecting subject matter that is not already covered elsewhere in this and other books.[2]

---

1 See also Fine (2003c).

2 There were other difficulties, especially in tracking down extensive numbers of references and quotations from incomplete drafts of long ago. In addition, authorships ranged across those by one or other of us alone, and heavy and/or uncertain mixes of these with heavy use of copying and pasting, commentary and amendments by the other, of which this draft is probably one, not least as it lies on the boundaries of where the two of us tended to specialise – Dimitris more focused on the past (of economics and economic history) and myself more on the more recent. There are for example drafts that are unambiguously drafted by Dimitris, if also commented upon extensively by myself, on Methodological Foundations of Economic History; Early Precursors of Economic History (Scottish Historical School, Smith, Marx, German Historical School); The Emergence of Economic History Proper (English Historical School, Tawney, Hammonds); and Economics and History after Marshall (Clapham, Rostow, Kuznets). By the same token, this chapter does seem to have been primarily drafted by me, not least given the files from which it derives as well as my files of extensive notes on the literature from which these drafts derive.

Consequently, although this chapter covers the emergence of the cliometric revolution, it only does so in a selective fashion, focusing on two themes. The first is so blatant in practice that it beggars belief that it scarcely appears (terminologically) in the literature on the cliometric revolution – that it was an ideal illustration, albeit with its own features, of economics imperialism. That cliometrics as economics imperialism should have been so little observed is undoubtedly, to a greater or lesser extent, the result of the relatively low profile played by Chicago, the explicit promoter of economics imperialism par excellence, in its success, as is discussed in Chapter 1. The second theme, perverse to some extent given the first, is to record just how much, and how wide-ranging, was the dissent against cliometrics for reasons that conform with its being seen, implicitly, as economics imperialism but without designating it as such. The curious absence of criticism by explicit reference to economics imperialism is a theme taken up in the previous volume (Fine, 2024b, especially Chapters 1 and 2). If only dissenting economic (and social) historians had rallied around critique of the application of mainstream economics to economic history as an example of economics imperialism, who knows what would have been the impact upon all three of economics, economics imperialism and economic and social history more generally.

1 Introduction

This chapter is concerned with the rise of the new economic history or the cliometric revolution whose origins can be dated from the mid-1950s. To a large extent, it can be considered to offer a classic illustration of the application of the old-style economics imperialism as laid out in the first two volumes in this series (Fine, 2024a and b). For, on the face of it, it is simply the application of neoclassical economics to history, and was explicitly motivated as such. This is covered in Chapters 6 and 7 of this volume, where the intellectual trajectory of Douglass North is laid out in some detail. As a pioneer of the self-styled revolution in economic history, it was made apparent that the new economic history should sweep out the old, it should involve the application of (perfect market) neoclassical history to the subject matter, irrespective of the (historical) realism of corresponding models and, as a consequence, abstract economic theory (of a particular type) with the history taken out, should, then, provide the standard by which to judge (economic) history itself.

From the more rounded social scientist, let alone social historian, this manifesto and its corresponding reductionism of economic history to the numbers that feed into estimating models, might be thought to be bad enough. For the cliometric revolution arose out of three intellectual developments: the taking of history out of economics (attached to the marginalist revolution but fully establishing itself with the formalist revolution of the 1950s) the taking of political economy out of both history and economics (we do not only sacrifice history but the social also) and the reduction of each of history and economics predominantly to as if perfectly working markets.

Such was the nature of economics imperialism as it applied to economic history in its first phase. It was as if Gary Becker, the arch economics imperialist, haunted the proceedings although he does not appear to have been present other than in spirit. Unsurprisingly, such slash and burn across the academic landscape was subject to considerable disquiet, if not outright opposition, possibly stronger in combination of breadth, depth and duration than for any other application of economics imperialism. As with the subsequent trajectory of economics imperialism itself, this inevitably gave rise to processes of bringing back in, BBI, what had been taken out by the reductionisms around history, political economy and perfectly working markets. Indeed, not least with Douglass North himself, see Chapters 6 and 7, reaction against, even rejection of, the new economic history gave rise to continuing contributions precisely along the lines of BBI. In his own idiosyncratic way (and he is by no means alone in this respect especially in light of continuing contributions of Deidre McCloskey) North can be seen to have eased his historical and social conscience as he moved from new to newer economic history (market imperfections economics as characteristic of the second phase of new economics imperialism) before embracing the newest economics history (market imperfections economics plus whatever variables take your fancy).[3]

Having established something of the nature of the new economic history in these terms, the remainder of the chapter will examine how and why it should have emerged in the form that it did, rapidly dominating the subject matter of economic history in the United States prior to being exported elsewhere in truly academic imperialist fashion. First, then, an account is given of cliometrics as economics imperialism, leading to a discussion of dissent against it (rarely if ever explicitly acknowledging it as economics imperialism as such). This opens the way for concluding remarks suggesting, over the longer term, that the cliometric revolution did, indeed, bring three processes together – the taking of history out of economics, the taking of political economy out of both

---

3 Note the dissonance in terminology. The *new* economic history or cliometrics is exemplary of the *old*, or first phase of, economics imperialism, meaning that the newer and newest economic history correspond, respectively, to the new and newer phases of economics imperialism. The same applies to the new, newer and newest development economics.

history and economics, and the reduction of each predominantly to as if (im) perfectly working markets (and, subsequently, the throwing in of other factors to suit).

2   Cliometrics as Economics Imperialism

Whilst the thrust of economics imperialism always incorporates some general characteristics, it also inevitably reflects in outcomes the peculiarities of the discipline or subject matter being colonised as well as broader intellectual and material contexts. There are some strikingly unique features of this success story for economics imperialism when it comes to cliometrics. First is the astonishing speed with which it established itself. As observed by McCloskey (1978, p. 14) spectators of the sport:

> will be astonished by the range and quality of actual play: in the twenty years or so that cliometrics has had an organized league the number of articles and books has expanded to several hundreds, growing exponentially.

And North (1974, p. 1) was equally sanguine over the venture's achievements:

> The new economic history has been with us now for almost a score years. Its practitioners have advanced from young revolutionaries to become part of the middle-aged establishment; and by all the criteria of publication and training of graduate students, it has indeed transformed the discipline in the United States.

Second, even if remarkable in establishing a position for itself, in a process that was sharp, full and fast, the revolution did not conquer and destroy all opposition, far from it. For the vanquished were never assimilated nor destroyed, and even prospered. There is a contrast, for example with the pervasive use of human capital across the social sciences for which there has been limited dissent and no recognisable alternative of equal stature, not even within the discipline of education itself (Jabbar and Menashy, 2022). The relationship between economic history and history is much more like that between social capital and (dissenting) social theory with the two existing side-by-side in parallel, with little critical engagement between the two with any enduring effects or resolutions (Fine, 2010a). For, recognisably (new, newer and newest) economic history as a field has been complemented by social history. They cover much the same subject matter, subject to inevitable differences deriving from their methodologies, methods and framings and, what have become, different traditions and preoccupations.[4]

Third, cliometrics is astonishing in (the speed of) its breadth of application. In his survey of the "The Achievements of the Cliometric School", McCloskey (1978, p. 23) suggests a recent turn to other subject matter than nineteenth century US history, such "novelties" being "congealed into reinterpretations ... in the making. The most finished is the denial of entrepreneurial failure in Victorian Britain". Possibly modesty discourages the mentioning of the role McCloskey (1971) played in posing economic performance in terms of entrepreneurial failure and settling the issue favourably for British capitalists through studies of iron and steel and coal – they were ok but were short of the necessary factor endowments (see also McCloskey, 1970).[5]

McCloskey (1978, p. 23/4) also recognises that, for at least a decade, cliometrics was "characteristically American" in the origin of its practitioners, focusing initially on economic growth in nineteenth century America, see below seventh. This subject matter became extended back to the origins of slavery (Fogel and Engerman, 1974) and forward to the Great Depression of the 1930s through the monetary history of Friedman and Schwartz (1963). Yet, this is already indicative of breadth of topic, from ante bellum slavery to modern financial crisis and depression. Not surprisingly, with accompanying references, McCloskey points to, "Tales of the adventures of *homo economicus* in unlikely places are beginning to accumulate, in nineteenth century India, for example, or medieval Europe or declining Rome ... Cliometrics has at least begun in the histories of Canada, Mexico, Brazil, Australia, Japan, China, India, Russia, West Africa, Israel, Italy, France, Central Europe, the Low Countries, Scandinavia, Ireland, and England", p. 25.

Fourth, unsurprisingly, the scale and scope of an accelerating cliometrics was dependent upon attracting an equally growing cohort of adherents. In a survey of articles in the leading journal for economic history in the USA, Whaples (1991, p. 294) reports, apart from young males being disproportionately involved:

> The data validate the conventional wisdom showing that the cliometric revolution swept the profession, as indicated by this JOURNAL's articles,

---

4   To a limited degree, this is reflected in location of my own publications straddling the two
    fields of social and economic history, and corresponding journals, Fine and Leopold (1990)
    and Fine and Milonakis (2003) as opposed to Fine (1990b, 1993a and 1999a) respectively.
5   For a critique of McCloskey on the British coal industry, see Fine (1990a).

in the 1960s and 1970s. Annual data show that the period of most rapid growth was between 1965 and 1970, when the cliometric portion of the pages grew from one-eighth to one-half.

Fifth, such ambitions across historical subject matter and academic personnel extends in scope to the subject matter of the social sciences other than economics. More specifically, if in retrospect, North (1974, p. 4) implicitly ties the new economic history to other ventures that had been made in the old-style economics imperialism since, "an equally promising extension of neo-classical theory is occurring in a more sophisticated approach to the household economy, with important implications for a theory of fertility", and that for political decision-making, "significant progress" is being made through "the work of Baumol, Buchanan and Tullock, and Anthony Downs ... (which) provides us with a promising starting point", p. 5.

Sixth, with the new economic history emerging rapidly and across diverse subject matters, drawing upon and being applied beyond economics to the terrain of other social sciences and, yet, limiting its approach to the narrowest of economic theory and statistical methods, it is hardly surprising that it should have been surrounded by continual controversy. In this respect, it stands out as different from most other examples of economics imperialism in which previous traditions have been treated with scant regard and to be discarded as lacking the formal and statistically grounded qualities of the new approach.

I discuss the wide-ranging controversies involved in the following section but, before doing so, it is worthwhile highlighting, seventh, what is already apparent from the discussion, that the cliometric revolution was especially strongly and initially, if not uniquely, an instance of economics imperialism centred upon the USA. Examining the reasons for this proves rewarding, not least through the work of Coats (1980, 1990 and 1995), even though his conclusions can be considered to have been premature if not, as a result, with just a little longer passage of time, entirely incorrect.[6] His emphasis on, and search for, the peculiarities of the US scene lead him to deny Schabas' (1995) claim that cliometrics, other than in the United States, had overshadowed traditional economic history. As evidence, he appeals to his own experience as an economic historian in England and perusal of the content of its leading journal, *Economic History Review* (Coats, 1995, p. 203).[7] Indeed, he concludes

---

6 See Chapter 1.
7 By mid-1990s, cliometrics has majority ownership of the UK's leading journal, the *Economic History Review* (Lamoreaux, 1998, p. 71). Its attaining maturity in university teaching is marked by the appearance of Floud and McCloskey (eds) (1981 and 1983). Note, at an early

with remarkable lack of foresight that, "cliometrics was a unique and essentially transitory episode in the development of economic history as an academic discipline", p. 203.

Not surprisingly, in order to make his case for US uniqueness in the rise rather than the origins of what was to be the spread of cliometrics, Coats ranges over a wide range of factors. He complements this with what he himself describes as his own rare attempt to situate the issues in intellectual history as opposed to resting on one side or the other of the debate over the rights or wrongs of cliometrics itself. He primarily compares the US and the UK, charting differences from the turn of the century. Thus, he points to the presence of a strong institutionalist tradition in the United States compared to Britain. Alfred Marshall is seen as responsible for taking traditional history out of economic theory but Keynes for retaining economic history within economics (so that it could monopolise the latter discipline's subject matter). The more "genteel" debate over the methodenstreit[8] had the effect in the UK of allowing for the emergence of economic history outside departments of economics.[9] By contrast, the US is seen to have depended on German influence in establishing economic history as an essential part and parcel of economics within economics departments rather than as an independent discipline, as economic factors were considered crucial for history alongside political and other factors. Teaching of economics within history departments as such even declined in the early years of the century, as "emphasis shifted away from political and economic towards a broader kind of social history" (Coleman, 1987, p. 6). Crucially, the core place of economic history within US economics departments was to be

---

stage, Hartwell (1971, p. 415) opines, with appropriate evidence: "The new economic history in Britain does now constitute, if not a threat, certainly a challenge, to the existing economic history establishment; this is a consequence of *not* believing, as Hughes [1971] does, that there are no possibilities for the development of new economic history in Britain that could parallel its development in the U.S.A".

8   Concerned with the relative merits of induction and deduction. For a full account, see Milonakis and Fine (2009). The debate, within and around the marginalist revolution, is concerned with the relative merits of induction and deduction with the presumption that marginalism won, within economics, for deduction at the expense of induction. This is false as there were no winners in the debate (with most commentators accepting the need for both induction and deduction in an appropriate balance). Nonetheless, deductive marginalism triumphed in practice. In any case, methodology cannot be reduced to the relative merits of induction and deduction even if these are symbolic of much more wide-ranging differences over methodology, theory, methods, conceptualisations and subject matter.

9   Coats (1990, p. 9) cites Coleman (1987, p. 46) to the effect that, for British economic history, "although in its early years it was nurtured more by history faculties than by economics, it later tended to become a separated entity, neither quite economic fish nor historic fowl".

sustained until after the cliometric revolution, after which it has been reduced considerably overall and to the application of economics to economic history. Or it has been discarded altogether, if not without considerable resistance from the dwindling number of economic historians within economics wedded to broader approaches as well as from mainstream economists seeking both to build upon the formalist revolution and to retain elements of history, see below. Also older generations of mainstream economists, even those leading the field of orthodoxy, had been trained in economic history, proper as it were, and were more sensitive to both its value and to the limitations of the formal apparatus of economics that they were themselves developing and promoting.

Significantly, from my own memory, the function provided by economic history in the USA in grounding students in economics realities was served in the UK by compulsory courses in what was termed applied economics or the like. This included discussion of the construction of national statistics, the role of government in practice, overviews of economic developments, options in (the making of) policy, and, indeed, anything else that took an instructor's fancy (if rarely imperialism, racism, sexism, power and hierarchy, etc). It was only much later than the USA's discarding of economic history as a reality check that the UK's counterpart in applied economics came to be dropped as a compulsory course, coincidentally or otherwise, making way for a core compulsory course on econometrics which has now become standardised alongside the continuing core courses of macro and micro.

The movement into the period after the Second World War is, then, most marked in both countries by developments within economics itself, and the consolidation of mainstream, orthodox, neoclassical economics, organised around a theoretical core. Unsurprisingly, the USA was in the lead in mainstream economics and, with that lead, even further in the lead, irrespective of whether it had been neck and neck with Britain in formalising economics, of appropriating economic history. Whilst economic history could prosper independently of economics in Britain, Coats (1990, p. 11) cites Rostow (1957, p. 520) to the effect that it was a "shapeless affair" in the USA.[10] This could hardly eradicate the boundaries between economic history and history as separate disciplines.

But, especially where in the US, economic history institutionally resided within departments of economics, the situation was open to different

---

10   Although he warns against ex post dismissals, "told in excessively gloomy terms by 'new'
      economic historians eager to promote a technicolor version of the magnificent cliometric
      dawn", and even advises of rediscoveries in the 1980s "by a younger generation, and by
      some of the older and wiser cliometricians", p. 11.

developments and new rigidly defined shapes in relations between economics and economic history. Rapid expansion of higher education in the US opened opportunities and a competitive struggle for intellectual leadership and position over how, and then whether, economic history would be taught within economics departments. This helps to explain why, for example, there could be a "remarkable rise to prominence of Purdue University, an institution with no prior standing in economic history which quickly became a leading center of cliometric evangelism, [and] illustrates the possibilities of a 'rags to riches' academic story" (Coats, 1990, p. 10). As their colleagues within economics narrowed their intellectual horizons, the presence of history as part of economics came under question, with survival depending upon conforming to the dictates of their home discipline. As Coats (1995, p. 192) reports, citing Hughes (1971, pp. 403/4) "whereas the organizers of the inaugural gathering had had difficulty in assembling a dozen or so interested scholars, six years later they had to ration invitations 'among the tens and then the scores of young scholars who wanted to attend'".[11]

In short, conditions that had allowed economic history to be established within economics departments were neither sufficiently powerful nor long lasting to allow it to survive there in shapeless form. For it to embrace the terms and conditions of its intellectual home was to release a torrent of activity. But, it should be added, the paradigm shift, to use Kuhn's term for scientific revolution, in economic history did not depend exclusively upon a younger generation to wait upon an older, entrenched conventional wisdom or normal science, and its practitioners, to die off and be replaced. Leading, established scholars were present from the beginning reflecting their command of economic theory from their own backgrounds from within economics departments. Nor, to pursue the Kuhnian framework further, did the new emerge out of the "anomalies" or unexplained problems from within the old. To the contrary, the latter was condemned for failing to generate clear refutable hypotheses at all, and corresponding controversy over them, and to be unduly flexible in failing to conform consistently to economic theory and the facts, usually interpreted as data for which insufficient energy had been engaged in discovering them in light of lack of interest in statistical testing or the weight and breadth of the empirical more generally.

---

11   Hughes adds, "I would not go so far as to say that the effort 'saved' economic history from extinction in economics departments, although that contrafactual history is easily constructed".

Although, as argued elsewhere,[12] whilst the Kuhnian approach is not appropriate as a model for studying intellectual change, let alone revolution, in general, its application can shed considerable light on the mechanisms of change even if these do not always conform to its framing. Such is the case not least for the cliometric revolution, and its US origins and trajectory from there and beyond. Essentially, the notion of scientific revolution as paradigm shift draws on three different aspects. The first is of "exemplar" or specific case study or approach that sets a new analytical standard that can be emulated across a range of problems. The papers by Meyer and Conrad (1957) and Conrad and Meyer (1958) are generally deemed to have launched the new economic history. They do serve the role of exemplar in many respects. The first specifically places emphasis on economic theory and statistical inference as the basis for economic history, and the second focuses on slavery as the subject of its case study, as indeed does what is still by far the most prominent and controversial contribution of cliometrics, Fogel and Engerman (1974). If the exemplar can handle slavery, it can surely handle more freely functioning markets! What is most important is that economic history should be understood in terms of the pursuit of self-interest in general and of profit in particular.[13]

The second meaning of paradigm, preferred by Kuhn himself if confined to one meaning alone, is of a community of scholars. The earlier discussion suggests this did not change too much in terms of its being drawn from the United States, even if from a younger generation albeit with a considerable dash of the old. Thus, the extent of change in the community rests on its deeper and more exclusive roots within mainstream economics and its academic departments. As already observed, the result was to mark social off from economic history, with a corresponding division of scholarly communities, with economics remaining in command of the economics of economic history at the expense of social history.

The third use of paradigm is at the opposite extreme of exemplar, pointing to the world vision shared by a community of scholars. In this respect, Coats (1980, p. 193) is interesting for pointing to the more general political context in which the cliometric revolution occurred, questionably distinguishing such external factors from the "internalist explanations ... nowadays fashionable among such historians and philosophers of science as Karl R. Popper, Thomas S. Kuhn, and Imre Lakatos". He considers the impact of McCarthyism and of the

---

12   See Fine (2001a, 2002b and 2004b) for discussion of Kuhn in light of economics imperialism, and vice-versa.

13   In many respects, the work of Fogel and Engerman was far in advance of what was immediately to follow and for this, and other reasons, atypical despite its prominence.

Cold War, and their implications for the thrust towards conservative scholarship. Certainly, cliometrics conformed to the "American way", with its emphasis on the pursuit of self-interest. Yet, it displaced a scholarship and vision that was no less supportive, and arguably more rhetorically functional for such.

For there are two conservative/dualities involved – one for or against mainstream economics and all that this entails, and the other being for or against old style economic history. Even these are very broad and rough and ready categories. Even so, there can be no presumption that being on the same side of the two sets of dualities is more or less automatic, certainly as far as influences from, and conformity with, political ideology is concerned. For example, as Coats recognises, such was overtly symbolised by Rostow's *Stages of Economic Growth: A Non-Communist Manifesto*, whose message to the world could not be clearer in the wake of the launch of the Sputnik in 1957 and the perceived threat of Soviet economic and technological catch-up. Whilst Rostow's ideological credentials could not have been stronger in support of US hegemony, and his volume was to go through numbers of editions and sell three hundred thousand copies, his own stance on economic history was not supportive of the single-minded theory and numbers characteristic of the emerging cliometric school. Indeed, at its birth, he had this to say (for example, Rostow, 1957, p. 518):

> Although economists may have done little in modern times to analyze long-period factors, they are well trained in listing exhaustively the factors they are assuming fixed; and this is most helpful.

In other words, economists have nothing to say on the major factors that need to change in order to serve as the engines of history. They simply take them as exogenous and, by implication, leave it to proper historians to address.

3   Discarding Dissent

The unsatisfactory division of variables between the exogenous and endogenous, with all the action in the first group, unexamined by the new economic history, as far as traditional historians are concerned, is just one of the sources of discontent with the cliometric revolution. This offers the opportunity to consider in greater depth and breadth, even than in Coats' wide-ranging accounts, the nature of the changes in method in moving through the cliometric revolution, the considerable dissent that they engendered, and how cliometrics' differences with past scholarship were overcome or, more exactly, set aside in both scholarship and, as has been suggested, by the institutionalised divisions between economic and social history.

The processes involved moved through three, closely related stages. First is the appeal to generally acceptable propositions but imparting them, wittingly or otherwise but surreptitiously, with a more controversial and specific content. Second is the narrowing down of the meaning and content of those general propositions. And, last is to proceed as if neither of the earlier stages had ever occurred. In detailing these stages, in part through Coats' contributions if not through his eyes, it is important to bear in mind that he sees the resistance to the revolution, wrongly, as having been successful in light of the scale and scope of the objections to which it could and did appeal. So his account of the temporary and confined rise of US cliometrics is diligent to some extent in discovering and bending dissent to his purpose of pigeonholing cliometrics as an idiosyncratic moment, not triumphant movement, in the evolution of economic history.

Thus, in the last of his three contributions, Coats (1995, p. 207) suggests that, "Most, but not all, of the cliometricians seem to have been epistemologically innocent", implying that worldly wisdom would soon prevail. Whilst guilty might be considered a more appropriate descriptor than innocence in view of what has often been the, admittedly naïve, positivism, of the cliometrician as economist, there is a sharp contrast with his earlier contribution in which Coats (1990, p. 16) argues, "In economics, positivism has been discredited these many years; Popperian falsificationism has been steadily losing adherents, given the mounting scepticism about the possibility of conclusive empirical testing; and there has been growing support for pragmatism and hermeneutics". Interestingly, though, Coats (1980, p. 203) initially assesses the cliometricians as having been methodologically reticent:[14]

---

14   Adding, that, "in this respect, as in others, their approach directly reflected the contemporary climate of academic opinion", something that might be doubted despite reference to the ascendancy of functionalist sociology and McCarthyism. For a useful overview of the emergence of cliometrics, see Freeman and Louçã (2001). Their view is that one of the two reasons for the triumph of cliometrics was "the emergence of positivism in economic history ... the hallmark of the scientific character of any discipline since the end of the nineteenth century", p. 16. This allowed a commitment of the discipline to some form of realism to be overturned. Otherwise, they suggest that cliometrics "challenged young researchers to use new and fancy techniques". See also Parker (1989, p. 540) in review of McCloskey's (1987) textbook which, "fails to emphasize how unreal most of the assumptions that lie behind the use of neoclassical economics really are. To disguise assumptions as logic is a familiar device of economists, and can lend to even absurd statements the air of unerring deduction".

Yet despite their insistence on the need to use explicit economic assumptions and formal models, the cliometricians were remarkably reticent about their own philosophical, political, and sociological preconceptions.

Indeed, as will be seen they had much over which to be reticent, not least in the immediate post-revolutionary years, when, alongside economics itself, it was as if postmodernism simply did not exist in other worlds, let alone their own.

Insofar as Coats charts a methodological course from rejection of falsification to innocence, with reticence as an intermediate stage, he would appear to be wrong.[15] Or, at most, momentarily true as mainstream economics, and cliometrics as its progeny, briefly flirted with Kuhnian notions and debate in order to claim a predominant and unchallenged position as normal science or whatever. Thus, for Gordon (1965, p. 123/6) in a piece that Coats (1969) himself reckons is the first to apply Kuhn to economics, such profound complacency is readily found:[16]

> [Adam] Smith's postulate of the maximizing individual in a relatively free market and the successful application of this postulate to a wide variety of specific questions is our basic paradigm. It created a "coherent scientific tradition" (most notably including Marx) and its persistence can be seen by skimming the most current periodicals ... I conclude that economic theory is much like a normal science and that, like a normal science, it finds no necessity for including its history as a part of professional training.

Indeed, Boylan and O'Gorman (1995, pp. 27 fwd) refer to a post-positivism phase as prevailing in economic methodology over the last quarter of a century, characterised by a desperate but unsuccessful attempt to rescue naïve falsifiability from its inescapable fallacies. Even this is too generous to the epistemologically naïve who have been more notable for their absence than their struggle for justifiable survival, as economic methodology has been confined

---

15   Note that Murphy (1965, p. 132) reckons that the new economic history is novel in converging on "what a modern empiricist might demand of it" together with "a really defensible set of techniques".

16   No doubt evidence for the last sentence is provided by those that come before it, and their extraordinary misrepresentation of the classics. See also Davis (1997, p. 289): "Since the *History of Political Economy* appeared nearly three decades ago, it seems as if most historians of economic thought have concluded that they no longer speak to other economists, and might accordingly focus entirely on thought that is no longer actively pursued by contemporary economists and on which history has closed the door".

primarily to a satellite status outside of the discipline itself (Lawson, 1997, for example). The major exception, that definitively proves the rule, is provided by a leading cliometrician (McCloskey, 1986a) whose highly popular appeal to "rhetoric" as what economists do, as opposed to science, significantly remains consistent with, and supportive of, the mainstream.

Coats does, however, highlight the two apparently reasonable axes upon which cliometrics thrust itself forward onto what is best described as a suspecting, if not suspicious, profession. This is why the application of the qualification "apparently" to "reasonable" is appropriate. For, the two arguments, for (more or better) theory and for (more or better) evidence also necessarily carried symbolic significance, at times but not always made explicit. And the nature and content of that significance has shifted over time. Today, when economists talk about testing theory against the evidence, they mean neoclassical theory and econometrics (and hence quantitative evidence and statistical methods). By contrast, there is no reason to doubt that Meyer, blaming lack of historical perspective, and cited in a personal communication to Coats (1980, p. 187) is being disingenuous in commenting on the response to their initial papers:[17]

> The two most shocked people ... were Conrad and myself as we behold the storm or "reaction" that we generated ... we really did not consider our papers to be particularly revolutionary or unconventional. Rather, we looked upon them as simple extensions of the teachings to which we had been exposed in our graduate student years, particularly of Schumpeter, Gerschenkron and Kuznets. We saw our papers as essentially an affirmation of their basic views on how historical quantification should be done in economics. In short, we hardly looked upon our presentation as

---

17 See also Meyer's (1997, p. 410) confession forty years later that is also highly revealing about pre-occupation with humanising rather than material social relations: "Many of the critiques of cliometrics over the years really trace back to one fundamental concern: that bringing numbers and economic theory into history somehow dehumanizes the activity. Admittedly, Conrad and I were spare in our treatment of these human aspects, but that probably mainly reflected our own deficiencies: we were economists and not historians, so we naturally emphasized what we knew best. Subsequent treatment of the slave question by 'real' economic historians, Robert Fogel and Stanley Engerman particularly coming to mind, has shown that cliometricians are quite capable of pursuing the qualitative as well as the quantitative. Certainly there is no inherent reason why they cannot do so". Note, this sort of commentary reflects a reduction of criticism to terms that are both compatible with, and answerable within, a cliometric framework.

revolutionary, but rather as an attempt to reassert much of what was best in the empirical traditions of American quantitative economics.

Here, the sting is in the tail of the last sentence, with those on the other side of the controversy no doubt more attuned to, and critical of, the potential reduction of economic history to the best traditions of what American quantitative economics was becoming or had already become.

Much more is involved here than the cutting down of other forms of evidence than the quantitative, such as literary, anecdotal or whatever. For the quantification was to be tied to a reduction in the variables considered, to those that could be accommodated within a calculus of self-interest, usually confined to the economic as supply and demand. Parker (1971, pp. 6/7) in retrospect, puts this in neat if conciliatory terms:[18]

> So modern economic history should teach us something. But what, pray, is it to teach? ... We believe, I venture to say, that these [Western] economies have grown rich and large and productive because people have followed their enlightened self-interest by and large and because the processes of competition within a price system translated those strivings into a growth of output and investment and productivity-raising improvement. This is in good part what the new economic history is about: it is a gigantic test of the hypothesis of economic rationality of a system and of the behavior of individuals within it. ... Using a favorite device of economics we have tried to consider the economy as a separately developing system within the context of the opportunities for growth offered to it by the social processes in the surrounding social space.

North (1990, p. 32) was to develop a more sophisticated but no less mainstream example:

> One issue is that of policing agents. The most extreme example concerns the relationship between a master and slave. There is, in fact, an implicit contract between the two; to get maximum effort from the slave,

18   He is more scathing later (Parker, 1989, p. 540): "The job of economic history in the world is not to apply a specific theory, but to discover, by applying it, where it falls short. Its discourse must not be limited to rational actors, perfect markets, smooth functions; it sweeps up irrationalities, obstructions, lumpiness, partial ignorance, social misery – the piles of brush of the 'real world' and throws them in the path of the social theorists of all sorts, with the challenge to tidy them up".

the owner must devote resources to monitoring and metering a slave's output and critically applying rewards and punishments based on performance. Because there are increasing marginal costs to measuring and policing performance, the master will stop short of perfect policing and will engage instead in policing until the marginal costs equal the additional marginal benefits from such activity. The result is that slaves acquire certain property rights in their own labor. That is, owners are able to enhance the value of their property by granting slaves some rights in exchange for services the owners value more. Hence slaves became owners too. Indeed it is only this ownership that made it possible for slaves to purchase their own freedom, as was frequently done in classical times and even occasionally in the antebellum South.

Stampp (1976, p. 2/3) however, borders on the sarcastic in observing that, "history is not an exact science – not even the 'New Economic History'", and specifically cites the ambition of the early North:

> However, a few historians dream of immortality [for their history] ... Douglass C. North, for another, believes that history can be "something more than a subjective reordering of the facts of the past as man's perspectives change with each generation". He, too, finds in the social sciences and in the methods of scientific research the tools for a "basic restructuring of historical inquiry". North suggests that the New Economic History, with its "well articulated body of theory and ... abundance of relevant quantitative data", is the discipline best equipped to accomplish the restructuring he thinks is needed.

As will be seen, the contrast with other strands of economic history that immediately preceded the cliometric revolution could not be stronger even though they drew upon both economic theory and quantitative evidence.

Here it is apposite to return to Rostow, and his stages of economic growth, a contribution both steeped in data and highly consistent in many respects with what had already become the classic growth theory of neoclassical economics contributed by Solow (1956 and 1957).[19] But, crucially, the ultimate causes of such growth are situated in a framework of modernisation, of breaking up of traditional societies and, correspondingly, of major shifts in political, cultural

---

19   See also Rostow (1957) where, to the consternation of commentators, economic historians are encouraged to focus on growth.

and social variables that are not reducible to the economic. This, no doubt, is a consequence of the older style economic history to which Rostow adhered, but it also reflects a keen commitment to distance his approach from the economic reductionism that he attaches to Marxism. Indeed, his book's last chapter is devoted to a critique of Marxism for its economic reductionism (making up 15% or so of the main body of the text).[20] The (mis)representation of Marx should not be taken too seriously except as a fascinating ideological text, reflecting (lack of) scholarly values of the time, but the contrast taken with this construct is instructive (Rostow, 1990, p. 149):[21]

> The first and most fundamental difference between the two analyses lies in the view taken of human motivation. Marx's system is, like classical economics, a set of more or less sophisticated logical deductions from the notion of profit maximization.

Of course, this is a better description of the neoclassical economics informing cliometrics. For Rostow, by contrast:[22]

> In the stages-of-growth sequence man is viewed as a more complex unit. He seeks, not merely economic advantage, but also power, leisure, adventure, continuity of experience and security; he is concerned with his family, the familiar values of his regional and national culture, and a bit of fun down at the local ... In short, net human behaviour is seen not as an act of maximization, but as an act of balancing alternative and often conflicting human objectives in the face of the range of choices men perceive to be open to them.

Thus, from his own perspective, Rostow more or less wittingly provides a manifesto of sorts more against the cliometrics of his time than Marxism by seeking to retain the notion of a more rounded individual than the former allows.

---

20   See also Rostow's (1957, p. 510) stated preference for interdisciplinarity "because I was repelled by Marx's economic determinism".

21   Compare with North (1978, p. 79) for whom the problem with Marxism is its lack of interest in testing hypotheses (and the same for the Annales school, p. 80).

22   In slightly different vein, see also Rostow (1957, p. 514): "The theorist has generally been uneasy if not awkward if forced to work outside Marshallian short-period assumptions; the historian – like the human beings he writes about – cannot avoid working in a world of changing tastes and institutions, changing population, technology, and capacity".

This, of course, reflects much broader divisions across the social sciences over the scope of the rationality/irrationality duality. To a large extent, in this light, antipathy to cliometrics is concerned with a different sort of individualism.[23] Thus, Elton (1983, p. 78) denies the role of "the past as a pattern of forces [except] to clarify one's understanding of circumstances and influences". In particular, "'Feudalism' is a categorizing concept invented to make discourse easier; it never existed in reality and cannot therefore have risen or declined", p. 79. This would be an example, Marxist in particular, of "historians who have fallen victim to the tendency to submerge the individual in the collectivity, or to clothe the abstract in a semblance of concreteness". Similarly, in more conciliatory fashion, for Fogel (1983, p. 24) "cliometricians ... apply the quantitative methods of behavioral models of the social sciences to the study of history" – but he does not confine such behaviour to that modelled by neoclassical economics. Instead, he points to six differences between the old and the new economic history. The first is subject matter, "'scientific' historians tend to focus on collectivities of people and recurring events, while traditional historians tend to focus on particular individuals and particular events", p. 42. Second is preferred types of evidence – quantitative versus literary, for example. Third are standards of proof and verification – the empirical-scientific as opposed to the legal model of calling witnesses to account. Fourth is the nature and role of controversy – estimating procedures versus quality of interpretation. Fifth is style of work with the traditional more loners and less collaborative. And sixth is that the traditional is more communicable to the general public. But he concludes that, p. 69/70:

> The genuine differences between "scientific" and traditional historians over subject matter, methods, and style should not obscure their more numerous and more fundamental affinities and complementarities ... each mode has a comparative advantage in certain domains of research, they supplement and enrich each other.

But Fogel's balanced view is one that heavily leans towards uncritical acceptance of the methods of neoclassical economics in principle, if only supplemented by the traditional that is, however, set aside in collective practice, often contemptuously.

---

23   Interestingly both Fishlow and Fogel (1971, p. 41) and North (1981, p. 21) look to the new economic history to provide an account of entrepreneurship. North even suggests that, "a satisfactory theory of the firm would contribute immensely to the development of a theory of the state".

This commentary conforms to the interpretation of gradual erosion of consciousness of the history of the past. Prior to and during the early phases of the cliometric revolution, this remains apparent from the two most significant symbols of past debates. One is reference to the Methodenstreit, and the necessity or not of some element of induction in theory, and the other is to Clapham's notion of economic theory as an empty box in the absence of historical content. Initially, these could both be referred to in shorthand. Soon they were to disappear almost entirely. Significantly, for example, Meyer and Conrad (1957, p. 524) open their account with the confession that:

> We wish to avoid *methodenstreit* and will therefore avoid arguments about precedence or relative importance. The literature is already over-burdened with the logbooks of intellectual voyages inspired by false charts of the history-theory dichotomy. We reject the possibility of such a dichotomy from the outset. Instead, we shall assert simply that economics as a science deals with historical processes and is dependent upon historical research.

This leads to an orthodox combination of economic theory and statistical inference to provide for economic history and, to a large extent, signals a path for the future that does not recognise its departure from earlier debates.

This, in retrospect, is also the rough justice delivered to those, such as Supple (1960, p. 549) seeking to open the empty box. He suggests:[24]

> It is not that the economist's conceptual tools are empty and useless boxes for purposes of economic analysis; rather it is that whatever limitations they have as tools of current analysis are doubly compounded when they are used as avenues of historical understanding.

But conciliation towards theory from a historical perspective was, if acknowledged, primarily appropriated to support neoclassical theory. Appeal for balance in light of limitations of the new economic history has fallen on deaf ears in practice if not in principle.[25]

Not surprisingly, then, discussion over the relationship between economic theory and historical specificity continued into the post-war period, prior to, during and after the rise of cliometrics. Search for balance between the two

---

24   See also Heaton (1957, p. 599).

25   See Goodrich (1960, 537/8) for the need to complement the quantitative with the qualitative.

was matched by considerable disquiet at the trend towards pure theory as the basis on which to incorporate historical evidence. For Hancock (1946, p. 149/50) for example, the idea that economic history could be reduced to economic theory applied to the facts begs the question of what theory and the dangers of the command of the contemporary. Similarly, Ashton (1946, p. 163) wishes "the young theorists ceased to twitter in their nests of indifference curves and fluttered down to earth". He is heavily critical of the interwar influence of economists for being out of touch with reality. He sees the need to chart a course between the economist's theory and the historian's facts, p. 177:[26]

> To sum up: the historian is increasingly feeling for the structure that underlies the surface of events, for explanation and interpretation. The economist is increasingly concerned not with static equilibrium, but with the transition from one equilibrium to another ... If they will take counsel together they may move towards that ideal in which no longer will one look at his facts in the hope of inducing from them a theory, and the other deduce from first principles a theory in the hope that it may be found to fit the facts, but in which the two cooperate so that ... the facts and the theory demonstrate each other.

Kuznets (1957, p. 546//7) reports of a debate over economics and history as the new economic history was emerging that, "On economic theory as a tool in the work of economic historians ... the discussants were concerned chiefly with the specific theory to be used, the implication being that there is no single accepted body of economic theory".

Subsequently, Pollard (1964, p. 294) is even more contemptuous of economic reductionism, following Robbins' interwar definition of economics as study of the allocation of scarce resources between competing ends in the middle of the deepest of recessions. For him, "economics was to be taken out of the muddy waters of political overtones, personal value judgements, social pressure and class interests in which real economic life takes place, to be studied in the serene clear waters of universally valid mathematical relationships, like the natural and neutral sciences". Cole (1967) suggests the economic historian should not be concerned with general or universal laws but with the particular. And Mathias (1970, pp. 381/2) also emphasises the need to take account of context at the expense of universality.[27] Chandler (in Fogel et al. 1970) does

---

26   See also Redlich (1968).

27   These all from inaugural lectures upon appointment to professorships in economic history in British universities.

not find the available economic theory to be much to his liking, being too much out of touch with reality. He prefers to draw upon other social sciences (Weber on bureaucracy, and Parsons for social action) suggesting the need for a grander vision, yet to be found in history (let alone, presumably, economics).

The result is transparent in the encroaching predominance of the deductive method. On the one hand, this involved a division of variables between endogenous and exogenous, (Freeman and Louçã, 2001, p. 15) a proxy for the rational and irrational. The historiographical framework is put particularly clearly by Davis (1970, p. 68) who divides history into four categories of susceptibility: to existing economic theory; to analysis other than economic theory; prospectively to one or other of the social sciences; to interdisciplinarity. Whilst potentially perceived as a neutral descriptive scheme for organising the literature, it is taken for granted that none of these categories, especially the first, is empty. On the other hand, a debate raged over the role of counterfactuals in economic history, so much so that, in a footnote, McCloskey (1978, p. 13) promises:

> This, by the way, will be the first essay on cliometric method not to discuss counterfactuals. The possible discussions lack point.

But there is a point, not least because of Fogel's (1967) view that all historians engage in counterfactuals and model-building whether they like, or are aware of, it or not.[28]

Such a stance follows from the presumption that it is reasonable to speculate about how the world would have been in the absence of some factor or other, something in which we all engage from time to time in order to assess the factor's importance. But there are huge differences in how such counterfactuals are interpreted causally. At one extreme, counterfactuals at most help us to organise a partial, possibly misleading explanation, of how various factors interact with one another. This is because of awareness of the interdependence of the excluded variable, for the counterfactual purpose, with those that remain. The excluded variable has both consequences and causes, and the latter cannot remain the same with the exclusion. At the other extreme, though, the counterfactual is simply an independent variable that can be included or excluded at will.

Leaving aside the shifting meaning of variables as they are included or excluded (what would have been the marginal product of a slave if in fact a

---

28   See also Fogel (1970, p. 129) where he insists "that counterfactual conditional statements cannot be banished from history ... we do not really have the freedom to avoid counterfactual conditional statements".

wageworker for example) the latter extreme immediately allows for econometric testing, and causation becomes synonymous with statistical significance. Thus, Meyer and Conrad (1957) spend much space providing a lesson in simple regression. Almost twenty years later, McLelland (1975) basically begins his understanding of causation by worrying around the meaning and significance of statements of the sort "if A then B". On this basis, he is inevitably drawn to the conclusion that, "The relationship between antecedent conditions and observed action in all causal explanations of history is probabilistic. The causes must be viewed not as leading inexorably to the effect, but rather as making the effect in question more probable, or at best, highly probable", p. 87/8.[29] This informs his discussion of counterfactuals, leading him to cite Schlesinger (1962, p. 768) to the effect that:

> Insofar as empirical social research can drive historians to criticize their assumptions, to expose their premises, to tighten their logic, to pursue and respect their facts, to restrain their rhetoric ... it administers a wholly salutary shock to a somewhat uncritical and even complacent discipline.

McClelland concludes, "Economics, as the most rigorous of the social sciences, might be expected to administer the most authoritative, shock", p. 104. Ultimately, a process of methodological slippage results in North's (1978, p. 77) dictum, "explanation means explicit theorizing and the potential of refutability".

4   Concluding Remarks

Remarkably, as will be seen in Chapters 6 and 7, North was unable to live by his own dictum, not only rejecting the cliometrics that he had played such a major role in inspiring, but also qualifying rather than rejecting his own theory, as it was demonstrably refuted by the simplest evidence of comparative economic

---

29   Fogel's discussion (Fogel et al. 1967), is considerably more sophisticated. But anticipating, or reproducing, problems within statistical inference, such as model mis-specification, merely pushes out the problem of the relationship between theory and history without addressing it. See Kuznets (1957, p. 549). For a rewarding discussion of the problems with such formalism, see Patinkin's (1976) account of Keynes' antipathy to, and reservations over, econometrics.

performance.[30] For, to reiterate, the cliometric revolution arose out of three intellectual developments – the taking of history out of economics, the taking of political economy out of both history and economics, and the reduction of each predominantly to as if perfectly working markets. The corresponding absence of market imperfections, institutions and other socio-economic and cultural variables entailed a violent rupture with the realism of older and, to some extent, continuing traditions in economic and social history. As an extreme resolution of the conflict between the rational and the irrational, and the economic and the non-economic, the initial phase of cliometrics had a limited life in time and content, not least as it tailed upon developments within mainstream economics. The result was to give rise in particular to the "newer" economic history, discussed in Chapters 8 and 9, as economics imperialism in general moved to an as if imperfectly working marker perspective, and to the "newest" economic history of North, each of which sought in its own way to renegotiate the absence of history from the economics that was to inform economic history.

---

30   Note how Thrupp (1957) and Easterbrook (1957), on comparative historical development, might just as well not have existed as far as the contemporaneous rise of cliometrics was concerned.

CHAPTER 6

From Principle of Pricing to Pricing of Principle: Rationality and Irrationality in the Economic History of Douglass North

Postscript as Personal Preamble

Douglass North no longer has the prominence he once held in both economics and economic history. There are the usual reasons for this associated with the passage of time, as new generations stand on the shoulders of the pioneers that have preceded them. Revolutionary new ideas become conventional wisdoms. There are, though, two remarkable aspects of North's contributions. The first is just how many he made of continuing significance. It began with the application of the standard mainstream economics of his time to economic history to play a major role in launching cliometrics and informing its initial trajectory. It continued with emphasis upon ideology, that institutions and history matter and ended with an odd foray into what is now known as neuroeconomics.

Second, then, whilst North was at the forefront of intellectual developments, pushing out the boat further and more explicitly than others, he did so with and with some degree of intellectual integrity irrespective of substantive content. He continually acknowledged that what he had done was inadequate, compelling him to move to another stage in the attempt to fix analytical lacunae. On a personal level, it is notable that he took the trouble to respond in correspondence to the criticisms that appear in this chapter, and his responses are reported below to some degree. In other words, he was acutely aware of the difficulties of staying afloat in the stormy seas of the relationship between the economic and the historical. In doing so, each of his fixes have sequentially become both commonplace and augmented by sundry others, as is characteristic of the third phase of economics imperialism, in which anything goes alongside a greater or lesser attachment to imperfect market economics.

In other words, North has been both eclipsed and swamped – as is covered in more detail below and in its broader context in Chapter 1, and so is not repeated here. His cause has not been helped by his ultimate resting point, as observed, in an idiosyncratic anticipation of what has become the, equally idiosyncratic, field of neuroeconomics. Nonetheless, whatever the degree of his fading star, the review of the trajectory of his work that follows sheds considerable light on the evolving relations between economics and economic history, serves as a case study of economics imperialism, and has continuing relevance for understanding the corresponding issues of today. Significantly, the piece reproduced here begins by locating developments in these respects at the time in terms of what I have dubbed the dual retreat from the excess of postmodernism and neoliberalism (and considers how these allowed both rational choice and its antitheses to prosper across the social sciences).

In addition, we were fortunate in being accepted for publication in *Comparative Studies in Society and History*, because of its willingness to allow for relatively long contributions. Even so, our initially drafted piece on North was at least twice as long as what appeared, leading us to detach the application of his principles to history from our original draft, and this was published separately elsewhere (Milonakis and Fine, 2007).

1   Introduction[1]

The current intellectual climate is marked by a dual retreat, faltering and uneven, from the excesses of neo-liberalism and postmodernism. First, the idea that the world is, and should be made as far as possible, like a perfect market, virtualism for Carrier and Miller (eds) (1998), is losing ground, giving way to an understanding organised around the more or less pervasive presence and influence of market imperfections and the need for the non-market to correct them. Second, obsessive interpretative and relativist deconstruction of the world associated with the cultural turn across the social sciences is increasingly conceding to a renewal of interest in material culture – how reality is both construed *and* created. Over the past decade, the extraordinary rise to prominence of two concepts in particular has symbolised these developments. In the lead, serving as a filter for a highly diverse range of approaches and topics, is globalisation.[2] Close behind in timing, weight and scope is social capital,

---

1   Originally published as Fine and Milonakis (2003). The title was neat, and funny, capturing the essence of the first and then the second steps in North's trajectory. This article was first drafted whilst I was in receipt of a Research Fellowship from the UK Economic and Social Research Council (ESRC) under award number R000271046 to study The New Revolution in Economics and Its Impact upon Social Sciences. Thanks to Douglass North, an anonymous referee and others for comments on earlier drafts. Note, in order to reduce numbers of citations and length, fuller reference to North's voluminous work has been deliberately limited.

2   For brief overview, see Fine (2002a, Chapter 2 and 2002d).

the counterpart in most respects to globalisation at the national or lower levels of community.[3]

For ideological and intellectual reasons, rational choice has prospered during the period governed by the strange co-existence of neo-liberalism and postmodernism. It has been complicit with neo-liberalism, both feeding and feeding upon it. Yet, because of its general lack of interest in, and capacity for, deconstruction, rational choice is essentially incompatible with postmodernism. But the latter has at least tolerated rational choice, not least in view of its own pre-occupation with subjectivity (of a different type, admittedly, as identity comes to the fore) and its abandonment of the economic field for those who have cared to claim it. Rational choice, neo-liberalism and postmodernism have thrived together.

These generalities aside, what are the prospects for rational choice as it loses its erstwhile bedfellows? An answer depends upon another major development across the social sciences, the growing success of economics imperialism. As argued elsewhere, economics is currently colonising the other social sciences as never before.[4] There has been a proliferation of new fields in and around economics, potentially appropriating the subject matter of other disciplines – the new institutional economics, the new household economics, the new economic sociology, the new welfare economics, the new political economy, the new growth theory, the new labour economics, the new economic geography, the new financial economics, the new development economics, the new economic history, and so on. Such economics imperialism is far from new. But previously it was based upon reducing the non-economic to the economic, treating the former as if it were equivalent to a perfect market even in its absence. It had significant but limited appeal and scope, most notably through the work of Gary Becker's "economic approach". For him, everything is reduced to the rational choices of individuals endowed with biologically determined preferences.

Just a decade ago, this was considered outrageous even by Becker's fellow mainstream economists (Swedberg, ed., 1990). In the interim, a new form of economics imperialism has come to the fore, emphasising the crucial impact of market (especially informational) imperfections. These are claimed in typical reductionist fashion, to explain economic *and* social outcomes, the latter as

---

3   See Fine (2001b) for a comprehensive and critical account, Fine (2010a) for a revisit and Fine (2023a) for most recent contribution.

4   Fine (2001b and 2002a) for detailed discussion and, for further accounts and references, website http://www2.soas.ac.uk/Economics/econimp/econimp1.html [this is no longer functional, but see Fine (2024a, Appendix)].

the potentially collective but individually rational response to market imperfections. Conformity to institutions, customs and culture become construed as rationality in light of feedback from historically evolving conditions.

In short, the new version of economics imperialism extends its explanatory power by inserting the rational individual into a world of statistical uncertainty and, equally, extends its appeal by adopting and adapting the language and concepts of colonised subject matter. Yet, as Zafirovski (2000) has perceptively documented in detail, all purveyors of rational choice rely upon a division between the rational and the irrational, between what they explain and what they find inexplicable (and generally to be dismissed or explained as irrational). Becker is an extreme example since he claims all behaviour is accommodated within his economic approach. More generally, others suggest rational choice resides somewhere between this extreme and limits set by pursuit of self-interest through the market. In the past, as recognised even by its most ardent practitioners, rational choice has its limits and limitations, where the irrational and the social take over and complement it. The position could not be more clearly stated than by Thaler (1987, p. 99):[5]

> I will end my remarks with the following two false statements.
> 1.   Rational models are useless.
> 2.   All behavior is rational.

Further, as Velthuis (1999) demonstrates for Talcott Parsons, it is not so much a matter of the subject of enquiry as the method of analysis in which the economic approach is concerned with the individual, and sociology with the social as a separate and legitimate approach (denied by the purist committed to rational choice).

Throwing these evolving elements together does not lead to identical outcomes in developments across the social sciences. How disciplines and topics respond to more general intellectual, and external, factors depends upon their own continuing traditions and debates. This chapter is critically concerned with recent developments in economic history and the way in which Douglass North, in particular, has dealt with the relationship between the rational and the irrational, and the accompanying baggage that goes with it.

North is an apt choice. He has had a major influence on economic history in a number of ways. As founding contributor to the new economics history,

---

5   See also Fine (2024b, especially Chapter 2).

or cliometrics, for which he was awarded a Nobel Prize in economics in 1993, he pioneered the application of mainstream neoclassical economics to history. Yet, he also rejected that earlier work, or its approach, for its inability to address the role of property rights and their foundation in institutions. These factors have themselves now fallen under the compass of "the newer economic history", one that draws upon the new micro-foundations or information-theoretic approach to economics. The rational, optimising individuals of mainstream economics still prevail but they inhabit an informationally imperfect world that leads them to form and conform with institutions and customs. North has remained dissatisfied with such reductionism, worrying over how the ideas for new institutions arise and stick. Ultimately, he rests his explanation on ideology or beliefs.

Thus, despite or even because of his intellectual foundations within neoclassical economics, North has recognised and emphasised its limitations. As the irrational has become rational, the exogenous rendered endogenous, so he has embraced, retained and strengthened his commitment to such dualities. This has had two important effects. First, it has led some to be confused about whether North's institutionalism is neoclassical or not, and whether it can or cannot be wedded to older institutional traditions.

Second, and more important, North's economics and economic history clearly both predate and cohabit with their current evolution and mutual interaction. For he is widely cited across these fields and the social sciences more generally for his role in what might be termed "bringing institutions and history back in" – from an economics and a (new) economic history that had been widely perceived to have omitted them, alongside power, conflict and the like. But, in restoring institutions and history, the questions of what (is) history and what (are) institutions remain vital.

In this light, this chapter shows that North's economics and economic history have, in some respects, remained fundamentally consistent with one another. That he should at times be perceived to be otherwise is a result of the failure to recognise that his undoubted methodological individualism persistently refuses to allow itself to be reduced to rational choice alone. In this respect, North remains faithful to the divisions between the social sciences, and the rationale for them, that were characteristic of the intellectual environment of his earliest work. In contrast, currently, there are those who seek to restore institutions and history without recognising the limitations of, and the limits to, explanations based upon rational choice. They can only draw approvingly upon North and his authority by ignoring the conundrums around ideology and beliefs with which North has puzzled over the last decades.

Such, in light sketch, are the analytical elements that form North's theory of history and its continuing significance. In section 2, we briefly outline the new and newer economic history so that the evolution of North's own stance can be brought into relief by way of departure as elaborated in sections 3 and 4, one covering his account of the economic, the other ideology. North's theoretical vision of history is shown to have traversed a path from the principle of pricing (resources and their allocation are everything) to the pricing of principle (ideology is decisive and open to implicit purchase) combining the rational with the irrational and mainstream economics with ideology, and with transaction costs, property rights and institutions bridging the divide between the two.

2   From New to Newer Economic History

Cliometrics is in its fifth decade. Its most enduring, and endearing, quality is navel-gazing. As one of its leading practitioners McCloskey (1978, p. 13) puts it:

> The members of the [Economic History] Association must be sick to death of "The Achievements of the Cliometric School". The health of a field, it is said, is inversely proportional to the percentage of essays on method, by which standard cliometrics itself was sick to death in childhood and is only just now recovering. The few essays on method appearing nowadays are usually commissioned, lack revolutionary fervor, and have become as predictable as sports writing: gee whiz, how extraordinary has been the growth of cliometrics; cliometrics is gravely limited by its attachment to neoclassical economics; do not be alarmed by counterfactuals.

McCloskey signals a schizophrenic response of the profession to the adolescent field. Ardent supporters faced off against dismissive critics. The former have stressed achievement. McCloskey summarises these as three:[6] to expose sloppy economics and reshuffle data; to engage in better counting; and, most important, to address grand questions of which the debates over the economics of slavery have been the most important.

Pre-occupation of cliometrics with itself is unique across the new fields being colonised by economics. In general, these have taken some old version as point of departure without benefit of a return ticket. Indeed, the old has been

---

6   See Lamoreaux (1998) for an account of the historiography of cliometrics from the perspective of the newer approach. See also Chapter 8 for a fuller account of her own contributions.

treated with scant respect for lack of "rigour" and "science" by the colonists, by which is meant formal mathematical models and falsifiability based on statistical techniques. It has been left to critics of the new not so much to defend the old as to observe that the new is not so novel after all with its insights fully understood and more fully grounded in earlier scholarship.[7] In many respects, the new and wider grasp of economics has been parasitic upon the old traditions and territories it seeks to colonise – requiring the latter to pose its problems and provide raw materials for its models and t-statistics – but otherwise it increasingly tends to be profoundly ignorant of its content unless through the selective prism of reductionist modelling (Lazear, 2000; Fine, 2002c for a critique).

Such qualities are commonplace in the cliometric literature. But so is a more circumspect element. This reflects a nagging historical conscience. We are dealing with major economic and social change, starkly revealed by the passage of time and scarcely reducible to the dull intersection of supply and demand. Should cliometricians themselves forget their broader mission in estimating the marginal product of the last slave deployed on the plantation, the softer side of the profession can serve a salutary reminder. In short, cliometrics has been particularly vulnerable to criticism from others as well as to critical self-reflection, especially by comparison to the encroachment of economics into other social sciences. The "irrational" continues to haunt the "rational".

The last decade has provided a striking illustration of the fragile self-confidence of the new economic history through the emergence of the *newer* economic history (Fine, 2000a).[8] Its leading representatives have been scathing of the old cliometrics and have posted a collective notice of *mea culpa* to earlier sceptics, now adjudged to have been exonerated. Specifically, it is accepted that the old cliometrics depended unduly upon perfect competition and absence of institutions. Institutions now matter, alongside customs, norms, and the like. But these are amenable to formal modelling by means of the new information-theoretic economics with its emphasis upon market imperfections. By embracing the corresponding latest models from neoclassical economics, apart from purporting to explain the presence of economic structures, non-market forms of interaction and apparent abandonment of (direct) pursuit of self-interest are also understood as an appropriate response to informational imperfections. From such analytical richness, rectifying the

---

7 For a selection, see Nelson (1997) on the new growth theory, Martin (1999) on the new economic geography, Ingham (1996) on the new economic sociology, Toye (1995) on the new institutional economics, and Fine (1998a) on new labour market theory.

8 See Fine (2000a) for a critical account of the newer economic history.

sins of omission of the past has, in its own mind, permitted the newer economic history both to command the field by incorporating the concerns of its erstwhile critics and to extend the scope of analysis from firms to industries and from industries to nations as reflected, respectively, in a sequence of volumes (Temin, ed., 1991; Lamoreaux and Raff, eds, 1995; Lamoreaux et al. eds 1999).

The newer economic history is marked by five fundamental features. First is its reductionism, comprising a number of elements. Despite claiming to break with mainstream economics, it only does so as far as the assumptions of perfect competition are concerned. Indeed, the newer economic history might be seen more as tagging upon recent developments within information-theoretic economics rather than as a responding to its critics within history. Significantly, in a relatively recent textbook, Atack and Passell (1994, p. xiv) comment:

> As new tools and insights have been added to the economist's toolbox – whether principal-agent problems, human capital theory, computable general equilibrium models, or game theory, to name a few – economic historians found that they provided better ways to interpret the past. Consequently, they have been quick to adopt them. At the same time economic history has not merely borrowed from economics but also contributed to our understanding of economics.

Yet, this promises too much, too early in terms of what the volume delivers, for the mentioned tools and insights scarcely figure, despite its 700 pages, and they are absent in index entries. Terms such as "principal-agents" and "moral hazard" do appear in a glossary, and presumably both introduction and glossary were drafted at a later stage, just as the newer economic history was coming rapidly to the fore. In any case, the basic reliance upon methodological individualism remains. The economy is made up of an aggregate of optimising individuals who are burdened by imperfect and asymmetric information and corresponding transaction costs. Consequently, it is possible for economic and social structures to be explained, together with institutions, customs, and norms, as the individually rational but collectively reproduced response to such market imperfections.

The newer economic history's second fundamental feature is that, methodologically, the newer approach depends upon a division of variables between endogenous and exogenous, an imperfect proxy for the rational and irrational, respectively. With the benefits of the new information-theoretic economics, the boundary between the exogenous and the endogenous shifts in the latter's favour. Consequently, whether it be preferences, technology and endowments, as in the old neoclassical model, residual explanation will always reside out-side the model – with some initial starting point for the triumvirate previously listed for example, even if they are endogenised with the passage of history through custom, learning, norms or whatever. Crucially, the division of varia-bles between endogenous and exogenous, wherever the boundary falls, leads to a corresponding definition of the scope of economic history and the con-tribution that economics can make. This historiographical framework is put particularly clearly by Davis (1970, p. 68) who divides history into four cate-gories of susceptibility: to existing economic theory; to analysis other than economic theory; prospectively to one or another of the social sciences; to interdisciplinarity. Whilst potentially perceived as a neutral descriptive scheme for organising the literature, it is taken for granted that none of these catego-ries is empty. It follows that any extension of economic theory must extend its scope of application to history. The newer economic history endogenises what was previously exogenous. It must be able to do more and better.

More specifically, the new approach brings history back in. Its previous departure under the old approach and its dependence on mainstream eco-nomics is pinpointed by McCloskey (1976, p. 434):

> Smith, Marx, Mill, Marshall, Keynes, Heckscher, Schumpeter, and Viner, to name a few, were nourished by historical study and nourished it in turn. Gazing down from Valhalla it would seem to them bizarre that their heirs would study economics with the history left out ... Yet this is what happened. It began in the 1940's, in some respects earlier, as young American economists bemused by revolution in the substance and method of economics neglected the reading of history in favor of macro-economics, mathematics, and statistics.

Third, then, for the new approach, *history* as "time and context" that *matters* is re-introduced as a matter of theory. But it is understood in a particular way as path dependence (or presence of dynamics and/or multiple equilibria). This understanding of history is seriously deficient. Despite allowance for path dependence, the models and concepts are ahistorical, asocial, timeless, and universal. History, time *and* context are confined to the random shock, or other haphazard factors which lead to one rather than another *pre-determined*, if stochastic, path to be taken. Thus, Greif (1997, p. 402) sees the neoclassical eco-nomics deployed by cliometrics to have been too narrow. In contrast:

> This new economic theory ... underscore[s] the importance of history in economic processes ... endogenous-growth models, and dynamic

general-equilibrium models ... posteriors, focal points, learning, coordination, sunk investment, historically determined interest groups, social groups, social norms, legislation, and preferences. Hence, economic theory has begun to support, rather than undermine, the claim regarding the importance of history and to provide conceptual frameworks within which path-dependence may be examined.

But, as is made clear in the volume of Bates et al. (1998)[9] to which Greif is a contributor, history at most serves to aid in the selection between otherwise ahistorical models or between equilibria for a selected model.

Fourth, as already apparent in its narrow understanding of history, the newer economic history remains more or less untouched by postmodernism and concern with the socially constructed meaning of its objects of study. This is inevitable for any analysis that draws upon mainstream economics, for the latter is unique across the social sciences in having been totally untouched by the influence of postmodernism. Quite apart from its own version of subjectivity, drawn from the preferences or utility of otherwise unexamined individuals over unexamined goods, it relies exclusively on universal categories such as utility, production, goods, and inputs for its analysis. Yet, the new economics does appeal to, and draw upon, notions of culture, trust, values, and so on. But the meaning attached to these is reduced to how individuals respond to informational uncertainties about the world. There is otherwise no socially- and historically-specific discursive content.

Last, and partly as a matter of style but significant in determining scope and appeal of the new approach, the formal modelling, and explicit assumptions and methodology upon which it rests, is often tempered by, even inconsistently incorporated with, informal analytical discourse. From broad propositions of the sort that institutions, customs, or history matter as a response to market imperfections, it is a simple step to allow for inclusion of any of the traditional variables of social theory, from culture and ideology to exploitation, power and conflict. Whether explicitly signposted as such, these ultimately derive from the opportunities or impediments created and sustained by optimising individuals in a world of imperfect information and imperfectly working markets.

From the preceding account of the newer economic history, a familiar pattern of analytical evolution presents itself. Because of the division between exogenous and endogenous, progress can be made by shifting variables from one to the other, respectively. What was previously a residual and unexplained

---

9   Somewhat paradoxically, the book is dedicated to North, Boniface and Sharman (2001).

becomes a variable and subject to explanation. The newer approach is exemplary illustration. Yet it is associated with one, as yet, unobserved anomaly. This is the relationship between the newer approach and Douglass North, one of the founding fathers of cliometrics and credited with having coined the expression "new economic history" (Goldin, 1995, p. 193). As will be seen, there are considerable affinities between North and the newer approach. He has for some time been highly critical of the old neoclassical model of perfect competition, especially in arguing that institutions and history matter. Yet North cannot be comfortably accommodated within the newer approach. One reason for this is because his own work has evolved informally and independently of it, not least because he commendably broke with its, and his own, early version prior to the rise of the new information-theoretic approach. The new and newer economic histories can in principle explain anything on the basis of rationality by pushing out the boundaries of the endogenous/rational, one by extending the scope of the as if perfect market, the other by appeal to market imperfections, respectively. By contrast, North has retained a continuing commitment to the role of ideology which occupies an uncomfortable position in straddling the rational/irrational divide.[10]

3 Shifting Vision of the Historian of the Western World

Since early cliometric years, North's thinking has evolved continually. At the outset, North (1963, p. 128) reports major change in the academic wind, "A revolution is taking place in economic history in the United States". The impact will be felt not only on the economic and the historical as such but also on the political and the social rather than vice-versa, p. 130:

> Moreover, this new emphasis in no way vitiates the contributions of the nonquantitative historian. It does promise to provide both the historian and economist with important new support. For the political and social historian, the basic revisions of our economic history should suggest some fundamental reinterpretations in political and social history.

The revolution involves the application of economic theory to economic history. North suggests taking any leading article and seeing whether it is

---

10   In what follows we concentrate exclusively on North's theoretical trajectory. For an assessment of its application to history, see Milonakis and Fine (2007).

susceptible to formal modelling even if needing to rely upon the most favourable (unrealistic?) assumptions. Most revealing of the primitive level of North's
(1965, p. 91) approach is his view on the viability of slavery:

> Only if the wages of free labor fell to the subsistence level, so that in fact
> the prices of slaves fell to below their reproduction cost, would the insti-
> tution become nonviable.

More generally, a manifesto is provided for the fledgling cliometrics, p. 91:

> In summary ... we need to sweep out the door a good deal of the old
> economic history, to improve the quality of the new ... and it is incum-
> bent upon economists to cast a skeptical eye upon the research produced
> by their economic history colleagues to see that it lives up to standards
> which they would expect in other areas of economics.

By the early 1970s, North adopts a more ambiguous stance towards neoclassical
economics and its application to history. It is roundly praised and perceived to
be essential (North, 1974, p. 3):

> Neo-classical theory has been a powerful tool of analysis of the new eco-
> nomic history and has demonstrated repeatedly that it can shed light
> upon our economic past. In fact, I would put it stronger: A theory of
> choice – the self-conscious application of opportunity cost doctrine – is
> essential to the framing of meaningful questions in economic history.

But, crucially, it is a theory that must know its limitations, p. 1:

> It is the systematic use of standard neo-classical economic theory which
> both has provided the incisive new insights into man's economic past
> and also serves to limit the range of enquiry.

The problem is the neglect of transaction costs and associated enforcement.
Indeed, p. 6:

> The growth or decline of economic systems is clearly a function of
> increasing or decreasing productivity of the two sectors – goods and ser-
> vices and protection and justice ... It is the interplay between the two
> sectors that is a key to an understanding of economic change. What leads

to the development of "efficient" or "inefficient" property rights and how do these "rules of the game" influence the output of goods and services?

Significantly, the complementary role of protection and justice is viewed as a sector of the economy, although it is subsequently tempered with the passage of time and the wise use of terminology less grating to the non-economist. Not surprisingly, he rejects the option of rejecting neoclassical economics altogether, simply because the economy rests cheek by jowl with the non-economic, p. 3:

> The approach I wish to suggest offers a common analytical framework to study the structure of economic systems. Standard micro-economic theory then becomes one part of a broader framework of analysis.

North's subsequent work has sought to fill out that broader framework, primarily building upon rather than setting aside what has gone before. Since the 1970's, his central task is to account for *change in economic history*. In this he considers neoclassical theory is inadequate:

> Neoclassical economics applied to economic development or economic history ... does not and cannot explain the dynamics of change.

This does not mean that neoclassical theory is useless for the historian. For it, "may account very well for the performance of an economy at a moment in time or, with comparative statics, contrasts in the performance of an economy over time" (North, 1981, p. 57). However, given its essentially static character, its usefulness in studying the dynamics of change is limited. Although, "explaining economic performance in history requires a theory of demographic change, a theory of the growth of the stock of knowledge and a theory of institutions, in order to fill the gaps of neoclassical theory", p. 7, the focus of his theoretical work became institutions.

The building blocks of this theory are, first, "a *theory of property rights* that describes the individual and group incentives", second, "a *theory of the state*, since it is the state that specifies and enforces property rights" and, third, "a *theory of ideology* that explains how different perceptions of reality affect the reaction of individuals to the changing 'objective situation'", pp. 7–8, emphasis added.

The key concept lying behind his theory of institutions is that of *transaction costs*, (North, 1989, p. 1319):

> What economists have not realized until recently is that the exchange process is not costless ... and [they] ignore the costs involved in exchange ... contending that such costs exist but are passive and therefore not important, or are neutral with respect to their consequences for economies.

Indeed, this observation is elevated to the highest level of importance, "In fact, the costs of transacting are the key to the performance of economies", p. 1319. Consequently, the work of Coase (1960) is singled out for its significance both in emphasising the presence of transaction costs and as a sorely neglected point of departure from mainstream economics, p. 1319:

> Coase pointed out that the neoclassical model, which has served as the basis of economic reasoning for most scholars in the Western world, holds only under the severely restrictive assumption of zero transaction costs.

The next theoretical task is to set the potential gains from trade against the pervasive presence of transaction costs. Consequently, development is understood in terms of the net advantage of one over the other, p. 1320:

> The result of all this is that resources devoted to transacting (although small per transaction) are large, while the productivity associated with the gains from trade is even greater; and high rates of growth and development have characterized Western societies.

Why should North have set up the problem of development in these terms? The answer is his wish to explain why some economies should perform better than others. If it were simply a matter of "fundamentals", availability of resources and technology, then differences would tend to be eroded by factor mobility and costless transactions.

Instead, as already indicated, North focuses on explaining how divergence in performance derives from differences in transaction costs. These, in turn, are explained by ascending a further analytical layer, to the level of *institutions*: "with positive transaction costs, institutions matter", p. 1319. At a relatively early stage, North (1981, pp. 201–2) defines institutions as "a set of rules and compliance procedures and moral and ethical behavioral norms designed to constrain the behavior of individuals in the interest of maximising the wealth and utility of principals". To highlight the importance, and potential variability, of institutions, North posits two extremes.[11] In "a simple model of personal exchange", there is a complete absence of "cheating, shirking, opportunism, all features that underlie modern industrial organisation theory" (North, 1989, p. 1320). Everyone knows everyone else so that it is impossible to walk away permanently as the beneficiary of a bum deal for others. Here we have pure integrity for fear of being exposed, but the division of labour is crucially limited by the absence of the impersonal market. By contrast, at the other extreme, "a pure model of this world of impersonal exchange", p. 1320, is rife with potential for cheating and other harmful behaviours.

Consequently, costly though it may be, these need to be discouraged, p. 1320:

> In order to prevent such activity, elaborate institutional structures must be devised that constrain the participants and so minimize the costly aspects ... As a result, in modern Western societies we have devised formal contracts, bonding of participants, guarantees, brand names, elaborate monitoring systems, and effective enforcement mechanisms. In short, we have well-specified and well-enforced property rights.

Property rights, then, are a core component of the institutional level, imperative for agents to be able to handle the uncertainties attached to increasingly complex and impersonal exchanges. There are two broad aspects to institutional structures. One is *the state* understood as an enforcement agency; the other is *social norms*, p. 1320:[12]

> The institutional requirements ... [are] the result, first, of the development of a third party to exchanges, namely government, which specifies property rights and enforces contracts; and second of the existence of norms of behaviour to constrain the parties in interaction, which will permit exchange where high measurement costs, even with third party enforcement, pose problems with respect to opportunism, cheating, etc.

Consider North's theory of the state. The *raison d'être* of the state is its power to specify and enforce property rights. These are designed to produce forms of economic organisation that would reduce transaction costs and promote

---

11   North (1990, p. 34/5) also identifies an intermediate stage of exchange, one based on, "impersonal exchange, in which the parties are constrained by kinship ties, bonding, exchanging hostages, or merchant codes of conduct".

12   Social norms also perform the function of explaining why economies differ in performance even though they share the same formal institutions.

economic growth. By doing so the state plays the role of the wealth maximiser for society. There is, however, a caveat; if this model is correct, what explains the widespread tendency of states to create and tolerate inefficient property rights? On the one hand, the state has two contradictory objectives; in addition to devising property rights in order to maximise societal output, the state, also tries to specify rules which maximise the income of its rulers. Indeed, the latter is of primary importance to North (1981, p. 43) but receives little analytical elaboration in later work:

> The state will specify rules to maximise the income of the ruler and then, subject to that constraint, will devise rules to lower the transaction costs (and promote economic growth).

Further, "This fundamental dichotomy is the root cause of the failure of societies to experience economic growth", p. 25. On the other hand, the ruler's maximising strategy is subject to two constraints which also help to produce inefficient property rights: first is a competitive constraint (from potential rulers within their own state or from rival states); second is a transaction cost constraint (referring to the costs of monitoring, metering and collecting taxes) p. 28.

This notion of the state is riddled with problems. First, the state is here treated as a Hobbesian institution standing above society, "a *deus ex machina* to define and sustain the idea of ownership" (Hodgson, 1988, p.154). As such it needs separate analysis. A transaction costs argument invoked in the explanation of most institutions is not applicable. Instead, North offers a functionalist explanation in terms of the state's services to society – the specification and enforcement of property rights and the maximisation of societal wealth (of its rulers). Second, a collectivity (the state) is here treated as if it were a rational maximising individual subject to constraints, albeit with a dichotomy of motives. This serves North's purposes well. If "inefficient property rights" arise, this is due to the first maximisation principle, whereas if efficient property rights prevail the second maximisation principle comes to the fore. Institutions emerge and persist according to whether they are functional to state objectives, however defined, in face of transaction costs. As seen below, in case of an individual's behavior contradicting the neoclassical rational cost/ benefit calculus, North appeals to the concept of ideology. Lacking a similar residual in the case of the state, he inculcates in its logic two self-contradictory objectives (maximisation postulates) drawing freely between them according to the explanandum.

With an institutional structure comprising government and norms, and a separate distinction between institutions as formal rules and informal norms, this completes North's analytical framework with the exception of one crucially important refinement of social norms that adds one last layer to be elaborated later. First, consider how this structure explains historical change and economic performance. There is one essential mechanism that straddles all of the analytical levels – *individual pursuit of self-interest with an as if market mechanism prevailing throughout society*. This is already explicit in the gains from behaviours such as cheating but for institutional impediments. But it penetrates everywhere, even to the determinants of ideology, with every principle having its price, p. 1322:

> To the degree that individuals believe in the rules, contracts, property rights, etc, of society, they will be willing to forego opportunities to cheat, steal, or engage in opportunistic behavior. In short, they live up to the terms of contracts. Conversely, to the degree that individuals do not believe in the rules, regard them as unjust, or simply live up to the standard wealth maximizing behavioral assumptions we typically employ in neoclassical economics, the costs of contracting, that is transaction costs, will also increase. Empirical evidence suggests the price we are willing to pay for our conviction is a negatively sloped function, so that ideological attitudes are less important as the price increases.

In this light, outcomes are path dependent, contingent upon the strength of bargaining parties and, not surprisingly, with (transaction costs) market imperfections as a starting point, can potentially lead to Pareto-inefficiency. The latter arises as those with power have an incentive to exploit it at the expense of efficiency, presumably in the absence of evolved mechanisms for transfer payments that could be more than provided for by the greater efficiency that is attainable in principle, p. 1321:

> (If) the revenue that can be raised by the rulers (is) greater with an inefficient structure of property rights...even when rulers wish to promulgate rules on the basis of their efficiency consequences, survival will dictate a different course of action, because efficient rules can offend powerful interest groups in the polity.

This means that history is the "endless struggle of human beings to solve the problems of cooperation so that they may reap the advantages not only of technology, but also of all the other facets of human endeavour that constitute civilization" (North, 1990, p. 133).

But what exactly does North mean by "history"? Essentially it is confined to the impact of path dependence. In moving from the opening of his book, "History matters" (North, 1990, p. vii) he adds the refinement, one hundred pages later, "Path dependence means that history matters", p. 100. But he considers that the literature has neglected the importance of transaction costs, without which past mistakes could be costlessly rectified, and explicitly refers to the work of Paul David and QWERTY, the setting of keyboard lay-out in stone (or, more exactly, plastic) p. 95:[13]

> If ... the actors initially have incorrect models and act upon them, they either will be eliminated or efficient information feedback will induce them to modify their models.

Once again, North's divergence from the mainstream is at most marginal and reflects no apparent sensitivity to the social as something distinct from the individual.

4   From Principle of Pricing to Pricing of Principle

North's analytical framework presented so far is consistent with the newer economic history. Indeed, the latter has engendered a positive response. For North (1997a, p. 412/13) "I am far more optimistic than I was in 1977", partly because of initiatives "exploring the 'black box' of the rationality assumption, confronting theorising in the real world of uncertainty (or ambiguity) exploring the implications of transaction costs for economic performance, modelling political-economic systems, examining the nature of preferences and so on". With the partial exception of reference to uncertainty and ambiguity, such sentiments could have been expressed by mainstream economists, or newer economic historians. North also shares a huge ambition in reach of historical explanation, as revealed by the title of his seventeen-page joint article of 1970, "An Economic Theory of the Growth of the Western World". Yet, North does not follow, or anticipate, the route taken by the newer approach, which is to

---

13   QWERTY is the typing keyboard laid out to minimise jamming for mechanical typewriters but now redundant for that purpose in the age of laptops, etc. Its use by David as an example of path dependence through technological lock-in has become a historical cliché. For a critique of path dependence as understood by David, see Fine (2000a) and Chapter 9.

elaborate ever more complex models of imperfect information on the basis of an ever-wider range of uncertainties. Rather, he critically departs from this path in response to one analytical and one empirical issue.[14] The latter concerns his acceptance that not all behaviour is reducible to economic rationality, even of the extended type associated with the conscious adoption of such things as custom for individual through collective gain. Simply put, behaviour remains anomalous by such criteria, most notably in the phenomenon of individual voting in elections where the negligible anticipated rewards (nil unless a tie) do not justify the effort.

Consequently, social norms become something more than, and different from, game-theoretic, long-term strategising. They incorporate, at one further level, ideology (North, 1989, p. 1322):

> Norms are codes of conduct, taboos, standards of behavior, that are in part derived from perceptions that all individuals form both to explain and to evaluate the world around them. Some of these perceptions are shaped and moulded by organized ideologies (religions, social and political values, etc). Others are honed by experience, which leads to the reaffirmation or rejection of earlier norms.

Ideology becomes a truly marvellous and powerful explanatory factor. For it encompasses whatever is not explained by rationality (the explanatory scope of which has itself been extended by appeal to market imperfections). This is a point of departure from the newer approach, certainly as promulgated by economists, for whom only rationality exists and appeal to any other form of behaviour is arbitrary and even unacceptable. North defines ideology as "the intellectual efforts to rationalise the behavioural pattern of individuals and groups" (North, 1981, p. 49). Again, as for the state, this approach changes little in his later work. But, unlike the state, much more analytical weight becomes placed upon ideology (possibly because the state is an institution that is itself seen as ideologically determined over and above the pursuit of self-interest).

For North, ideology performs two critically important analytical functions. The first is to act as a constraint on a simple hedonistic, individual calculus of costs and benefits. It does so by legitimising a given set of property relations thus helping to reduce enforcement (transaction) costs. "Strong moral

---

14   Hence Vandenberg's (2002) notion that North inconsistently combines different approaches where he departs from the neoclassical economics with which he began.

and ethical codes of a society is the cement of social stability, which makes an economic system viable", p. 47.

Second, a positive theory of ideology is necessary to explain secular change, mostly as an initiator of, and fuel for, large group action. As a historian mindful of change through time, North is not surprisingly devoid of reliance upon an equilibrium in which ideology is a self-reproducing artefact complementing, interacting and integrating with the material world. Indeed, for North (1990, pp. 43/4) "it is simply impossible to make sense out of history (or contemporary economies) without recognizing the central role that subjective preferences play". North (1999, pp. 10/11) is acutely aware, not least for methodological individualism, that for the world and for its institutional structures to change, someone must do it. "Secular change has occurred not only because of changing relative prices but also because of evolving ideological perspectives that have led individuals and groups to have contrasting views of the fairness of their situation and act upon them" (North, 1981, p. 58).

Further, "individuals change their ideological perspective when their experiences are inconsistent with their ideology", p. 49. "Individuals will attempt to force change as a result of injustice and alienation they feel". In other words, individuals may attempt to change the system because of a "deep seated conviction" that the system is unjust, p. 12. There must not only be incentive but conception, as revealed in this sweeping summary of his approach (North, 1999, pp. 10/11):

> The reality of a politico-economic system is never known to anyone, but humans do construct elaborate beliefs about the nature of that reality – beliefs that are both a positive model of the way the system works and a normative model of how it should work. The belief system may be broadly held within the society, reflecting a consensus of beliefs; or widely disparate beliefs may be held, reflecting fundamental divisions in perceptions about the society. The dominant beliefs, that is, those of political and economic entrepreneurs in a position to make policies, result over time in the accretion of an elaborate structure of institutions, both formal rules and informal norms, that together *determine* [emphasis added] economic and political performance. The path dependence that results typically makes change incremental, although the occasional radical and abrupt ... akin to punctuated equilibrium change in evolutionary biology can occur in economic change as well ... the rate of change will depend on the degree of competition among organisations and their entrepreneurs ... resulting in alterations of the institutional matrix. What follows are revisions to perceptions of reality.

Thus, at the end of the day or, more exactly, on the top layer of the analytical structure, resides ideology or beliefs as underlying, explanatory factor. Indeed, for North (1994b, p. 385) "It is belief systems that are the underlying determinant of path dependence, one of the most striking regularities of history". But as Rutherford (1994, p. 46) puts it, "North does not provide ... a theory (of ideology) so that his treatment of institutional change and stability now rests on the change or stability of a factor that is, in significant part, exogenously determined". It is a remarkable destination for an analytical journey that begins with optimising individuals (with given preferences) in a perfect market. In turning full circle and returning to the individual, by way of markets, property rights and institutions, at last a more rounded human being emerges, one with values and beliefs. By the same token, a more rounded economic history is created, one that straddles the other social sciences. Yet, if use of fundamentals depends on transaction costs, and institutions depend on ideology, the latter is ultimately decisive. How has it been understood by North?

First, there is some lack of clarity in the way North treats ideology. Having defined structure as "the characteristics of society which we believe to be the basic determinants of performance", he goes on to include in this "the political and economic institutions, technology, demography, and ideology" (North, 1981, p. 3). Ideology, therefore, becomes part of the structure of society on a par with technology and demography! The problem with this formulation is that in treating ideology as part of the structure of society the analytical distinction between structure and human agency or, in David Lockwood's (1964) terminology, between "system integration" and "social integration", is completely blurred since an aspect of the latter (human agency, social interaction) is simply treated as part of the former (structure, system integration). Thus, one of the basic problems that has puzzled social theory from its inception, from Karl Marx and Max Weber to David Lockwood and Anthony Giddens, appears to evaporate unless it be the result of a huge and complex mechanism of simultaneous interdependencies over time. Ideology, however, whatever the exact meaning one chooses to attach to it, by its very nature implies a subject. Although *socially constructed*, it involves intellectual processes and is therefore *subjectively held* by individuals. As such, it is an indispensable part of human agency. Structures, on the other hand, refer to objectively identified properties and positions within a social system. As such, in Giddens' (1979, pp. 65–6) words, "structures are necessarily (logically) properties of systems and collectivities, and *are characterised by the absence of a subject*". Hence, ideology cannot legitimately be treated as part of the structure of society but is itself part of the social process through which objective determinations in the form of structural positions and properties are translated into subjective action (Callinicos, 1987, pp. 39–40; Anderson, 1980, p. 17).[15]

Second, despite its crucial analytical significance for his framework, North's treatment of ideology is admitted to be superficial although, he claims, through no fault of his own. North (1989, p. 1323) writes of ideology as:

> That complex of ideas, customs, dogmas, values, ethical standards, etc, which make up our understanding of the world around us, establish our normative standards, and help define the choices we make. While some norms are externally enforced, others are internally enforced codes of conduct, like honesty or integrity. It would be an immense contribution to have a testable general theory of the sociology of knowledge and therefore an understanding of the way overall ideologies emerge and evolve.

Ideally, there would be a theory of how ideologies arise and are reproduced. But North declares himself dissatisfied with what is available, p. 1330:

> The immense literature on the subject from Marx and Mannheim to Merton is not very convincing, although Robert Merton's chapters written in 1949 are still a good summary of the state of the art.

Because the literature does not provide a general theory of the sort he seeks, North sets most of it aside altogether (although, if such a theory were available and passed the test, it would close his model of history for good!).

What does North derive from Merton's (1967) account?[16] The answer seems to be very little despite the decisive importance of ideology for his theory of history. Indeed, with one minor and heavily distorted exception to be taken up as the next point, North's approach is marked by a rejection of Merton, especially in two respects. So much taken for granted that it does not bear stating, Merton is concerned with the *social* determinants of ideology – through

---

15   In commenting on an earlier draft of ours in personal communication, North accepts he was wrong in his 1981 book to "imply that ideology is part of the structure". He also claims that he has since "conspicuously stayed away from the term because it is so loaded; and I have really been more concerned with the way in which beliefs evolve and the way in which learning takes place".

16   In commenting in communication on an earlier draft, North reports that he "sat in on Merton's graduate seminar at Columbia in 1949 ... I have tried to modify his framework in terms of what we have since learned about institutions, organizations, and culture, but a lot of my approach is derived from [what] I have learned from Merton and, for that matter, from Marx too".

class, structure, etc – even if harshly dismissive in his commentary of such factors being decisive in of themselves. North's treatment of ideology proceeds exclusively from the individual, each of which deciding to change perception of reality as they would a production technique or colour or design of clothing. Further, in seeking to avoid excessive determinism, Merton necessarily ranges over a wide set of explanatory variables and processes. By contrast, North chooses to focus upon one ideological determinant alone, stripped to its bare essentials – the costs and benefits to an individual of holding to, or changing, an ideology. Otherwise, with frequent reference to the work of Herbert Simon, and others working on (ir)rationality from the perspective of the individual's cognition and system of beliefs, North is most readily interpreted as always reconstructing social theories of ideology through the prism of methodological individualism, of agents making sense of their external environment by interacting with, and internally contemplating, it. In short, for North (1995a, p. 822):[17]

> A theory of learning would model the way in which the initial genetic architecture, collective learning ... from past generations, and the players' experiences together shape the mental models of the player to thereby provide the resultant belief systems.

Third, in confining himself to work surveyed up to 1949, North entirely overlooks the postmodernist period, and before, in which ideology is seen to be concerned not only with its attachment to cause and effect but also irreducibly with its own meanings. This theme is not absent from Merton's work but is more easily read into it retrospectively rather than its jumping out of the page. In contrast, there is little or no evidence throughout North's writings that he is aware of such considerations. Accordingly, he feels entitled to revert to an outlook based on the as if market price for principles, p. 1323:

> In the absence of such a theory, we can still derive an important and potentially testable implication about norms at a more specific microlevel of analysis, which is derived from an understanding of institutions. Specifically, the structure of rules and their enforcement help define the costs we bear for ideologically determined choices; the lower the costs, the more will ideas and ideologies matter.

---

17   For North (1993a, p. 161) in short again, it would tell us, "what is the relationship between the way the mind works and the formation of institutions?".

In effect, from starting with the principle of pricing in establishing the old version of the new economic history, and then applying it successively to resource allocation, property relations and institutions, North can be neatly adjudged to have moved to a position of the pricing of principle. It is a theme that recurs throughout his later work, although consistent with what has gone before. As it were, ideology, etc, is complicated; we do not have a complete theory; so the focus will be on one effect alone. Thus, North (1990, p. 22) suggests:

> Institutions basically alter the price individuals pay and hence lead to ideas, ideologies, and dogmas frequently playing a major role in the choices individuals make.

He confirms that ideas, etc, respond to the prices implicitly charged by institutions for our beliefs, even if we cannot decipher other determinants, p. 26:

> If our understanding of motivation is very incomplete, we can still take an important forward step by taking explicit account of the way institutions alter the price paid for one's convictions.

North uses this forward step to explain changing attitudes towards the family and to the role of women in society, p. 84, and towards slavery, p. 85:

> What perhaps needs stressing more than anything else is that individuals could express their abhorrence of slavery at relatively little cost to themselves and at the same time exact a high price from slave owners.

Nonetheless, had the North foreseen the cost of the Civil War, it might never have taken place.

Fourth, as already remarked, North definitely departs from the neoclassical version of ideology, one that reduces it to biologically determined preferences that are, nonetheless, potentially influenced by random as well as optimally chosen experience. North (1981, pp. 50/1) explicitly distinguishes himself from the pure form of rationality associated with Stigler and Becker (1977). He argues that they neglect the formation of different individual ideological stances on the basis of the same experiences, and that ideology contains moral/ethical judgements (especially around fairness and equity). For North, ideology is seen as theory-driven, if at times unconsciously so, and as a means to simplify decision-making; it is "inextricably interwoven with moral and ethical judgements" and altered when inconsistent with experiences. North (1990, p. 23) is particularly favourably inclined towards the bounded rationality approach of Simon, quoting him at length and concluding, that he:

> captures the essence of why ... the subjective and incomplete processing of information plays a critical role in decision making. It accounts for ideology, based upon subjective perceptions of reality ... It brings into play the complexity and incompleteness of our information and the fumbling efforts we make to decipher it.

Fifth, as already apparent, absence of a general theory justifies North in choosing arbitrarily across ideological determinants. Pricing of principle is one example but, equally prominent, is the idea that whilst formal rules and institutions can be changed overnight, ideology and the informal evolve incrementally and are slow to adjust, a critique of a caricatured Marx for his base-superstructure model (North, 1999). It is worth emphasising, something more than a polemical point, that the modern economics literature through formal models, has sought to demonstrate that North's conclusion of the inevitability of incrementalism is simply wrong. Relatively small changes in some arena can lead to huge changes in others as a result of multiple equilibria, complex dynamics and path dependence, quite apart from catastrophe and chaos theory. In adding the informal, and unmodelled, there is no reason to believe that this should be otherwise. Nonetheless, in drawing many of the separate elements of his approach together, and recognising that preferences are strongly subjective and interpretative as distinct from the one-dimensional subjective rationality of mainstream neoclassical economics, North (1990, p. 83) concludes:

> The agent of change is the individual entrepreneur responding to the incentives embodied in the institutional framework. The sources of change are the changing relative prices or preferences. The process of change is overwhelmingly an incremental one.

Presumably, North wishes to deny that revolutionary change is possible, on the basis of normative as well as of historical judgement. Paradoxically, he borders on the dialectical in denying the revolutionary, p. 90/1:

> Although ideological commitment is a necessary condition for mass support of a revolution, it is difficult to sustain. Giving up wealth and income for other values is one thing in face of a common and hated oppressor but the value trade-off changes as the oppressor disappears. Therefore, to the extent that the new formal rules are built on an incentive system

that entails ideological commitment, they are going to be subverted ... the formal rules change, but the informal constraints do not. In consequence, there develops an ongoing tension between informal constraints and the new formal rules ... Although a wholesale change in the formal rules may take place, at the same time there will be many informal constraints that have great survival tenacity because they still resolve basic exchange problems among the participants, be they social, political, or economic. The result over time tends to be restructuring of the overall constraints – in both directions – to produce a new equilibrium that is far less revolutionary.

Thus, with resource allocation and pricing nested in a structure that ultimately rests on an informal system of beliefs, change can only be slow and incrementally cumulative as the higher layers in the hierarchy of determinants act as a buffer on those below (North, 1994a, 1995 and 2000).

Last, having departed the neoclassical world, a whole new world is opened up for North from which to explain the ideologies we adopt. Apart from technology, demography and institutions to address the evolution of fundamentals, he embraces cognitive analysis as a means to understand ideology. Somewhere inside our psyche, human history is waiting to be told or, more exactly, to unfold. In short, the simultaneous weakness of North's treatment of ideology and its strength as an explanatory factor is a consequence of his failure to have drawn from the immense literature on the topic, most notably that ideology is subject *socially* to what might be termed the six Cs. It is constructed, construed, chaotic, contradictory, contextual and contested.[18] This is to be contrasted with North's (1997b, p. 13/14) understanding of culture:

> Culture is more than a blending of different kinds of knowledge; it is value-laden with standards of behaviour that have evolved to solve "local" exchange problems (be they social, political, or economic). In all societies there evolves an informal framework to structure human interaction. This framework is the basic "capital stock" that defines the culture of a society.

---

18   See Fine (2002a) for this in the context of the culture of consumption. Note, though, that North (1995), for example, accepts inconsistencies in beliefs. The 6 Cs at the time of writing were eventually expanded to 10C (Fine, 2013 and 2024b, Chapter 5; with Bayliss and Fine, for a fuller account).

Thus, in reviewing the theme of comparing North with Merton, one over-whelming difference stands out between the two. Whilst, in the context of the social, Merton is committed to avoiding reductionism and rigid determin-ism, whether to the economic or otherwise, North ultimately settles on the strongest form of reductionism and determinism at, and to, the level of the individual. The impact of other factors is acknowledged if only to be sidelined in deference to the "pricing of principle". The as if market mechanism works its way up through his analytical framework from resource allocation, property rights, and institutions, to ideology. One reason for what might be thought of as an ironic revenge upon Marxism, whose practitioners would surely blush at the extent of the economic reductionism, is the substitution of the individual for the social in this parody of a base-superstructure model (with intermediate levels). Throughout his work, North remains inseparably attached to method-ological individualism, however much it may be complemented by property rights, institutions and culture.

As a result, his most recent interest in cognitive science is understanda-ble and entirely compatible with the evolution of his thinking. But this work remains underdeveloped both in itself and in its results. For, in addressing the notion of the social construction of ideology, North suggests that,[19] "you can-not understand the way the mind works without intimately understanding the connection between the mind and its social environment" and, in order to take this further, "what we would like to understand is the way in which the external signals that the mind receives from the environment get structured into neu-ral nets that produce the beliefs that human beings have". As signalled in the Preamble, this is to enter the world of neuroeconomics which has exploded far and wide beyond North's initial prognostications.[20]

5   Concluding Remarks

North's starting point in his post-cliometric phase has been a critique of neo-classical theory as a framework for analysing change in history. Since "the neo-classical world is a frictionless one where no institutions exist" and in which "change occurs via a change in relative prices in an impersonal market", neo-classical theory can account for neither the institutional framework nor for

---

19   This, and the following, come from North's commentary on an earlier draft of ours.

20   For some critical accounts, see Koshovets (2019) and Primrose (2022). See also Fine (2011), with appendix entitled, "Attaching economics to the brain or from free to choose ... to 'motor responses to brain chemistry'", quotation taken from Hands (2010, p. 644).

change in history (North, 1981, pp. 5, 8). In addition, neoclassical theory with its individualistic calculus is considered inadequate for a host of other reasons: first, it does not tackle the free rider problem and as such cannot explain "large group action" which, for North is a major source of change; second, it cannot account for altruistic behavior; and, third, it cannot explain stability ("why do people obey the rules of society ... when an individualistic calculus would suggest cheating, shirking, stealing, assault and murder should be everywhere evident?"). "Indeed", North (1981, p. 11) goes on, "a neoclassical world would be a jungle and no society would be viable".

To account for all this, one has to go beyond the individualistic account of costs and benefits of neoclassical economics. Hence the introduction of institutions through a transaction costs argument and of ideology as a means of overcoming the free rider problem and of accounting for all forms of behavior that do not conform to individual rational choice calculus. This is, according to North, the task of the social sciences. "The task of the social scientist is to broaden the theory to be able to predict when people will act as free riders and when they will not", p. 46. In other words, for North, the task of social sciences is supplementary to the "economic approach" in order to deal with situations in which the latter fails, as is the case with altruistic behavior, large group action, secular change, etc. The rational individual, however, remains the starting point as well as the most pervasive element in North's problematic. Having extracted the social from the picture by starting his analysis with the asocial, ahistorical rational individual, he then reintroduces it from without to account for the theoretical lacunae created by the very act of leaving the social out of the picture in the first place.

What is more, he does so *on the basis* of the individualistic rational choice postulate. This is obvious in the way he treats both institutions and ideology. He regards both simply as constraints on individual maximisation. Institutions in particular, although of central importance in North's theoretical discourse, are not taken as a point of departure but are themselves explained in terms of the individual motivation of agents that comprise them, p. 44 and (North, 1990, pp. 3–6). The state, on the other hand, is treated as if it were a maximising individual. All is attached to a static and timeless framework.

This is how North (1990, p. 5) himself summarises his approach:

> Defining institutions as the constraints that human beings impose on themselves makes the definition complementary to the choice theoretic approach of neoclassical economic theory. Building a theory of institutions on the foundation of individual choices is a step toward reconciling differences between economics and other social sciences. The choice

theoretic approach is essential because a logically consistent, potentially
testable set of hypotheses must be built on a theory of human behavior ...
Institutions are the creation of human beings. They evolve and are altered
by human beings; hence our theory must begin with the individual.

But North's methodological individualism also goes beyond the utility maximisation of mainstream economics to encompass a more complete human
being, purportedly drawing upon and integrating social science as a whole. As
North (1990, p. 17) puts it:

All theorizing in the social sciences builds, implicitly or explicitly, upon
conceptions of human behavior ... traditional behavioral assumptions
have prevented economists from coming to grips with some very fundamental issues ... a modification of these assumptions is essential to further progress in the social sciences. The motivation of the actors is more
complicated (and their preferences less stable) than assumed in received
theory.

His approach might be best understood as a combination of rational choice
theory with irrational choice theory, the latter comprising whatever is left aside
by the former. Yet, the approach is admitted to be flawed. The first, rational,
element is unable to explain action other than in self-interest. The second has
proved so elusive that, in a remarkable non sequitur, North focuses systematic
analysis on the pricing of principle. Yet, if there is one thing to be learnt from
the literature on ideology, it is that, however widely cast, its origins, meanings
and evolution cannot be found within the individual. Ideology, although individually held, is *socially* constructed. Having taken social and historical specificity out of the analysis in the first instance by appeal to universal categories
such as transaction costs, division of labour, factor endowments, and ideology
itself, it is hardly surprising that North should face severe difficulties in reintro-
ducing the social and the historical at a later stage.

North's overt influence, then, has been to establish economic history as (a
shifting) mainstream economics plus ideology, with transaction costs, property rights, and institutions bridging the divide between the two. His covert
influence has been to deter those who look for something else from their history – to classes, movements, power and conflict, with corresponding theory
to suit. The result in the past has been a great divide between economic and
social history, in which there has been a corresponding if inexact division of
responsibility between material and cultural factors, respectively. This division
is breaking down as economics increasingly purports to be able to address the

social, the cultural, the institutional and so on. The example of North's work reveals how limited are these claims derived, as they are, from methodological individualism, for which a division is necessarily drawn between the rational and the irrational, the endogenous and the exogenous, and the economic and the ideological. Nonetheless such methods will prevail to the extent that "social" historians fail to grasp the nettle of providing economic alternatives to the principle of pricing and the pricing of principle. For the latter will be influential if not central amongst those, such as North himself, who are dissatisfied with exclusive reliance upon formal modelling and reductionism to rational choice (with history as path dependence and model choice).

These approaches, as in the newer economic history, have already introduced the richer language of history and social science by reference to culture, institutions, norms, trust and so on. North offers an alternative in allowing for the irrational, something outside the modelling itself, but only at the expense of a continuing commitment to methodological individualism however much it might be disguised by the adoption and adaptation of concepts and terminology drawn from genuine social theory. Thus, North has become a standard reference in providing authority for the newer economic history (especially if citing work before his cognitive turn) but also for those who wish to engage on a wider compass whether in social history, political science, the new institutional economics, or the new development economics and studies.

What is the alternative? First is to recognise the current intellectual climate as one of dual retreat from the extremes of neo-liberalism and postmodernism. Unavoidably for North, the non-market and ideology matter, although each is narrowly construed. Second, North's own intellectual voyage, despite setting out under the mast of individualism, eventually leads him to the troubled waters of collectivities, power and conflict. Third, these should be taken as an analytical starting point, historically grounded in the societies under consideration for which capital and capitalism, for example, are more appropriate as both material and cultural categories than are the universal notions of property, institutions and ideology.

CHAPTER 7

Douglass North's Remaking of Economic History: a Critical Appraisal

Postscript as Personal Preamble

This is the second of two chapters on Douglass North's contributions to economic history. The first, Fine and Milonakis (2003), deals primarily with his theory of economic history and how it begins by deploying the first phase of economics imperialism before critically departing from it, first by way of institutions, second by way of ideology, and third by engaging with neuro-science if never abandoning his previous constructs altogether. This chapter offers an overview of what came before in the earlier chapter, even though the two chapters initially were a single piece, being much too long to be accepted as a single publication. As such, its precis of his theory is more marked by the later, idiosyncratic shift in his thinking. But the main purpose of this chapter is to assess North's applications of his theoretical contributions to economic history proper.

They are found to be sorely lacking in and of themselves, and by reference to contributions from other economic historians covering the same histories. The main problems are those of consistency and veracity of explanation, ability to explain diversity of outcomes, and the absence of factors, or their arbitrary inclusion, other than pricing, incentives, institutions and ideology – his turn to neuroscience scarcely having given rise to historical application.

As a result, North made a big splash in economic history and beyond, not least with his nostra that institutions matter and history matters. But he did not create longer lasting waves. He did provide convenient stepping stones for the new and newer economic history, see Chapters 1, 8 and 9, and for the new and newer institutional economics. His historical studies, though, alongside his pioneering contributions in the new(er) economic history and institutional economics have scarcely been subjected to critical scrutiny as opposed to warm citation. As a result, his own self-criticism and lack of satisfaction in what he had achieved also tends to be overlooked, not least with his early embrace of neuroscience on the historical stage, used with the intention of pinning down a theory of ideology. If far from being forgotten, even with the subsequent rise of neuroeconomics, North's own contributions have been more or less swamped by principles, institutions and ideologies other than the ones he proposed even if they opened the way to what was to become the latest phase of economic history as economics imperialism – for which we throw in any variable we please, whether consistent or not with market (im)perfection economic principles.

1   Introduction[1]

> I set out to understand what make economies rich or poor because I viewed that objective to being the essential prerequisite to improving their performance. The search for the Holy Grail of the ultimate source of economic performance has taken me on a long and certainly unanticipated journey, from Marxism to cognitive science, but it has been this persistent objective that has directed and shaped my scholarly career
>
> NORTH, 1997C, p. 3

Douglass North remains one of the most influential economic historians of our times. He is widely cited both as economic historian and as economist. And his influence extends far beyond his immediate field to the other social sciences, Fogel (1997, p. 25). The reason for this prominence arises out of his serving as a point of reference for the study of institutions and economic performance or, to put it more generally, the relationship between the economic and the social. This has itself come to the fore across the social sciences in the 1990s,[2] coinciding with the opportunely timed award to North of the Nobel Prize in Economics in 1993.[3]

Somewhat surprisingly, North's work has been subject to a limited level and depth of critical assessment.[4] This is despite his significance and well-known role in founding cliometrics, the application of the deterministic and individualistic neoclassical economics to history. Rather, it is enough that he should have raised the importance of institutions or the nostrum that "history

---

1 Originally published as Milonakis and Fine (2007).

2 With the dual intellectual retreat from the extremes of postmodernism and neo-liberalism and the rise of a new aggressive strain of "economics imperialism" as it seeks to colonise the other social sciences. For a discussion in the context of economic history, see Fine and Milonakis (2003) and Fine (2003c).

3 This was followed by a flush of papers representing, promoting but adding little to his approach.

4 Fenoaltea (1975), Field (1981) and Ankarloo (2002) represent three notable exceptions.

matters" for others to appeal to his authority and proceed to offer their own histories (or contemporary analyses). In short, North has served as a powerful catalyst across the social sciences in allowing institutions to be addressed in a variety of manners – ranging, often in combination, from continued commitment to neoclassical economics through to descriptive narratives.[5]

Elsewhere, Fine and Milonakis (2003), we have offered a close account of North's intellectual trajectory, identifying four stages in what we dub the passage from the principle of pricing to the pricing of principle.[6] In brief, in the initial promotion of cliometrics, concern is focused on scarce allocation of resources in response to the price system. But, moving on, efficacy of the allocative mechanism is dependent on property relations – ownership and enforcement. These, in turn, at the next analytical stage, require institutions (formal and informal) to command conformity to property relations given primacy of pursuit of self-interest. One further step allows institutions to be changed (or not) by ideology, itself heavily conditioned by self-interest (the price you pay for your beliefs in supporting slavery or not for example). Ultimately, now moving into the 1990s, North shifts towards explaining ideology in terms of cognition, even neural responses to external stimuli![7]

This late flight of analytical fancy is studiously ignored in the literature, apart from those few social theorists wedded to behaviouralism. North is most heavily referenced from around 1990 with little acknowledgement that he then remained dissatisfied with his own theoretical account of historical (and institutional) change.

The purpose here, though, is to focus on what has been neglected even more than critical account of North's analytical edifice, its application to history in

---

5   Not least in combination, for example, in the *Analytic Narratives* of Bates et al. (1998) where history is allowed for in choice of game, model, equilibrium or path. More specifically, referencing North to whom their volume is dedicated, p. 8: "Institutions ... induce choices that are regularized because they are made in equilibrium ... Behavior becomes stable and patterned, or alternatively institutionalized, not because it is imposed, but because it is elicited".

6   For concise summaries of the evolution of his thought, see Sutch (1982), North (1990, pp. 6–10) North (1997c) and Myhrman and Weingast (1994).

7   Thus, Eggertsson (1996, p. 20) cites North as concurring with Schelling (1990, p. 196) to the effect that, "If I were to start all over again, I think I would ask for several years to study the recent developments in the brain sciences". See also North (1997c, pp. 11–2) in conclusion: "Two modern developments provide promise of future development. The first is the growth of cognitive science, blending research on the brain in neural sciences with research on the mind in philosophy and psychology ... The second is the fascination of social scientists with game theory that has forced them finally to confront directly the rationality issue, because the foundations of game theory ultimately rest on the way human beings think and what is meant by common knowledge".

practice. The rationale for doing so is to bring out the consequences of his approach more fully in light of his historical endeavours.

In short, both for his theory and for his history, North is worthy of close critical attention because of the great clarity that his work brings to both the strengths and weaknesses of initiatives such as the New Institutional Economics. Our focus will be North's history in the middle phase of his career; after his abandonment of cliometrics in its pure, neoclassical form (of limited interest to the more rounded treatments of today with their emphasis on market imperfections and the non-market responses to them) and prior to his cognitive turn. Interestingly, the latter marks a total reversal of the brash confidence attached to the rise of cliometrics.[8] Indeed, the last decade has witnessed a collapse in North's strictly historical contributions in favour of repetition of his analytical prognostications. Before turning to his history, we begin with a short account of a few theoretical preliminaries to be found in North. This provides the basis for an overview of his main historical contributions followed by critiques of both his theory and his history, before drawing a brief conclusion.

2   Theoretical Considerations

North's central task in his post-cliometric phase has been to account for change in economic history and to find possible explanations for the diverse economic performance experienced in different parts of the world at different points in time. In doing so, institutions and institutional change became the primary focus of attention. "Institutional change shapes the way societies evolve through time and hence is the key to understanding historical change" (North, 1990, p. 3). However, none of the then existing theories, according to North, provided an adequate framework for analysing the dynamics of change in economic history.

Hence his starting point is a double rejection and a critique. First reject is (old) institutionalism, despite its overwhelming emphasis on the role of institutions, for its lack of a coherent theoretical framework (North, 1997c, p. 6).

---

8   Thus, he recognises that little progress has been made in knowing how to go from A to B in transitional economies (North, 1997a, p. 413). Indeed (North, 1997b, p. 16): "We simply do not know how to create efficient political markets ... We simply have no good models of policies in Third World, transition, or other economies. The interface between economics and politics is still in a primitive state in our theories, but its development is essential if we are to implement policies consistent with intentions". As North confesses much the same is true of ideology, we are left with little more than an inadequate neoclassical economics!

Second, the Marxian framework is also rejected, despite its being as North (1981, p. 61) puts it, "the most powerful of the existing statements of secular change because it includes all of the elements left out of the neoclassical framework: institutions, property rights, the state, and ideology".[9] Unlike his followers, North recognised Marxism as a powerful alternative and, like others such as Rostow (1960), dismissed it for what was understood to be an undue degree of economic determinism, a heavy irony in view of the degree of determinism of most of today's institutional economics and its disregard of Marxism as an alternative.

Neoclassical economics, on the other hand, for North (1997c, p. 6) despite its economism (or rationality to use its own vernacular) has some virtue in focusing on scarcity, competition and the individual as basic unit of analysis. But its strengths are complemented by weaknesses in being unable to explain the presence of large-group behaviour, especially in view of the potential for free-riding, and the corresponding stability that this enables. In short, "why do people obey the rules of society ... when an individualistic calculus would suggest cheating, shirking, stealing, assault and murder should be everywhere evident ... Indeed, a neoclassical world would be a jungle and no society would be viable" (North, 1981, p. 11).

Thus, the neoclassical world cannot fill out history by itself, and the extent to which it does prevail depends upon non-market elements. How these are incorporated reflects North's intellectual trajectory. Initially, he recognises that dealing with the deficiencies of neoclassical economics requires an analytical "retooling". As he puts it (North, 1997c, p. 5):

> Retooling turned out to radically change my scholarly life, since I quickly became convinced that the tools of neoclassical economic theory would not explain the fundamental societal change that had characterized European economies from medieval times onward.

First port of call in this respect is through the work of Coase (1937 and 1960). The common ground, according to North (1995b, p. 19) between new institutional economics and neoclassical economic theory, is that the former also:

> begins with the scarcity hence competition postulate; it views economics as a theory of choice subject to constraints; it employs price theory as an

---

9 Note that Hughes (1982, pp. 4–5) reports North as being a self-proclaimed Marxist in his youth – but in love with price theory.

essential part of the analysis of institutions; and it sees changes in relative prices as a major force inducing change in institutions.

Notwithstanding these common starting points, the new institutional approach also modifies and extends neoclassical theory:[10]

> In addition to modifying the rationality postulate, it adds institutions as a critical constraint and analyses the role of transaction costs as the connection between institutions and costs of production. It extends economic theory by incorporating ideas and ideologies into the analysis, modeling the political process as a critical factor in the performance of the economies, as the source of the diverse performance of economies, and as the explanation of "inefficient" markets.

The key concept lying behind his theory of institutions is that of transaction costs, (North, 1995b, p. 18):

> The incomplete information and limited mental capacity by which to process information determines the costs of transacting which underlies the formation of institutions ... The costs of transacting arise because information is costly and asymmetrically held by the parties to exchange.

But, further, "when it is costly to transact, institutions matter". This explains the entry of institutions into North's analysis to assume central importance in the explanation of differential performance. He defines them as (North, 1990, p. 3):

> the rules of the game in a society or, more formally, the humanly devised constraints that shape human interaction [and which] in consequence structure incentives in human exchange, whether political, social, or economic.

The key role of institutions, which North divides into formal rules (constitution, statute law, common law) and informal constraints (conventions, norms of behaviour and self-imposed codes of conduct) is that, "they reduce uncertainty by providing a structure for everyday life" and by defining and limiting the set of choices of individuals, pp. 3–4 and (North, 1995b, p. 23).

---

10   In this light, not surprisingly, North (1992, p. 13 and 1993b, p. 73) is favourably inclined towards Herbert Simon's view of bounded rationality.

Institutions and institutional change then became the primary focus of attention in North's writings. At the outset, institutions change smoothly and efficiently in response to evolving economic conditions. Unfortunately, such postures are rudely denied by historical experience – dramatic differences in economic performance and corresponding levels of efficiency. The result is to allow for inefficiency of institutions but to leave the analytical framework as before. As North (1995b, p. 7) puts it:[11]

> In North and Thomas (1973) we made institutions the determinants of economic performance and relative price changes the source of institutional change ... we had an essentially efficient explanation; changes in relative prices create incentives to construct more efficient institutions. The persistence of inefficient institutions ... did not fit into the theoretical framework.

Hence, in *Structure and Change in Economic History*, North abandons the efficiency view of institutions and tries to account for the persistence of inefficient institutions. At the same time North also feels the need to tackle two more theoretical problems: first, the question of the sources of institutional change and, second, the riddle of the free rider problem associated with the rationality assumption. In trying to account for these problems he adopts three basic building blocks: property rights, the state since it enforces them, and ideology since it explains how individuals respond to the "objective situation" (North, 1981, pp. 7–8).

Thus, in accounting for the unprecedented growth of Western economies in the modern era, North (1989, p. 1320) singles out the establishment of "well-specified and well-enforced property rights" as the single most important institution. Efficient property rights, however, in contrast to earlier work, are no longer seen as the only possible outcome. Inefficient property rights can also prevail. The existence and persistence, however, of inefficient property rights needs some explanation, and the state steps in to offer a solution. Although wavering between treating the state as a ruler that maximises its own as opposed to society's welfare,[12] its dual constraints suffice to explain how inefficiency can arise: "a competitive constraint (the threat of being replaced by competitors for the ruler) and a transaction cost constraint (efficient rules

---

11   See also North and Thomas (1970).

12   Thus, North and Weingast (2000, p. 414) highlight, "'the fundamental political dilemma' of an economy", that any government strong enough to enforce property rights, etc, can abuse its power to confiscate wealth.

might have such higher costs of tax collection that the ruler's revenue would be decreased)" (North, 1997c, pp. 8–9). The state puts its own welfare above that of efficiency and would lose power if it sought to do otherwise. These two constraints on the state's actions then become the basic source of inefficient property rights (North, 1981, Chapter 3).[13]

With inefficient property rights explained by resort to the state, North deploys ideology to solve the issue of altruistic behaviour, etc.[14] For North, the existence of the free rider problem means that, "change and stability in history require a theory of ideology to account for these deviations from the individualistic rational calculus of neoclassical theory" (North, 1981, p. 12). Between them, in these broad terms, the state and ideology have the free-floating, universal power to explain more or less anything that happens and, correspondingly, figure prominently in North's analysis. This is especially so in light of the looseness with which they are defined individually and in relationship to one another. Even so, the most pervasive element remains his use of neoclassical tools and analytical methods including methodological individualism, rational choice and comparative statics. This is evident in almost every single aspect of his theoretical excursion. What is more, even when he departs from the neoclassical framework through the introduction of institutions and ideology, he does so in a complementary way, in order to make up for some deficiency in this underlying framework. As such these concepts cannot but remain residual to this neoclassical framework. Thus, as seen already, ideology, is introduced as a means of overcoming the free rider problem and of accounting for all forms of behaviour that do not conform to a rational choice calculus.

Further, despite the prominence of dynamics and change in North's vocabulary, he relegates social and institutional change to incrementalism through changes driven by relative prices. Thus, for North (1990, p. 84) "institutions change and fundamental changes in relative prices are the most important sources of that change". Change is handled in a typically neoclassical comparative-static fashion rather than as a *process* of change.[15] And it is driven by the actions of individuals (North, 1995b, p. 23):

---

13   In a later work North (1990, p. 16) gives another explanation for the existence of inefficient institutions based on conflicting interests and relative bargaining power: "Institutions are not necessarily or even usually created to be socially efficient; rather they, or at least the formal rules, are created to serve the interests of those with the bargaining power to devise new rules".

14   For a fuller exposition and critique of North's concept of ideology see Fine and Milonakis (2003).

15   See also Dugger (1995, p. 455) and Vandenberg (2002).

> Economic change is a ubiquitous, ongoing, incremental process that is a consequence of the choices individuals and entrepreneurs of organizations are making everyday.[16]

Granted this, it is not surprising that North fails to provide a theory of revolution or as he calls it "discontinuous change" and that, although he admits the possibility of its occurrence, he underplays its importance in the historical record (North, 1990, pp. 89–91).

3   Making Economic History

North's history has evolved in parallel and in dialogue with his theoretical move from the principle of pricing to the pricing of principle. Given the highly abstract nature of his theory, the connection between it and his history is heavily conditioned by what he cares to leave in and out. In this respect, it displays a degree of arbitrariness albeit conditioned by the intellectual environment as he both promotes and moves beyond neoclassical theory in his own idiosyncratic fashion. Thus, a striking feature of his history is the introduction of population change as a basic explanatory variable. It complements transaction costs, the power of the state and a transhistorical notion of competition. All these elements are attached to a (ir)rational choice framework whereby history is presented as a result of choices made either by the state ("rulers") or by individuals ("entrepreneurs"). Given that the richness, diversity and complexity of historical experience are not reducible to these few simple nostrums, North amplifies through the inclusion of select elements drawn from history itself. The result is profound for the nature of his scholarship: arbitrary inclusion or exclusion of important factors with a corresponding rough relationship to existing scholarship.[17]

North argues that there is a general tendency for population to grow. It comes up against natural barriers leading to what North calls "the basic structural tension" between population and resources. But this tension is tempered by technology. Whether or not population growth leads to diminishing

---

16   As he puts it elsewhere, "incremental change comes from the perceptions of the entrepreneurs in political and economic organizations that they could do better by altering the existing institutional framework at some margin" (North, 1990, p. 8).

17   Our critique here bears resemblance to that of C. Wright Mills in his *Sociological Imagination* of what he called the 'abstracted empiricism' of Talcott Parsons' 'grand theory'. Our thanks to Michael Keaney for bringing our attention to this point.

returns depends on the rate of advance of technology. This is determined by the rate of growth of the stock of knowledge, and its application through the system of property rights. The latter corresponds to the prevailing forms of economic organisation, and its associated structure of (dis)incentives devised to reduce transaction costs, (North, 1981, Chapter 2; North and Thomas, 1973, Chapters 2–4).

For North, there have been two major discontinuities in the population/ resource base, what he calls the First and Second Economic Revolutions. The first witnesses emergence of settled agriculture. The second, located prior to the industrial revolution, is driven by productivity increase and overcomes the problem of diminishing returns to natural resources that had previously been an ever-present constraint.

North offers two alternative explanations for the First Economic Revolution, Chapter 7. First, and in typical neoclassical fashion, the emergence of settled agriculture and of stock raising is perceived to be the result of a choice made by the "band" for settled agriculture over pre-existing hunting and gathering. This choice is based on respective marginal products of labour across the two systems that, in the absence of a market to determine relative prices, are determined by the band's own introspective calculations. The alternative explanation North offers takes population growth as central in provoking Malthusian crises. According to him, diminishing returns and declining living standards may have led to efforts to curtail population growth, alongside competition between tribal bands to exclude others from the utilisation of certain resources. This competition led to the development of exclusive (communal) property rights over a territory (the first "efficient" economic institution to appear in history by displacing common property rights). Thus arose the rate of private return to acquiring knowledge about the resource base, bringing about the First Economic Revolution associated with settled agriculture and stock raising.

For North (1981, p. 109) "population growth was the most important underlying factor of ancient history". Population pressure and Malthusian crises lay behind the ever more sophisticated forms of economic organisation that made their appearance throughout ancient history and beyond, such as exclusive individual property rights, slavery, the state, etc. Thereby was "promoted productivity increase leading to periods of sustained economic growth", p. 110. Thus, for example, the state, as "the most fundamental achievement of the ancient world", p. 94, eased the increasing difficulty of decision making that was the result of the increased specialisation and division of labor associated with the emergence of exclusive (communal) property rights. "The improving institutional organisation of the state that we observe in the sequence from

Egypt to Persia, to Greece to Rome", on the other hand, "led to the reduction in transaction costs, growing regional specialisation, and widening of markets", p. 110.

Population growth, however, only provides the necessary condition for the growing sophistication of economic organisation. For the actual emergence of these institutions some additional power is needed. In the case of the First Economic Revolution, it was provided (in North's second explanation) by the competition between bands, which resulted in the emergence of exclusive (communal) property rights and, hence, to settled agriculture as a more efficient means to organise their labour. The emergence of slavery, on the other hand, was the result of a deliberate choice by the state, since it was "more profitable to the rulers" thus satisfying the state's first maximisation principle: the maximisation of the rulers' own revenue (North, 1981, p. 43). Last, the emergence of serfdom is considered to be the result of the initiative of the lords in face of "high transaction costs involved in trading goods ... in the general absence of a market economy" (North and Thomas, 1973, p. 32; North, 1981, p. 130).

Yet another source of decline and change in North's historical endeavour is the struggle over distribution, both within and between states. Once again, what triggers this process is population growth. It figures as the "deep underlying influence in shaping the pattern of conflict and adjustment" (North, 1981, pp. 113–4). It is "a major factor in internal and international conflict, political instability and decline", p. 110. Thus, for example, population growth in the ancient world, by bringing about a fall in "wages",[18] lies behind both the increased competition from other states and the rising tension and conflict between peasants and landowners over the distribution of income. Population growth also brings an increase in the price of land, intensifying the process of colonisation and conquest as well as the struggle over land, thus prompting the creation of exclusive private property rights. Ultimately, the causes of decline of the ancient world, for North, are to be found in the loss of its military superiority and the growing costs of bureaucratic control. Corresponding tax demands generated dysfunctional disincentives, Chapter 9.

Similar arguments are brought to bear on the later Middle Ages. Population growth leads to diminishing returns on common fields and to attempts to provide exclusive ownership rights by restricting access to land through land law and the enclosure movement. Further, the Malthusian crisis of the fourteenth century increased the land/labor ratio, bringing about a shift in bargaining

---

18   Note here the ahistorical way that North uses the notion of wages specific to capitalism.

power from lords to peasants, raising "wages" as lords competed for labour, eventually liberating serfs and leading to the emergence of "fee-simple own-ership of land". The same trends also gave rise to the centralisation of political coercion on the part of the lords in order to collude and prevent wages from rising (North and Thomas, 1973, pp. 23–4; North, 1981, pp. 134–5, and 1990, p. 89).

A further element in these changes is alterations in military technology,[19] especially the imperatives of scale. Thus is explained the increase in the size of the state in the ancient world, as well as the obsolescence of the feudal lord and alteration in the optimal size of the political unit of feudalism. Such changes feed into the radical alteration in property rights and to the growth of nation-states (North and Thomas, 1973, p. 17; North, 1981, p. 66).

Both population growth and changes in military technology are also identi-fied as the basic underlying factors behind the changes in property rights that occurred in early modern Europe. By themselves, however, they cannot account for the nature of these property rights and for the fact that similar changes and trends in these factors gave rise to vastly different outcomes (growth rates) in different parts of Europe at the dawn of the modern era. In particular, "efficient" property rights only emerged in England and Netherlands, and not in Spain and France that were left behind. For North, such differentiation is explained by the development of the nation-state. On this occasion, however, property rights, rather than being the result of a rational choice by the nation-state, as in the case of slavery and serfdom, are the outcome of the conflict between government and its subjects over the issue of taxation (North, 1981, pp. 147–8).

Once the new set of property rights are in place, a transaction costs argu-ment is revisited to explain both absence of crisis in seventeenth century England, as well as the exceptional growth rates of modern economies. Thus, the reduction in transaction costs associated with private property rights, laid the economic foundation that "allowed England to escape the Malthusian check that both France and Spain suffered during the seventeenth century", p. 157. This reduction of transaction costs in England and Netherlands boosted the incentive for individuals to use factors of production more efficiently and to engage in inventive and innovative activities, thus promoting the expan-sion of trade and commerce and giving rise to intensive growth. In France and Spain, on the other hand, "the absolute level of taxation and the specific forms by which fiscal revenues were obtained resulted in personal incentives to do just the opposite", p. 148.

---

19   Although "military technology" is the term used by North, a better term might be "military capability" or "capacity" which includes both fighting and resources.

North's account of the Industrial Revolution is both innovative and at odds with traditional explanations, both chronologically and theoretically. For, p. 159:

> The Industrial Revolution was an acceleration in the rate of innovation the origins of which go back well before the traditional chronology (1750–1830). It was better specified property rights … which improved factor and product markets … The resultant increasing market size induced greater specialisation and increased division of labor, which increased transaction costs. Organisational changes were devised to reduce these transaction costs and had the consequence of radically lowering the cost of innovating at the same time that the increasing market size and better specified property rights were raising the rate of return on innovating.

The combination of well-defined property rights with the consequent reduction in transaction costs is also invoked by North to explain the Industrial Revolution. "The most convincing explanation for the Industrial Revolution", he writes, "is one drawn from straightforward neoclassical theory in which a combination of better specified and enforced property rights and increasingly efficient and expanding markets [following upon the reduction of transaction costs] directed resources into new channels". The origins of this process, however, "go back in time well before the traditional chronology … Productivity increase as a result of declining transaction costs had been going on since at least 1600", p. 166. The Industrial Revolution, as North perceives it, "was initiated by increasing size of markets (which) induced changes in organisation, away from vertical integration as exemplified in home and handicraft production to specialisation. With specialisation came the increasing transaction costs of measuring traded inputs and outputs", thus leading to new organisational forms in production (from handicraft production to the putting out system to factory production) to replace the market. The factory system, through the introduction of supervision and monitoring of the production process and the system of team production, led to a reduction in the cost of technical improvements and an increase in productivity, pp. 167–8. At the same time, "the increasing market size and better-specified property rights over inventions were raising the rate of return on innovating. It was this set of developments, which paved the way for the real revolution in technology" which for North was the "wedding of science with technology" as he calls the Second Economic Revolution, p. 159 and Chapter 13.

Just as the first explanation for an invented Revolution relied upon an as if market calculation (prior to the emergence of the market) so the second draws upon a historically undifferentiated state and an unexplored relationship between science and technology (other than at the level of transaction costs and pressure on resources); and both yield to exogenous population pressures and deploy micro as macro arguments.

Further, in accounting for social stability, decline and change of an economic order, North introduces the role of ideology as at most an auxiliary factor. Indeed, over his spectacular bird's eye view of the whole historical epoch from the First Economic Revolution to the present, North only introduces the concept of ideology at two points. One occasion is in accounting for social stability in ancient Egypt where, in face of unequal distribution of output and increasing conflict over it, ideology and religion are deemed to have helped in reducing the costs of enforcing the rules and property rights, Chapter 5 and p. 64. Religion, according to North, played this role through the identification of the ruler with god in the form of the face of the Pharaoh. Otherwise, ideology only enters North's historical account through the great religious movements of Judaism and Christianity that, according to North, were a further factor contributing to the process of change in the ancient world.

4   Theoretical Considerations: a Critique

At the theoretical level, despite the prominence of institutions and ideology in North's analysis, the individual remains the basic unit of analysis, the point of departure as well as the most pervasive element. Methodological individualism is his most sacred analytical principle. Everything from the existence of institutions to structural change is seen as the result of the (rational) action of individuals. Thus, despite the prominence of the structural framework in North's problematic (individual) agency takes precedence over structural factors and the latter are either treated as the result of individual action (in the form of rational choice) or else are taken as exogenously given and, as such, are not explicable from within the model. Thus, institutions are seen either as the result of choices made by individuals or by the state which, however, is also treated as if a maximising individual. Once in place, institutions influence behaviour by acting as constraints on individual action. Ideology, on the other hand, is an exogenously given factor, which also acts upon society by influencing and constraining individual action.

The way, however, North treats the relation between structure and agency is problematic, quite apart from how the state relates to the possibly broader variables of ideology and institutions. He defines structure, as "the characteristics of society which we believe to be the basic determinants of performance", and includes within it "the political and economic institutions, technology, demography, and ideology" (North, 1981, p. 3). But, as we have argued elsewhere, ideology, although socially constructed, is subjectively held by individuals and as such it is part of human agency (Fine and Milonakis, 2003, p. 561). Granted this, it cannot at the same time be part of the structure of society without blurring or flattening the distinction between structure and agency.[20] The residual rationale for doing so can only be that the individual is the source of everything, structure as well as agency, with everything otherwise potentially depending upon everything else (if selectively so according to analytical predilections).

In the methodological structurist approach adopted here and briefly outlined below (see Lloyd, 1986, p. 37) and contrary to North's methodological individualism, the social whole is given analytical primacy. This is done, however, without totally disregarding the role of human agency, as in various forms of methodological holism.[21] The social is taken as a point of departure, and social wholes and collectivities assume an autonomous existence, independent from its individual members. This is so in two senses: first, that the social whole is more than a mere aggregation of its individual parts (members) as methodological individualists would have it; and, second, that the social whole significantly influences and conditions the behaviour or functioning of its parts, but does not totally determine this behaviour. At the same time, agency (both individual and collective) is not a passive responder to the structural imperatives but is actively involved in the shaping of these structures. This is how Lloyd describes the principle of methodological structurism, p. 37:[22]

> Action always takes place within structures of relations, rules, roles and classes. But structures are not agents in the way some functionalists and holists seem to believe. They do have powers of a *conditioning* kind, which set parameters for the exercising of human agential action, but they do not cause themselves to change. This means that humans are not pure agents because their power is limited and constrained both internally

---

20   Repeating from the previous Chapter, in a personal communication, North accepts he was wrong in his 1981 book to "imply that ideology is part of the structure". He also claims, reflecting his cognitive turn, that he has since, "conspicuously stayed away from the term because it is so loaded; and I have really been more concerned with the way in which beliefs evolve and the way in which learning takes place".

21   See Rutherford (1994, Chapter 3) for a comprehensive discussion of the different forms of methodological individualism and methodological holism.

22   In this passage we would substitute the words "limited and constrained" with the words "filtered through and conditioned by", since we consider social structures as not simply constraining, but also enabling and conditioning human behaviour (see also below).

and externally and it also means that individual and collective action is the fundamental agent of history. This methodological structurism is not reductionist, holding that explanations of mechanisms have to be given on both the micro and macro levels.

In such a framework, structures refer to objectively identified properties and positions within a social system.[23] As such, in Giddens' (1979, pp. 65–6) words, "structures are necessarily (logically) properties of systems and collectivities, and *are characterised by the absence of a subject*". Agency, on the other hand, which involves "conscious, goal directed activity" (Anderson, 1980, p. 19) is synonymous with (individual or collective) action and, as such, it necessarily implies a subject. Only people, either individually or collectively, can become bearers of purposeful activity. The implications of such a delineation of the relationship between structure and agency for North's problematic are many.

---

23   By 'objectively identified' we simply mean that a structural property does not depend on the ideas or actions of any single individual. Within our framework a social structure refers to an abstract structural property possessed by a social system. It represents a set of relations between individuals that may be acknowledged or unacknowledged by the individuals involved, but are external to any given individual, although not external to all the individuals involved. Although a structure does not exist apart from all individuals comprising it, it may exist apart from any one individual (Hodgson, 2004, pp. 12–6, 36). It is in this sense that a social structure is described as a set of locations or a set of empty spaces. This is more than a metaphor. It is an abstraction. It is, however, a real abstraction, in the sense that the nature and existence of a class does not depend on the identity of the agents comprising it (individual traits) but is independent of it. Much less so does it depend on behaviour of the individuals involved, which takes place at the level of social practices. This, however, does not make it any less real as Giddens (1979) seems to imply in several places, p. 63 for example. As Hodgson (2004, p. 33) puts it "a relation is real, but it is an association, not a singular entity. Individuals may confront these structures, even if they do not have the memories, ideas or habits that are associated with them". A social structure provides the template, and social practices in the form of the activities of individuals fill in its blanks. Social systems, according to Giddens, by contrast to structures, "are constituted by social practices", p. 73. More analytically, social systems "involve regularised relations of interdependence between individuals or groups, that typically can be best analysed as recurrent social practices. Social systems are systems of social interaction; as such they involve the situated activities of human subjects, and exist syntagmatically in the flow of time. Systems in this terminology, have structures, or more accurately have structural properties; they are not structures in themselves. Structures are necessarily (logically) properties of systems or collectivities, and are characterised by the absence of a subject", p. 66. "'Structure' refers to 'structural property', or more accurately, to 'structuring property', structuring properties providing the 'binding' of time and space in social systems", p. 64.

First, since individual action never takes place in a social vacuum, it has to be located within its proper historical and social context from the outset. In this way, individual motivation becomes a function of structures and collective interests and the fact that individual behaviour is shaped by social factors is explicitly taken into account as a point of departure. As Heilbroner and Milberg (1995, p. 8) put it, "the recognition of the inextricably social roots of all social behaviour leads to the view that macrofoundations must precede microbehaviour, not the other way around". In other words, structure takes precedence over agency at the level of the individual, and the social is incorporated into the analysis ab initio rather than emerging as a consequence of the actions of (asocial, ahistorical, rational) individuals. At the same time, structures cannot be treated simply as constraints on individual behaviour, but rather as positively shaping that behaviour. As Giddens (1979, p. 70) puts it, "every process of action is a production of something new, a fresh act; but at the same time all action exists in continuity with the past, which supplies the means of its initiation. *Structure thus is not to be conceptualized as a barrier to action, but as essentially involved in its production*". This does not mean that individual behaviour is totally determined by these properties of collectivities, only that individual action is necessarily *filtered through* and *conditioned by* these structural and social factors and institutions.

In such a framework, the individual is no longer the asocial, ahistorical, rational individual of standard economic theory, but a social individual situated within a proper social and historical context. In other words, the "homo economicus" of neoclassical theory (with more or less occasional fits of irrationality, institutional conformity and ideology) is replaced by "homo socioeconomicus". Human subjects become bearers of specific histories, and are treated as members of particular classes, cultures and communities both in determining continuity and change, with structural factors assuming central importance. But this is not a one-way process. Agency itself acts upon, shapes and reshapes the structural framework, which provides its own context of action.[24] This is close to Giddens' (1979, p. 69) notion of structuration:

> The concept of structuration involves that of the *duality of structure*, which relates to the *fundamentally recursive character of social life, and expresses the mutual dependence of structure and agency*. By the duality of structure I mean that the structural properties of social systems are

---

24   As Marx (1972, p. 120) has said, "men make their own history, but they do not make it just as they please; they do not make it under circumstances chosen by themselves, but under circumstances directly encountered, given and transmitted from the past".

both the medium and the outcome of the practices that constitute those systems.

In other words, social structure is both the "unacknowledged condition" and the "unintended consequence" of human action, p. 70. Human action in this respect involves both individual and collective agency.

Second, collectivities and collective action are either absent from North's theoretical map or, to the extent that they are present, they are stripped of intrinsic collective character. They are treated in terms of "the individualistic rational calculus of neoclassical economics", as mere aggregations of their individual parts. For North (1981, pp. 61–2) only individual agents exist (hence, paradoxically, the state as a collective individual) and action is mostly individualistic in character, although through the influence of ideological factors to overcome the free rider problem, collective action is possible but only if seen as an aggregation of individual actions. Aggregating over thousands of individual acts, however, does not change their character as individual action. Simple aggregation cannot transform individual action into collective action. The latter implies coordinated action on the part of individual agents to achieve some common objective. For this, the identification of a collective agent is necessary. Such an agent is totally absent from North's analysis. Granted this, it comes as no surprise that in North's framework, evolution and change is seen as being mostly the result of individual action. "The active agents of change were overwhelmingly individuals with a direct interest in altering the system. The great bulk of the population was typically passive and inert", pp. 116–7. Consequently, history is made mostly by individuals, inevitably from above, indicatively by "rulers" and "entrepreneurs".

Take the example of class. North (1981, p. 61) defines class as a simple aggregation of individuals "determined by commonality of interest". The emphasis here is on commonality of interest among individual agents. What is lacking is the structural determination of these shared interests. This is because, as Callinicos (1987, p. 134) puts it, "agents have shared interests by virtue of the structural capacities they derive from their position in the relations of production ... [and] they draw their powers in part from structures ... which divide them into classes with conflicting interests". In similar fashion, the bases of collective action also "comprise not just agents but the structures from which they derive the power to realise their ends". Hence the identification of the structural determination of what North calls "commonality of interests" forms the basis of both class as a collective agent and of collective action itself. Social structures or the positions agents hold within a social system form the necessary conditions for class to become a collectivity. On their own, however, they do not suffice. In order for class to become a collectivity and for a collectivity to give rise to collective action, something more is needed at the level of social practices. What transforms class from a mere position within a social system (a structural property) into a collectivity, is what in the Marxist literature is known as class consciousness or ideology.[25]

So, third, collectivities are closely intertwined with the concept of ideology. As Callinicos (1987, p. 137) argues, "collectivities exist if and only if their members coordinate their actions in the light of the identity they believe themselves to share. This raises the issue of the beliefs agents have about society, in other words, the question of ideology". Ideology, which can be defined as "a set of widely held beliefs ... whose acceptance is socially caused", p. 138, is an indispensable part of human agency and provides sufficient conditions for collective action. Whatever meaning one chooses to attach to it, ideology by its very nature implies a subject. As such, ideology cannot legitimately be treated as part of the structure of society as North does at times, but is itself part of the social process through which objective determinations in the form of structural positions and properties are translated into subjective action. It becomes the mediator through which structure affects agency. It is a mediator, however, which ceases to be an exogenous, complementary factor to "account for ... deviations from the individualistic rational calculus of neoclassical theory", p. 12. Instead of being yet another *deus ex machina* standing above and outside society, ideology now becomes an endogenous variable situated within society. The mystery of its existence within North's framework can now be transcended through the identification of its many social determinations and coordinates.

In short, what one learns from the literature on ideology is that, however widely cast, its origins, meanings and evolution cannot be found within the individual. Because ideology, although subjectively held by individuals

---

25 Again what is involved here is a distinction between class as a structural element of a social system, and class as a collectivity at the level of "recurrent social practices", what Marx called class in itself and class for itself. In dealing with classes as social structures we abstract from the specific identity and actions (individual traits) of the agents comprising them, in order to concentrate on their common attributes. Identifying the criterion of what should constitute the basis of this commonality has been a matter of debate within social science. Marx's answer is that since the first act of human existence has always been production, then this common criterion should be searched for in the production process of each social system. In this way he came down to the relation individuals have with the means of production and to labour power as the basic criterion in identifying social classes at the level of social structure.

through intellectual processes, is first and foremost socially constructed.[26] This is closely related to the notion of interests. "The primary sense in which ideologies are socially caused is that they are articulations of interests. They are attempts to give conscious expression to the needs of agents occupying particular positions within the relations of production", p. 125.

Fourth, the notion of interests brings forth the issue of power and conflict. Both of these concepts are noticeable for their absence from North's theoretical framework in his *Structure*. Neither in his theory of the state, of institutions, nor in his account of change in history does he allow for any role for power and conflict.[27] In his *Institutions*, however, North did at first try to introduce power in his theoretical framework through concepts such as group interests and group dominance, only to abandon it again at a later stage in favour of the orthodox perspective (North, 1990; Nilsson, 1993).[28] This is a necessary consequence of the absence of true collectivities and collective action in his approach. Individual interests are not simply derived internally or biologically endowed but arise *"by virtue of their membership of particular groups, communities, classes, etc"* (Giddens, 1979, p. 189). So, once again, at the first level of analysis, interests are objectively, structurally determined by the positions the actors hold in the social system.[29] Whether or not agents are able to realise

---

26   As such, ideology is subject to the 6Cs: it is constructed, construed, chaotic, contradictory, contextual and contested, Fine (2002a) in the context of consumption. See also Fine (2013) and Bayliss and Fine (2021) for fuller account and extension to 10Cs.

27   As we shall see below, when it comes to applying his theoretical tools to history, he does introduce power and conflict as explanatory variables at various points. He treats conflict, however, in an individualistic way as a bargaining process.

28   According to Nilsson (1993, pp. 46–7) "one of the oddest aspects of this book is that North offers two quite different, perhaps contrary, approaches to understanding the institutions regulating a given economy. On the one hand, North explicitly introduces politics and power into the analysis. Collective organization appears with sufficient power to create and protect the institutions that benefit the members of the organization ... But after remarks along these lines early in the book, North abandons this perspective to embrace the quite contrary orthodox perspective: that the institutions which exist are the outcome of the choices of atomized individuals responding to relative prices in a world of imperfect information and purely voluntary exchange".

29   Here it is perhaps necessary to clarify further the concept of interests by making a distinction between "interests" and "wants". Wants are subjective attributes of subjects and as such cannot exist outside and independently of the subject's consciousness. Interests on the other hand, are objectively defined as the structural properties of collectivities. In this way, the concept of objective interests is linked with with the notion of "collective interests". The problem with this conception is that it breaks the relation between interests and wants, the two being now seemingly unrelated. One way around this problem suggested by Giddens is to conceive interests as a means to achieve given wants, p. 189: "Interests presume wants, but the concept of interest concerns not the wants as

their interests depends on the power they hold relative to other agents, and the particular outcomes of their actions. Power refers to the relative capacity of agents to achieve their aims, and is itself based on the position and control of resources different actors bear within the social system. If the positions different actors hold are based on a "structural asymmetry of resources" (e.g. ownership/non-ownership of the means of production) then these positions lead to contradictory interests, which form the basis of (class) conflict. So, although interests arise as a result of the structural properties of collectivities, their formation, and realization or not, depends crucially on the transformative action of (collective) agents in relationship to other agents, p. 88.

Last, and putting aside detail, North's approach is built through reliance upon universal categories, and then applied to a more or less amenable history rather than being drawn from, and rooted in, contextually delimited periods of history. To be blunt, structure, agency, ideology, and the state only take on a meaningful life if delineated by their different context through history – for feudalism, capitalism, and so on for a Marxist approach and even for simple narratives. Significantly, North rejects such commonplace categories with little or no critical assessment. At one level, this is inevitable since the use of capital(ism) for example, as a socio-economic category is precluded by the universal use of capital or resource as setting the basis for transhistorical economic performance. At another level, disregard for the conventional categories is a consequence of the approach itself, as it draws upon the more or less (im)personal extent to which individuals make transactions. Thus, one way in which North (1990, pp. 34–5) periodises history is by identifying two extreme stages, one of personal exchange, one of impersonal exchange (the market) providing for an intermediate stage of "impersonal exchange, in which the parties are constrained by kinship ties, bonding, exchanging hostages, or merchant codes of conduct".

---

such but the possible modes of their realisation in social analysis; and these can be determined as objectively as anything in social science". In this way interests become a. objectively determined, b. related to, but, c. not identical with wants. Again only individual agents can have interests (even if they are not aware of them) but this is the result of their membership of particular social groups. So although only people have interests, these can be shared with other people belonging to the same group, class, etc (Callinicos, 1987, p. 129). Interests in this conception refer to objectively identified courses of action in order to achieve given wants. These courses of action are a function of the agent's position in the social system and his/her membership of particular social entities within the social system.

5   North's Journey from Theory to History: a Critique

In moving from theory to history one striking feature is the relegation of the role of ideology, in contrast to North's mature theoretical work, and the simultaneous elevation of demographic change as the basic motor of history. Following in the tradition of Postan (1950 and 1966) and Le Roy Ladurie (1974), North offers a Malthusian theory of population tempered by a technological constraint. Population changes by causing Malthusian crises leads to the development of new forms of economic organisation through the changes in relative prices they prompt. So the chain reaction runs from population increases to diminishing returns from available land and resources, to Malthusian crises, to changes in relative prices of land and labor, to changes in the organisational structure and property rights.

The difficulties faced by attempts to explain long-term historical evolution by appealing to demographic movements are many. For one thing, neo-Malthusianism has come under heavy fire for its inability to account for the divergent paths of development in different parts of Europe in the face of similar demographic trends. As Brenner (1976, p. 21) puts it, demographic interpretations of historical change "break down in the face of comparative analysis. Different outcomes proceeded from similar demographic trends at different times in different parts of Europe". Thus, for example, population decline in the fourteenth and fifteenth centuries was accompanied by the demise of feudalism in Western Europe and by the re-enserfment and the tightening of feudal bonds in Eastern Europe (the so-called "second serfdom"). In order to explain these divergent paths of development in the face of similar demographic trends something more is needed than mere appeals to population changes (Field, 1981, p. 190).

Further, North treats population as an exogenous variable determined outside his model, so that demographic trends are left completely untheorised (North and Thomas, 1973, p. 26). As North (1981, p. 68) himself admits, he does not advance any theory of demographic change but simply offers some assertions about population changes based on empirical observation. Demographic change, however, cannot simply be regarded as externally given. Issues like fertility, average age of marriage, etc, are heavily influenced by the prevailing social norms and values of each epoch as well as by the average level and distribution of wealth and affluence of each society. Thus, population changes rather than being an exogenous variable are a function of the social and economic conditions prevailing in each epoch. Therefore, any adequate theory of demographic change has explicitly to take into account its social environment.

This is hardly the place to offer a theory of population. However, casual observation of the figures North himself gives can help to prove our contention. Between 1AD and 1750 the annual rate of growth in population may have been .056 percent whereas from 1750 to 1950 it increased tenfold to an average of .57 percent. Such spectacular change cannot just be taken for granted but has to be addressed. It is impossible to imagine that such a dramatic increase in the rate of population growth was simply an accident and had nothing to do with the establishment of capitalist relations and the consequent eruption of the industrial revolution. In fact, it seems clear that this change in social structure made it possible to sustain such high growth rates in population through the huge increase in the productive potential it brought about.[30] A similar explanation can be invoked for the spectacular increase in population growth between the periods prior to and after what North calls the First Economic Revolution. If this is correct, however, North's chain reaction is inverted, since now the rate of population growth is the result of a change in the social structure and not vice-versa. This is not meant to deny that there is a general tendency of population to grow, but only to show that the pace and rhythm of this growth are dictated by the prevailing socio-economic conditions. Once a population trend is established on the basis of these conditions it can, in conjunction with changes in the productive forces, have its own independent impact on these conditions.

Further, the notion of Malthusian crisis arising out of the tension between population and resources points in the direction of some form of natural barrier to population growth, in the form of a fixed factor, land, p. 60. However, in the same sense that population changes are socially determined, so the limits to further growth in population are imposed by the prevailing social relations of production. Both population changes and changes in the productive potential are functions of the social structure. The prevailing social relations both dictate the pace and rhythm in the development of productive forces, which make possible the growth in population as well as setting the limits to the further development in both. Thus, the feudal crisis of the fourteenth century was not simply the result of population growth reaching the limits imposed by nature, thereby leading to diminishing returns in agriculture and to productivity crisis. The limits were imposed by the feudal organisation of the countryside. The crisis was not a natural fact. "It was, rather, built into the interrelated structure of peasant organisation of production on the one hand, and, on the

---

30   A possible chain reaction is from capitalist relations to increases in productivity, to increases in wealth, to changes in the attitudes towards marriage (e.g. lower average marriage age) to increases in fertility and hence to accelerated population growth.

other, the institutionalised relationships of serfdom by which the lord was able extract a feudal rent" (Brenner, 1976, p. 31). Accordingly, the structural limits imposed by the small size of plots coupled with "the heavy surplus extraction by the lords from the peasants and the barrier to mobility of men and land which were themselves part and parcel of the unfree surplus-extraction relationship", hindered the further development of the productive forces. These social limits imposed by the feudal social structure itself explain the productivity crisis of the fourteenth century.

North himself on many occasions, in his more historical writings, seems to allow for a socially determined explanation of demographic change, thereby contradicting his otherwise Malthusian theory of population (as in North and Thomas, 1973, p. 11; North, 1981, pp. 92, 109, 115, 117 and 132). Thus, for example, he attributes the slow growth of population in Ancient Egypt to "the extremely unequal income distribution which kept the peasants at a very low level of well-being" (North, 1981, p. 117). At another point he attributes the expansion of both population and economic activity witnessed in the Middle Ages to the "order and security" granted by the feudal order (North and Thomas, 1973, p. 11; North, 1981, p. 132). He nowhere, however, makes any attempt to incorporate these observations into a theory of population, which is totally lacking.

Similar considerations apply to North's treatment of military technology. For him, it becomes yet another exogenous variable to be drawn upon for additional explanatory power. Thus, for example, in the case of the radical alteration in property rights in the early modern period, the sufficient conditions were laid by the changes in military technology which led to the obsolescence of the feudal lord and the alteration in the optimal size of the political unit of feudalism (North and Thomas, 1973, p. 17; North, 1981, p. 66). Again, however, the development in military technology is left completely untheorised, although it is considered crucial for the evolution in the size and structure of the state in history (North, 1981, p. 68). Had North taken social structure as his starting point and had he allowed for power and conflict to enter his analysis, such a theorisation would, in principle, be possible. To take the example of feudalism again, what lies behind the growing military sophistication of feudal lords was the "parcellisation of sovereignty" characteristic of the feudal structure coupled with the lords' competitive struggle for power that such parcellisation carried with it (Anderson, 1974b, p. 148). This, in addition to the colonisation of new lands and the increased consumption of luxury goods, led to what Brenner has called "political accumulation", part of which is the building up of larger and more effective military organisations. Since, under feudalism, military might in conjunction with possession of land and conspicuous consumption are symbols of power and strength, the need for military expenditure was the direct result of the nature of this social system (Brenner, 1982, pp. 236–242; Milonakis, 1993-4, pp. 397, 408–9).

Despite their absence from his theoretical map, North on many occasions introduces power and conflict as additional (hence residual) sources of change in history. It is interesting in this respect that in his treatment of serfdom, following criticism (Fenoaltea, 1975), North switches from treating it as a contractual relation (North and Thomas, 1973, pp. 20 and 31) to dealing with it as a power relationship where "the warrior class was analogous to the mafia in extracting income from the peasantry" (North, 1981, p. 130). This is an astonishing concession by North that, if taken on board, could have serious implications for his rational choice framework. It is not surprising then that North nowhere draws out the full implications of this position. For, if the lord/peasant relation is a mafia-like power relation, this makes conflict an endemic feature of feudal society, something that North fails to take into account in his analysis of social change (Holton, 1985, p. 62). Further, if the lord/peasant relation is indeed a power relation, then clearly its emergence cannot simply be regarded as the result of the lord's choice in face of transaction costs. It is a process that must necessarily involve some form of coercion in order for peasants to be dragged into this relation and held within it.[31] As is well established, this takes the form of extra-economic, politico-legal compulsion (Dobb, 1963, pp. 35–6; Anderson, 1974b, pp.147–8; Hilton, 1978, p. 14; Milonakis, 1993-4, pp. 392–5).

What lies behind all of this is North's treatment of feudal power as an empirical factor rather than as a necessary part of the theoretical construction of class relations. For the latter, the concepts of surplus and surplus extraction are necessary, something that is again missing from his framework. Given this absence, and the individualistic nature of his analytical framework, it is not surprising to find North summarily dismissive of the concept of class as a "primary unit of action" (North, 1981, p. 61).

In accounting for the emergence of new property rights in the early modern period, it is strikingly appropriate that North totally departs from his rational choice and transaction costs framework. Thus, as we have seen, new property rights are not considered as the simple result of a rational choice on the part of some agent or institution (in this case the nation-state) in order to maximise its revenue or in order to minimise the transaction costs, as was the case with the institutions of slavery and serfdom. Rather, they are the outcome of the conflict between government and its subjects "with respect *to the expansion*

---

31   Faced with these difficulties, it is not surprising that North, in his later writings, has fallen back to his original position of treating serfdom as a contractual relation (North, 1990, p. 96).

of the state's right to tax" since "each emerging nation-state was desperate for revenue" (North, 1981, pp. 147–8). In short, the divergent paths of development in early modern Europe were the result of the installation of different types of property rights dependent on "the particular way each nation-state evolved", which, in turn, was a function of the bargaining power of the monarchy vis-à-vis its constituents, Chapter 11.

There is a striking resemblance between North's analysis at this point and Brenner's account of the causes of the divergent paths of development in different parts of Europe at the dawn of modern era. For both, the divergent routes followed in each case were the result of the outcomes of a conflict involving the specific form of evolution of the absolutist state. For Brenner, following the disintegration of serfdom, the basic conflict was over the control of surplus between the feudal aristocracy, the monarchical state and the peasantry. Thus, in France, the development of essentially freehold property by the peasants offered itself for exploitation by the monarchical state, which developed as a "class-like phenomenon" antagonistic to the lord's power. In England, on the other hand, the peasantry did not manage to establish freehold rights on the land, thus depriving the absolutist state of a "potential financial base" for exploitation. Here the centralised state developed "in relationship to and ultimate dependence upon the landlord classes" rather than in opposition to them as in France. As a result of the peasants' failure to establish freehold control over land in England, English landlords by the end of the seventeenth century controlled an overwhelming proportion of cultivable land. At the same time, given the precarious nature of peasant leasehold, they were able to "engross, consolidate and enclose, to create large farms and to lease them to capitalist farmers" thus giving birth to "the 'classic' landlord/capitalist farmer/ wage-labourer structure which made possible the transformation of agricultural production in England". In contrast, in France, the state by virtue of its ability to intervene between the landlords and the peasants to ensure peasant freedom, managed to increase its power to extract surplus from the peasants in the form of taxation. At the same time, given the security of the peasant freehold and their protection by state-supported law, the French landlords did not manage to consolidate their holdings and the landlord/capitalist farmer/ wage-worker synthesis did not materialise (Brenner, 1976, pp. 46–63).

Appearances to the contrary, there are substantial differences between Brenner's and North's accounts of the emergence of modern property relations. First, for Brenner, power and conflict form an integral part of his analysis right from the start and represent major sources of change in history rather than simply a residual source of explanatory power. For him, feudal crisis is the result of heavy surplus extraction of the lords from the peasants rather than of population pressure running against some natural barrier, pp. 31–6.[32] Second, power and conflict are introduced as part and parcel of the class structure, which represents Brenner's starting point. As he puts it, "different class structures, specific property relations of surplus-extraction relations, once established, tend to impose rather strict limits and possibilities, indeed rather specific long-term patterns, on society's economic development ... In sum, fully to comprehend long-term economic developments ... it is critical to analyse the relatively autonomous processes by which particular class structures, especially property or surplus-extraction relations, are established, and in particular the class conflicts to which they do (or do not) give rise. For it is in the outcome of such class conflicts ... that is to be found perhaps the key to the problem of long-term economic development" (Brenner, 1976, p. 12). In other words, class power and class conflict form the basis of his analysis rather than conflict between or within states or between states and their constituents.

Third is the way each treats the issue of property relations. In North's hands, this concept is reduced to "property rights", which he defines in juridical terms as "the right to exclude" (North, 1981, p. 21). Such a narrow definition of property relations, however, is problematic. North makes a general distinction between "efficient" and "inefficient" property rights. "Efficient" property rights give rise to "sustained economic growth", whereas "inefficient" property rights produce stagnation and decline, pp. 6, 22–3. Although inefficient property rights have been the rule rather than the exception in history, "sustained economic growth", according to North, is not confined to the two hundred years since the industrial revolution. According to him, Mesopotamia, Egypt, Greece, Rhodes and the Roman Empire, all experienced "sustained economic growth".

North uses the term "sustained economic growth" in very general terms to mean the cases in which "output has grown at a more rapid rate than population", p. 22. Given this general, all-embracing definition, North is able to use this term to describe such disparate phenomena as modern economic growth experienced by capitalist societies, and the improvements in productivity that all societies he cites (and some others, see below) have experienced. This, however, is done at the cost of obscuring the qualitative differences involved. Although these ancient societies did experience improvements in productivity and a certain development in their productive forces, they did not in any sense experience sustained economic growth. The latter term implies "the systematic and continuous pressure to increase the efficiency of production which is the *sine qua non* of modern economic growth" (Brenner, 1986, p. 33) and forms

---

32   For a critique of Brenner's position, see Milonakis (1993-4 and 1997).

an integral, indeed indispensable, part of capitalist societies. Sustained economic growth in this sense is clearly absent from all previous societies.

Yet, for North, all these societies were characterised by "efficient property rights". How then can this qualitative difference in their growth trajectories be accounted for? Further, Western feudalism, although it does not figure in North's list, and despite what many commentators believe, did exhibit substantial dynamism. In addition to the extensive form of development to hitherto uncultivated land, the period between the eleventh and the thirteenth century witnessed considerable advances in technique and in productivity.[33] If, however, "efficient" (i.e. well-defined) property rights is a necessary prerequisite of growth and given the precarious nature of feudal property rights, how can this dynamism be explained? To be more specific, quiritary ownership under Roman law approximated absolute ownership and yet Western feudalism with its conditional property rights witnessed higher levels of productivity than the Roman Empire.[34] In North's framework, with its narrow, juridical conception of property rights this represents an anomalous situation.

To shed light on this "anomaly", and other questions posed by history, one has to go beyond North's narrow conception to something more embracing.[35] This is not to deny that secure property rights play an important role in promoting growth. Only, first, it is not an absolute condition for growth (as the case of feudalism testifies). Second, even if it were, it cannot, on its own, account for the substantial differences in growth rates between societies that did experience a certain degree of development in their productive forces (as, for example, capitalism compared to ancient Rome). North's conception of property rights is too narrow. The notion of property *relations* or social relations of production denoting mostly social relations between production agents, does provide a

---

33   According to Duby (1968, pp. 102–3): "A great change in productivity, the only one in history until the great advances in the eighteenth and nineteenth centuries, occurred in the countryside of Western Europe between the Carolingian period and the dawn of the thirteenth century ... Mediaeval agriculture had at the end of the thirteenth century reached a technical level equivalent to that of the years which immediately preceded the agricultural revolution".

34   For a concise comparative discussion of the legal systems of Ancient Rome and of Western feudalism, see Anderson (1974a, Part III).

35   In discussing the Property Rights School, Hodgson (1988, p. 153) refers to the tendency: "to reduce the concept of property to a relation between an individual and a good, whereas through its institutional connection with social customs and the state, it is simultaneously a relationship between persons as well as things. This stripping of the social and institutional aspect of the property concept enables the school to mistakenly treat 'property rights' largely or wholly as a set of incentives and disincentives for the owner: as simply an amended Benthamite calculus of pleasure and pain".

way out of this problem. Property rights in the juridical sense form only a necessary part of this wider social concept, which encompasses "a specific totality of economic relationships" (Therborn, 1976, p. 371).

Through this conception, the feudal dynamic can be seen as the result of specific features of its social structure including the "possession" (but not ownership) of the means of production (a plot of land and the instruments of production) by the peasants which gave them an incentive to improve their productivity, the "parcellisation of sovereignty" with the (political) competition between lords it carried with it, etc. Similarly, the unprecedented growth witnessed under capitalism is, in this context, not simply the result of "efficient" property rights in the form of absolute private property but of the specific attributes of the capitalist relations of production. These include the existence of capital itself conceived as a social relation (exploitation of wage labour to yield surplus value appropriated in the form of profit), the monetisation of the means of production and their distribution among individuals, the transformation of labour-power into a commodity, the (economic) competition between individual capitalists, etc. These attributes of the wider web of capitalist relations of production form the basis for the unprecedented growth experienced in the last two hundred years. Further, they explain the qualitative difference between modern economic growth and the "growth" experienced, for example, by the Roman Empire.

6   Transaction Costs in History: a Critique

We have saved for last the critique of the concept of transaction costs as applied to history by North, not least because of its significance both in North's problematic and in his historical discourses. This is how he locates transaction costs within his analysis (North, 1981, pp. 33–4):

> To account analytically for economic organisation we use a theory of transaction costs together with a theory of the state. A theory of transaction costs is necessary because under the ubiquitous condition of scarcity and therefore competition, more efficient forms of economic organisation will replace less efficient forms under the ceteris paribus conditions ... Abstracting from the role of the state, the choice of organisational form will be dictated by the relative amount of resources required for a given amount of output. A market price system is costly because it is costly first to measure the dimensions of the good or service transacted and then to enforce the terms of exchange ... In contrast ... the costs of [hierarchical

forms of organization] are the costs of measuring the performance of agents; the inefficiencies associated with imperfect measurement; and the costs of enforcement.

A general critique of transaction costs economics is not possible here. Our main concern, though, is North's application of transaction cost analysis to explain organisation in history. Before we embark on this critique, however, a few general comments help to put the critique in context. Coase's (1937) main aim was to open up what for neoclassical economics was a "black box" by addressing the question, "why do firms exist?". Both his and Williamson's (1975 and 1985) answer to this question is that firms exist because they economise on transaction costs (including measurement, search and information, bargaining and enforcement costs) associated with the operation of the market. In this argument, the markets assume the status of a universal category or a primordial system (the original institution): "I assume, for expositional purposes", says Williamson (1975, p. 21) "that 'in the beginning there were markets'" (Ankarloo and Palermo, 2004). This conception, however, is internally inconsistent since exchange cannot take place without production (Engels, 1976, p. 180; Fourie, 1993, p. 44). As Ankarloo and Palermo (2004, p. 421) put it, "markets cannot exist without institutions that solve the production problem ... so, logically, the firm precedes the market and not vice versa". Coase's is an explicit attempt "to extend neoclassicism, using its marginalist techniques to explain the nature and boundaries of internal organisation" (Coase, 1937, p. 386; Slater and Spencer, 2000, p. 65). Both he and Williamson offer a static and timeless approach, which does not break with the neoclassical (Walrasian) framework. They do so through the use of universalistic and ahistorical concepts such as transaction costs to explain the existence of firms while totally neglecting the historical dimension of their emergence and the question of uncertainty (as opposed to calculable risk) (Fourie, 1993, p. 44; Slater and Spencer, 2000; Pitelis, 1998; Toye, 1995, pp. 65–6).

In North's hands transaction costs has become a catchall phrase to be used as an explanatory tool in almost any historical or theoretical context.[36] Thus he first uses it to explain the existence of alternative forms of exchange ("alternative contractual arrangements") prior to the emergence of organised markets in the form of the Athenian agora in the sixth century B.C. "Two considerations militated against the existence of price-making markets prior to the 6th

---

36   It seems that the only historical period he excludes is the one prior to the historical emergence of organised markets (North, 1981, pp. 41–2) but see also below.

century B.C. One was the transaction costs considerations ... the second was the wealth maximising objectives of the rulers of the state" (North, 1981, p. 42). In the absence of well-defined and enforced (private) property rights, the argument goes, the high transaction costs this implies for organised markets mean that alternative forms of contractual arrangements will prevail.

A similar transaction cost argument is invoked in order to explain the emergence of serfdom in Western Europe in the tenth century. "Labor services", he maintains, "were the result of extremely high transaction costs of forming organised markets precluding specialisation and exchange ... It was less expensive for the lord to employ labor dues owed to him to grow the goods he desired than to negotiate with his serfs every time he wished to consume different goods during the next season" (North, 1981, p. 129; North and Thomas, 1973, pp. 20–1). Here, the state, previously deployed by North as the second pillar in an explanation for the existence of organisations (see above and also North, 1981, p. 33) is left on one side, with its place being taken by an individual, the lord.[37] Serfdom here is presented as the result of rational choice on the part of the lords in the presence of high transaction costs associated with trading goods (in the absence of well-defined and enforced property rights). In responding to criticism that markets were far more widespread between the tenth and twelfth centuries than had been implied in an earlier work (North and Thomas, 1973, p. 20) and that therefore the transaction costs of acquiring a bundle of goods through the market was not a higher cost alternative than allocating labor services, he pushes his syllogism even further by maintaining that this "argument is not inconsistent with the view that the *earlier* existence of labor services could have come from high transaction costs *before* the growth of money economy" (North, 1981, p. 130, emphasis added).

There are two basic elements in North's argument: first, serfdom is the result of a choice on the part of the lords between labor services and buying goods from his serfs, a choice that is, secondly, conditioned by the prevalence of higher transaction costs associated with trading goods compared to commanding labour services. Leaving aside the rational choice nature of his position on this point, it is clear that North is once again putting forward a logical, not a historical argument. His proposition, however, suffers on both logical and historical grounds. It is logically inconsistent since serfdom, similarly to the case of the capitalist firm discussed above, is a production institution, and as such it logically precedes the market, which is an exchange institution, so that

---

37   This is possible in North's framework, since the state itself is treated as if a maximising individual.

the former cannot be theoretically explained as a substitute for the latter. The relevant question is not why serfdom substitutes for the market, but why it substitutes for other production arrangements, e.g. slavery (see also Ankarloo and Palermo, 2004, p. 422) and below. In addition, there still remains the question of whether it is legitimate to consider the trading of goods, as a real, actual alternative before the historical emergence of markets. In other words, given this absence, is it historically possible to substantiate the existence of such a choice on the part of the lords? Given the rational choice nature of the argument, the answer must be in the negative. In the absence of markets, explaining the (historical) existence of another institution (labour services) through a cost/benefit analysis in relation to the market is historically meaningless. As Ankarloo (2002, p. 26) puts it, "If there was no market how could one visualize it, and economise upon it?". And he adds:

> Considering the persistence of serfdom, even if individuals could calculate on a non-existent market, how could they act on this knowledge? Labour mobility was heavily restricted by the serf's bondage to his or her lord, which means that even if market opportunities were present, individuals could not take advantage of them.

Similar considerations apply to the transaction costs argument of North and Thomas (1973, pp. 31–2) on why lords selected labour obligations rather than any of the alternatives available to them such as "fixed wage payments in kind, fixed rents in kind, or an arrangement for sharing either inputs or outputs". Fenoaltea (1975, pp. 394, 397) in fact, after a careful examination of the transaction costs involved in labour services compared to rents in kind or in money, reaches the conclusion that:

> There is every reason to believe that labor dues did not minimize transaction costs even among forms of direct barter, and on both logical and empirical grounds it is difficult to accept the notion that these were in fact the only available arrangements in "the general absence of markets" ... From the perspective of transaction costs, then, the superiority of rents over labor dues is clear, whether the lord was to be paid in goods or in money.

In this light, North's own criticism of neoclassical theory of the firm can easily be turned against him. "Modern neoclassical literature", he writes, "discusses the firm as a substitute for the market". The usefulness of such a perspective for the economic historian, North continues, is limited "because it ignores a crucial fact of history: hierarchical organisation forms and contractual arrangements in exchange predate the price-making market" (North, 1981, p. 41). Does not the same apply to cases like the emergence of serfdom where, all the institutions North and Thomas consider as "alternatives", are in fact absent in the specific historical conjecture? If this is not accepted, then it becomes possible in principle to explain the existence of any institution in history by invoking the high transaction costs of some other theoretically possible institutions. But simply asserting that an institution exists because it is a lower cost alternative to some other theoretical possibility is no explanation at all of the historical emergence of the specific institution. Even if the logic of transaction costs is accepted, this logic is only valid in conditions in which the alternative forms considered had an existence prior to the decision to reject and substitute for them. The same applies for socially inefficient ex ante choices in which rulers benefit disproportionately at the expense of efficiency.

Even, however, if one accepts the logic of the argument that the presumed high transaction costs associated with markets might be an explanation for the absence of markets (as indeed is North's argument for the period prior to the first emergence of markets) and of the prevalence of self-sufficient units, in what sense can it be an explanation for the presence of a specific social arrangement such as serfdom? In other words, high transaction costs might explain the prevalence of some form of institution other than the market but why serfdom in particular? Why not slavery for example? The explanation given by North and Thomas (1973, p. 20) is again based on the higher transaction costs in the form of high enforcement and high supervision costs associated with slavery relative to serfdom. This argument, however, is associated with their treatment of serfdom as a contractual relation where the peasant, entering voluntarily into serfdom, had more incentive to work efficiently and had no incentive to flee, as opposed to slave and slavery involving higher enforcement costs. Once, however, the contractual nature of serfdom is set aside, as North (1981, pp. 130–1) himself does, this argument collapses. For one thing, it is beyond doubt that serfs, while working in the lord's demesne lands, had a strong incentive to shirk. Given the oppressive, mafia-like nature of serfdom, it is also highly probable that their incentive to flee was similar to that of slaves. Granted this, it is safer to assume that both the supervision and enforcement costs of serfdom were high.[38]

---

38   In fact North and Thomas themselves explicitly say so on more than one occasion, see North and Thomas (1973, pp. 20, 39, 62).

Whether they were higher or lower than for slavery is a different question and difficult to settle. The obvious quantification and measurement problems involved in such an exercise can give rise to arbitrary explanations, which are susceptible to subjective bias.[39] North and Thomas contend that slavery involved higher enforcement and supervision costs relative to serfdom, a fact they relate to the self-sufficient nature of the manor which would have made it "costly to direct and supervise slaves in the many types of tasks involved" (North and Thomas, 1973, p. 20). According to this argument, slavery is economically preferable to serfdom only in cases where each production unit is engaged in the production of only one crop (as in the case of a plantation involved in market production) involving large-scale and repetitive operations, which help to lower supervisory costs, p. 20. The so-called "second serfdom" east of the Elbe, however, provides a historical example that runs counter to this contention. This refers to the expansion and consolidation of labour services which accompanied the expansion of grain exports in Eastern Europe in the sixteenth century, "the heyday of Eastern export agriculture" (Anderson, 1974b, p. 258). If the analysis of North and Thomas were correct, one would expect the expansion of the export trade to take place in slave plantations producing exclusively for the market. As it happened, however, the expansion of the export trade led "to arable cultivation for the market on the large estates on the basis of serf labor".

The arbitrary and subjective nature of North's (and Thomas') transaction cost arguments is obvious in most of their historical illustrations. Take the example of feudalism itself, i.e. of the feudal ties between king and lords, which takes the form of the exchange of land for military services. These ties, according to North and Thomas (1973, p. 32) were the most efficient way to organise "quasi-national or regional government defense", in the absence of a market economy, since the alternative of a standing or mercenary army involved higher transaction costs in the form of higher negotiation costs. As North and Thomas themselves admit, however, feudalism also involved high transaction costs in the form of high enforcement costs deriving from its decentralised and unstable nature. Granted this, for feudalism to be a more efficient way to organise defence than a standing army, it has to be explicitly shown (rather than simply asserted) that the negotiation costs of the latter exceed the enforcement costs of the former. Given that North and Thomas do no such thing, it is quite legitimate to consider their argument as arbitrary. Indeed, it is highly questionable

---

39   For the problem of measurement as a critique of transaction cost economics see inter alia
      Matthews (1986, p. 917).

whether such a comparison is feasible given the non-quantifiable nature of many transaction costs.

All these questions and problems associated with North's analysis arise out of the ahistorical and universalistic nature of transaction costs theory. In such a framework it is possible, in principle, to "step into history at some point in time" without regard to what has gone on before. Such an exercise, however, is only possible, as North and Thomas (1973, p. 9) themselves admit, at the expense of doing "violence to (history's) essential continuity". In other words, this amounts to taking history itself out of history. Transaction costs theory provides a static and timeless framework, which can do no justice to the richness, diversity and complexity of historical evolution. Attempting to provide an explanation of the emergence of serfdom without any reference to what has gone on before is a futile exercise. The causes of the collapse of slavery in ancient Rome, the Gallo-Roman heritage in conjunction with the institutions of the Germanic invaders, the transitional institution of the *coloni*, the Carolingian State, "the turmoil and repeated barbarian invasions ... [of] the period between the collapse of the Roman Empire and the start of the author's narrative (900 AD)" (Field, 1981, p. 180) to name but a few, all form part of the historical heritage which must be the starting point of any adequate explanation of the emergence of serfdom (Anderson, 1974b, Part II). Given its ahistorical nature, it is not surprising that in North's analysis so little history is present.

Further, as North (1981, p. 130) accepts the argument that after the tenth century trading goods through the market was no longer a higher cost alternative to serfdom, then how can this change in the transaction costs associated with the market be explained? The implication is that the mere presence of markets makes them a lower cost alternative to labour services. Even if this is correct, something that cannot just be taken for granted, it still leaves open the question of why did markets emerge in the first place given that prior to their emergence they represented a higher cost alternative to labour services, p. 131. Clearly to account for the emergence of markets a transaction cost argument will not do. To make things worse, well-specified property rights, which are considered as an absolute prerequisite for the emergence of markets, are absent in the feudal context. Given the precarious nature of feudal property rights and the fact that markets represent a high cost alternative before their actual appearance, their emergence under feudalism becomes yet another riddle in North's theoretical framework. It therefore seems that the observation of Fischer (1977, p. 322) quoted in Hodgson (1988, p. 200) is warranted:[40]

---

40   Toye (1995, p. 65) reaches a similar conclusion: "Transaction cost ends up as an all-purpose tool of explanation, pressed into service to "solve" any and every puzzle – but

> Transaction costs have a well-deserved bad name as a theoretical device, because ... there is a suspicion that almost anything can be rationalised by invoking suitably specified transaction costs.[41]

Yet, North's writings have been quite influential even outside academia, as is evidenced in the World Bank's citation of North's emphasis on institutions in its World Development Report, 2002. This despite North's admission of failure in identifying how these institutions are supposed to emerge, and his recognition that his framework has little to offer in forging contemporary historical change in transitional economies, such as those of the former Soviet Union.

7   Concluding Remarks

Douglass North is considered by many as "building bridges" between different schools of thought, with the resulting eclecticism considered to be a major strength (see inter alia Groenewegen et al. 1995; Rutherford, 1995; Vandenberg, 2002). North does not hesitate to draw elements from different theoretical currents in order to offer a fuller account of the why's and how's of history, especially with regard to the causes of change in history and of the divergent performance of different economies at different points in time. At the same time his history is on the grand scale, almost unlimited in scope and sweep. This contrasts with the more mundane case studies that he has inspired, reinforcing the lack of critical analytical attention, with an equal disregard for the larger historical questions that ought, at least in principle, underpin the role of institutions, etc, in economic performance.

Although North's work has been subject to criticism here, it is important to recognise the virtues that he brings to economic history as these are more observed in the breach than his vices by those who appeal to the new

---

in fact empty of explanatory power ... (I)t is quite possible for the concept to support a tautological functionalism of the sort beloved by conservative economists".

41   Strongly associated with this ex post rationalisation of all that has happened is North's eurocentrism and the implication that the superior development of Europe and North America, compared to the rest of the world, rests upon the innate rationality of its inhabitants and their good sense to minimise transaction costs by moving towards market-based systems founded upon strongly-upheld property rights. As Blaut (1993) details, various populations in Africa and Asia were as developed as Europe; it was the conquest and looting of the Americas that gave Europe the advantage. But this is a fact again conveniently excised from this sort of history. We thank Michael Keaney for emphasising this point.

institutionalism. For, in part, because of the intellectual environment and influences upon him, North has felt the need to go beyond neoclassical economics, to address the role of property relations, institutions, the state and ideology, and to recognise Marxism as a powerful approach to such issues. In short, North's nostrum that institutions matter has become a conventional wisdom, a point of departure for the (partial) break with neoclassical economics in studying economic history and contemporary economic performance.

What is now required is the incorporation of all the elements of North's analytical tool-kit in a different methodological and theoretical framework, which would radically break away from methodological individualism and neoclassicism, by taking the social as a point of departure and focusing on forces internal to the system as the basic motors of history. Such a framework would have to combine structural factors with human agency in accounting for change in history, hence providing a truly dynamic theory of historical evolution based on endogenous forces. The Marxian notion of the mode of production coupled with the concept of collective action, seen through a methodological structurist prism, which allows for both structure and agency to assert their perspective roles, thus avoiding the deterministic aspects of some traditional interpretations of Marx's schema, could provide one such analytical template.

From New to Newer Economic History

Postscript as Personal Preamble

As highlighted in Fine (2024a, Chapter 4) I had in Fine (1997a) published a "Polemic" on the new revolution in economics, arguing that a new aggressive form of economics imperialism was well under way through the incorporation of the "social", through seeing it analytically as the individualistically-motivated, but potentially collective, response to market imperfections. Other than to the first phase of cliometrics, based on as if perfectly working markets, there is no reference in this polemic to economic history. This was soon to change, and dramatically, as I came across a stream of publications that appeared soon after my polemic – although there were earlier signals that I appeared to have overlooked. In a nutshell, it was almost as if the contributors were deliberately seeking to confirm my hypothesis and, consequently, immediately drew my critical attention, especially as I had been granted a two-year ESRC research professorship, running from 1999 to 2001, to study economics imperialism and its impact across the social sciences (although my first, main target was social capital).[1]

Significantly, my first published piece on social capital was situated in relation to the work of Joe Stiglitz and his launching of the post Washington Consensus (Fine, 2003d). As is well-known, Stiglitz is the economist of imperfect information, imperfectly working markets, par excellence. As covered in Fine (2024a) his work, mine on social capital (and why such different creatures as Pierre Bourdieu, Gary Becker and, the not so different, James Coleman) should all be using the same term, and the application of market imperfections to underpin the post Washington Consensus (the newer in place of the new development economics) all came together in a rush. As if that were not enough, the newer economic history, taking the new as its critical point of departure, followed hard on the heels of these other assaults.

In light of its individualistic orientation, the newer economic history derived from applying market imperfection economics within business history. From there it was a small analytical step to extend big and wide. The rest, as they say, is history. The new and the newer economic history drew my close critical

---

1 See especially Fine (2001b) followed by Fine (2010a) and Fine (2023a) most recently.

© BEN FINE, 2024 | DOI:10.1163/9789004689275_009

attention, and an even closer collaboration with Dimitris Milonakis to draw out the shifting relations between economic theory (and political economy) and economic history, extending back to before the marginalist revolution, and, prospectively, forward to the newest economic history, corresponding to the newer economics imperialism, in which market imperfections economics is supplemented by whatever considerations take the historian's, or the economist's, fancy to bolster what imperfect markets with optimising actions cannot explain, just as imperfect markets themselves were allocated the task of remedying the explanatory deficiencies of perfect market economics. This chapter, though, is situated in the interregnum – as the newer is putatively displacing the new economic history and, consequently, the nature of the shifts involved, and the analytical ambitions on the narrowest of principles, is that much more transparent than the muddied waters of the newest economic history (as an example of the newer economics imperialism). What remains startling is the knowing innocence with which this is done – there is never a mention of economics imperialism by name by the practitioners of the newer economic history, and practically none by its critics.[2]

1 Introduction[3]

In Fine and Milonakis (2003) and Milonakis and Fine (2007), we have charted, especially through the initial trajectory of Douglass North's contributions, how the rise of cliometrics in the post-war period signified the bringing back together of economic theory and economic history. Essentially, the new economic history provides an exemplary illustration of old-style economics imperialism although Keynesian accounts of the past have prospered alongside those more committed to understanding the past in terms of an as if perfectly working market.[4] Keynesianism or, for example, admitting the possibility of

---

2   The reasons for this are discussed in Chapter 1, but see also Fine (2024b, Chapter 2) for the more general neglect of economics imperialism as a driving force in the shifting relations between economics and the other social sciences.

3   This chapter was primarily drafted for a book on economic theory and economic history, to be co-authored with Dimitris Milonakis, that was never completed. But see Fine (2000a and 2003c) and my own drafts on record indicate Dimitris' influence on the text but not his own major contribution otherwise in drafting. The book became so long, though, that it was turned into two. These were sufficiently advanced to have been titled and designated as coming out with Routledge in 2005: *Economic Theory and History: From Classical Political Economy to Economics Imperialism*; and *Inventing the Past: Method and Theory in the Evolution of Economic History*.

4   See Eichengreen (1995).

entrepreneurial failure (a favoured pastime of British economic historians) accepts that markets (or its agents) might work imperfectly. Nevertheless, there is an implicit assumption that history is at most some deviation from an otherwise perfectly working market outcome as standard.

Not surprisingly, such an approach was heavily rejected by more historically-minded historians. In principle, the result is otherwise to relegate what are perceived to be non-market or non-economic factors to a second level of importance. At most, institutions, politics, culture and so on, are an impediment to the market, itself the conduit through which rational, optimising individuals are able to allocate resources more or less efficiently. In practice, such broader historical considerations were often relegated from second-order importance in principle to an absence altogether (other than as an as if market).[5]

Inevitably, the relationship between economic theory and economic history has changed with the changes in economic theory over the intervening period to the present. With the emergence of the new phase of economics imperialism, based on market imperfections, economic theory as history is enabled to incorporate institutions, politics, etc as the rational, if collective, response of individuals to the imperfect market. The old economics imperialism treats the non-market as if market or as obstacle to its efficacy and so source of deviation from an ideal outcome. The new accepts the inevitability of market imperfections and explains market and non-market outcomes as their consequence. It is a moot point, from a broader perspective, how different are these two approaches. Is the bottle of (non)market (im)perfections half-empty of half-full? As will be seen in Chapter 9, in discussion of path dependence, this is not an idle quip. Does the non-market correction of market imperfections demonstrate that the market works well or not?

An approach based on market imperfections does, however, make a considerable difference to those working within the new paradigm. This chapter selectively charts the outcome for economic history of the new phase of economics imperialism. It does so by focusing on the most immediate and explicit version of what will be termed the newer economic history, one that takes perfectly working markets and the new economic history as its critical points of departure. It is an exemplary illustration of the impact of the new phase of economics imperialism on economic history. In retrospect, it also offers a stepping stone to the newest economic history which, by adding other variables at

---

5   See discussion of North's intellectual trajectory in Fine and Milonakis (2003) and Milonakis and Fine (2007) with his seeking both to deploy the principle of pricing and ultimately to move beyond it as inadequate.

will than those generated endogenously by responses to market imperfections, can use the newer as its own critical point of departure.

2   New and Improved: from as if Perfect to Imperfect Markets

As elaborated in previous chapters, the emergence of cliometrics had the effect of creating a schism within history between those embracing and those rejecting it. For unquestioning supporters of cliometrics, more trained and attuned to economics than history, this has been far from troublesome. It is simply a matter of banging out a model with corresponding stylised facts or regressions. But, for those more historically inclined, there has remained a nagging doubt and guilty conscience over the excision of a more rounded historical approach in such endeavours. Possibly more than for any other incursion of economics imperialism across the social sciences, history has engendered a deep-rooted antipathy whether by virtue of its methods, traditions or subject matter. However, once economics imperialism entered a new phase, based on market imperfection economics, it allowed some to appease their sense of unease. For, emphasis upon the lingering effects of market imperfections has offered space for a conscience-clearing exercise. In particular, in a sequence of edited conference volumes, organised from the National Bureau of Economic Research, an explicit attempt has been made to bring economists and historians back together despite the confessed failures that have accompanied the enterprise in the past following the incursions of the first phase of cliometrics or new economic history (Temin, ed., 1991; Lamoreaux and Raff, eds, 1995; Lamoreaux et al. eds, 1999).[6] Their collective enterprise, what I will term the newer economic history,[7] has the virtue of making explicit its organising principles and motivation, thereby locating itself both in relation to the cliometrics of the future and the economic theory of the present.

First is rejected the previous basis on which economics has sought to collaborate with economic history. What is termed "traditional" neoclassical economics, and continuing interpretations of it, are perceived to have relied

---

6   See also Lamoreaux et al. (1997) and Lamoreaux (1998a).

7   Note the necessary but unfortunate dissonances in terminology for phases of economics imperialism (old, new and newer) as opposed to cliometrics and beyond. The latter began, as an instance of old economics imperialism, as the new economic history, and so, respectively, continues in parallel as newer and newest, respectively. The same happens for the new development economics (as old economics imperialism).

unduly upon unacceptable and simplistic assumptions associated with the model of perfect competition.[8] Thus, for Lamoreaux et al. (1997, p. 62):

> Traditional neoclassical theory assumed that economic actors were rational beings who made optimizing decisions on the basis of perfect information and foreknowledge. This highly stylized view of human behavior was a useful simplification that enabled economists to deal with certain kinds of otherwise intractable problems, especially concerning markets, in an effective way.

As a result, despite the presumed ability to deal with markets effectively, the firm is reduced to a "black box – as an equation-solving entity that determined prices and output by setting marginal revenue equal to marginal cost", p. 62. By contrast, whilst the theory has some purchase over the behaviour of differentiated consumers, it is not able to address the complex and varied ways in which firms exist and function as organisations (Lamoreaux et al. 1999, p. 6):

> Firms as such figured in the analysis only in such detail as was necessary to make the models of markets work. This treatment was no different from that which the theory accorded to other economic actors, but because firms typically are complex organizations composed of people who often have conflicting interests and goals, the effect was particularly unworldly. Neoclassical theory endowed firms with perfect knowledge ... and with the ability to act both instantaneously and effectively. Whereas consumers were portrayed as maximizing utility, a concept that at least paid lip service to the idea that human beings may have different preferences, firms were depicted as maximizing the more objective concept of profit.

In short, whilst traditional economics can handle consumers and markets, it is ill-equipped to deal with firms and organisations.[9] For Temin (1991, p. 7)

---

8 Note that it is common for those working *within* neoclassical economics to place themselves as lying outside of, or departing from, it by stressing that they do not accept models of perfect competition as realistic. But reliance upon market imperfections is a longstanding tradition for the mainstream. The claim of breaking with the mainstream through appeal to market (as informational) imperfections is especially true of Stiglitz for example. Similarly, in a retrospective on transaction cost economics perceived by others as a point of departure from the lack of realism of the mainstream, Coase (1998, p. 72) sees the latter by contrast as, "more and more abstract over time, and ... little concerned with what happens in the real world".

9 Note, however, as argued in Fine and Leopold (1993, Chapter 4) and Fine (1995, 1997b and 2002a) the neoclassical theories of consumption and of production are essentially identical, with consumers understood as mini-firms producing utility at minimum cost. See later footnote on omission of consumption as indicative of limited attention to "culture".

"traditional economic theory ... is of only limited use to business historians", not least because of its inability to deal with firms, wants, strategies and organisation.[10] Mokyr (1985, p. 2) a leading practitioner, concurs in many respects:[11]

> The New Economic History has shown itself best qualified to answer questions that it itself poses, often well-defined questions that yielded clear, refutable hypotheses. Indeed, the very definiteness of the new methods has confined them to a narrow range of problems.

This raises questions of how the new economic history can both improve what it does and on a wider canvas – the newer economic history begins to provide an answer through developments from within the economics upon which it draws.

For, second, the new economics adopted to resolve these conundrums continues to be drawn from the neoclassical tradition, relying upon the economics of informational imperfections and asymmetries. As a result, attention can be given to the different effects of such market imperfections as well as the non-market forms of responding to them, not least in opening up the black box of intra-firm organisation and behaviour. As Temin (1991, p. 2) puts it in the opening introduction to the first volume, in highlighting their novelty:

> The first theme is analytic ... information is the key element to the functioning of an enterprise.

---

10   This assessment of the old, then the new, was anticipated by Redlich (1965, p. 482) on the twenty-fifth anniversary of the Economic History Association: "Traditional economic history deals primarily with the development of economic institutions and secondarily with processes taking place therein. The new approaches tend to deal primarily with and directly with economic processes while more or less neglecting economic institutions".

11   This downside, whatever its validity since cliometrics has also been parasitic in order to find problems to address, has for Mokyr to be set against the claimed superior intellectual standards of the economist, on which see below for the newer approach also, p. 2: "Most important, the New Economic History has imposed certain standards of economic logic upon the field. Economists are not less prejudiced and politically biased than other social scientists, and they certainly do not monopolize common sense ... But economics allows at least fewer logical lapses than other social sciences and when an economist commits them, he or she can count on other economists to point them out mercilessly". Of course, this logic is questionable running from methodological questions through to those that are conceptual, theoretical and empirical, not least concerning the Cambridge critique of capital theory and the validity and usefulness of both old and new growth theory for example. See discussions in Fine (2024a and b).

Thus, the approach begins modestly with intra-firm issues, in which the out-side environment is taken as given. But analytical ambition has broadened, moving to inter-firm relations and, ultimately, to the economy as a whole. It is simply a matter of shifting out the boundaries of the scope of analysis to deal with common intra-and inter-organisational informational problems. In the second volume, Temin (1995, p. 315) calls for extension of "concern with infor-mation to include the coordination of activity both within and between firms". And for Lamoreaux et al. (1999, p. 10) in the third volume:[12]

> Although ... previous volumes dealt with learning processes, the present volume moves this theme to center stage by asking explicitly how firms, industries, and even nations can learn to overcome uncertainty ... The essays in this volume thus mark a transition from focussing on problems that are common to a whole class of firms or industries to explaining why firms, groups, and nations can differ in important and persistent ways.

In addition to dealing with learning and uncertainty within and between such organisations, the theory is able to address their own divisions as in where one firm ends and another begins. Temin (1991, p. 3) observes:

> The vertical relations within business enterprises have many important common characteristics ... the problems and the solutions are similar at the level of employee compensation, the direction of business units, and the finance of enterprises as a whole. In fact, the solutions to these infor-mation problems are important determinants of where the boundaries of business enterprises lie.

Information, then, is the decisive variable in analysing economic performance, and the universal applicability of the information-theoretic approach renders it extensive in scope, from lowest to highest levels of analysis.

Third, closely related to the elevation of information to such prominence, is the notion that apparently diverse applications have a common analytical core. For Lamoreaux et al. (1999, p. 15) commenting on a variety of case studies:

> All of the authors take the imperfect state of information as their starting point, and all aim to illuminate the ways in which this condition effects

---

12   See also Lamoreaux et al. (1999, p. 14/5): "More than any other factor, the ability to col-lect and use information effectively determines whether firms, industry, groups, and even nations will succeed or fail".

the playing out of economic life. This common preoccupation then leads to a deeper source of coherence – the structural unity behind all these various topics. The information problems that firms face in their internal operations are not so different from those faced by firms and other economic actors when they interact with one another. Further, the solutions adopted in response to these information problems typically have many features in common, even though they often result in the creation of capabilities that are specific to the organization.

Thus, different issues can be handled analytically in the same way and still provide, to be taken up again below, for organisational and historical specificity.

Fourth, aware of its reliance upon formal mathematical models with claims of universal applicability, the new approach is sensitive to the charge from historians of neglect of what it terms "time and context". However, the new theory presents itself as free from or, less vulnerable, to such charges because it deploys game theory in which history matters and for which outcomes and future strategies depend upon paths taken from or around multiple equilibria in the past. In short, for Lamoreaux and Raff (1995, p. 5):

> The historian critics should take heart from the way the economists' literature developed ... The first game theorists had sought unique equilibrium solutions to their problems. These would inevitably be independent of history. But, as research advanced, it became clear that the games frequently possessed multiple equilibria. Because only one outcome could actually happen, theorists needed to think about selection principles. Players' expectations came to be recognized as quite important, as did the history of relations between the players. Time and context mattered after all.

So, despite formal models, history figures in the form of "time and context". Information, then, is the decisive variable in analysing economic performance. But such potential variability in outcomes carries a potential cost because the wide range of different models, and the multiple equilibria potentially attached to each, suggest difficulties in coming to firm conclusions (Lamoreaux et al. 1999, p. 9):[13]

---

13   See Hounshell (1991, p. 39) and also Sutton (1995, p. 98) for whom: "A decade of work on game-theoretic models in industrial organization has made it plain that, in representing any market of interests, there will usually be many a priori reasonable models, whose design differs in respect of features we cannot observe, identify, or proxy empirically. Now

But the richness of this literature is also its Achilles' heel, because it gives the appearance that anything can happen in the absence of good – that is, cheap – information. Of course, this impression is false – there are many constraints operating to limit the choices that actors make. At the simplest level, the desire to pay one's bills or make a profit can limit the number of actions that seem wise; similarly, competitive forces can constrain the alternatives that are reasonable to take.

Despite the indeterminacies that are characteristic of the new economic theory, there is no reason for rejecting it as causally empty because it builds in constraints on potential outcomes. We may not be able to explain what did happen but we can explain some of what did not.

Fifth, the indeterminacies attached to the new economic theory delineate a distinctive role for the historian; it is to filter out unrealistic models and to uncover the historically feasible relationship between information and choice, (Lamoreaux et al. 1999, p. 9):[14]

Historians can offer economists intellectual discipline simply by focusing their efforts on what they are well-trained to do: elucidating what economic actors actually know at any given point in time, how they use their knowledge to make informed choices, and how they learn from their past decisions.

There is some awareness that this might appear to place business historians in a servile status relative to economists (Lamoreaux et al. 1997, p. 77):

-----

if *all* outcomes are possible, we are in the historian's realm of accident and personality; and the business historian need pay little heed to what the economist has to say. But this is not, in fact, the case. Many outcomes are possible, but by no means all. It turns out that there are certain competitive mechanisms whose operation across *all* reasonable candidate models constrains the set of possible outcomes. These 'robust' mechanisms include, notably, the process of price competition and the process of competitive escalation of competitive efforts –whose operation serves to delimit the set of outcomes that can emerge". Sutton (1991) refers to his own work on how (endogenous) fixed costs and increasing returns to scale interact with market size to determine industrial structure. For a critique, see Fine (1999b).

14   Note here how what the historian has to offer is posed entirely in terms of the knowledge and choice of (individual) economic actors, signalling total capitulation to the economists' "intellectual discipline".

We do not see business historians as research assistants for economists who engage in a higher level of thinking.

Rather, it is intended that they should internalise the new economic theory in order to discover the commonalities across what would otherwise be diverse case studies (Lamoreaux et al. 1997, p. 77) continuing from above and closing this article:

> Although we hope that a byproduct of this dialogue will be better modelling by economists, our main concern is that the work of individual business historians redound to the credit of the field of business history as a whole. The real benefit of recent theoretical developments in economics is that they enable business historians to recognize the essential unity that underlies a great number of the problems with which they are concerned. As a result, studies on one topic can resonate with studies on others, strengthening them all and, in turn, the field as a whole.

Economic history essentially becomes the application of an appropriately identified model to the problems of informational imperfections.

Sixth, there is no need for economic historians to become fully trained in the esoteric mathematical modelling attached to the new economics (Lamoreaux et al. 1999, p. 9):

> There is no requirement that historians adopt formal theoretical approaches in their work or even that they weave their narratives around abstract economic models.

Economic historians need be motivated less by "formal economic theory, in a direct or self-conscious way", and more by "questions growing out of this literature" (Lamoreaux and Raff, 1995, p. 5). The technical high ground attached to mainstream economics can be incorporated by historians by embracing the results of the new theory into their thinking and research.

3   Testing the New Product

The preceding account has presented the new(er) approach to business history on its own terms. In the attempt to do so fairly and without misrepresentation, it has drawn heavily upon extensive quotation, as does the critical assessment that follows. This is in order to avoid the danger of addressing a constructed straw product, and to blow it away unfairly with rhetorical and radical huff and puff.

First and foremost, an inescapable aspect of the new approach, shared in common with the traditional neoclassical economics with which it purports to break, is its reductionism. This has a number of critical components, which are distinct but interrelated. At the analytical level, the social is reduced to the aggregated behaviour of optimising individuals and does not exist independently of such atomised behaviour. Indeed, the new informational economics prides itself on such methodological individualism and congratulates itself for extending the scope of analysis by incorporating informational imperfections as an explanatory tool and the non-economic and social as an explanatory outcome. But this involves a tension as far as influence over social theory is concerned. For, whilst the social is addressed where previously it was taken as given, undoubtedly an attraction and selling point, the basis on which it is done is ultimately individualistic and denies the independent existence of the social, a drawback for other approaches within social science that rejects rational choice theory. It means an absence of independently given social relations, structures, agencies and tendencies, as well as their analytical accompaniments such as power and conflict.

But here it is already possible to illustrate the difficulty in pinning down the nature and intent of the new approach. For is power, for example, inevitably absent both from the information-theoretic approach and, as a corollary, from its counterpart in the newer economic history? The information-theoretic approach has in part recognised its limitations as far as the absence of power is concerned. Thus, Stiglitz's (1993, p. 111) offers the following response to the relatively mild suggestion from Bowles and Gintis (1993) that exchange is not only institutionally driven but also "contested":

> There are good economic reasons, beyond the exercise of "power" (whatever that much-used term means) for the existence of hierarchical relationships.

However, in part, meaning has, for example, been given to the notion of power within neoclassical economics by appeal to *incomplete* contracts. These are deemed to arise when outcomes are either unforeseeable or unenforceable and, consequently, cannot be subject to complete, if contingent, bargaining. Who bears residual gains and losses in such circumstances is a matter of power over the incomplete aspects of the contract, with outcomes, apparently appropriately, depending on the distribution of those property rights that are recognised and enforceable.

This all raises a host of tricky problems that are food and drink to those engaged in the technicalities of the information-theoretic approach. One is to endogenise contracts themselves – what issues are contracted quite apart from the prices involved. Another is to relate the terms and scope of the contract to broader optimising decisions – if a particular asset yields power, it will tend to attract over-investment, and a corresponding under-investment where residual rights are limited. For Rajan and Zingales (1998), for example, addressing "Power in a Theory of the Firm", this explains why a state regulating health provision may find it necessary itself to become a provider or rely upon providers who are insufficiently invested in specialisation for lack of residual rewards. Not surprisingly, then, similar explanations emerge for the existence of a host of non-market institutions. But the fundamental starting point for the approach, as correctly formalised by Rajan and Zingales, is the power that derives from what *cannot* be contracted, p. 387:

> The smaller the space of contracts that can be written and enforced the more important the role of residual rights of control, and hence of power.

But this, from the perspective of social theory departing from methodological individualism, is the opposite of the case. Power derives from what *is* contracted, from the recognition and enforcement of established property relations, from the state as an instrument of power rather than as its antithesis, and so on. Inevitably, the neoclassical approach takes as given and subject to unproblematic contracting what are the defining characteristics of one society as opposed to another, even though they are subject to continuing conflict and redefinition over shorter or longer periods of history.

Significantly, Lamoreaux (1998c) explicitly, if informally, seeks to modify Hart's (1995) theory of incomplete contracts, unwittingly anticipating the results of Rajan and Zingales, by positing a range of contractual forms, pointing to the use of economic muscle on the part of agents.[15] Each adopts varying degrees of "firmness", with corresponding facility to "hold-up" joint activities. She concludes that, p. 70:

> Incomplete contracts and power are keys to understanding the structure of economic institutions.

---

15   Hart is a leading exponent of incomplete contract theory, for which he received the Nobel Prize in 2016.

In such terms, the underlying methodology based on individual optimisation evaporates from immediate view.[16]

Indeed, the new approach to economic history does not advertise its dependence upon methodological individualism, the unshifting ingredient in its (continuing) reliance upon a shifting neoclassical economics. It is far more concerned to emphasise outcomes in terms of explaining social organisation within and between firms. Yet, the reductionism of the approach is made clear at times (Lamoreaux et al. 1999, p. 9/10) requoting the last sentence from above to pinpoint the role of both historians and history:[17]

> For business historians to provide theorists with this kind of intellectual discipline, they have to communicate their findings in a way that economists can appreciate ... All that is necessary is that they share with economists a few fundamental assumptions about how human beings behave. Too often, historians have reacted to the limitations of the neoclassical approach by attacking the notion of economic rationality itself – by challenging the idea that at its heart economic behavior is fundamentally a matter of weighing the expected outcomes of alternative decisions in a systematic fashion. But this is throwing out the baby with the bath water. One does not have to assume that economic actors are all-knowing to believe that they make the most advantageous choices they can on the basis of the limited information they possess. Thanks to recent developments, economists are now employing a more commonsensical notion of rationality – one that business historians should be able to embrace without doing violence to any of their deeply held beliefs about the importance of context, ideas, or culture. As a result, historians can offer economists intellectual discipline simply by focusing their efforts on what they are well-trained to do: elucidating what economic actors actually know at any given point in time, how they use their knowledge to make informed choices, and how they learn from their past decisions.

---

16   Further, US radical political economy has in part been won to these forms of argument. For example, for an explicit account of power as arising out of incomplete contracts, see Bowles and Gintis (2000), and also Slater and Spencer (2000) for a critique of such transaction costs economics.

17   Note the previously observed role being assigned to historians as providers of raw materials to economists to allow model selection and specification of initial conditions.

At risk of pedestrian pursuit of metaphor, it is the social in the form of the bath itself that has been discarded even if retaining and refining its prior contents – optimising babies, only awash in a douche of imperfect information.

Further, just as the new economics is ahistorical in building up timelessly from the idea of optimising individuals in a world of imperfect information, contracts and markets, so it is *asocial* in other respects. As is apparent from the assertion of the last two sentences of the last quotation, the notions of context, idea and culture are simply being reduced to the distribution and use of "information", which is itself understood unproblematically. Context, ideas or culture are about a more commonsensical notion of rationality. This is all to set aside entirely, not to incorporate as discussed later, the lessons to be learnt from the postmodernist, and preceding, understandings of knowledge as socially constructed. Information is not given and either known or unknown, it is the consequence of its contextually contested, chaotic, contradictory and constructed interpretation and use. Discarding perfect competition and information or, more exactly, seeing them as a special case, does not match up to incorporating the cultural which is thereby reduced to informational imperfections and how they are handled. As Lipartito (1995, p. 34) neatly puts it in his assessment of the role of culture (or lack of it) in business history:

> Some economic models today treat firms as temporal, intentional actors, acknowledging that they acquire new knowledge and correct past mistakes. But all this learning is rather more like that of the smart machine than the human mind.

Nor is this corrected by disaggregating the firm, firms or the nation into smart machines and nor is this learning attached to social and economic relations, structures, agencies and conflicts other than as a collection of individual interpersonal connections.

The new approach, then, like its underlying economic theory, is asocial as a result of its being ahistorical.[18] As this charge is liable to be denied in view of the inclusion of "time and context", it needs to be carefully laid out and justified. Essentially, the "historical" can be understood in at least three different senses.[19] First is the simple passage of (chronological) time, the sequence in which events unfold. Second is the marking of distinct breaks in the nature of society or its processes that have a more or less close correspondence to

---

18   Note Hobsbawm (1997, p. 96) refers to cliometrics as "retrospective econometrics", "because of its a-historicity and the highly restrictive nature of its models". See also p. 112.

19   See Fine (2003d) for a discussion in the context of social capital as ahistorical category.

chronology but which inevitably contain a significant analytical element – the idea, for example, that feudalism precedes capitalism or that production precedes consumption. We cannot make sense of such statements in the absence of an analytical framework, one in which feudalism and capitalism, and production and consumption are defined and related to one another. Third is the recognition that the meanings of our categories of analysis are specific to the society and milieu in which they arise and are used. Production within capitalism is different from production within feudalism or within the home for example. This is obvious in the case of consumption, when it is a slave as opposed to a slave-owner (or a modern wage-worker) that is involved. For one it is a matter of directly reproducing the capacity to work; for the others there is a much greater distance from such mundane considerations. More generally, there is a need to ensure that the categories of analysis that we use are appropriate to their object of study. Why is it that slaves or serfs do not earn a wage or that landlords do not make a profit as opposed to drawing a rent?

It is in this last respect that the new, like the old, approach fails to handle time and context properly. For, fundamentally, the theory depends upon universal categories that have no social or historical specificity – utility, production, technology, factor inputs, etc, and information. This deficiency is only reinforced by adding notions such as, institutions, organisation and information. Ultimately, terms like capital and the firm, and the analytical results attached to them, whilst rooted by origin in capitalist society, are derived transhistorically from the universal categories deployed within neoclassical economics. Further, the models remain deterministic if not determined. One feature is that there are numbers of models from which to choose, with multiple equilibria attached to them. Consequently, history in the form of time and context only arises in order to make model choice and determine initial conditions, or to allow for path dependence. Significantly, all such terms originate with the physical sciences and not with social theory nor the humanities.

Two further features illustrate the reductionism of the new approach. One is its own path dependence. As observed above, it has moved from intra-to inter-firm to national concerns, seamlessly raising the same informational concerns, and their corresponding analytical principles, to a higher or, more exactly, broader stage. It is not difficult to see why. For the theory needs to take as given the conditions within which optimising individuals determine their imperfectly informed decisions. Consequently, it is a simple matter to endogenise such exogenously given constraints by extending the new approach to them. It is an extension that not only creeps from firm to nation (and globe?) but also from economic to non-economic and through history. Where do you stop without relying on unexplained exogeneity? Ultimately, something must be taken as given, and it will tend to be the inappropriately naturalised categories of capital, prices, wages, etc, as well as the individuals as "smart machines" that deploy them. Or will it be the inherited customs and institutions, "the time and context", from which each new round of history proceeds anew?[20] These conundrums surrounding the definition of boundaries between exogenous and endogenous, however, can only be satisfactorily lifted by adopting an alternative methodology, not least one which takes a starting point at the opposite extreme to methodological individualism and its associated reductionism, one in which socially and historically specific are critically unravelled. In short, reflecting the final and most overt reductionism, is capitalism let alone the whole of human history nothing more than the market and non-market response to informational imperfections?

So much for reductionism. In summary, it derives from methodological individualism combined with an understanding of both the economic (market) and non-economic (non-market) worlds as the consequence of consistent interpersonal interactions in response to market (informational) imperfection. Formally, the economic models involved are universal in application so that time and context (history and society) do not enter ab initio. This provides for a blank sheet on which history and society can be filled out by empirical study. Its inclusion focuses upon path dependence (as the way of choosing between model equilibria) and differences in institutions or whatever as the concrete form taken by one path as opposed to another. Universal theory necessarily takes out history. So it can be brought back in when required to confront reality. What better way than by appeal to path dependence and institutions?

The use of institutions for this purpose has been interrogated in Fine and Milonakis (2003) and Milonakis and Fine (2007), in assessing the work of Douglass North, possibly the most prominent economic historian emphasising the role of institutions in history. Path dependence will be taken up in the next chapter through close examination of its use by Paul David, who is significant for having been a strong critic of cliometrics in its earliest phases.[21] First, though, in closing this section, consider how the reductionism of the newer

---

20   Whilst welcoming cliometrics for clarifying hypotheses and arguments and for using counterfactuals as a "nonsense detector", Hobsbawm (1997) suggests that its circularity (given rather than explained constraints) is one of its four weaknesses, the others being ahistorical theory, exclusive preoccupation with rational choice, and undue dependence on unreliable and invented data.

21   Again, neatly and inconveniently motivating the (false) idea that appeal to path dependence is a break with mainstream economics rather than its (potentially) imperialistic enrichment.

economic history imparts a particular flavour to its understanding of both the character of the discipline and its evolution. For the tensions between economic history and economics,[22] it is tempting to understand this in parallel with, or as a parody of, the new approach itself. It is a temptation that a leading practitioner finds irresistible (Temin, 1995, p. 316):

> Research, expressed in the formal, mathematical terms beloved of economic theorists, is not very accessible to business historians. This clash of cultures gives rise to a problem of information flows in our disciplines that mirrors the problems we analyze.

In a nutshell, drawing primarily on the experience of the United States, initial divisions within business history at the turn of the century are perceived to have focused on theory versus description. The latter is implicitly criticised for seeking generalisation out of accumulation of case studies rather than investigation of "the discipline of the market that ... could provide insight into larger economic processes" (Lamoreaux et al. 1999, p. 3). Lack of appropriate theory ultimately motivated and paved the way for neoclassical theory to be introduced, prompting the meteoric rise of cliometrics but with a greater emphasis upon markets than entrepreneurship. Its influence grew "to dominate the Economic History Association", leading to the formation of the rival Business History Conference, "to provide historians fleeing the cliometric revolution with a new organizational base" (Lamoreaux et al. 1999, p. 5). Their emphasis was placed more on the cultural and social side of economic history, and designated as social history.

Such institutional and intellectual fragmentation of economic history is in part explained by the weaknesses of the "traditional" neoclassical economics, most notably its excessive reliance upon perfect markets and its inability to explain long-run development. In this light, Lamoreaux comes to the conclusion that the cliometric revolution has not only run its course, as suggested by Field in having successfully established itself, but has failed. This is so in two senses. First, it has been an intellectual failure precisely because of its narrow foundation within neoclassical economics. Second, it has been an institutionalised failure. Despite its renewal through the information-theoretic approach, that purports both to accept blame for past crudities and to correct them, cliometrics now finds itself in an intellectual ghetto. Lamoreaux suggests that, for "the cliometric revolution ... over the long term its impact has been relatively

---

22   See especially Lamoreaux et al. (1997 and 1999) and Lamoreaux (1998a).

limited", p. 59 and, in closing her piece, she "highlights the intellectual costs that disciplinary fragmentation can entail", p. 77. Having bitten the forbidden fruit of market imperfections in the original cliometric garden of as if perfectly working markets, the newer economic history finds itself banished from the Eden of social history.

The picture that emerges then is one of an unfortunate early and over-zealous application (by "'Young Turks'", p. 63) of an inappropriate economic theory to economic history. This had the effect of fragmenting the discipline of history across borders that hardened and became increasingly difficult to cross. The major exception is to be found amongst the new brand of economic historians who have broken from the earlier version of cliometrics. They command the necessary historical skills as well as the necessary economic theory. The pity is, by virtue both of the difficulties of economic theory itself and the institutionalised and entrenched fragmentation of history, that considerable obstacles persist to the acceptance and flourishing of the new approach. Thus, the account of the rise of cliometrics, and the assessment of its current state and prospects, represents a remarkable self-application of the new approach! Path-dependent intellectual developments are promoted or impeded by the institutions to which they give rise and respond.

The downbeat assessment of the prospects for cliometrics in its new-found form is possibly a consequence of the novelty at its time of writing in the mid-1990s. This was just as the new phase of economics imperialism had yet to accelerate its influence across other social sciences as well as economic history. Putting this aside as well as the favourable embrace offered to the information-theoretic approach, there are some parallels between her account and our own of the rise, if not for me, the fall, of cliometrics. But closer examination of her account reveals considerable absences and/or anomalies. First observe, though, how much there is an affinity with orthodox approaches to the history of economic thought within neoclassical economics. These view the contributions of the past through the prism of the present, presumed to be correct, and setting the standard and understanding towards which the past has evolved. Tick off Smith, Ricardo and Marx to the extent to which they anticipate general or partial equilibrium and its constituent components. Similarly, Lamoreaux offers a parallel reading of how the economic history of the past is, or is not, evolving, adding the twist of path-dependent institutionalised obstacles to adoption of best practice. In short, transposing from wealth to ideas, the approach offers an answer to the question jokingly posed to economists, "if you are so smart, how come you are not rich".

Significantly, emphasis upon the thwarted fortunes of the new approach by the intellectual traditions and institutions of the discredited past corresponds exactly to what Stiglitz claims of his own attempts to shake up old-style neoclassical economics through promotion of the information-theoretic approach.[23] It is surely no accident that these common sources of frustration are to be found in the United States. This points to the significance of factors other than the intellectual in the evolution of economics, economic history and the relations between them. To be fair, Lamoreaux does make fleeting references to the external world, not least in suggesting that fragmentation of history as a discipline was promoted in the post-Sputnik period, as money became available from government and private foundations "to support initiatives in the hard social sciences", p. 63. Further, "the spread of cliometrics abroad depended in large measure on its intellectual appeal, which in turn was limited by the perceived narrowness and conservatism of the neoclassical models on which it was based", p. 70. As a result, its basis in perfectly working markets proved far from palatable to Latin American dependency theory, and the same applied to the assumption of economic rationality in French historical circles. In addition, she suggests that an econometric revolution and econometric imperialism originally promoted cliometrics in the United States, recognising that, "in recent years as American-style neoclassical economics has spread internationally, so has cliometrics", p. 71. Yet, whilst it is inappropriate to draw crude and direct intellectual implications from US hegemony, much greater emphasis must be placed on how economic history has forgotten political economy in its turn to the "hard social sciences". This is so not only in the United States, where the latter might be expected to flourish, but also, under US leadership, in and from Latin America, France and elsewhere.

Unfortunately, the squeezing out of political economy in the rise of cliometrics is an important but overlooked element in Lamoreaux's account and, it might be added, in her own economics. It is neglected either by simple omission or by a reading of the past through the prism of the thwarted rise of the information-theoretic approach. A section on "Economic History before Cliometrics", for example, makes no reference to Schumpeter, and he is only mentioned after the event as the inspiration for a source of opposition to cliometrics from those seeking to emphasise entrepreneurship as a creative act rather than, presumably, an optimising one, p. 68. More generally, the pre-cliometrics period is seen as being based more on ideological rather than theoretical or methodological differences. For, "progressive historians typically focused on the negative, exploitative aspects of capitalism, whereas economic historians were more likely to appreciate the material gains that economic

---

23   Stiglitz (2002) for example.

development brought and to seek to understand the institutional foundations of that improvement", p. 61.

With exploitation implicitly overlooked as a category for examining capitalism theoretically, it is not surprising that the awkward-to-include contributions of Rostow immediately preceding the emergence of cliometrics, are also overlooked. Instead, the post-war period is assessed in terms of reducing scholars such as Landes and Chandler to a stance in which they "felt that neoclassical theory had little to contribute to the study of entrepreneurship. After an active search for a usable alternative, they turned to Parsonian sociology instead ... [and] consistently employed concepts and addressed debates at the heart of this sociological literature, even when they did not make extensive use of its rather arcane vocabulary and categories of analysis", p. 63. In contrast, the turn to cliometrics is explained as a result, particularly strong in the United States as opposed to Europe, of the wish "to make the study of the past more systematic and objective, less subject to ideological contamination or bias", p. 59.

In Lamoreaux's short account of the rise of cliometrics, it is understandable, even excusable, for there to be omissions. But, as is apparent, the substance that is there, whatever its deficiencies in terms of descriptive content and ideological biases, is framed in a way that interprets its analytical content as inferior and obstacle to own contribution. This is primarily a result of its simply serving as a side-show in the emergence of the new approach. For the latter, as already observed, is deemed to occupy the higher intellectual ground. Lamoreaux (1998a, p. 75) effectively claims that economics is difficult but history is easy, with historians unable or unwilling to keep up with advances in scholarship:[24]

> Not only have the two groups of academics deprived themselves of the benefits of cross-fertilization of ideas, but because practitioners on either

---

24   Here, though, she is in agreement with Hobsbawm (1997, p. 58): "I have ... had close contact with a discipline which does call for considerable brain-power, or at least nimbleness, namely economics at Cambridge, UK and USA, and I have never forgotten this salutary but depressing experience of trying to keep up with a much cleverer body of people". However, he continues from his Marshall Lectures of 1980, p. 95: "For economics, or rather that part of it which from time to time claims a monopoly of defining the subject, has always been a victim of history. For lengthy periods, when the world economy appears to be rolling on quite happily with or without advice ... proper economics has the floor, improper is tacitly excluded, or consigned to the twilight of past and present heterodoxy, the equivalent of faith-healing or acupuncture in medicine ... However, from time to time history catches economists at their brilliant gymnastics and walks off with their overcoats".

side of the divide have failed to keep abreast of developments on the other, they have not upheld the profession's minimal standards of scholarly competence. Because keeping up with the economic history literature required more effort for historians than the reverse did for cliometricians, the negative consequences have been particularly apparent on the historical side ... [who] continue to evince an often painful naiveté about economic concepts, equating, for example, market behavior with the narrow pursuit of profits and suggesting that the mere existence of markets can somehow force a supply response from unwilling participants.

On the other hand, the new approach boasts scholars of a different calibre, p. 76:[25]

> All these economic historians are well read in the historical literature, and many of them have done extensive archival research. Their studies are of high quality and should be of great interest to historians working in related areas. Whether, however, it is possible to communicate this relevance over the wall that currently divides economic history from the rest of the profession is a matter of serious concern.

Indeed, not only does this inequality in capabilities prevail currently, it has also characterised the past. For, in the context of *Time on the Cross*, Lamoreaux suggests that because critics of cliometrics "did not themselves have the knowledge or skills to determine the effect on the models of changing assumptions they found unreasonable, they tended to dismiss the whole literature as suspect, a reaction that was reinforced by the underlying ideological divisions between cliometricians, on the one hand, and most historians, on the other", p. 74. Some historians did challenge *Time on the Cross* on its own terms, especially David et al. (1976), "from its philosophical underpinnings to the correctness of its economic theory to the appropriateness of its quantitative tests to its handling of historical data", p. 73. But this had the effect of consolidating fragmentation, with other (less ably-equipped) historians no longer taking the trouble to read and engage with cliometrics, p. 75.

---

25   See also Raff (1998, p. 57) who posits perceptions by economists of traditional business histories in the following terms: "The typical example contains much admiring prose, not much analysis, very little comparison, and practically no explicit theorizing. The best works provide provocative food for thought: but most will suggest to economists that business history is a subject better suited to the Department of Public Relations than to the Department of Economics".

This assessment is remarkably lacking in circumspection and, unhappily, accepts too readily what has long been and remains a common weapon used by mainstream economists against its opponents – that they lack the technical skills to understand the significance of mathematical models and empirical testing. Lamoreaux sees it as ironic that cliometrics should be gaining influence abroad from the late 1980s just as it was losing influence in the United States. This was, however, not only a result of the antipathy displayed by historians but also, equally ironically, of economists to cliometrics as they increasingly dedicated themselves to mastering mathematical techniques at the expense of "historical knowledge and research skills", p. 71. Indeed, "as a result, economic history increasingly came to be seen as an unaffordable luxury, and [economics] departments began to cut positions and eliminate required courses from the curriculum", p. 72. Is it surprising in such circumstances that those who opposed cliometrics should fail to rise to its challenge? Debate was precluded by developments within economics itself. In addition, this raises questions over the supposed intellectual superiority of economists and economics. If it is so much harder than the softer social theory in general, and history in particular, why should economists have been unable to acknowledge the limitations of their assumptions and approach for so long. And, as we have seen, how is it that they continue to do so even with the adoption of the new approach to economic history?[26]

Whatever the relative intellectual merits of economists and other social sciences, Lamoreaux exaggerates the significance and duration of the impact of the mathematical and econometric turn (more exactly, obsession) of economics in the 1970s in terms of the discipline's introspection with respect to economic history and more generally.[27] After an initial scarcity of mathematical economists, these were soon being turned out in conveyor belt quantities and training their eye on the other disciplines. Initially, in the 1970s, mathematical economics was inspired by the New Classical Economics that represented the extreme academic version of monetarism – assuming agents are rational in all respects, including processing of information, and that all markets work perfectly and instantaneously. This allows for the conclusion that government intervention is at best ineffective and at worst a source of inefficiency.

---

26 Note that Gary Becker (1990, p. 29) takes a different view, explaining modestly (false or otherwise) why he became an economist in the following terms, "After reading Parsons, I decided sociology was just too difficult for me".

27 Her suggestion that "research in economic history appeared to have fewer direct policy implications", p. 72, is also short-sighted, not least in how it has engaged with development economics and the scholarship and ideology of the World Bank.

Increasingly, over the last two decades, these developments around macroeconomics have been transplanted into the microeconomics of the information-theoretic approach, with a more measured stance on the virtues of government and markets.

This is, of course, the origin of Lamoreaux's hopes around a new economic history. For her, p. 75/6:[28]

> Abandoning the convenient but unrealistic assumptions of traditional neoclassical theory ... economists have begun to reconceptualize the world as a place where information is scarce, imperfect, and costly, where people build institutions in order to cope with problems of imperfect information, where human beings' 'bounded rationality' affects their economic decision making, and where economic processes can have multiple outcomes depending on participants' perceptions of each other's actions.

The anomaly here is that such reconceptualisations are far from new as well as the criticisms of mainstream economics that have accompanied them. This means that the novelty lies precisely in their adoption by mainstream economics with a corresponding conformity to its methodology. This is rendered obvious by what is the most striking anomaly in Lamoreaux's account – the manner in which she suggests that the concerns of historians have been met by the new approach.

In a section entitled the "'Linguistic Turn' in History *and* Economics", emphasis added, there is an explicit identification between the concerns of postmodernism and the information-theoretic turn in economics, with the latter displaying "parallels in intriguing ways [to] the emergence of critical theory in the humanities", p. 75. For, it is suggested that, p. 76:

> The questions at the heart of this new work – how do economic actors know what (they think) they know, and how does what (they think) they know affect their behavior? – are remarkably similar to those that inform the work of the new cultural historians.

---

28   Significantly, Lamoreaux cites North as having abandoned the original cliometrics for the failings of neoclassical economics, p. 69. But, as revealed in Fine and Milonakis (2003) and Milonakis and Fine (2007), North's reservations run much deeper and different than can be accommodated by the information-theoretic approach.

This is simply and fundamentally incorrect but significant in revealing how limited is the understanding of the cultural and the social more generally in the new approach. On the one hand, the postmodernist and cultural, let alone the linguistic, turns of social theory have proceeded without touching (mainstream) economics at all. Even and especially in its new information-theoretic approach, the concerns of social theory with the meaning of categories both to agents and within analysis itself has been totally absent.[29] In effect, the only thing that the recent developments in economics share with the linguistic turn is the terminology of culture, norms and the like. Not surprisingly, there is no recognition on the part of the new approach that its notion of information (and culture itself!) borders on the cultureless, as is apparent from a vast historical and other literature on the nature of culture.[30] In short, through its filter, the scope of economic and social theory that is recognised by the new approach is extraordinarily narrow.[31]

Indeed, Lamoreaux's account of the thwarted evolution of the new approach needs to be turned upside-down, or is it inside-out? If dubious comparisons are to be made between the difficulty of doing economics and history, surely the evidence suggests how more demanding is (the theoretical element of) history, especially for those trained in economics both before and after recent developments. The latter's special type of methodological individualism does not simply display an unwillingness and inability, however critically, to incorporate the contributions made by postmodernism and any genuinely social theory more generally – lest it be to reconstruct it parasitically in its own image. Rather, there is a virtue made out of ignorance along the lines of what we do not understand (and/or cannot incorporate into a deterministic model subject to econometric testing) is not of relevance. Further, these failings on the part of economics, and its application through the newer economic history where

---

29   Hence absence of consideration of consumption in the new approach, the site par excellence of postmodernism's preoccupation with meaning, identity, etc.

30   Temin (1997) does encourage reference to culture in studying industrial performance, contrasting Anglo-Saxon with Japanese, the individualistic with the collective, respectively, wrapping each in the equally superficial terminology of social capital. He cites Aoki (1988) for proposing the notion of the J-firm as a coalition of stockholders and labour. As the title of his book reflects, Aoki has played a leading role in transposing the information-theoretic approach to the study of East Asia on which see especially Hayami and Aoki (1998).

31   Even by the standards of the current author as economist rather than historian by training! But see Misa (1999, p. 251): "Given the present diversity of approaches in business and economic history (a short list must include Chandlerian, institutional, evolutionary, and cultural approaches) ... [it] needs more explicitly to justify its approach and to relate its approach to these others".

culture, etc are, thereby, reduced to information-theoretic problems, lead it to ratchet up its highly esoteric technicism and formalism. This is used to explain why its superior intellectual stances are failing to prosper – as a result of ignorance, inability and backyard intellectual protectionism.

For, whilst there are now a group of younger Turks, trained both in the new techniques and as historians, Lamoreaux remains pessimistic over whether the wall between them and historians can be bridged since the latter are, "more interested in understanding specific historical circumstances", p. 76. Once again, then, the deficiencies of historians are emphasised both in terms of their parochial focus in scholarship and their inability to recognise the value of more abstract reasoning, as purveyed by the proponents of the new approach. For, p. 76:

> The models they build are highly abstract and mathematical and, to the uninitiated observer, appear to bear little or no connection to actual circumstances, whether current or historical.

By contrast, the problem is that the models do not bear any connection to circumstances. Such a perspective casts a very different light on why the newer economic history should emerge in the current intellectual milieu. For the limitations of economics as a methodology for investigating history had long been recognised and accepted by economists themselves in the traditional division between the social sciences, with those such as Becker seen as rogue exceptions.[32] The information-theoretic approach has blown away such reservations as all social theory, and history, comes within its compass. It does so at a price – the need to set aside the "traditional" but far from the universal ideological nostrum of the old-style neoclassical economics – that markets work perfectly and the non-market works like the market. But it is a cost that can be easily borne as it renders the new approach more rounded in its understanding of the individual and of the social, and more palatable to other social scientists sufficiently intimidated by its technicism and sufficiently deceived by its reductionist claims. Further, far from the new approach beginning to incorporate the concerns of the postmodernist turn in cultural history, it denies them in all but name. And its success in suggesting otherwise depends on the

---

32   Note, as argued by Velthuis (1999), Parsons insisted upon a separation between economics and sociology, not so much for their subject matter as for their methods, one dealing with the individual and the other with the social, respectively. Presumably this would imply, to the extent that economic history draws upon sociology, that it should not draw simultaneously upon economics!

current dual turns away from both postmodernism and neo-liberalism across the social sciences.

4   Concluding Remarks

In short, in Lamoreaux's hands, the only social theory recognised in the making of cliometrics is Parsonian sociology, with postmodernism as a latter day source of guilty conscience. And neoclassical economics is the only representative of economic theory. All other relevant history and theory is reduced to, and dismissed as, atheoretical and/or anti-theoretical descriptive investigation! Not surprisingly, her narrative is one of the eventual movement of the intellectual vanguard away from flawed traditional economics to an uncritically accepted new approach, which the uninformed or incapable are either personally or institutionally discouraged from embracing. The idea that the past rejection of the new economic history, as well as its newer version, might be on the basis of alternative methods and theory is effectively not acknowledged.[33] Rather, conveniently, the rejection of the earlier assault from economics is seen as justified in principle on grounds of its attachment to perfect competition even if it was often rejected in practice for what were the wrong reasons by those perceived to be anti-theoretical. This allows the new economics to be projected as delivering the traditional from its deficiencies, for continuing resistance to be explained but interpreted as unjustified, and for alternative criticisms of the economic theory and its interaction with social theory to be overlooked together with its associated alternatives. Perhaps such rough justice to historiography is to be expected since what constitutes the economic has merely been moved marginally from traditional neoclassical economics to incorporate informational imperfections and asymmetries, with a corresponding understanding of the non-economic as non-market response to market imperfections. Effectively, from a position of having excluded the social, or treating it as the economic by other means, the social has been brought back in on the narrowest of bases, with the result that the vast majority of economic and social history and theory remains excluded from consideration as such.

These developments, and the way in which Lamoreaux interprets them, follow from the nature of economics as a discipline on which the new approach,

---

33   It is ironic, for example, that Lamoreaux's (1998a) contribution should lie cheek-by-jowl in an edited collection with Ross' (1998) study of social history which covers, for example, the influence of the Annales School which, presumably, must be judged by its omission by Lamoreaux to be unconcerned with economic issues.

like the old, so heavily draws. For it has been heavily associated with the extraordinary process of eliminating heterodox alternatives to the mainstream both in terms of methodology and technique. Mathematical models, methodological individualism and econometrics rule the profession to an unprecedented degree in what has been termed the internationalisation or Americanisation of the discipline by neoclassical economics.[34] Inevitably, in the US academic heartland, the colonisation of economic history will rely more or less exclusively on mainstream economics as much in the past as in the new future. It is worth recalling the earlier warning sounded half-jokingly by Heaton (1965, p. 467) on the occasion of the twenty-fifth anniversary of the Economic History Association:

> In fact, American research on European topics was so all pervading that some nasty-minded person may one day describe it as Yankee academic imperialism.

Despite the different traditions within the UK both in terms of economics and economic and social history, Lamoreaux (1998a, p. 71) is still able to report a 50% cliometric content for the *Economic History Review* for 1994. In short, the understanding of her and her colleagues' approach by Lamoreaux, as a break with the new economic history is wrong, other than minimally in adding market imperfections into the mix. That these being absent is the reason for the break between the new economic history and social history is also wrong. And last, and by no means least, that the newer economic history will put such wrongs to rights is fanciful. On the contrary, the newer economic history has paved the way for the breach between economic and social history to be sustained and strengthened as well as preparing the ground for the newest economic history in which the past is viewed through the prism of the

---

34   See Coats (ed.) (1996). Particularly disturbing is the declining number of US students taking PhDs in economics whilst those studying there from abroad continue to increase (Coats, 1996). See also Hodgson and Rothman (1999, p. F165) who report that over 70% of the editors of the "top" thirty economic journals are located in the United States, almost 40% in twelve institutions alone. Two-thirds of articles are of US authorship, the top twelve institutions accounting for over 20%. As they conclude, "the degree of institutional and geographical concentration of editors and authors may be unhealthy for innovative research". For the UK, in the light of study of the impact of the Research Assessment Exercise on the discipline of economics, see Lee and Harley (1998) who suggest that non-mainstream economics could be eliminated from British economics departments within ten years! More recently, for the (US) dominance of the mainstream and decline of heterodoxy, see Aigner (2021) and Javdani and Chang (2019).

consequences of market imperfections plus the addition of other, more or less random variables to suit – all in line with developments of economics imperialism in its own third phase.

In this light, it would be unfortunate if those who have been, or are, unwilling to embrace the newer economic history respond by retreating into culturalist analysis. For this would be to concede the economic in economic and other history. It is imperative both to offer and develop alternatives that appropriately incorporate an economic *and* a "cultural" content. Such alternatives depend upon not falling into the clichéd patterns of analysis which are portrayed by the new approaches as filling out what they do not or cannot cover themselves. It is necessary to embrace theory and to make it explicit, not least to draw upon a political economy which is appropriate to the issues being addressed, with a social and historical content sensitive to the specific period and object under study. Most often, if not always, this involves an understanding of capital and capitalism, as both economic and cultural. The challenge is particularly urgent for, just as economics is seeking to colonise the other social sciences, so the extreme form of influence of postmodernism is on the wane. The chances are that the role of economics across the social sciences is set to increase as they incorporate a more substantial concession to material realism. What content and form such economics is to take is yet to be determined. But the outcome will depend upon the extent to which and the way in which a colonising economics is either accepted, incorporated or resisted, in business history as more generally across other social sciences.[35] It would be surprising if economic and social history were to be totally colonised by a newer economic history, given the institutionalised separation that has resulted from past assaults. But, both for the sake of history and economics, it would also be unfortunate if the response were to be one of flight to the cultural "ghetto" through neglect of the economic and economic theory.[36]

---

35   Irrespective of the validity of its judgements in practice as opposed to principle, the imperative implied by Douglas and Isherwood (1996, p. xxvi) in the new introduction to the *World of Goods*, can only be applauded: "Methodological individualism is now so much under attack that the only thing wanting for its defeat is a range of alternative assumptions to take its place, and several are in the air".

36   Fine (2001b, Chapter 2) develops some analytical propositions in the context of alternatives to social capital, and Fine (2000c) discusses how culture and economics might be satisfactorily combined in historical studies (of consumption) with Auslander (1996a and b) and Coffin (1994) for example, cited as exemplary illustrative case studies.

CHAPTER 9

From QWERTY to Microsoft and Beyond

Postscript as Personal Preamble

In preparing a separate book, then two, on the relationships between political economy, economic theory, economics imperialism and economic history, Dimitris Milonakis and myself had much material already drafted from around the turn of the millennium. We had also made extensive preparation, and some drafting, for what were rapidly evolving and expanding assaults from the new (as if perfect market) and the newer (as if imperfect market) economic history. Ultimately, the economic history books were never completed and published (even though designated to appear with Routledge in 2005). As a result, the material presented here derives from drafts untouched from before 2005, long before even our more general books on economics imperialism (Fine and Milonakis, 2009; Milonakis and Fine 2009) were published.

It means that the explicit specification of the newer phase of economics imperialism, and the corresponding, newest economic history had yet to be identified, as this only occurred immediately after the two books were published, with reference to the "suspension" of the core principles of mainstream economics (optimisation, production and utility functions, general equilibrium, etc) so that more or less any variable could be included in economic analysis irrespective of its compatibility with those principles. The term suspension is deployed since the core principles continue to play a major organising role, either being added to, however much coherently and consistently, or as the centre around which deviations are explained by the addition of other considerations – as it were, this is why the moon is not made of cheese.

In short, the material offered here is on the cusp of the entry of the newest economic history onto the scene (and our realisation of it). This is clear in the reference to narrative economics (and economic history) which has taken off in a small way subsequently. The attention to Paul David and path dependency was prominent at the time but is less so now. It does mark a key insight into the nature of how history matters is interpreted. The response by Liebowitz and Margolis was considered less important, a fanciful and even ridiculous promotion of neoliberal scholarship. The text on them was drafted to be an appendix, a curiosum, but is included here as a section. There is also passing reference to path dependence as a weapon in the battles with Microsoft over software. At the time, this was early days. Others, such as Google, Facebook and Apple, are now embroiled over such issues which now also encompass gaming, artificial intelligence, social media and so on.

1   Introduction[1]

As discussed in passing elsewhere in this volume, the new, newer and newest economic history are marked by two enduring aspects, in tension with one another and, as a result, subject to more or less conscious accommodation, never entirely satisfactorily whether, in their combination, at one extreme, the other or somewhere in between. The first aspect is to conform closely to the dictates of the corresponding phases of economics imperialism – the economic and the social as if perfectly working markets, as if (the response to) imperfectly working markets, and as if some combination of the other two with other considerations added to suit as old is replaced by new and then newer economics imperialism. The second aspect is for training in history, and its very subject matter and methods – dealing in the long terms and non-economic causes and consequences (and their attachments to more rounded social science more generally) – to leave a residual sense of doubt and guilt over the reductionisms involved in succumbing to the dictates of economics imperialism.

The result has been for a flourishing inclusion of any number of historical and social factors to augment analyses, to bring back in, BBI, what has been left out, but also inevitably to reduce these also to the thrust of economics imperialism. This chapter offers a critical presentation of a small selection of case studies. I begin in section 1, with one example and contributor, path dependence and Paul David, respectively, not least because he has attracted some prominence in light of the appeal of his compelling case study of the persistence of, QWERTY, or the familiar standard keyboard – from manual typewriter

---

1   Apart from the introduction and concluding remarks, the content of this chapter was primarily drafted before the mid-noughties. The chapter was initially intended to be combined with the previous to serve as a single chapter for the study of the relationship between economic theory and economic history under the second (new, market imperfection) phase of economics imperialism and the corresponding second phase of cliometrics, the newer economic history. In the body of the text, little attempt has been made to take account of developments around the case studies in the intervening twenty years or so, other than to remark on the relationship to the newer economics imperialism and newest economic history, each's third phase (neither of which were dubbed as such at the time of initial drafting although the associated developments were both apparent and observed).

to any number of electronic devices – despite its dissonance with even more knowledge of, and familiarity with, the more longstanding standard alphabet.

This is followed by an account of the endearing riposte to Paul David by Liebowitz and Margolis. They are subject to what Carrier and Miller (eds) (1998) term "Virtualism: The New Political Economy" – an approach which wishes everything worked like a perfect market, scarcely recognises that it does not, and is (to be) made to do so by the non-economic acting to bring about a perfect market when the market does not work perfectly itself. There is, correspondingly, little need for state intervention. Hayek and efficacious spontaneous order on speed is embraced across both market and non-market. It is a bit of that old chestnut – if something were worth doing, it would have been done already, whether by the market or otherwise. As a result, there is little or no (inefficient) path dependence; where it persists, it is not worth the effort of putting it right; and in the unlikely event that it is worth putting right, it would have happened already. We live in the best of worlds if left best to individuals to get on with it.[2]

---

2 Lest you think I lampoon and exaggerate, consider the summary from Puffert (2019, pp. 1589/ 90) with apologies for length: "The most prominent skeptics of the importance of path dependence, S.J. Liebowitz and Stephen E. Margolis (1994, 1995a) argued that forward-looking optimizing behavior is likely to override Arthur's mechanisms for path dependence in any context where outcomes truly matter. In their analysis, adopters who choose among alternative technologies would typically have foresight into future payoffs of their choices, not just current payoffs. Furthermore, adopters and other agents would have opportunities to coordinate adopters' choices through communication, various sorts of market transactions, and the ownership and profit-seeking promotion of alternative competing products or technologies – in short, actions that internalize the mutual externalities of adopters' choices. Thus, they argued, purposeful, incentivized behavior can frequently override nonsystematic or random elements in a selection process, and path dependence can only affect aspects of the economy that no economic agent has an opportunity or incentive to change. Liebowitz and Margolis allowed that path dependence might affect (1) aspects of the economy with no implications for efficiency or else (2) outcomes whose efficiency consequences had previously been unforeseeable and thus not subject to rational economic behavior. In the second case, agents might later express naïve regret that an outcome with higher payoffs had not been chosen, but Liebowitz and Margolis argued that it would not be meaningful to call the chosen outcome inefficient. Efficiency, they urged, should be defined in relation to what can be pursued on the basis of available information and feasible purposeful actions. In contrast to the first two cases, Liebowitz and Margolis expressed skepticism that path dependence would affect outcomes in a further case, where (3) an inferior outcome is locked-in despite the existence, at some point in time, of both the foresight and the means to direct a selection process to a superior outcome. In that case, they argued, path dependence would be the result of irrational errors, or inefficiencies that are (or had been) profitably remediable but nonetheless remain unremedied. They urged that economists cease looking for causal significance in small events or historical accidents, except perhaps in analyzing error-prone

Section 4 offers some commentary on what is a friendlier approach to market imperfections, highlighting especially the BBI of narrative. This is itself indicative of the continuing BBI of institutions, culture and the like, anticipating the move towards the newest economic history. Nonetheless, Section 5 gets back to business as usual with the core of the newer economic history through select reference to the contributions of Nic Crafts. Section 6 also offers a return, to the work of Lamoreaux, covered in some detail in the previous chapter, but focusing here on finance in particular. The concluding remarks re-emphasise the historian's dilemma through the phases of economics imperialism and its associated phases of economic history – how to be both an historian and an economist.

2   David and the Two Goliaths – Economics and History

Paul David has been well-known for his antipathy to the new economic history as it emerged and for posing an alternative based on path dependence. Significantly, much of the thrust from within the newer economic history, and economics imperialism more generally in its assault upon other social sciences, as market imperfections come to the fore, can draw upon path dependence not least because the new-found theories of market imperfections allow for it so readily in terms of the impact of hysteresis, multiple equilibria, complex dynamics, and the corresponding influence of initial or random conditions.[3] More specifically, it is possible to boil down the idea of path dependence to two approaches depending on how it understands context and contingency, distinguishing between weak and strong versions (Fine, 2001b, Chapter 7). The weak version is fully compatible in its theoretical form with mainstream economics, essentially dependent on the continuing effect of market and non-market responses to market imperfections across all of the factors listed at the end of the penultimate sentence. The strong version understands path dependence (and contingency and context) in an entirely different way that is analytically incompatible with the weak version. For the latter is entirely deterministic (other than in a stochastic sense) but, more important, continues to

---

government actions, and focus instead on "the neoclassical model of relentlessly rational behavior leading to efficient, and therefore predictable, outcomes" (Liebowitz and Margolis 1995, 207)". Puffert offers an excellent overview of path dependence but see also debate across Kay (2013 a and b) Arthur (2013) and Margolis (2013).

3   Note that random effects need not be exogenous (or due to shocks) but can be generated within the system – by probabilistic strategic behaviour, for example.

be ahistorical and asocial in failing to confront the shifting meaning of the concepts that it deploys, most notably in reference to capital, labour and so on, but also in, for example, the cultural in corporate culture other than as a strategic or inherited response to market imperfections.[4] This is simply methodologically and theoretically inadequate, for concepts need to be consciously socially and historically rooted in, and delimited by, the societies to which they are applied. This is one justifiably enduring lesson to be learnt from postmodernism, although it does not originate there.

How does David's work reflect these conundrums? In recent papers, he has provided a two-page set of references to his own work entitled, "A Chronological Listing of Selected Works by Paul A. David on Conceptual and Methodological Aspects of Path Dependence in Economics",[5] and these have been consulted as far as possible along with others not listed. It is relatively easy to place him in relation to the new economic history as it evolved. From the first listed paper (David, 1969) a commentary on Fogel's assessment of the importance of railways to the United States' economic development, he emerges as a critic of the older-style cliometrics. He does so from a position of emphasising the significance of market imperfections. In retrospect, in an opening footnote (David, 1993, p. 210) he describes himself as an "economist-economic historian" but not one of the "the 'new' economic historians ... pretty near indistinguishable from the mass of practitioners of neoclassical economics ... My case, however, is rather different. Most of my working life has been spent as a member of a small dissenting sect –advocating *historical* economics – within the more-or-less tolerant (albeit largely indifferent) society of academic economists". Initially, then, David was caught between the two Goliaths of history and economics. Path dependence has been the means by which he has sought to reconcile their competing claims upon him. As a result, David is best seen as having anticipated subsequent developments both within economics and economic history.[6]

But what exactly is meant by "historical economics"? The answer to this question is closely bound up with the sorts of market imperfections incorporated by David. He did not anticipate the future information-theoretic economics as such. Rather, his concern from the outset has been with the possibly self-reinforcing interactions between systemic components of the economy,

---

4   For an astute critique along these lines, see Lipartito (1995).
5   No longer available but plenty of resources on the internet.
6   Note that David (1999a) reports that McCloskey, despite hostility to his work, acknowledges that it effectively pre-dates (mainstream, neoclassical) endogenous growth theory, on which see Fine (2000b).

thereby imparting path dependence as these become locked together. Thus, David (1971, p. 180) explains limited mechanical reaper adoption in Victorian Britain in terms of the costs of an early start that gave rise to a "farming land-scape" and "of *technical* interrelatedness between equipment and long-lived physical plant". Interestingly, even at this early stage, discussion of his paper concluded that the key issue was how high would be the transaction costs concerning the multiplicity of changes around farm sizes and technology or "the costs of negotiations and of forming a market", p. 214.

A more substantive elaboration of historical economics emerges with the set of papers given at the AEA meetings in December, 1984, organised to deal with the issue, "Economic History: A Necessary though not Sufficient Condition for an Economist".[7] Kindleberger (1986, p. 83) describes it as "one of the most enthusiastically received sessions on the program" and expresses concern that the technicalities attached to economics will squeeze out "a true contact with the facts", p. 90. Whilst there is a more general concern with the extent to which history had been taken out of economics (Parker, 1986a)[8] equally important, if less explicit, is anxiety over the fate of economic history itself.[9] There is considerable disquiet with Arrow's (1986) metaphor of economics as like geology, with history allowing it to apply the universal laws of physics and chemistry. More acceptable is Solow's (1986) view of the limitations, if necessity, of axiomatic models since they are heavily circumscribed by extraneous circumstance and unconsidered factors such as culture, and so a more traditional acceptance of division of labour between the economic and the non-economic and the rational and irrational.

In short, the session was concerned with the role of economics in history and of history in economics at the time just before the new microfoundations, and the new economics imperialism, were about to emerge. A justifiable fear concerned the trend towards historyless economics and economists. David's (1986) own paper to the session has become a cliché, dealing in the lessons to

---

7   Parker (ed.) (1986) includes (some longer versions of) the papers that first appeared in the *American Economic Review*, Papers and Proceedings, vol 75, no 2, 1985, as well as some other papers.

8   See also Parker (1986b) who summarises what economic history might do for economists, observing that all agree that it is appropriate "to encourage the exposure of economists to economic history", p. 93. Rostow (1986, p. 70) like Arrow (1986), regrets lack of knowledge of history of "most contemporary economists". He opines that theorists must acknowledge limitations of models and econometrics, render dynamic what is static for reasons of tractability, and be pragmatic about what can be achieved in light of data availability.

9   In most extreme form in McCloskey's (1986b, p. 69) stance that, as story telling, "economics does not merely have a lot to learn from history: history is what it is".

be drawn from the QWERTY keyboard, put in place when typing was mechanical and with danger of proximate keys jamming if used in close sequence. Once we have learnt to type with QWERTY, there are considerable costs to changing even if it could be arranged, given long lasting machines and skills with them. Accordingly, David emphasises the importance of "technical interrelatedness, scale economies, and irreversibilities due to learning and habituation", p. 46, drawing the more general conclusion that there are, "many more QWERTY worlds lying out there in the past ... to draw adventurous economists into the study of essentially *historical* dynamic processes and so will seduce them into the ways of economic history and a better grasp of their own subject matter", p. 47.[10]

Within a few years, such hopes seem to have been realised.[11] David (1993, p. 29/30) first puts QWERTY in perspective by describing it as:

> most frivolous and, at the same time the most evocative of these tales. A path-dependent process is 'non-ergodic': systems possessing this property cannot shake off the effects of past events, and do not have a limiting, invariant probability distribution that is continuous over the entire space. In the case of deterministic systems, the property of path-dependence manifests itself most immediately through the outcome's 'extreme sensitivity to initial conditions'.

Significantly, however, David then observes that, p. 30:

> In several of my recent essays that have a more explicitly theoretical cast, attention has been drawn to the happy circumstance that those who share similar hopes and visionary delusions can read some favourable signs for the future of our discipline in the latest fashions among economic model builders. More and more frequently theorists are acknowledging the existence of local or global *positive feedback* effects – and consequent

---

10   At the time, the IBM golf ball electric typewriter head seemed to have rendered QWERTY potentially redundant (although latest generations have no idea what it is alongside slide rules).

11   But note that Snooks (1993a, p. xv) remains concerned that: " While most of the significant real-world problems emerge from longrun dynamic processes in society, economics is an abstract and deductive science that employs a shortrun static approach to these problems. There is, in other words, a mismatch between the nature of economic theory and the nature of economic reality. If economics is to develop a realistic longrun dynamic approach, it must not only develop path-dependent theoretical models but also attempt to reconstruct the process of change through time".

multiple equilibria, arising from a variety of mechanisms at the microe-
conomic level. Rather than shunning models with multiple equilibria on
account of their indeterminacy, economists working on central problems
across a surprisingly broad range of specialties in international trade and
finance, location theory, industrial organization, so-called 'new' growth
theory, macroeconomics, and time-series analysis, and still others –
increasingly seem content to leave open a door through which transient
influences, including minor perturbations specific to historical context,
can play a critical part in 'selecting' the particular equilibrium solution
that emerges.

David then does not offer anything by way of critical departure but simply
elaborates that:

> Many underlying sources of positive feedback processes in the economy
> are being elucidated as a consequence of the renewed interest among
> theoretical and empirical researchers in the implications of econo-
> mies of scale, scope and coordination, of Marshallian externalities and
> local network externalities, of endogenous technical progress through
> learning-by-doing and learning-by-using, of habituation phenomena
> affecting tastes and behaviours, and of adaptive cognitive processes
> (such as Bayesian information processing) affecting the formation of
> expectations.

Economists are now understood as seeing such effects everywhere where previously they seemed to be invisible, reflecting the passage of economics' own
path dependence, p. 30/31, and, in particular, the error of having taken history
out of social science, with the latter having been subject to an understanding
based on natural laws, pp. 31–35. In short, for David, economics has begun to
bring history back in, with the prospect of "witnessing a significant intellectual
'regime change' ... with the hopeful prospect of an eventual escape from the
trap of ahistorical economic analysis", p. 36.

It is striking how, from his own perspective, David is describing the foundations of the latest phase of economics imperialism and, for economic history
itself, the renewed process of its colonisation on the basis of the newer and
improved models of market imperfections. Substantively, he puts forward a
number of features that need to be incorporated in future work, p. 38/40: the
presence of hysteresis; because of feedback, the need for inner motivation of
agents to be considered; the presence of multiple and punctuated equilibria;
cognitive uncertainty; and acceptance of the idea that mechanisms of resource

allocation and the structures of material life resemble biological mechanisms, in that they have evolved historically through a sequence of discrete adaptations. Now, with minor exceptions such as token allowance for cognition and values, none of these is incompatible with latest developments in mainstream economics around market imperfections. Of further interest is David's explanation for this regime change in economics and economic history. He sees the timeless and deterministic models of the past as reflecting an intellectual tradition of drawing parallels between society and natural laws that includes and goes back long before Adam Smith.[12] Consequently, as the natural sciences have become increasingly concerned recently with not only what happens but also how as a path-dependent process through time, so have economists grasped the same nettle, especially as enhanced computer power has allowed the qualitative properties of complex dynamic systems to be examined, p. 36.

In this light, it would be easy to conclude that David has been overtaken by and, subsequently, has run alongside, the new developments within and around economics. Indeed, it can be argued that he never departed mainstream economics other than in commitment to the consequences of market imperfections in the form in which he has recognised them. Much writing in the historical economics vein is about adding history to the otherwise unquestioned apparatus of mainstream economics. Thus, David (1975, Chapter 1, p. 2) points to the confusion of understanding technical change in terms of a shift in an aggregate production function. However, the latter is not rejected as an illegitimate analytical device:

> But rather than eschewing any reliance on the neoclassical construct of a smooth, continuous production function, the subsequent studies restrict themselves to employing it circumspectly, at low levels of aggregation.

This is amply demonstrated in his Chapter 2, for example, in restoring the Rothbarth-Habbakuk thesis concerning the direction of induced labour-saving technical progress as a result of availability of cheaper raw materials

---

12   Thus, with selective citation, and reductionist interpretation, of selective authors to make the point, p. 31: "The dominant ahistorical formulation of much modern economic theory has its roots in the bedrock of Western philosophical and scientific traditions ... (and) far antedate the introduction of formal mathematics into our discipline (which) owe their beginnings to lines of thought in Western science that stretch back (well before Adam Smith) to Pascal, Descartes, and farther, all the way to the teleological reasoning of Aristotle". Note that Snooks (1993b, p. 17) disagrees, arguing that the deductivism of economics is modern and arises out of the vulgar promotion of career opportunities.

with which to experiment and produce. As another illustration, David (1993) uses the apparatus of the Edgeworth box to explain how history gets us to one place or another on the contract curve because of a sequence of trading at non-equilibrium prices.[13] Finally, leaping to the present, David (1999a) even defends "blackboard economic theory" against the critique of its use by McCloskey, and posits that the quantitative significance of path dependence is appropriately assessed by use of a path-integral, an implicit acknowledgement of formal mathematical modelling to address the impact of path dependence.[14] Indeed, David (1997) admits that his earlier work (David, 1975) "was written before I was aware of the availability of mathematical techniques for studying stochastic systems that exhibited interesting behaviors (of the path dependent sort) with which my historical investigations were concerned".

These are all examples of the reliance upon mainstream economics that could have been made at any time over David's longstanding commitment to path dependence, an ante-diluvian feature of his approach as far as recent developments in and around economics are concerned. But it also significant to trace the direction taken by his work after, possibly as a result of, the new directions taken by economics. In particular, it is appropriate to focus on two closely related aspects: on the one hand, in what respect is David's analysis historically "open" in relying upon path dependence;[15] second, how is his analysis contextual or dependent upon drawing from historical and social specificity.

As has been shown, David explains the determinism (lack of path dependence) in mainstream economics and (the new) economic history by a longstanding predilection to ape the natural sciences. This is made explicit in David (1975, pp. 11/2) where he reveals a preference for abandoned biological over mechanical analogues. These are better able to accommodate his commitment to path dependence, with evolution as the appropriate metaphor. For, the

---

13 See also David (1997) where the same device is used to argue that path dependence might not lead to inefficiency.

14 For a particularly striking appeal for rapprochement between mainstream modelling and history, see Snooks (1993b, p. 1/2): "The most telling observation about modern economics is that the dimension of real time has been lost. As an abstract, deductive, and mathematical science, economics has focused upon shortrun, comparative-static analysis of both a partial and general kind ... The argument here is that we should not abandon what has been achieved by deductive economics, rather we should augment it with an historical analysis of both shortrun and longrun economic problems ... In this way it may even be possible to construct more realistic path-dependent models". See also Snooks (1993c, pp. 42/3).

15 The lack of openness in neoclassical methodology is especially emphasised by the critical realist approach, on which see Lawson (1997) – and Fine (2004d) for a critique.

economy, like the evolution of animal species, may not be ergodic as a result of hysteresis effects, "and marked divergences between ultimate outcomes may flow from seemingly negligible differences in remote beginnings", p. 16. The same point is made almost twenty years later as reported above (David, 1993, pp. 38/40). It would, however, be a mistake to see David's preference for the biological over the physical world to represent some sort of ontological position – that we are closer to plants or animals. Rather, it is simply a matter of the contingent availability of the sorts of models that the two areas of science tend to furnish and whether these are better or not at capturing the sort of path dependence that he has in mind.

Such a conclusion is reinforced even by a casual account of David's shifting model selection, both from less reliance on the informal and more on the formal (mathematical) and by choice within the formal. First note, however, as reported above, his disdain for models drawn from the physical sciences has evaporated as they have become more concerned, according to his account, with process as well as outcome. As a result, economics has itself adopted more appropriate models, ones that draw upon more complicated mathematics and allow for more complex and varieties of dynamics around multiple equilibria. In short, it is a matter of linking path dependence to mathematical modelling with the result that (David, 1997):

> The core notion of path dependence has been seen to be concerned with *stochastic processes of historical change* – the probabilistic motions of systems through unidirectional time.

A preferred technique is that of Markov chain analysis, for example, relying upon probabilistic movement within and between overlapping local networks, with illustrative application to probabilistic interdependence between preferences which gives rise to different equilibria depending on the strength of demonstration effects between consumers. Significantly, in an earlier paper considering the adoption of new technology, David and Foray (1994) rely upon the Pólya urn model with random selection of coloured balls from an urn with over-replacement that, only if sufficiently strong, will lead to convergence to an urn population of single colour ball.[16] From there, the analysis moves through Markov chain models to "percolation" to allow diffusion to be understood in terms both of "connectivity" and "receptivity" between agents.

---

16   See also David (1997).

From all of this, two messages are clear. First, there is a convergence between David and the new economics. His work is becoming or is already indistinguishable from the mainstream since the latter is now providing the necessary models for what he has always done in the past.[17] The only difference is that the previously informal presentations, whether rightly or wrongly in terms of his own views, allowed for alternative interpretations in which the social, the historical and the systemic were endowed with a much richer content. At most, there is flirtation with ideas of evolution and, interestingly, the national system of innovation approach to technological change (David,1986, 1990 and 1991 for example). But close consideration of David's fleeting attachments to the NSI approach reveals just how much there is a failure to engage with its (historical and social) openness, not least its wish to develop a theory of underlying tendencies and associated long waves that ultimately underpin technological systems, corresponding institutions and its own versions of path dependence.[18]

To some extent, the affinity between David and the mainstream has been cloaked by his continuing disputes with it over the nature of path dependence. In particular, he observes that path dependence has now become trendy within the economics profession as, at times, a superficial way of recognising that history matters (David, 1997). For him, in and of itself, this is an inadequate grasp of the idea of path dependence and of historical economics. It allows history to be treated as a residual factor of minor significance. For this reason, admittedly as a minor terminological quibble, he is unhappy about the use of the term path dependency by converts such as Williamson, North and Mokyr since this suggests a factor of secondary importance. But what are the substantive issues involved over path dependence/dependency? For David, two are important. The first is that path dependence, and QWERTY-like lock-ins to particular technologies, etc, may or may not lead to economic inefficiency. This, however, is not the main analytical point. Rather, second, *path* dependence should not be confused with the weaker form or special case of *past* dependence. For the latter, initial conditions, for example, affect the path taken but, once embarked upon, the path is set. More generally, David's path dependence is not to be

17   This is evident, for example, from his favourable reference to the papers by Durlauf (1991), Heckman (1991), Krugman (1991) and Milgrom et al. (1991) in the AEA meeting's session on "Path Dependence in Economics: The Invisible Hand in the Grip of the Past".

18   See Edquist (2001) who reveals how ad hoc and descriptive the NSI approach can be. For a critique that it tends to overlook the role of economic and political power and conflict and, in this light, to be insufficiently historically and socially specific in tracing the evolution of technological systems, see Fine (1993c) with reference to apartheid South Africa.

reduced to a stationary or state dependent sequence of events in the statistical sense in which where you go next only depends upon where you are now. As important is how you got to where you are in determining where you are going. In a nutshell, as David makes explicit and is already abundantly clear from above, his notion of path dependence is stochastic in the statistical sense. As a result, he is highly critical of a series of papers by Liebowitz and Margolis for being deterministic in the statistical sense, and interpreting him as such.[19]

Whilst of decisive importance to David, the rejection of past for path dependence by addition of a stochastic content is merely to randomise an otherwise unreconstructed determinism. David's method is to understand the world on the basis of models that are constructed independently of it. A further example is telling. For David (1999b) also offers a critique of Krugman's new economic geography.[20] The latter depends upon a notion of space simply as the sites on which various dynamic outcomes of market imperfections are concentrated or not. It is a wonderful illustration of the colonisation of economic geography by economics, even the heterodox, not least with the appropriation of terms such as uneven development, core and periphery and so on. Yet David's critique does no more than to refine Krugman, to suggest he has neglected a wider range of heterogeneities in the geography of development, externalities on the demand as well as the supply side, and the importance of the state in promoting competitive bidding through offering subsidies to footloose firms.[21]

---

19   See below and Liebowitz and Margolis (1990, 1994, 1995a and b, and 1998a and b). As is clear, they are on a sort of neo-neo-liberal crusade in which market imperfections are recognised primarily as a logical possibility but of limited historical and contemporary significance. Apart from seeking to debunk QWERTY, Liebowitz and Margolis are prominent for their defence of Microsoft on non-lock-in grounds of software sub-systems, also see below.

20   For my own later critique in the context of the embrace of NEG (the new economic geography) by the World Bank, see Fine (2010b).

21   See also David et al. (1998) where colonisation by economics is consolidated by using a model to bring together spatial and technological dualism (through Markov chains). For an outstanding critique of the new economic geography that parallels the one offered here of the newer economic history, see Martin (1999) and, especially germane for the latter, p. 76: "The "history" referred to is not real history: there is no sense of the real and context-specific periods of time over which actual spatial agglomerations have evolved (and, in many cases, dissolved) ... Thus, while the claim that 'history matters' is certainly correct, the treatment of history in the new economic geography is more metaphorical than real and, despite the importance assigned to path dependence, this notion remains a conceptual and explanatory black box".

As a result, what David and Krugman share is more important than where they differ, and much the same could be said of his disputes with others over the meaning of path dependence. In particular, the assault by Krugman upon economic geography leads to the setting aside, as if it never existed, of the intellectual tradition that sees space as socially and historically (re)constructed.[22] In other words, reference to the meaning of space itself is totally absent and taken to be unproblematic just as capital, labour and so on are merely factor inputs for mainstream economics. David's acceptance of the unproblematic nature of space within the new economic geography is indicative of a parallel to the weakness in his understanding of openness through path dependence. Where the latter is analytically concerned with the nature of outcomes, contextual content depends upon how social and historical specificity is drawn upon from the outset through the nature and legitimacy of the concepts deployed?[23]

It is fortuitous that the limited contextual content of David's notion of path dependence is revealed in a particular way by his having addressed the new economic geography. More telling, if far from accidental given the preoccupations of the new directions taken by mainstream economics, is what is revealed in his work on the relationship between science and technology, not least because it deals explicitly with the issue of knowledge itself. The broad thrust of this work is that what distinguishes science and technology is less the

---

22   For a short discussion of the bifurcation of geography and opposition to the new economic geography in the context of space as a form of cultural capital, see Fine (2001b, Chapter 4).

23   For salutary lessons on how to undertake Evolutionary Economic Geography, EEG, consider the advice on its critical reconstruction offered by Essletzbichler et al (2023, pp. 10–11): "First, following insights from evolutionary biology and developmental systems theory … *transformational change* should be added to the conceptual apparatus of EEG. Transformational change allows for a better understanding of paradigm shifts, structural breaks, modularity and ruptures and emphasizes an understanding of evolution in relation to particular historical conjunctures … Second, evolution occurs only in particular *historical and geographic contexts* … Third, in order to understand inequality or climate change it is necessary to examine how these macrogeographies affect local innovation systems in the current (not past) historical conjunctures. In order to address big questions, EEG thus needs to incorporate *economic development, historical analysis* and *macro-scale analysis* in its conceptual apparatus. The inclusion of macro-scale analysis requires the augmentation of a territorial conceptualization of space with a *relational understanding* … Fourth … attempts to estimate *value extraction and transfers* in combination with the analysis of power relations and rent extraction … would offer an important complementary analysis to EEG work on the localized dimensions of regional competitive advantage. More work is needed to understand better how patterns of uneven development result from localized technological and industrial branching processes and/or integration in global chains of value creation and extraction".

outcomes and processes attached to each (such as pure and applied science) and more the ethos with which they are approached. Science is more open, collaborative and cooperative, and technology more commercially oriented. Thus, Dasgupta and David (1987, p. 527) deny that:[24]

> the most useful distinctions to notice between science and technology are the ones most often drawn ... according to the intended or realized characteristics of their 'products'. A more promising approach is to be found by focusing, not upon the production of varieties of information, but upon observable differences in the *social ethos* of research, as reflected by researchers' attitudes and actions in regard to the *transmission* of information.

This all leads to a discussion of interaction between public and private research and the need to sustain social ethos through adequate public support for science – otherwise a low level equilibrium is liable to result in science-technology interaction.

As is apparent, the notion of knowledge itself is not taken to be problematic, only how it is produced and shared or not. As a result, knowledge is taken as given (if subject to discovery and use) but differentiated according to how it is exchanged (through the market or otherwise more or less open science and technology). Further, Cowan et al. (1999), in which David is a co-author, provide an appropriate critique of tacit knowledge as being used by mainstream economics, as the knowledge that is not or cannot be passed on. A distinction is drawn between knowledge that can be codified or not, and whether it is or not depends upon context in the sense of how different systemic components interact with one another.[25] Not only can there be disputes about tacit

---

24   It is no surprise that collaboration with Dasgupta should lead to a contextually limited understanding of knowledge, etc. For, in his own work, Dasgupta treats trust, custom, culture, etc in a similar way. For a critique in the context of social capital, see Fine (2001b, Chapter 7).

25   See also Dasgupta and David (1994) for a discourse on codified and tacit knowledge, interaction between systems, public and private research, and intellectual property rights and open science. To establish "a new economics of science", p. 492: "We will be building upon the foundations laid down by the classic contributions in the sociology of science, adding to the insights provided by the 'old' economics of science some new ones that are drawn principally from the rapidly growing analytical literature that treats problems of behavior under incomplete and asymmetric information (including the economic theories of agency and optimal contract, or 'mechanism design' theory) as well as issues in the dynamics of racing and waiting games".

knowledge, there may or may not be methods of resolving them. As a result, the boundaries between the various sorts of knowledge are endogenous, and not simply as a result of intellectual property rights and the objective nature of the knowledge itself. It also depends upon how the science and technology systems are formed and interact with one another and the rest of society. It is transparent that knowledge is simply being treated like other things within a path dependent framework, although certain special features are incorporated. Thus, whilst intriguingly, "*context* – temporal, spatial, cultural and social – becomes an important consideration in any discussion of codified knowledge", our hopes for elaboration are shattered. For, "as economists, and not epistemologists, we are substantively more interested in knowledge transactions or activities ... rather than where knowledge of different sorts may be said to reside". Consequently, David's notion of knowledge is essentially reduced to that of a system for generating, disseminating and deploying information.[26]

Such conclusions are reinforced by consideration of David's (1998) broader historical sweep across the origins and progress of "open science". For, once again, the problem is set in the terms of the conventions of mainstream economics, p. 16:

> In brief, the norm of openness [in scientific interaction] is incentive-compatible with a collegiate reputational reward system based upon accepted claims to priority: it also is conducive to individual strategy choices whose collective outcome reduces excess duplication of research efforts and enlarges the domain of informational complementarities.

This approach, or informal model, is explicitly detached from its historical content and dubbed a "'logical-origins' style of explanation for the institutions of modern science and (technology) ... unconcerned with the details of their actual historical evolution". In order to avoid a "creationist fiction", the history is provided by an account of the patronage system of the seventeenth century,

---

26   See also David (1992, p. 222) where, in the context of "the growth of the stock of scientific knowledge", epistemological connections are understood as "the way in which scientific knowledge is gained". This is in order to criticise the trickle-down theory of technological progress from scientific advance, given more "feedbacks and interactions between advances in technology and science". In other words, trickle-down is supplemented by trickle-up and trickle-across. For a critique of trickle-down, in the context of food knowledge, which does deal with the nature of knowledge and its origins in exploring the articulation between food and information systems, see Fine and Leopold (1993), Fine et al. (1996), Fine (2002a) and, especially, Fine (1998b).

under the heading of "The Argument: Noble Patrons, Mathematicians, and Principal-Agent Problems". As science was funded by nobles, for unexplained utilitarian and ornamental motives, with no expertise of their own, "it was left to the initiative of the parties dependent upon such patronage to organize the production of credible testimonials of their own credibility and scientific status", p. 18. Consequently, under the heading, "Common Agency Contracting, with Rival Principals – The Legacy of European Feudalism", it is explicitly acknowledged that, p. 19:

> The foregoing sketch of the early modern court patronage system presents features recognizable to economists as those of "common agency contracting," involving the competition of incompletely informed rival principals for the dedicated services of an expert agent.

In short, not only are new microfoundations being applied transhistorically, willy-nilly for each of capitalism and feudalism, the same applies to the nature of (open) science and knowledge itself.[27]

3   Hayekian Revenge on Path Dependence

No doubt David's concern with public versus private science is motivated by disquiet at the commercialisation and appropriation of knowledge, something which has itself become more prominent in the age of the so-called "new economy", the increased pre-occupation with intellectual property rights and, in the academic arena, the information-theoretic approach. Significantly, path dependence indicates that outcomes may be inefficient and longstanding (by path as well as by dead-weight loss). It encourages an antipathy to neo-liberalism – the market might not work well and warrants correction by the state.

   Not surprisingly, those continuing to emphasise the virtues of the market beg to disagree, viewing the incidence and impact of market imperfections as insignificant (and to be proven case-by-case with presumption of innocence until guilt is demonstrated). Crucially, as will be seen, this can involve a common analytical approach to that of market imperfections, something that might disturb its proponents who believe themselves to be breaking with

---

27   For an excellent, if less theoretically ambitious, account of how open science is being routed by rampant commercialism, see Press and Washburn (2000).

the old laissez-faire mould. Indeed, the neo-liberal response to path dependence has taken David's QWERTY case study as its point of departure, especially through the work of Liebowitz and Margolis (2001).[28] They have engaged, for reasons that will become apparent, on something of a crusade based on accepting path dependence in principle but of denying it as important in practice. They question whether the world is riddled with QWERTY examples, arguing instead that if a superior keyboard layout were available, then it would almost certainly be adopted as long as short-run transition costs did not outweigh long-run continuing benefits. By re-examining the historical evidence, they claim that there is no case for the availability of a superior keyboard layout. In short, whilst there ought to be lots of QWERTY worlds, p. 14, "not even QWERTY offers us a QWERTY world and ... other QWERTY worlds are awfully hard to find", p. 50.

It is not my intention to review this debate over QWERTY. Rather it is to highlight the extent to which an analytical framework is *shared* by both sides. This is brought out extremely sharply by Hirshleifer, himself a leading economics imperialist of the old type,[29] in his foreword (and most effective summary of the approach) to Liebowitz and Margolis (2001). His first words are to concede that, "History matters" as market failures can materialise with technological lock in due to network effects when "initial mistaken (or only temporarily correct) choice retains a kind of natural monopoly over a superior one ... Everyone is supposedly aware of the inefficiency, yet no single rational decision-maker – having to conform to the actions of everyone else – is in a position to correct it". p. xi. This is history mattering like the accident of different countries driving on different sides of the road before the emergence of international trade in motor vehicles. As a result, it is accepted that, "inefficient outcomes due to network effects are indeed theoretically possible in a market economy, though only under rather stringent conditions. These outcomes are a matter for empirical study ... path dependence is inefficient only when an inferior product survives at the expense of a superior one *and* if the costs of changing over do not exceed the value of the postulated quality improvement", p. xi/xii. Those who emphasise inefficiency tend to suffer from the "Nirvana fallacy: comparing a real-world actuality with a hypothetical ideal not within the range of feasible options", p. xii.

---

28 Significantly, this is published by The Independent Institute, Oakland. Note also that Liebowitz is a member of the Mont Pèlerin Society, in 2013 if not 2010, https://www.des mog.com/mont-pelerin-society/.

29 See Hirshleifer (1985) for example.

As will be apparent, there is a focus upon networks on the demand side where one another's consumption is complementary – having a phone or speaking the same language for example, or learning keyboard layout. Networks are perceived as natural monopolies. As a consequence, especially where privately owned, they will appear, potentially wrongly, to be uncompetitive and inefficient both in outcome (single supplier) and process (marketing behaviour). For if inefficiency arises, new technology can displace old by "low introductory price or money-back guarantee ... [firms might] subsidize the cost of the user's changeover, and even commit to pay the cost of changing back", p. xiii. This amounts to what could be predatory pricing – lowering price in the first instance in order to drive out and discourage competitors in pursuit of longer-term monopoly. The important point, though, is that predatory pricing as such, and potentially all commercial shenanigans, are compatible both with elimination of rivals to forge a monopoly, on the one hand, and the appropriate way to establish the presence of a superior product in face of network effects, on the other. In particular, in markets with rapid technological progress, it is to be expected that we will observe serial monopoly and increasing quality with falling prices, as in the shift in word processing from WordStar to WordPerfect and then to Microsoft Word.

Analytically, the substance of Liebowitz and Margolis's book adds very little to Hirshleifer's account. For them, QWERTY is a myth that lives on despite their critique and its being economic quackery, p. 266.[30] Their methodology is one of mathematical models tested against the facts. Indeed for them, economics is mathematics except that its object is the real as opposed to a hypothetical world, and hence only as good as its assumptions against which it must be tested, p. 49/50, and the idea "that some issues are not empirical [is] a questionable position", p. 236.[31] In the context of network effects (the term used instead

---

30   Krugman is cited as having accepted the QWERTY myth, p. 11, but is later noted to have redeemed himself p. 18, fn 3. There is, of course, a paradox here if Liebowitz and Margolis are correct – why is there persistence of the QWERTY myth if it is so unreasonable. Why does their approach not apply to the world of ideas to render redundant their own view of, as it were, the lock-in of the lock-in approach.

31   See also Liebowitz and Margolis (1995a) on rival paradigms for the role of history, with no doubt over their own preference between the limited menu of choices that they offer: "One holds that efficiency explanations are important and the economic history, at least, is the search for purpose in past actions ... Technology responds to scarcities, technique responds to price, and so on. The other holds that history is important only to the extent that, for one reason or another, agents do not successfully optimize. History then is the tool to understand what rationality and efficiency do not explain, that is, the random sequence of insignificant events that are not addressable by economic history. We leave it to the reader to decide which paradigm promises greater returns to the study of history".

of externality since the latter has pejorative associations with market failure) they draw upon Coase (1960) as the framework for examining networks, "to see activity set in motion to internalize externalities", p. 21. It is a matter of establishing property rights and bargaining over their use, leading to "being first on the market, patent and copyright law, brand names, tie-in sales, discounts, and so on", p. 22. The persistence of inefficient lock-in means no individual is prepared to break through the externality by internalising, despite the availability of the full gamut of commercial initiatives, "things like consumer and trade magazines, trade associations, guarantees, advertising, brand names, word of mouth, and so on", p. 58.

So Liebowitz and Margolis do accept path dependence, positing a taxonomy of three degrees, p. 51/5: the first degree is attached to decisions with pre-determined and fully available perfect information, qualified by durability of investments – too large a house in anticipation of having children for example – or, it might be added, owning an umbrella even if it is not always raining; the second degree depends upon imperfect foresight that would have been corrected in advance if possible; and the third degree is the only one involving inefficiency and is due to lack of co-ordination. As such, it is subject to remediable action through internalising the externality involved through some form of collective behaviour. Elsewhere Liebowitz and Margolis (1995a, p. 224) indicate how they believe the third degree is likely to be outflanked, for:

> Where there is a knowable and feasible improvement from moving onto a better path, those who will benefit from the improvement, and who know it, will be willing to pay to bring the improvement about. Where simple spot market transactions are insufficient to bring these improvements about, institutional or strategic innovation seems a likely response, especially if the improvement is important enough that the innovator is likely to be well paid.

And, further (Liebowitz and Margolis, 1996):

> There is an enormous body of evidence in support of this proposition that market participants do find ways around the traps posed by entrenched standards and established technologies. For if they could not, we would still be riding horses, wearing animal skins, and living in caves.

In this light, not surprisingly, David (1999a) is disturbed by the continuing resistance to path dependence and supposes it to be due to dogmatic commitment by economists to laissez-faire. He reasonably responds that, for

Liebowitz and Margolis, "'third-degree path dependence', has led from 'nirvana economics' in which markets work perfectly to a more fanciful 'nirvana political economy' – in which optimal public ordering will be there to save the day when private ordering fails!" (David, 1997).

Nor is this all simply of academic and ideological interest because the QWERTY cliché and path dependence more generally has been an important source of contention in the anti-trust case being brought against Microsoft by the US government and numbers of states.[32] In principle, as already highlighted, the avoidance of inefficient path dependence rests on processes (predatory pricing) and outcomes (serial monopoly) that appear to be inefficient if not illegal as Microsoft ensures its putatively superior product is collectively adopted.[33] This leads Liebowitz and Margolis to warn against too vigorous anti-trust policy and action, especially where motivated by the QWERTY myth. Certainly, Microsoft can be interpreted as engaging in dirty tricks from exclusion of access to its software for hardware manufacturers not complying with its presence alone, through infringement of copyright, to insisting that its internet browser icon be most readily, if not exclusively, accessible.[34] Particularly important, in dispute with Netscape, is the predatory pricing of making its internet browser available free of charge but insisting that it be installed – a "tie-up" to sustain a serial monopoly for its operating system. On the other hand, this may simply have been a means to accrue network effects across operating and browser system use.

The crucial point is that the same empirical evidence can be interpreted either way.[35] Or, to put it otherwise, path-dependence economics is capable of explaining whatever happens in whatever way is required. Consequently, Microsoft's trials have been graced by rival industrial economists. Franklin Fisher, MIT professor, testified for the US Government at a price of $500 per

---

32   For a, necessarily dated, narrative and chronology, see Auletta (2001) and, for an account of the analytical issues from orthodox perspectives, see Eisenach and Lenard (eds) (1999).

33   See McKenzie (2000) for emphasising how, in the Microsoft case, all evidence of anti-competitive behaviour can be interpreted as its opposite.

34   See Rohm (1998) for an account of the numerous dirty tricks perpetrated against other companies by Microsoft. Typically, Auletta (2001, p. 316) reports that Microsoft made a settlement with Caldera, a Salt Lake City software company, for $275 million, against the claim that illegal means had been used to put them out of business. Of course, this allowed it not to face the possibility of being found guilty, p. 316. See also Quittner and Slatalla (1998, p. 267) on Microsoft's threat to withdraw Windows from Compaq if it did not desktop icon Microsoft Explorer, and Wallace (1997) on stealing Stac data compression or not (an award against Microsoft of $120 million), etc.

35   See also Fine (2016).

hour, the irony being that he had previously testified for IBM against the Justice Department in its case, with corresponding acrobatics over whether large market share indicates inefficient monopoly or not. Further, taking his corporate place and testifying for Microsoft was his own pupil, Richard Schmalensee, at $800 an hour. Under cross-examination, it was found that he had published an article in 1997, arguing that, "'A clear signal of low barriers to entry is provided only by effective, viable entry' into the market 'that takes a nontrivial market share. There is a substantial difference between toehold entry and substantial entry that provides real pressure on established firms' profits" (cited in Brinkley and Lohr, 2001, p. 145). Indeed, introduced as evidence were "several academic papers by Mr. Schmalensee over the years that held opinions contradicting statements he had made in court. Mr. Schmalensee said his views had evolved", p. 256, forcing him to confess that he had no quantitative proof that Microsoft was constrained from raising prices by competition, (Auletta, 2001, p. 297). Out of court, Schmalensee appeared to be more frank, observing of Judge Jackson that, "He did not believe a word I said after 'Good morning, Your Honour!'".

In practice, if not in principle, as anything can be accommodated as a "tie-up" market, the work of Liebowitz and Margolis is insular for neglecting the wider environment in which network effects occur. This follows from their exclusively micro-orientation. Theirs is a world in which there is no unemployment, no need to control workers, no financial crises and no consideration of David's previously discussed concern over the relative merits of private versus public science.

The latter has been a controversial matter around software.[36] There can be little doubt that the operating system and tie ins and ups associated with Microsoft have been deliberately designed not only to exclude other commercial operators but also the ethos and practice of offering freely available programmes, with ease of use. Instead of a public facility, freely used and potentially developed by all, what Microsoft does and can do is heavily constrained by the vagaries of the financial system. As Wallace (1997, p. 293) reports, someone who had purchased shares when Microsoft went public in 1986 would have

---

36   See Williams (2002) and Stallabrass (2002) for a review. See also Quittner and Slatalla (1998) for the movement out of the National Center for Supercomputing Applications (NCSA), University of Illinois, where the Mosaic software originated. "Anybody who wanted one could make a copy of Mosaic for free and use it. The method of distribution over the Internet was a time-honoured tradition at NCSA, originating as far back as the debut of NCSA Telnet ... It was common in the Unix world for programmers to post source code publicly", p. 52.

seen them worth 123 times in 1996. On a judgement confirming Microsoft mal-
practice in 1999, its share price fell by over 11% in a day, representing an $80
billion fall in market value. The next three weeks witnessed a further fall twice
as large (Auletta, 2001, p. 364). Are we to believe this is the basis on which
externalities are internalised?

4   Culture, Institutions, Narrative and All That Jazz

Yet the most striking omission in the account of Liebowitz and Margolis
is that their economic theory is entirely free of consideration of the role of
uncertainty. Whilst software fortunes are supposedly built out of the inven-
tion of something new and possibly unforeseeable, the neo-liberal posture of
Liebowitz and Margolis is significant for its total conformity to current developments within mainstream economics. This is to include mathematics and
empiricism, the acceptance of market imperfections in principle, *and* the writing out of neo-Austrian insights. If not necessarily in this form, this has the
effect of alienating those historians whom Liebowitz and Margolis might seek
to attract other than through their neo-liberalism. Path dependence, whether
in the welcoming embrace of David or the doubting hands of Liebowitz and
Margolis, remains predominantly, almost openly, cultureless, as reflected in its
formal methods.

The same is not true, however, of others, coincidentally of a neo-liberal
bent, who have explicitly sought to incorporate "narrative", Bates et al. (1998)
for example, who entitle their collective endeavour, *Analytic Narratives*. On
the analytic side, there is little novelty, although the scope of the approach is
claimed to cover both history and development, p. 8:

> Institutions ... induce choices that are regularized because they are made
> in equilibrium ... Behavior becomes stable and patterned, or alternatively
> institutionalized, not because it is imposed, but because it is elicited.

But they seek to offer more than reliance on rational choice with the wish to
"blend rational choice analysis and narration". Thus, "Our approach is narrative; it pays close attention to stories, accounts, and context. It is analytic in
that it extracts explicit and formal lines of reasoning, which facilitates both
exposition and explanation", p. 10. It also "focuses on choices and decisions.
It is thus more micro than macro in orientation", p. 13. But it does offer some
macro, partly endogenous, partly exogenous, p.13:

> The models that we mobilize presume that some variables are con-
> strained, whereas the values of others can be chosen; they presume that
> alternatives have been defined, as well as the linkages between actions
> and outcomes.

There is much more in this vein that could be quoted at length but, apart from
the idea of turning thick narrative into thin analytics, it is difficult to discover
what exactly makes up the narrative.

Rather, considerable care is taken to pre-empt objections. Thus, it is argued
that politics is not absent because of attention to force, territorial expansion,
conquest, state-building and war; "coercion is as much a part of that life coercion, as are production, consumption and exchange ... [so] although based on
models of rational choice, our work is not apolitical", p. 8. It is also recognised
that data are unlikely to lead to the rejection of a model as, "the dominant
response to disconfirmation is thus reformulation, not falsification", p. 16. This
is hardly surprising as the problem is also acknowledged of the huge range of
models that might remain consistent with the facts. Accordingly, models are
to be chosen if they are more powerful (in their scope of explanation) or more
general (including others as a special case) p. 17/8. Again, this adds nothing to
the narrative as opposed to the analytic.

Such postures inevitably reveal the absence of "narrative" rather than its
presence. For context is used at most to establish the problem and not its specificity in terms of categories of analysis. This is inadvertently made explicit by
Greif (1994) for whom history and culture literally become the games people
play. He offers the following definitions, p. 943:

> Cultural beliefs (how individuals expect others to act in various con-
> tingencies) and organizations (the endogenous human constructs that
> alter the rules of the game and, whenever applicable, have to be an
> equilibrium).

On this basis, p. 930, "The Maghribs and the Genoese experienced over time a
specific alteration in the merchant-agent game", and "The rationale behind the
different responses of the Maghribis and the Genoese to the same exogenous
change in the rules of the game is clear once one considers the impact of cultural beliefs on equilibrium selection", p. 931. Thus, Greif and others are simply
adopting the language of narrative, just as they have done in case of culture,
institutions and so on. As Boniface and Sharman (2001) suggest in review, the
project of analytic narratives is seeking to bridge the incompatible, and they
observe that "subjective factors are all too frequently ignored in these scholars'

analytic models (or are developed merely as an afterthought to account for unexplained variance)", p. 484. One problem is that if models are sensitive to historical conditions, they are not generalisable and history is brought in as an added factor to explain what would otherwise be anomalies.

5   Crafting the Newer Economic History

In short, the narrative in analytic narratives plays three roles: one is to court those historians suspicious of the scope and content of analytics; another is to shift out the boundary of the exogenous; and the third is to accommodate history's annoying capacity to throw up contra-evidence to the models by which it is supposed to be tracked. In each of these respects, the work of Nic Crafts represents an equal if much more transparent dependence upon developments in neoclassical economics as applied to history, with an equally reductionist approach to earlier contributions. Thus, Crafts (1999a, p. 6) puts forward the idea that Gerschenkron can be interpreted in terms of the new microeconomics. Indeed, p. 18:

> Gerschenkron on development from conditions of economic backwardness still deserves to be read and might usefully be revisited from the perspective of modern microeconomics.

Nonetheless, whilst he "can be construed in terms of modern microeconomics ... [this] does not mean that his underlying view of the role of the state in the development process is acceptable", because of his neglect of sources of total factor productivity, TFP, and the dangers of government as opposed to market failure.

Crafts has, however, moved from discussing measurements of TFP, and the reasons for them, to new growth theory. Here the idea is that technical progress can be explained within the model by clusters of endogenously-induced "micro-inventions" following upon an exogenously given "macro-invention".[37] This is not the place to rehearse the legion theoretical and empirical deficiencies of the new growth theory, in general and as applied to history.[38] Suffice it

---

37   Crafts (1995b) borrows the idea from Mokyr (1993). Note that the latter's position has shifted to embrace the theories of technological change associated with the new growth theory whereas previously he was left pondering, "Is it possible to analyze technological change with the traditional tools of the economist, the rules of supply and demand?" (Mokyr, 1985, p. 28). He has subsequently moved to the cultural, see below.

38   See Fine (2003e) for an overview.

to observe how the exogenous has become the endogenous, the dependence upon neoclassical economics, and the reinterpretation of both evidence and previous contributions through the newly created framework. For, in the context of the industrial revolution, Crafts (1995a, p. 772) judges that:[39]

> Growth theorists have ... found useful ways of formalizing ideas long discussed by economic historians, and the way may now be open for some fruitful interaction between economics and economic history.

This is an updated manifesto for the new economic history!

Even so, because the endogenous (and explanation) ultimately rest upon the exogenous (and unexplained) it is not surprising, possibly intended, that major historical episodes such as the British Industrial Revolution should be considered to be accidental (who gets the accidental shock or favourable initial conditions). Hence, in debate with Landes (1994 and 1995), Crafts (1995, p. 597) concludes that:[40]

> Unlike Landes, then, I am still prepared to contemplate a role for accident in economic history or, in terminology that I would prefer, to think in terms of economic models which both permit a role for exogenous

---

39   Crafts may even be referring to himself as being formalized since, before the emergence of new growth theory, he anticipated it in explaining how demand might affect growth, Crafts (1981, p. 131): "In the short run supply does not create its own demand ... the level of output depends on the level of aggregate demand, which may not be that which achieves full employment in the short run. Levels of demand that push the economy towards full employment in the short run might elicit greater investment and productivity increase, thereby enhancing the growth rate of the productive potential. Levels of demand that push the economy towards full employment in the short run might elicit greater investment and productivity increase, thereby enhancing the growth rate of the productive potential ... The long-run rate is made up of a large number of these short-run spells, and so the economy's rate of growth will depend on levels of demand. The majority of recent English economic historians of the eighteenth century have (*possibly unconsciously*) written in this vein. (emphasis added)". This has also been cited in Fine and Leopold (1993, p. 162) in a broader critical discussion of the eighteenth century as a consumer as opposed to an industrial revolution and whether the latter can be reduced to a matter of supply and demand.

40   Thus, Mokyr (1985, p. 7) in commenting on Crafts, concludes: "The ultimate success of Britain is thus largely inexplicable. A good analogy is the tossing of a fair coin: once it is tossed and heads comes up, there seems little point in explaining why that has occurred". Note how the inexplicable is confounded with the accidental on which see immediately below in terms of the exogenous becoming the endogenous.

technological shocks and also allow on occasions for wide ramifications of these shocks.

By the same token, the boundaries between exogenous and endogenous are ever restless, moving in favour of the latter alongside the new phase of economics imperialism, as yesterday's accident becomes today's ramification. Crafts (1997), for example, seeks to examine the determinants of innovation (as opposed to R&D) to become more Schumpeterian, suggesting, p. 69:

> One of the most exciting avenues of research for economic historians and economists to pursue together using an endogenous innovation frame-work is the political economy of growth. This should aim for an understanding both of what the key effects of policy on growth have been and also of how the incentive structures facing politicians and private agents generate growth-retarding or growth-enhancing interventions.

This is economics imperialism applied to Schumpeter and politics just as previously it was imposed on Gerschenkron.

Crafts (1999a-c) has also extended his economic history to the present not least in discussion of east Asian economic miracle and crisis. He perceives economic performance as dependent upon factor inputs and "social capability". For Crafts (1999b, p. 112):

> Catching-up is not automatic, therefore, and absence of social capability may be a crucial obstacle to growth and development.

He also stresses the role of imperfect information and financial systems. On the basis of highly questionable total factor productivity and other empirical work, he concludes, "this analysis tends to reinforce the conclusion that the Asian developmental state has been much more successful in promoting high levels of investment than in achieving exceptional productivity performance", p. 116.[41] Thus, "present problems are a result of earlier success which propelled the leading Tigers to a point at which more emphasis needed to be placed on strong productivity performance, and reform of the developmental state

---

41   As Stiglitz (1998) comments, "I do not believe, however, that East Asia has grown through investment alone. Any visitor to the cities and factories in East Asia comes away impressed by the enormous technological progress in the last decades".

model seemed appropriate", p. 120.[42] Consequently, Crafts (1999c, p. 155/7) has been able to conclude:

> Initially backward countries have an opportunity for rapid catch-up if they take radical measures to promote development through institutional innovations and controlled capital markets ... this would tend to leave a legacy of institutions different from the standard U.S. model and that, especially in the longer term, there were a number of downside risks of this type of strategy ... A clear risk ... is that it is perverted into opportunities for rent-seeking and corruption that ultimately undermine economic growth ... A second danger ... is that it spawns government policies that serve the interests of special interest groups and actually inhibit economic growth by inducing misallocation of resources, for example, through so-called "industrial policy".

Crafts' explanatory reliance upon industrial policy, financial regulation and cronyism has been effectively demolished by Chang (2000) on simple empirical grounds. There is no evidence that these factors were sufficient or sufficiently different than in the past or from other countries, with the resulting danger of having generated the Asian crisis of 1997/98 for example.[43] But the more important point is to observe how the broadening scope of mainstream economics is being deployed, with supplementary variables being added to its core principles to allow for anomalies from them in light of historical variations.

6   Finance before Financialisation

This is an opportune moment at which to return to the new approach propounded by Lamoreaux and others. For finance is prominent as a case study in

---

42   See also p. 124, "the 1997/8 crisis reflects weaknesses in the institutional arrangements of the East Asian developmental state model in the age of financial liberalization".

43   See also Chang et al. (1998, p. 735) who argue: "The crisis resulted from uncoordinated and excessive investments by the private sector, financed by imprudent amounts of short-term foreign debt, which in turn had been made possible by rapid and ill-designed financial liberalisation (especially capital account liberalisation) and a serious weakening of industrial policy ... While it has some important shortcomings, Korea's supposedly pathological corporate governance system was neither the main source of the current crisis, nor something that has to be radically restructured if Korea is to regain its growth momentum, as many observers outside and inside Korea currently believe".

the new approach – it is a market or, more exactly, many markets, with asymmetric information between borrowers and lenders, and diverse features across time and place. The new financial economics has been at the forefront of the information-theoretic approach to economics and is an exemplary illustration of the new phase of economics imperialism. In a nutshell, it works out and up from the informational asymmetries between optimising agents in financial markets (including government that may need to gain credibility for its monetary policy) to systemic properties of the economy. In particular, for the latter, a distinction is drawn between two archetypal banking systems. One, the market-based as represented by the US and the UK, is deemed to function primarily by offering short-term loans against collateral to guard against default and misrepresentation, with no other influence over, or concern for, corporate strategy. On the other hand, the bank-based system, associated with Japan and Germany, allows for long-term loans, and support over troubled periods, with bank representation in corporate management to monitor performance and safeguard financial interests. It is presumed to be superior for levels and stability of industrial investment, although it has the disadvantage of tying particular corporations to particular banks in contrast to the greater flexibility of the market-based system.

There are a number of theoretical and empirical problems with this approach.[44] First and foremost, it does not link finance to questions of economic and political power, other than at most as exogenous constraints, themselves differentiated through stages of economic development that might also be taken as given. Thus, Fine (1997c) offers a critique of the new financial economics for its focus on intrinsic contracting between borrower and lender rather than the extrinsic conditions in which they operate. He uses apartheid South Africa as a case study for which a few highly concentrated individual corporations have controlled access to both finance and industry. Failure to invest and to coordinate investment could have nothing to do with asymmetric information between borrowers and lenders who, in this case, are pretty much one and the same![45]

Second, whilst the nature of agents and their trustworthiness are important aspects of all transactions, such knowledge is highly dependent upon the class and other characteristics of the agents concerned. In other words, both the nature of informational asymmetries and how they are interpreted and acted upon derive from the question of position within a particular stage of

---

44   We do not address what has been shown to be the questionable and simple empirical
     division between market-and bank-based systems.
45   See also Aybar and Lapavitsas (2001).

development of an economy and its own peculiar characteristics (Lapavitsas, 2003, for a discussion). These conditions not only set the basis for the narrow preoccupation on asymmetric information in determining the level, composition and outcome of investment but also have a direct bearing on the workings of finance.

For, third, the confidence or otherwise in financial transactions derives as much if not more so from the external environment as from the asymmetries of information between borrowers and lenders. Apart from the stage and character of development of the economy itself, the state plays a significant role through its monetary and other policies (which is why Gerschenkron cannot be reduced to modern microeconomics as suggested by Crafts). Thus, the strength of the Japanese financial system in promoting industrialisation followed from the commitment of the state to coordinate and promote industrial investment, as has also been the case for South Korea.

Fourth, underpinning each of the earlier points, is the inadequate theory of money and finance that is being deployed. Essentially, it is universal not only across time and place but also across different types of finance as well as for markets other than finance. It is simply a matter of the nature and incidence of informational imperfections between those who wish to lend and those who wish to borrow. It is hardly surprising that questions of power, the state, and of the role of finance in promoting industrialisation, industrial restructuring and other broader socio-economic transformations simply do not figure.[46]

In short, the new approach to finance can be seen to be inside-out. It takes informational asymmetries as given, alongside broader external conditions that at most evolve alongside institutionally-constrained optimisation. Thus, White (1998, p. 30/1) addresses the decline of the US commercial banking sector, and the rise of other financial institutions, in the following terms, p. 30/1:

> The dominant position of commercial banks among financial intermediaries in the late nineteenth century may thus be interpreted as the best solution to the asymmetric information problem between borrowers and lenders when there were few technologically feasible alternatives. The twentieth-century decline in the prominence of banks as intermediaries can be traced back to the development of alternative markets and the improvement of information collection that began during the National Bank Era.

---

46 See Itoh and Lapavitsas (1999) for an alternative.

In commenting, Lamoreaux (1998b) adopts the same approach but suggests a fuller picture in which borrowers' needs became more geographically spread, undermining significance of local bank knowledge as local lending declined. Such factors are important but they need both to be set in the socio-economic positions of the agents concerned and the broader economic and political developments, themselves connected to finance, as in the geographical spread of borrowers' needs (or larger scale capitals). Interestingly, in the same symposium, Temin (1998, p. 51) in commenting on Fohlin's (1998) suggestion that the differences between pre-WWI German and British banking systems were not so great, implicitly accepts these points by appeal to Gerschenkron. He refers to the different role of different banking systems at different stages of development and the need to interrogate the differences in more than balance sheets (and asset composition) and, in voluntaristic and vulgar terms, the need to take account of the wider context:

> Were the German universal banks that have been both glorified and vilified over the years simply banks along the lines that we know them, loaning money to firms and earning money by choosing good risks? Or were they like the man pulling the levers behind the curtains in the *Wizard of Oz*? And if they were pulling the levers, how were they being paid for doing so?

In her own, earlier work on early nineteenth century US banking, Lamoreaux (1994) points to the widespread practice of insider lending whereby entrepreneurs set up their own banks and used them in order to gain access to funds for investment – or corruption. Such practices accommodated development of both industry and finance but, equally, degenerated into scandal and failure from time to time. But, no doubt reflecting on the current financial liberalisation pursued by the IMF, World Bank and others, Lamoreaux closes her account in more rounded fashion, p. 165:

> Other societies, of course, have had very different histories and operate in accordance with different value systems. In many other parts of the world, for example, favoritism toward kinsmen and other close associates is still an accepted part of daily life. It is important, therefore, that we do not react moralistically when confronted with the insider lending that often characterizes financial institutions in such societies. The lesson of our own history is that under certain circumstances a banking system based on insider lending can function very well. Rather than attempt to impose our own modern values and institutions on others, therefore,

our efforts at assistance might better be directed toward helping these societies arrange incentives in a way that puts insider lending to productive use.

This is exactly what has emerged out of the micro-finance (Grameen Bank) schemes that are so closely associated with the World Bank in practice and the asymmetric information approach to finance in theory.[47]

It is indicative of a theory of finance in which it inevitably functions successfully only at the risk of allowing for individual corruption on a greater or lesser scale. It can also give rise to bubbles and bursts at an aggregate level as agents follow market (price) information that is all that is readily available to them. In fact, this is no theory of finance at all and could equally be applied to any market, as indeed it is. Finance is inextricably linked to money-making but without guarantees of success because of its dependence upon the real accumulation of capital, something that is systemic and lies beyond, and is not reducible to, appropriately informed or regulated optimising agents.

7   Concluding Remarks

The account offered here of recent developments within economic history has both begun and ended with the simple application of the information-theoretic approach. In between, it has ranged over path dependence, narrative and market imperfections and endogeneity more generally. In each case, the extent and nature of reliance upon recent developments in economic theory is different as is the way in which it is complemented by other elements such as institutions and culture, etc. Such is common practice for the new economics imperialism. As it rampages across the social sciences, it retains to a greater or lesser extent the mathematical and statistical formalism of its origins, shedding these more for more informal narrative as needs be according to subject matter and/or audience. What all the contributions considered in this chapter have in common, warranting the title the newer economic history, is an ultimate reliance upon the single-mindedly optimising individual, albeit one who is prepared to make compromises in light of the longer view, bounded rationality, imperfect information and markets, and the like.

---

47   For a critique of such self-policing schemes, especially in the context of the burst bubble of micro-credit, see Bateman et al. (2018).

Thus, the old economics imperialism which, for some at least, knew its place and limitations, has been set aside in deference to the new, with corresponding shifts between the new and the newer economic history. Each generalises from the previous by no longer assuming (as if) perfect markets, absence of institutions, etc. Such virtue is only gained at the expense of no longer accepting strict boundaries to the approach. In the academic world, even history, memories are short. Consequently, it takes one of those, Douglass North, who pioneered the new economic history to recall and emphasise the limitations of exclusive reliance upon the optimising individual, even if it is applied in its newer information-theoretic version, see Chapters 6 and 7. However, where for North, neuroscience provided the answer for the origins of change (to ideology, and so institutions, and so how history matters) a different tack has been adopted by economics imperialism and economic history in their latest, newer and newest, phases, respectively. It has been to add whatever considerations appear relevant, however consistently and coherently, or even at the expense of those attached to the optimising individual in context of imperfect markets. There are hints of this in this chapter in the form of narrative, culture writ narrow as an analytical device – one of appeal to historians.[48] This reflects the starting point taken in the introduction to this chapter – highlighting the tensions between being a rounded historian and succumbing to the unsubtle charms of economics imperialism. As economic history and economics imperialism have co-evolved so these tensions have only intensified, with mixed and shifting results across individual scholars, how they contribute and the corresponding uneasy co-existence between economic history as such and social history as its alter ego.

---

48   See, for example, McCloskey (1981) for rhetoric, Mokyr (2017) and Shiller (2019).

References

Acemoglu, D., G. Egorov, and K. Sonin (2021) "Institutional Change and Institutional Persistence", in Bisin and Federico (eds) (2021), pp. 365–90.

Acemoglu, D., S. Johnson and J. Robinson (2001) "The Colonial Origins of Comparative Development: an Empirical Investigation", *American Economic Review*, vol 91, no 5, pp. 1369–1401.

Aigner, E. (2021) "Global Dynamics and Country-Level Development in Academic Economics: an Explorative Cognitive-Bibliometric Study", Department of Socio-Economics, Institute for Multi-Level Governance & Development, Vienna University of Economics and Business, Social-Ecological Discussion Paper in Economics, no 7, https://www-sre.wu.ac.at/sre-disc/sre-disc-2021_07.pdf.

Alston, L., T. Eggertsson and D. North (eds) (1996) *Empirical Studies in Institutional Change*, Cambridge: Cambridge University Press.

Anderson, P. (1974a) *Lineages of the Absolutist State*, London: Verso.

Anderson, P. (1974b) *Passages from Antiquity to Feudalism*, London, New York: Verso.

Anderson, P. (1980) *Arguments Within English Marxism*, London: Verso.

Andreano, R. (ed.) (1970) *The New Economic History: Recent Papers on Methodology*, New York: Wiley.

Ankarloo, D. (2002) "New Institutional Economics and Economic History", *Capital and Class*, no 78, pp. 9–36.

Ankarloo, D. and G. Palermo (2004) "Anti-Williamson: a Marxian Critique of New Institutional Economics", *Cambridge Journal of Economics*, vol 28, no 3, pp. 413–29.

Aoki, M. (1988) *Information, Incentives, and Bargaining in the Japanese Economy*, Cambridge: Cambridge University Press.

Arestis, P. and M. Sawyer (eds) (2004) *The Rise of the Market*, Camberley: Edward Elgar.

Arrow, K. (1986) "History: the View from Economics", in Parker (ed.) (1986), pp. 13–20.

Arthur, W. (2013) "Comment on Neil Kay's Paper: Rerun the Tape of History and QWERTY Always Wins", *Research Policy*, vol 42, no 5–6, pp. 1186–7.

Ashman, S., B. Fine and E. Karwowski (2021) "The Relevance of Financialization for African Economies: Lessons from South Africa", SOAS Department of Economics Working Paper, no 245, https://www.soas.ac.uk/economics/research/workingpapers/file156232.pdf.

Ashton, T. (1946) "The Relation of Economic History to Economic Theory", vol 13, no 50, pp. 81–96, reprinted in Harte (ed.) (1971), pp. 161–179.

Assa, J. (2017) *The Financialization of GDP: Implications for Economic Theory and Policy*, London: Routledge.

Assa, J. (2019) "Gross Domestic Power: a History of GDP as Numerical Rhetoric", *Annals of the Fondazione Luigi Einaudi*, vol LIII, no 2, pp. 81–96.

Aston. T. and C. Philpin (eds) (1985) *The Brenner Debate: Agrarian Class Structure and Economic Development in Pre-Industrial Europe*, Cambridge: Cambridge University Press.

Atack, J. and P. Passell (1994) *A New Economic View of American History from Colonial Times to 1940*, second edition, New York: W. W. Norton.

Atkins, F. (1991) *A Reconsideration of Land Reform: an Analysis of Underlying Theories with Reference to Jamaican Experience*, University of London, unpublished PhD thesis.

Atkinson, P., S. Delamont, A. Cernat, J. Sakshaug and R. Williams (2020) *SAGE Research Methods Foundations*, online, London: Sage, https://research.manchester.ac.uk/en/publications/sage-research-methods-foundations.

Auletta, K. (2001) *World War 3.0: Microsoft and its Enemies*, London: Profile Books.

Auslander, L. (1996a) *Taste and Power: Furnishing Modern France*, Berkeley: University of California.

Auslander, L. (1996b) "The Gendering of Consumer Practices in Nineteenth-Century France", in de Grazia and Furlough (eds) (1996), pp. 79–112.

Aybar S. and C. Lapavitsas (2001) "Financial System Design and the Post-Washington Consensus", in Fine et al. (eds) (2001), pp. 28–51.

Baffigi, A. (2019) "Stefano's Face, Comment on 'Spleen: the Failures of the Cliometric School' by Stefano Fenoaltea", *Annals of the Fondazione Luigi Einaudi*, vol LIII, no 2, pp. 31–48.

Ball, M. (1980) "On Marx's Theory of Agricultural Rent: a Reply to Ben Fine", *Economy and Society*, vol 9, no 3, pp. 304–26, reproduced within Fine (ed.) (1986, Chapter 5), pp. 114–87.

Baran, P. and P. Sweezy (1968) *Monopoly Capital*, Harmondsworth: Penguin.

Bateman, M., S. Blankenburg and R. Kozul-Wright (2018) *The Rise and Fall of Global Microcredit: Development, Debt and Disillusion*, London: Routledge.

Bates, R., A. Greif, M. Levi, J.-L. Rosentahl and B. Weingast (1998) *Analytic Narratives*, Princeton: Princeton University Press.

Bayliss, K. and B. Fine (2021) *A Guide to the Systems of Provision Approach: Who Gets What, How and Why*, Basingstoke: Palgrave MacMillan.

Becker, G. (1990) "Gary S. Becker", in Swedberg (ed.) (1990), pp. 27–46.

Ben-Schachar, A. (1984) "Demand vs Supply in the Industrial Revolution: a Comment", *Journal of Economic History*, vol XLIV, no 3, pp. 801–5.

Bina, C. (1985) *The Economics of the Oil Crisis*. London: Merlin Press.

Bisin, A. and G. Federico (2021) "Merger or Acquisition? An Introduction to the Handbook of Historical Economics", in Bisin and Federico (eds) (2021), pp. XV–XXXVIII.

Bisin, A. and A. Moro (2021) "LATE for History", in Bisin and Federico (eds) (2021), pp. 269–96.

Bisin, A. and T. Verdier (2021) "Phase Diagrams in Historical Economics: Culture and Institutions", in Bisin and Federico (eds) (2021), pp. 491–524.

Bisin, A. and G. Federico (eds) (2021) *The Handbook of Historical Economics*, London: Academic Press, https://www.sciencedirect.com/book/9780128158746/the-handbook-of-historical-economics.

Blaut, J. (1993) *The Colonizer's Model of the World: Geographical Diffusionism and Eurocentric History*, New York and London: The Guildford Press.

Boniface, D. and J. Sharman (2001) "An Analytic Revolution in Comparative Politics?", *Comparative Politics*, vol 33, no 4, pp. 475–93.

Bowles, S., J.-K. Choi and S. Naidoo (2021) "How Institutions and Cultures Change: an Evolutionary Perspective", in Bisin and Federico (eds) (2021), pp. 391–434.

Bowles, S., and H. Gintis (1993) "The Revenge of Homo Economicus: Contested Exchange and the Revival of Political Economy", *Journal of Economic Perspectives*, vol 7, no 1, pp. 83–102.

Bowles, S. and H. Gintis (2000) "Walrasian Economics in Retrospect", *Quarterly Journal of Economics*, vol 115, no 4, pp. 1411–39.

Boylan, T. and P. O'Gorman (1995) *Beyond Rhetoric and Realism in Economics: towards a Reformulation of Economic Methodology*, London: Routledge.

Boyns, T. (1987) "Rationalisation in the Interwar Period: the Case of the South Wales Steam Coal Industry", *Business History*, vol XXIX, no 3, pp. 282–303.

Braudel, H. (1974) *Capitalism and Material Life, 1400–1800*, New York: Harper and Row.

Breen, T. (1986) "An Empire of Goods: the Anglicisation of Colonial America, 1690–1776", *Journal of British Studies*, vol XXV, no 4, pp. 467–99.

Brenner, R. (1976) "Agrarian Class Structure and Economic Development in Pre-Industrial Europe", *Past and Present*, no 70, pp. 30–75, reprinted in Aston and Philpin (eds) (1985), pp. 10–63.

Brenner, R. (1982) "The Agrarian Roots of European Capitalism", *Past and Present*, no 97, pp. 16–113, reprinted in Aston and Philpin (eds) (1985), pp. 213–327.

Brenner, R. (1986) "The Social Basis of Economic Development", in Roemer (ed.) (1986), pp. 23–53.

Briggs, A. (1958) *Friends of the People: the Centenary History of Lewis's*, London: Batsford.

Brinkley, J. and S. Lohr (2001) *U.S. v. Microsoft*, New York: McGraw-Hill.

Broadberry, S. (2021) "The Industrial Revolution and the Great Divergence: Recent Findings from Historical National Accounting", in Bisin and Federico (eds) (2021), pp. 749–72.

Bromley, S. (1991) *American Hegemony and World Oil: the Industry, the State System and the World Economy*, London: Polity Press.

Bruland, K. (1985) "Say's Law and the Single-Factor Explanation of British Industrialisation: a Comment", *Journal of European Economic History*, vol XIV, no 1, pp. 187–91.

Brunskill, I., B. Fine and M. Prevezer (1985) "The Ownership of Coal Royalties in Scotland", *Scottish Economic and Social History*, vol 5, no 1, pp. 78–89.

Buxton, N. (1970) "Entrepreneurial Efficiency in the British Coal Industry between the Wars", *Economic History Review*, 2nd series, vol XXIII, no 3, pp. 476–97.

Caicedo, F. (2021) "Historical Econometrics: Instrumental Variables and Regression Discontinuity Designs", in Bisin and Federico (eds) (2021), pp. 179–212.

Cain, L. and P. Uselding (eds) (1973) *Business Enterprise and Economic Change: Essays in Honour of Harold F. Williamson*, Kent, OH: Kent State University Press.

Callinicos, A. (1987) *Making History: Agency, Structure and Change in Social Theory*, Cambridge: Polity Press.

Campbell, C. (1987) *The Romantic Ethic and the Spirit of Modern Consumerism*, Oxford: Blackwell.

Cannadine, D. (1984) "The Present and the Past in the English Industrial Revolution 1880–1980", *Past and Present*, vol 103, issue 1, pp. 131–72.

Carrier, J. and D. Miller (eds) (1998) *Virtualism: the New Political Economy*, London: Berg.

Chandler, A. (1990) *Scale and Scope: the Dynamics of Industrial Capitalism*, Cambridge: Belknap Press.

Chang, H.-J. (2000) "The Hazard of Moral Hazard: Untangling the Asian Crisis", *World Development*, vol 28, no 4, pp. 775–88.

Chang, H.-J. (ed.) (2003) *Rethinking Development Economics*, London: Anthem Press.

Chang, H.-J., H.-J. Park and C. Yoo (1998) "Interpreting the Korean Crisis: Financial Liberalisation, Industrial Policy and Corporate Governance", *Cambridge Journal of Economics*, vol 22, no 6, pp. 735–46.

Christophers, B. (2013) *Banking across Boundaries: Placing Finance in Capitalism*, Chichester: Wiley-Blackwell.

Church, R. (1986) *The History of the British Coal Industry, Volume 3, 1830–1913: Victorian Pre-Eminence,* Oxford: Clarendon.

Cioni, M., G. Federico and M. Vasta (2021) "The Two Revolutions in Economic History", in Bisin and Federico (eds) (2021), pp. 17–40.

Coase, R. (1937) "The Nature of the Firm", *Economica*, vol 4, no 4, pp. 386–405.

Coase, R. (1960) "The Problem of Social Cost", *Journal of Law and Economics*, vol 3, no 1, pp. 1–44.

Coase, R. (1998) "The New Institutional Economics", *American Economic Review*, vol 88, no 2, pp. 72–74.

Coats, A. (1969) "Is There a 'Structure of Scientific Revolutions' in Economics?", *Kyklos*, vol 22, no 2, pp. 289–96.

Coats, A. (1980) "The Historical Context of the 'New' Economic History", *Journal of European Economic History*, vol 9, no 1, 185–207.

Coats, A. (1990) "Disciplinary Self-Examination, Departments and Research Traditions in Economic History: the Anglo-American Story", *Scandinanvian Economic History Review*, vol 38, no 1, pp. 3–18.

Coats, A. (1995) "Comments on Schabas: the Nature and Significance of the 'New' Economic History: a Response to 'Parmenides and the Cliometricians'", within Little (ed.) (1995), pp. 183–209.

Coats, A. (1996) "Report of Discussions", *History of Political Economy*, vol 28, Supplement, pp. 369–91.

Coats, A. (ed.) (1996) *The Post-1945 Internationalization of Economics, History of Political Economy*, vol 28, Supplement.

Coffin, J. (1994) "Credit, Consumption, and Images of Women's Desires: Selling the Sewing Machine in Nineteenth-Century France", *French Historical Studies*, vol 18, no 3, pp. 749–83.

Coffin, J. (1996) "Consumption, Production, and Gender: The Sewing Machine in Nineteenth Century France", in Frader and Rose (eds), pp. 111–41.

Cole, A. (ed.) (1932) *Facts and Figures in Economic History: Articles by Former Students of Edwin Francis Gay*, Cambridge: Harvard University Press.

Cole, W. (1967) "Economic History as a Social Science", Inaugural Lecture delivered at the University College of Swansea, 24th October, reproduced in Harte (ed.) (1971), pp. 349–66.

Cole, W. (1983) "Factors in Demand, 1700–1860", in Floud and McCloskey (eds) (1983), pp. 36–65.

Coleman, D. (1987) *History and the Economic Past: an Account of the Rise and Decline of Economic History in Britain*, Oxford: Clarendon Press.

Conrad, A. and J. Meyer (1958) "The Economics of Slavery in the Ante Bellum South", *Journal of Political Economy*, vol 66, no 2, pp. 95–130.

Cowling, K. (1982) *Monopoly Capitalism*, London: Macmillan.

Crafts, N. (1981) "The Eighteenth Century: a Survey", in Floud and McCloskey (eds) (1981), pp. 1–16.

Crafts, N. (1995a) "Exogenous or Endogenous Growth – The Industrial Revolution Reconsidered", *Journal of Economic History*, vol 55, no 4, pp. 745–772.

Crafts, N. (1995b) "Macroinventions, Economic Growth, and 'Industrial Revolution' in Britain and France", *Economic History Review*, vol 8, no 3, pp. 591–8.

Crafts, N. (1997) "Endogenous Growth", in Kreps and Wallis (eds) (1997), pp. 38–78.

Crafts, N. (1999a) "Development History", Symposium on Future of Development Economics in Perspective, Dubrovnik, 13–14th May, now available at https://www.lse.ac.uk/Economic-History/Assets/Documents/WorkingPapers/Economic-History/2000/wp5400.pdf.

Crafts, N. (1999b) "Implications of Financial Crisis for East Asian Trend Growth", *Oxford Review of Economic Policy*, vol 15, no 3, pp. 110–31.

Crafts, N. (1999c) "East Asian Growth before and after the Crisis", *IMF Staff Papers*, vol 46, no 2, pp. 139–66.

Cunnington, C. and P. Cunnington (1972) *Handbook of English Costume in the Eighteenth Century*, London: Faber.

Damodaran, S., S. Gupta, S. Mitra and D. Sinha (eds) (2023) *Development, Transformations and the Human Condition: Volume in Honour of Professor Jayati Ghosh*, New Delhi: Routledge, forthcoming.

Dasgupta, P. and P. David (1987) "Information Disclosure and the Economics of Science and Technology", in Feiwel (ed.) (1987), pp. 519–542.

Dasgupta, P. and P. David (1994) "Towards a New Economics of Science", *Research Policy*, vol 23, no 5, pp. 487–521.

Dasgupta, P. and G. Heal (1979) *The Economics of Exhaustible Resources*, Cambridge: Cambridge University Press.

David, P. (1969) "Transport Innovation and Economic Growth: Professor Fogel on and off the Rails", *Economic History Review*, vol 22, no 3, pp. 506–25, reproduced in David (1975), pp. 291–314.

David, P. (1971) "The Landscape and the Machine: Technical Interrelatedness, Land Tenure and the Mechanization of the Corn Harvest in Victorian Britain", in McCloskey (ed.) (1971), pp 145–214, reproduced without discussion in David (1975).

David, P. (1975) *Technical Choice, Innovation and Economic Growth: Essays on American and British Experience in the Nineteenth Century*, Cambridge: Cambridge University Press.

David, P. (1985) "Clio and the Economics of QWERTY", *American Economic Review*, vol 75, no 2, pp. 332–37.

David, P. (1986) "Understanding the Economics of QWERTY: the Necessity of History", in Parker (ed.) (1986), pp. 30–49, longer version of David (1985).

David, P. (1990) "The Dynamo and the Computer – An Historical Perspective on the Modern Productivity Paradox", *American Economic Review*, vol 80, no 2, pp. 355–61.

David, P. (1991) "The Hero and the Herd in Technological History: Reflections on Thomas Edison and the Battle of the Systems", in Higonnet et al. (eds) (1991), pp. 72–119.

David, P. (1992) "Knowledge, Property, and the System Dynamics of Technological Change", *World Bank Economic Review*, Supplement, pp. 215–48.

David, P. (1993) "Historical Economics in the Longrun: Some Implications of Path-Dependence", in Snooks (ed.) (1993), pp. 29–40.

David, P. (1997) "Path Dependence and the Quest for Historical Economics: One More Chorus of the Ballad of QWERTY", University of Oxford Discussion Papers in Economic and Social History, no 20, now at https://personal.utdallas.edu/~liebo wit/knowledge_goods/david2.htm.

David, P. (1998) "Common Agency Contracting and the Emergence of 'Open Science' Institutions", *American Economic Review*, vol 88, no 2, pp. 15–21.

David, P. (1999a) "At Last, a Remedy for Chronic QWERTY-Skepticism!", paper prepared for presentation to the European Summer School in Industrial Dynamics, L'Insitute d'Etudes Scientifique de Cargèse (Corse) September.

David, P. (1999b) "Krugman's Economic Geography of Development: NEGS, POGS, and Naked Models in Space", *International Regional Science Review*, vol 22, no 2, pp. 162–72.

David, P. and D. Foray (1994) "Dynamics of Competitive Technology Diffusion through Local Network Structures: the Case of EDI Document Standards", in Leydesdorff and van den Besselaar (eds) (1994), pp. 63–78.

David, P., D. Foray and J.-M. Dalle (1998) "Marshallian Externalities and the Emergence of Spatial Stability of Technological Enclaves", *Economics of Innovation and New Technology*, vol 6, no 2/3, pp. 147–82.

David, P., H. Gutman, R. Sutch, P. Temin and G. Wright (1976) *Reckoning with Slavery: a Critical Study in the Quantitative History of American Negro Slavery*, New York: Oxford University Press.

Davies, G. (1989) "Governments Can Affect Employment: a Critique of Monetarism, Old and New", in Shields (ed.) (1989), pp. 49–144.

Davis, J. (1997) "New Economics and Its History: a Pickeringian View", in Davis (ed.) (1997), pp. 289–308.

Davis, J. (ed.) (1997) *New Economics and Its History, History of Political Economy*, vol 29, Supplement 1, Durham, NC: Duke University Press.

Davis, L. (1970) "'And It Will Never Be Literature': the New Economic History: a Critique", in Andreano (ed.) (1970), pp. 67–84.

de Grazia, V. and E. Furlough (eds) (1996) *The Sex of Things: Gender and Consumption in Historical Perspective*, London: University of California Press.

de la Escosura, L. (2019) "Pace Baudelaire? Comment on 'Spleen: the Failures of the Cliometric School' by Stefano Fenoaltea", *Annals of the Fondazione Luigi Einaudi*, vol LIII, no 2, pp. 25–30.

Deaton, A. and N Cartwright (2018) "Understanding and Misunderstanding Randomized Controlled Trials", *Social Science and Medicine*, vol 210, pp. 2–21.

Diebolt, C., and M. Haupert (2018) "A Cliometric Counterfactual: What If There Had Been Neither Fogel Nor North?", *Cliometrica*, vol 12, no 3, pp. 407–434.

Diebolt, C. and M. Haupert (2019a) "Measuring Success: Clio and the Value of Database Creation", *Annals of the Fondazione Luigi Einaudi*, vol LIII, no 2, pp. 59–80.

Diebolt, C. and M. Haupert (2019b) "Introduction", in Diebolt and Haupert (eds) (2019), pp. V–XVI.

Diebolt, C. and M. Haupert (2022) "The Role of Cliometrics in History and Economics", Bloomsbury History: Theory and Method, http://dx.doi.org/10.5040/9781350927 926.117.

Diebolt, C. and M. Haupert (eds) (2019) *Handbook of Cliometrics*, New York: Springer, second edition.

Dietz, B. (1986) "The North-East Coal Trade, 1550–1750: Measures, Markets and the Metropolis", *Northern History*, vol XXII, no 1, pp. 280–94.

Dintenfass, M. (1985) *Industrial Decline: Four British Colliery Companies between the Wars*, PhD thesis, Columbia University, but see *Managing Industrial Decline: British Coal Industry Between the Wars*, Columbus: Ohio State University Press, 1992.

Dobb, M. (1963/1946) *Studies in the Development of Capitalism*, London: Routledge and Kegan Paul.

Douglas, M. and B. Isherwood (1996) *The World of Goods: towards an Anthropology of Consumption*, second edition with new introduction, London: Routledge.

Drobak, J. and J. Nye (eds) (1997) *The Frontiers of New Institutional Economics*, London: Academic Press.

Duby, G. (1968) *Rural Economy and Country Life in the Medieval West*, Columbia: University of Carolina Press.

Dugger, W. (1995) "Douglass C. North's New Institutionalism", *Journal of Economic Issues*, vol XXIX, no 2, pp. 453–58.

Durlauf, S. (1991) "Multiple Equilibria and Persistence in Aggregate Fluctuations", *American Economic Review*, vol 81, no 2, pp.70–74.

Easterbrook, W. (1957) "Long-Period Comparative Study: Some Historical Cases", *Journal of Economic History*, vol 17, no 4, pp. 571–95.

Eatwell, J., M. Milgate, and P. Newman (eds) (1998) *The New Palgrave's Dictionary of Economics and Law*, London: MacMillan.

Edquist, C. (2001) "The Systems of Innovation Approach and Innovation Policy: an Account of the State of the Art", Lead paper presented at the DRUID Conference, Aalborg, June 12–15, http://www.obs.ee/~siim/seminars/edquist2001.pdf.

Eggertsson, T. (1996) "A Note on the Economics of Institutions", in Alston et al. (eds) (1996), pp. 6–24.

Eichengreen, B. (1995) "Macroeconomics and History", in Field (ed.) (1995), pp. 43–90.

Eisenach, J. and T. Lenard (eds) (1999) *Competition, Innovation and the Microsoft Monopoly: Antitrust in the Digital Marketplace*, Norwell:Kluwer.

Elton, G. (1983) "Two Kinds of History", in Fogel and Elton (eds) (1983), pp. 71–122.

Engels, F. (1976) *Anti-Duhring*, Peking: Foreign Language Press.

Erasmo, V. (2023) "The Impossibility of a Paretian (Il)liberal: a Historical Review Around Sen's Liberalism (1970–1996)", *History of Economic Thought and Policy*, issue 1, pp. 91–116.

Essletzbichler, J., M. Scholz-Wäckerle, L. Gerdes, H.-P. Wieland and C. Dorninger (2023) "Geographical Evolutionary Political Economy: Linking Local Evolution with Uneven and Combined Development", *Cambridge Journal of Regions, Economy and Society*, https://doi.org/10.1093/cjres/rsad014, forthcoming.

Evans, T. and B. Fine (1980a) "The Diffusion of Mechanical Cutting in the British Inter-war Coal Industry", Birkbeck Discussion Paper, no 75, University of London.

Evans, T. and B. Fine (1980b) "Economies of Scale in the British Inter-war Coal Industry", Birkbeck Discussion Paper, no 76, University of London.

Eversley, D. (1967) "The Home Market and Economic Growth in England, 1750–1780", in Jones and Mingay (eds) (1967), pp. 206–259.

Feiwel, G. (ed.) (1987) *Arrow and the Ascent of Modern Economic Theory*, London: MacMillan.

Fenoaltea, S. (1975) "The Rise and Fall of a Theoretical Model: the Manorial System", *Journal of Economic History*, vol 35, no 2, pp. 386–409.

Fenoaltea, S. (2019) "Spleen: the Failures of the Cliometric School", *Annals of the Fondazione Luigi Einaudi*, vol LIII, no 2, pp. 5–24.

Field, A. (1981) "The Problem of Neoclassical Institutional Economics: a Critique with Special Reference to the North/Thomas Model of Pre-1000 Europe", *Explorations in Economic History*, vol 18, no 2, pp. 174–198.

Field, A. (ed.) (1995) *The Future of Economics*, London: Routledge.

Fine, B. (1973) "The Prisoner's Dilemma and Moral Philosophy", Birkbeck Economics, Working Paper, no 10, November.

Fine, B. (1974) "Interdependent Preferences and Liberalism in a Paretian Society", Birkbeck Economics, Working Paper, no 15, January 1974.

Fine, B. (1975) "Individual Liberalism in a Paretian Society", *Journal of Political Economy*, vol 83, no 6, pp.1277–81.

Fine, B. (1978) "On the Origins of Capitalist Development", *New Left Review*, 109, pp. 88–95.

Fine, B. (1979) "On Marx's Theory of Agricultural Rent", *Economy and Society*, vol 8, no 3, pp. 241–78, reproduced within Fine (ed.) (1986, Chapter 5), pp. 114–87.

Fine, B. (1980a) "On the Historical Transformation Problem", *Economy and Society*, vol 9, no 3, pp. 337–39, reproduced within Fine (ed.) (1986, Chapter 5), pp. 114–87.

Fine, Bh. (1980b) *Economic Theory and Ideology*, London: Edward Arnold.

Fine, B. (1980c) "On Marx's Theory of Agricultural Rent: a Rejoinder" *Economy and Society*, vol 9, no 3, pp. 327–31, reproduced within Fine (ed.) (1986, Chapter 5), pp. 114–87.

Fine, B. (1980d) "The Historical Approach to Rent and Price Theory Reconsidered", Birkbeck Discussion Paper No. 69, University of London, published in *Australian Economic Papers*, vol. 22, no 4, 1983, pp. 132–43.

Fine, B. (1982a) *Theories of the Capitalist Economy*, London: Edward Arnold.

Fine, B. (1982b) "Landed Property and the Distinction between Royalty and Rent", *Land Economics*, vol 58, no 3, pp. 338–350.

Fine, B. (1983) "The Order of Acquisition of Consumer Durables: a Social Choice Theoretic Approach", *Journal of Economic Behaviour and Organisation*, vol 4, no 2/3, pp. 239–248.

Fine, B. (1988) "The British Coal Industry's Contribution to the Political Economy of Paul Sweezy", *History of Political Economy*, vol 20, no 2, pp. 235–50.

Fine, B. (1990a) *The Coal Question: Political Economy and Industrial Change from the Nineteenth Century to the Present Day*, London: Routledge, reprinted as Routledge Revival, 2013.

Fine, B. (1990b) "Featherbedding Cartel or Economies of Scale: the Case of the British Interwar Coal Industry", *Economic History Review*, vol XLIII, no 3, pp. 438–49. See Chapter 3.

Fine, B. (1993a) "Is Small Beautiful? Mine Size in the British Inter-War Coal Industry", *Economic History Review*, vol XLVI, no 1, pp. 160–62. See Chapter 3, Appendix.

Fine, B. (1993b) "Resolving the Diet Paradox", *Social Science Information*, vol 32, no 4, pp. 669–87.

Fine, B. (1993c) "Economic Development and Technological Change: From Linkage to Agency" in Liodakis (ed.) (1993), pp. 111–30.

Fine, B. (1994) "Coal, Diamonds and Oil: towards a Comparative Theory of Mining", *Review of Political Economy*, vol 6, no 3, pp. 279–302. See Chapter 4.

Fine, B. (1995) "From Political Economy to Consumption", in Miller (ed.) (1995), pp. 127–163.

Fine, B. (1997a) "The New Revolution in Economics", *Capital and Class*, no 61, Spring, pp. 143–48.

Fine, B. (1997b) "Playing the Consumption Game", *Consumption, Markets, Culture*, vol 1, no 1, pp. 7–29.

Fine, B. (1997c) "Industrial Policy and South Africa: a Strategic View", NIEP Occasional Paper Series, no 5, Johannesburg: National Institute for Economic Policy.

Fine, B. (1998a) *Labour Market Theory: a Constructive Reassessment*, London: Routledge.

Fine, B. (1998b) *The Political Economy of Diet, Health and Food Policy*, London: Routledge.

Fine, B. (1998c) "The Triumph of Economics: Or 'Rationality' Can Be Dangerous to Your Reasoning", in Carrier and Miller (eds) (1998), pp. 49–73.

Fine, B. (1999a) "'Household Appliances and the Use of Time: the United States and Britain since the 1920s' – A Comment", *Economic History Review*, vol LII, no 3, pp. 552–62.

Fine, B. (1999b) "Competition and Market Structure", *Metroeconomica*, vol 50, no 2, pp. 1–25.

Fine, B. (2000a) "New and Improved: Economics' Contribution to Business History", SOAS Working Paper in Economics, no 93, amended version.

Fine, B. (2000b) "Endogenous Growth Theory: a Critical Assessment", *Cambridge Journal of Economics*, vol 24, no 2, pp. 245–65, a shortened and amended version of identically titled, soas Working Paper, No 80, February 1998, pp. 1–49.

Fine, B. (2000c) "Consumption for Historians: An Economist's Gaze", SOAS Working Paper in Economics, no 90.

Fine, B. (2001a) "Economics Imperialism as Kuhnian Revolution?", *International Papers in Political Economy*, vol 8, no 2, pp. 1–58.

Fine, B. (2001b) *Social Capital versus Social Theory: Political Economy and Social Science at the Turn of the Millennium*, London: Routledge.

Fine, B. (2002a) *The World of Consumption: the Material and Cultural Revisited*, London: Routledge.

Fine, B. (2002b) "Economics Imperialism and the New Development Economics as Kuhnian Paradigm Shift", World Development, vol 30, no 12, pp. 2057–70.

Fine, B. (2002c) "'Economic Imperialism': a View from the Periphery", *Review of Radical Political Economics*, vol 34, no 2, pp. 187–201.

Fine, B. (2002d) "Globalisation and Development: the Imperative of Political Economy", Paper for the Conference "Towards a New Political Economy of Development: Globalisation and Governance", Sheffield, July, published as Fine (2004c).

Fine, B. (2003a) "Political Economy and Nature: From ANT and Environmental Economics to Bioeconomics?", *Journal of Interdisciplinary Economics*, vol 14, no 3, pp. 357–72.

Fine, B. (2003b) "Callonistics: a Disentanglement", *Economy and Society*, vol 32, no 3, pp. 496–502.

Fine, B. (2003c) "From the Newer Economic History to Institutions and Development?", *Institutions and Economic Development*, vol 1, no 1, pp. 105–36.

Fine, B. (2003d) "Social Capital: the World Bank's Fungible Friend", *Journal of Agrarian Change*, vol 3, no 4, pp. 586–603.

Fine, B. (2003e) "New Growth Theory", in Chang (ed.) (2003), pp. 201–17.

Fine, B. (2004a) "Debating Production-Consumption Linkages in Food Studies", *Sociologia Ruralis*, vol 44, no 3, pp. 332–42.

Fine, B. (2004b) "Economics Imperialism as Kuhnian Revolution", in Arestis and Sawyer (eds) (2004), pp. 107–44.

Fine, B. (2004c) "Examining the Idea of Globalisation and Development Critically: What Role for Political Economy?", *New Political Economy*, vol 9, no 2, pp. 213–31.

Fine, B. (2004d) "Addressing the Critical and the Real in Critical Realism", in Lewis (ed.) (2004), pp. 202–26.

Fine, B. (2005) "From Actor-Network Theory to Political Economy", *Capitalism, Socialism, Nature*, vol 16, no 4, pp. 91–108.

Fine, B. (2009a) "Enigma in the Origins of Paul Sweezy's Political Economy", *Review of Political Economy*, vol 21, no 1, pp. 157–61.

Fine, B. (2009b) "The Economics of Identity and the Identity of Economics?", *Cambridge Journal of Economics*, vol 33, no 2, pp. 175–91.

Fine, B. (2010a) *Theories of Social Capital: Researchers Behaving Badly*, London: Pluto.

Fine, B. (2010b) "Flattening Economic Geography: Locating the World Development Report for 2009", *Journal of Economic Analysis*, vol 1, no 1, pp. 15–33, http://users.ntua .gr/jea/JEA%20Vol.%20I,%20No%20I,%202010/jea_volume1_issue1_pp15_33.pdf.

Fine, B. (2011) "Prospecting for Political Economy", *International Journal of Management Concepts and Philosophy*, vol 5, no 3, pp. 204–17.

Fine, B. (2013) "Consumption Matters", *Ephemera*, vol 13, no 2, pp. 217–48, http://www .ephemerajournal.org/contribution/consumption-matters.

Fine, B. (2016) *Microeconomics: a Critical Companion*, London: Pluto.

Fine, B. (2019) "Post-Truth: an Alumni Economist's Perspective", *International Review of Applied Economics*, vol 33, no 4, pp. 542–67, shortened version of, SOAS Department of Economics Working Paper No. 219, 2019. https://www.soas.ac.uk/econom ics/research/workingpapers/file139489.pdf.

Fine, B. (2023a) "Social Capital: the Indian Connection", in Damodaran et al. (eds) (2023) forthcoming.

Fine, B. (2023b) "Mathematical Economics as Aid or Obstacle to Heterodox Economists?: a Personal Experience", Special Issue for Duncan Foley and Anwar Shaikh, *New School Economic Review*, vol 12, no 1, forthcoming.

Fine, B. (2024a) *Economics Imperialism and Interdisciplinarity: Before the Watershed; Critical Reconstructions of Political Economy*, Volume 1, Leiden: Brill, and Chicago: Haymarket.

Fine, B. (2024b) *Economics Imperialism and Interdisciplinarity: the Watershed and After; Critical Reconstructions of Political Economy*, Volume 2, Leiden: Brill, and Chicago: Haymarket.

Fine, B. (ed.) (1986) *The Value Dimension: Marx versus Ricardo and Sraffa*, London: Routledge and Kegan Paul.

Fine, B. and O. Dimakou (2016) *Macroeconomics: a Critical Companion*, London: Pluto.

Fine, B. and L. Harris (1975) "The British Economy since March 1974", *Bulletin of Conference of Socialist Economists*, vol 4, no 3, issue 12, pp. 43–62.

Fine, B. and L. Harris (1976) "The British Economy from May 1975 to January 1976", *Bulletin of Conference of Socialist Economists*, vol 5, no 2, issue 14, pp. 1–24.

Fine, B. and L. Harris (1979) *Rereading 'Capital'*, London: MacMillan.

Fine, B. and L. Harris (1985) *Peculiarities of the British Economy*, London: Wishart.

Fine, B. and L. Harris (1987) "Ideology and Markets: Economic Theory and the 'New Right'", in Miliband et al. (eds) (1987), pp. 365–92.

Fine, B., M. Heasman, and J. Wright (1996) *Consumption in the Age of Affluence: the World of Food*, London: Routledge.

Fine, B., C. Lapavitsas and J. Pincus (eds) (2001) *Development Policy in the Twenty-First Century: Beyond the Post-Washington Consensus*, London: Routledge.

Fine, B. and E. Leopold (1900) "Consumerism and the Industrial Revolution", *Social History*, vol 15, no 2, pp. 151–79. See Chapter 2.

Fine, B. and E. Leopold (1993) *The World of Consumption*. London: Routledge.

Fine, B. and P. Mendes Loureiro (2020) "A Note on the Relationship between Additive Separability and Decomposability in Measuring Income Inequality", *Review of Social Economy*, vol 80, no 4, pp. 550–65.

Fine, B. and P. Mendes Loureiro (2021) "From Social Choice to Inequality-Decomposition: In the Spirit of Arrow and Atkinson by Way of Sen and Shorrocks", *International Review of Applied Economics*, vol 35, no 1, pp. 765–91.

Fine, B. and D. Milonakis (2003) "From Principle of Pricing to Pricing of Principle: Rationality and Irrationality in the Economic History of Douglass North", *Comparative Studies in Society and History*, vol 45, no 3, pp. 120–44. See Chapter 6.

Fine, B. and D. Milonakis (2009) *From Economics Imperialism to Freakonomics: the Shifting Boundaries between Economics and Other Social Sciences*, London: Routledge.

Fine, B. and A. Murfin (1984a) *Macroeconomics and Monopoly Capitalism*, Brighton: Wheatsheaf.

Fine, B. and A. Murfin (1984b) "The Political Economy of Monopoly and Competition: a Critique of Monopoly and Stagnation Theory", *International Journal of Industrial Organisation*, vol 2, no 2, pp. 133–46.

Fine, B., K. O'Donnell and M. Prevezer (1985a) "Coal before Nationalisation", in Fine and Harris (1985), pp. 285–319.

Fine, B., K. O'Donnell and M. Prevezer (1985b) "Coal after Nationalisation", in Fine and Harris (1985), pp. 167–202.

Fine, B. and G. Pollen (2018) "The Developmental State Paradigm in the Age of Financialisation', in Hyland and Munck (eds) (2018), pp. 211–27.

Fine, B. and Z. Rustomjee (1992) "The Political Economy of South Africa in the Interwar Period", *Social Dynamics*, vol 18, no 2, pp. 26–54.

Fine, B. and Z. Rustomjee (1995) "'Afrikaner Nationalism, Anglo American and Iscor: the Formation Of The Highveld Steel And Vanadium Corporation, 1960–70' – A Comment", *Business History*, vol 37, no 3, pp. 111–14.

Fine, B. and Z. Rustomjee (1997) *South Africa's Political Economy: From Minerals-Energy Complex to Industrialisation*, Johannesburg: Wits University Press.

Fine, B. and Z. Rustomjee (1998) "Debating the South African Minerals-Energy Complex", *Development Southern Africa,* vol 15, no 4, pp. 689–70.

Fine, B. and A. Saad Filho (2016) *Marx's 'Capital'*, London: Pluto, sixth edition.

Fine, B., J. Saraswati and D. Tavasci (eds) (2013) *Beyond the Developmental State: Industrial Policy into the 21st Century*, London: Pluto.

Fine, B. and J. Simister (1995) "Consumption Durables: Exploring the Order of Acquisition", *Applied Economics*, vol 27, no 11, pp. 1049–57.

Fischer, S. (1977) "Long-Term Contracting, Sticky Prices, and Monetary Policy: a Comment", *Journal of Monetary Economics*, vol 3, no 3, pp. 317–24.

Fishlow, A. and R. Fogel (1971) "Quantitative Economic History: an Interim Evaluation: Past Trends and Present Tendencies", *Journal of Economic History*, vol 31, no 1, pp. 15–42.

Flinn, M. (1984) *The History of the British Coal Industry, Volume 2, 1700–1830: the Industrial Revolution*, with the assistance of D. Stoker, Oxford: Clarendon Press.

Floud, R. and D. McCloskey (eds) (1981) *The Economic History of Britain since 1700, Volume 1, 1700–1860*, Cambridge: Cambridge University Press.

Floud, R. and D. McCloskey (eds) (1983) *The Economic History of Britain since 1700, Volume 2, 1860–1939*, Cambridge: Cambridge University Press.

Fogel, R. (1967) "The Specification Problem in Economic History", *Journal of Economic History*, vol 27, no 3, pp. 283–308.

Fogel, R. (1983) "'Scientific' History and Traditional History", in Fogel and Elton (eds) (1983), pp. 5–70.

Fogel, R. (1997) "Douglass C. North and Economic Theory", in Drobak and Nye (eds) (1997), pp. 13–27.

Fogel, R., S. Bruchey and A. Chandler (1970) "Comments on Conrad Paper", in Andreano (ed.) (1970), pp. 129–50.

Fogel, R. and G. Elton (eds) (1983) *Which Road to the Past?: Two Views of History*, New Haven: Yale University Press.

Fogel, R. and S. Engerman (1974) *Time on the Cross: the Economics of American Negro Slavery*, Boston: Little, Brown.

Fohlin, C. (1998) "Banking Systems and Economic Growth: Lessons from Britain and Germany in the Pre-World War I Era", *Review of the Federal Reserve Bank of St Louis*, vol 80, no 3, pp. 37–47.

Forty, A. (1986) *Objects of Desire: Design and Society from Wedgwood to IBM*, London: Thames and Hudson.

Fourie, F. (1993) "In the Beginning There Were Markets?", in Pitelis (ed.) (1993), pp. 41–65.

Frader, L. and S. Rose (eds) (1996) Gender and Class in Modern Europe, Ithaca: Cornell University Press.

Frankema, E. (2021) "Why Africa Is Not That Poor", in Bisin and Federico (eds) (2021), pp. 557–84.

Freeman, C. and F. Louçã (2001) *As Time Goes By: From the Industrial Revolutions to the Information Revolution*, Oxford: Oxford University Press.

Friedman, M. and A. Schwartz (1963) *A Monetary History of the United States, 1867–1960*, Princeton: Princeton University Press.

Gaski, J. (1982) "The Causes of the Industrial Revolution: a Brief, 'Single Factor' Argument", *Journal of European Economic History*, vol XI, no 1, pp. 227–33.

Geary, F. (1984) "The Cause of the Industrial Revolution and 'Single Factor' Arguments: an Assessment", *Journal of European Economic History*, vol XIII, no 1, pp. 167–73.

Gerstenberger, H. (2022) *Market and Violence: the Functioning of Capitalism in History*, Leiden: Brill.

Giddens, A. (1979) *Central Problems in Social Theory*, London: MacMillan.

Gilboy, E. (1932) "Demand as a Factor in the Industrial Revolution", in Cole (ed.) (1932), pp.–39, reproduced in Hartwell 620 (ed.) (1967), pp. 121–38.

Goldin, C. (1995) "Cliometrics and the Nobel", *Journal of Economic Perspectives*, vol 9, no 2, pp. 191–208.

Goodrich, C. (1960) "Economic History: One Field or Two?", *Journal of Economic History*, vol 20, no 4, pp. 531–47.

Gordon, D. (1965) "The Role of the History of Economic Thought in the Understanding of Modern Economic Theory", *American Economic Review*, vol 55, no 2, pp. 119–27.

Greasley, D. (1993) "Economies of Scale in British Coalmining between the Wars", 2nd Series, *Economic History Review*, vol XLVI, no 1, pp. 155–59.

Greenwood, J., N. Guner and K. Kopecky (2021) "The Wife's Protector: a Quantitative Theory Linking Contraceptive Technology with the Decline in Marriage", in Bisin and Federico (eds) (2021), pp. 903–44.

Gregory, T. (1962) *Ernest Oppenheimer and the Economic Development of Southern Africa*, Cape Town: Oxford University Press.

Greif, A. (1994) "Cultural Beliefs and the Organization of Society: a Historical and Theoretical Reflection on Collectivist and Individualist Societies", *Journal of Political Economy*, vol 102, no 5, pp. 912–50.

Greif, A. (1997) "Cliometrics after Forty Years", *American Economic Review*, vol 87, no 2, pp. 400–3.

Groenewegen, J., F. Kerstholt and A. Nagelkerke (1995) "On Integrating New and Old Institutionalism: Douglass North Building Bridges", *Journal of Economic Issues*, vol XXIX, no 2, pp. 467–75.

Hancock, W. (1946) "Economic History at Oxford: an Inaugural Lecture Delivered before the University of Oxford on 1 February 1946", reproduced in Harte (ed.) (1971), pp. 143–160.

Hands, D. (2010) "Economics, Psychology and the History of Consumer Choice Theory", *Cambridge Journal of Economics*, vol 34, no 4, pp. 633–48.

Hansen, G., L. Ohanian and F. Ozturk (2021) "Dynamic General Equilibrium Modeling of Long-and Short-Run Historical Events", in Bisin and Federico (eds) (2021), pp. 297–334.

Harriss, J., J. Hunter and C. Lewis (eds) (1995) *The New Institutional Economics and Third World Development*, London and New York: Routledge.

Hart, O. (1995) *Firms, Contracts, and Financial Structure*, Oxford: Oxford University Press.

Harte, N. (ed.) (1971) *The Study of Economic History: Collected Inaugural Lectures, 1893–1970*, London: Frank Cass.

Hartwell, R. (1965) "The Causes of the Industrial Revolution: an Essay in Methodology", *Economic History Review*, vol XVIII, no 164 –82, reproduced in Hartwell (ed.) (1967), pp. 53–80.

Hartwell, R. (ed.) (1967) *The Causes of the Industrial Revolution*. London: Methuen.

Hartwell, R. (1971) "Is the New Economic History an Export Product?: a Comment on J. R.T. Hughes ", in McCloskey (ed.) (1971), pp. 413–22.

Harvey, C. and J. Press (1990) "Issues in the History of Mining and Metallurgy", *Business History*, XXXII, no 3, pp. 1–14.

Haupert, M. (2017) "The Impact of Cliometrics on Economics and History", *Revue d'Economie Politique*, vol 127, no 6, pp. 1059–1082.

Haupert, M. (2019) "A Brief History of Cliometrics and the Evolving View of the Industrial Revolution", *European Journal of the History of Economic Thought*, vol 26, no 4, pp. 738–74.

Haupert, M. and C. Diebolt (2020) "Cliometrics", in Atkinson et al. (eds) Sage Research Methods, *Econometrics*, https://doi.org/10.4135/9781526421036818809, cited from, Working Paper, no 1, 2018, Association Française de Cliométrie, https://ideas.repec.org/p/afc/wpaper/01-18.html.

Hausmann, W. (1984a) "Cheap Coals or Limitation of the Vend? The London Coal Trade, 1770–1845", *Journal of Economic History*, vol XLIV, no 2, pp. 321–8.

Hausmann, W. (1984b) "Market Power in the London Coal Trade: the Limitations of the Vend, 1770–1845", *Explorations in Economic History*, vol XXI, no 4, pp. 383–405.

Hayami, Y. and M. Aoki (1998) *The Institutional Foundations of East Asian Economic Development*, London: Palgrave Macmillan.

Heaton, H. (1957) "Summary of Discussion", *Journal of Economic History*, vol 17, no 4, pp. 596–602.

Heaton, H. (1965) "Twenty-Five Years of the Economic History Association: a Reflective Evaluation", *Journal of Economic History*, vol XXV, no 4, pp. 465–79.

Hecht, J. (1956) *The Domestic Servant Class in Eighteenth-Century England*, London, Routledge & Paul.

Heckman, J. (1991) "Identifying the Hand of the Past: Distinguishing State Dependence from Heterogeneity", *American Economic Review*, vol 81, no 2, pp. 75–79.

Henley, A. (1988) "Price Formation and Market Structure: the Case of the Inter-War Coal Industry", *Oxford Bulletin of Economics and Statistics*, vol 50, no 3, pp. 263–78.

Hidy, R. and M. Hidy (1955) *History of Standard Oil Company (New Jersey): Pioneering in Big Business, 1882–1911*, New York: Harper and Bros.

Higonnet, P., D. Landes and H. Rosovsky (eds) (1991) *Favorites of Fortune: Technology, Growth, and Economic Developments since the Industrial Revolution*, Cambridge: Harvard University Press.

Hilton, R. (1978) "Introduction", in Hilton (ed.) (1978), pp. 9–30.

Hilton, R. (ed.) (1978) *The Transition from Feudalism to Capitalism*, London: Verso.

Hirshleifer, J. (1985) "The Expanding Domain of Economics", *American Economic Review*, vol 83, no 3, Special Issue, December, pp. 53–68.

Hobsbawm, E. (1997) *On History*, London: Weidenfeld and Nicolson.

Hodgson, G. (1988) *Economics and Institutions*, Cambridge: Polity Press.

Hodgson, G. (2004) *The Evolution of Institutional Economics: Agency, Structure and Darwinism in American Institutionalism*, London and New York: Routledge.

Hodgson, G. and H. Rothman (1999) "The Editors and Authors of Economics Journals: a Case of Institutional Oligopoly?", *Economic Journal*, vol 109, no 453, pp. F165–86.

Holton, R. (1985) *The Transition from Feudalism to Capitalism*, London: Macmillan Education.

Hogarth, R. and M. Reder (eds) (1987) *Rational Choice: the Contrast between Economics and Psychology*, Chicago: Chicago University Press.

Hounshell, D. (1991) "Comment", in Temin (ed.) (1991) within pp. 7–40.

Hughes, J. (1971) "Is the New Economic History an Export Product?", in McCloskey (ed.) (1971), pp. 401–12.

Hyland, M. and R. Munck (eds) (2018) *Handbook on Development and Social* Change, Cheltenham: Edward Elgar.

Ingham, G. (1996) "Some Recent Changes in the Relationship between Economics and Sociology", *Cambridge Journal of Economics*, vol 20, no 2, pp. 243–75.

Inkster, I. (1983) "Technology as the Cause of the Industrial Revolution: Some Comments", *Journal of European Economic History*, vol XII, no 3, pp. 651–8.

Innes, D. (1984) *Anglo American and the Rise of Modern South Africa*, London Heinemann.

Itaman, R. (2021) "The Finance-Growth Nexus Enigma: Bringing in Institutional Context and the Productiveness Debate", *Journal of Economic Surveys*, forthcoming, https://doi.org/10.1111/joes.12454.

Itoh, M. and C. Lapavitsas (1999) *Political Economy of Money and Finance*, London: Palgrave Macmillan.

Jabbar, H. and F. Menashy (2022) "Economic Imperialism in Education Research: a Conceptual Review", *Educational Researcher*, vol 51, no 4, pp. 279–88.

Javdani, M. and H-J Chang (2019) "Who Said or What Said?: Estimating Ideological Bias in Views among Economists", Institute of Labor Economics, IZA, Bonn, Discussion Paper, no 12738, https://www.iza.org/publications/dp/12738/who-said-or-what-said -estimating-ideological-bias-in-views-among-economists, published in *Cambridge Journal of Economics*, 2023, beac071, https://doi.org/10.1093/cje/beac071.

Johnson, B. (1987) *A Lady of Fashion: Barbara Johnson's Album of Fashions and Fabric*, London: W. W. Norton.

Jomo, K. S. and B. Fine (eds) (2006) *The New Development Economics: after the Washington Consensus*, Delhi: Tulika, and London: Zed Press.

Jones, E. (1973) "The Fashion Manipulators: Consumer Tastes and British Industries, 1660–1800", in Cain and Uselding (eds) (1973), pp. 198–226.

Jones, E. and G. Mingay (eds) (1967) *Land, Labour and Population in the Industrial Revolution: Essays Presented to J. D. Chambers*, London: Edward Arnold.

Kafka, A. (2016) "The Lives of Deirdre McCloskey: Her Gender Change May Be the Least Iconoclastic Thing about Her", *The Chronicle Review*, March 20, https://www .deirdremccloskey.com/docs/pdf/ChronicleProfile2016.pdf.

Kay, N. (2013) "Rerun the Tape of History and QWERTY Always Wins", *Research Policy*, vol 42, no 5–6, pp. 1175–85.

Kindleberger, C. (1986) "A Further Comment", in Parker (ed.) (1986), pp. 83–92.

Kirby, M. (1973) "The Control of Competition in the British Coal Mining Industry in the Thirties", *Economic History Review*, 2nd series, vol XXVI, no 2, pp. 273–84.

Kirby, M. (1977) *The British Coalmining Industry, 1870–1946: a Political and Economic History*, London: MacMillan.

Knowles, R. (1983) *The First Pictorial History of the Business Oil and Gas Industry, 1859–1983*, Athens: Ohio University Press.

Koshovets, O. (2019) "Neuroeconomics: New Heart for Economics or New Face of Economic Imperialism", *Journal of Institutional Studies*, vol 11, no 1, pp. 6–19.

Koxhoorn, N. (1977) *Oil and Politics: the Domestic Roots of US Expansionism in the Middle East*, Frankfurt: Peter Lang.

Koyama, M. (2019) "Political Economy", in Diebolt and Haupert (eds) (2019), pp. 727–60.

Kreps, D. and K. Wallis (eds) (1997) *Advances in Economics and Econometrics: Theory and Applications*, Volume II, Cambridge: Cambridge University Press.

Krugman, P. (1991) "History and Industrial Location: the Case of the Manufacturing Belt", *American Economic Review*, vol 81, no 2, pp. 80–83.

Kuznets, S. (1957) "Summary of Discussion and Postscript", *Journal of Economic History*, vol 17, no 4, pp. 545–53.

Lamoreaux, N. (1994) *Insider Lending: Banks, Personal Connections, and Economic Development in Industrial New England*, Cambridge: Cambridge University Press.

Lamoreaux, N. (1998a) "Economic History and the Cliometric Revolution", in Molho and Wood (eds) (1998), pp. 59–84.

Lamoreaux, N. (1998b) "Commentary", *Review of the Federal Reserve Bank of St Louis*, vol 80, no 3, pp. 33–36.

Lamoreaux, N. (1998c) "Partnerships, Corporations, and the Theory of the Firm", *American Economic Review*, vol 88, no 2, pp. 66–71.

Lamoreaux, N. and D. Raff (1995) "Introduction: History and Theory in Search of One Another", in Lamoreaux and Raff (eds) (1995), pp. 1–10.

Lamoreaux, N. and D. Raff (eds) (1995) *Coordination and Information: Historical Perspectives on the Organization of Enterprise*, Chicago: Chicago University Press.

Lamoreaux, N., D. Raff and P. Temin (1997) "New Economic Approaches to the Study of Business History", *Business and Economic History*, vol 26, no 1, pp. 57–79.

Lamoreaux, N., D. Raff and P. Temin (1999) "Introduction", in Lamoreaux et al. (eds) (1999), pp. 1–18.

Lamoreaux, N., D. Raff and P. Temin (eds) (1999) *Learning by Doing: In Markets, Firms, and Countries*, Chicago: Chicago University Press.

Landes, D. (1994) "What Room for Accident in History?: Explaining Big Changes by Small Events", *Economic History Review*, vol 47, no 4, pp. 637–56.

Landes, D. (1995) "Some Further Thoughts on Accident in History: a Reply to Professor Crafts", *Economic History Review*, vol 8, no 3, pp. 599–601.

Lapavitsas, C. (2003) *Social Foundations of Markets, Money and Credit*, London: Routledge.

Lawson, T. (1997) *Economics and Reality*, London: Routledge.

Lazear, E. (2000) "Economic Imperialism", *Quarterly Journal of Economics*, vol 115, no 1, pp. 99–146.

Le Roy Ladurie, E. (1974) *The Peasants of Langeudoc*, Urbana: University of Illinois, originally published in French in 1966.

Lee, F. and S. Harley (1998) "Peer Review, the Research Assessment Exercise and the Demise of Non-Mainstream Economics", *Capital and Class*, no 66, pp. 23–51.

Lemire, B. (1984) "Developing Consumerism and the Ready-Made Clothing Trade in Britain,1750–1800", *Textile History*, vol xv, no 1, pp. 21–44.

Lenin, V. (1899) *The Development of Capitalism in Russia: the Process of the Formation of a Home Market for Large-Scale Industry*, https://www.marxists.org/archive/lenin/works/1899/devel.

Lenzen, G. (1970) *The History of the Diamond Production and the Diamond Trade*, London: Barrie Books.

Levine, D. and S. Modica (2021) "State Power and Conflict Driven Evolution", in Bisin and Federico (eds) (2021), pp. 435–62.

Lewis, P. (ed.) (2004) *Transforming Economics: Perspectives on the Critical Realist Project*, London: Routledge.

Leydesdorff, L. and P. van den Besselaar (eds) (1994) *Evolutionary Economics and Chaos Theory: New Directions in Technology Studies*, London: Pinter.

Liebowitz, S. and S. Margolis (1990) "The Fable of the Keys", *Journal of Law and Economics*, vol XXXIII, no 1, pp. 1–25.

Liebowitz, S. and S. Margolis (1994) "Network Externality: an Uncommon Tragedy", *Journal of Economic Perspectives*, vol 8, no 2, pp. 133–50.

Liebowitz, S. and S. Margolis (1995a) "Path Dependence, Lock-In, and History", *Journal of Law, Economics and Organization*, vol 11, no 1. pp. 205–26.

Liebowitz, S. and S. Margolis (1995b) "Are Network Externalities a New Source of Market Failure?", *Research in Law and Economics*, vol 17, pp. 1–22.

Liebowitz, S. and S. Margolis (1996) "Market Processes and the Selection of Standards", https://personal.utdallas.edu/~liebowit/standard/standard.html, earlier version of a paper that appeared in *Harvard Journal of Law and Technology*, vol 9, no 2, pp. 283–318.

Liebowitz, S. and S. Margolis (1998a) "Path Dependence", in Eatwell et al. (eds) (1998) Volume 3, pp. 17–23.

Liebowitz, S. and S. Margolis (1998b) "Network Effect", in Eatwell et al. (eds) (1998) Volume 2, pp. 1329–1333.

Liebowitz, S. and S. Margolis (2001) *Winners, Losers and Microsoft: Competition and Antitrust in High Technology*, Oakland: The Independent Institute, second edition.

Liodakis, G. (ed.) (1993) *Society, Technology and Restructuring of Production*, Athens: V. Papazissis (in Greek).

Lipartito, K. (1995) "Culture and the Practice of Business History", *Business and Economic History*, vol 24, no 2, pp. 1–42.

Lister, A. (1988) *I Know My Own Heart: the Diaries of Anne Lister (1791–1840)* New York: New York University Press.

Little, D. (ed.) (1995) *On the Reliability of Economic Models: Essays in the Philosophy of Economics*, New York: Springer.

Lloyd, C. (1986) *Explanation in Social History*, Oxford: Basil Blackwell.

Lockwood, D. (1964) "Social Integration and System Integration", in Zollschan and Hirsch (eds) (1964), pp. 244–57.

Lucas, A. (1937) *Industrial Reconstruction and the Control of Competition: the British Experiments*, London: Longmans, Green and Company.

Mader, P., D. Mertens and N. Van der Zwan (eds) (2020) *International Handbook of Financialization*, London: Routledge.

Majumdar, T. (1969) *Growth and Choice*, Oxford: Oxford University Press.

Malm, A. (2019) "Against Hybridism: Why We Need to Distinguish between Nature and Society, Now More than Ever", *Historical Materialism*, vol 27, no 2, pp. 156–187.

Margo, R. (2021) "The Economic History of Economic History: the Evolution of a Field in Economics", in Bisin and Federico (eds) (2021), pp. 3–16.

Margolis, S. (2013) "A Tip of the Hat to Kay and QWERTY", *Research Policy*, vol 42, no 5–6, pp. 1188–90.

Marks, S. (1985a) "Southern Africa, 1867–1886", in Oliver and Sanderson (eds) (1985), pp. 359–421.

Marks, S. (1985b) "Southern and Central Africa, 1886–1910", in Oliver and Sanderson (eds) (1985), pp. 422–92.

Martin, R. (1999) "The New 'Geographical Turn' in Economics: Some Critical Reflections", *Cambridge Journal of Economics*, vol 23, no 1, pp. 65–91.

Marx, K. (1972/1852) *The Eighteenth Brumaire of Louis Bonaparte*, in Marx et al. (1972), pp. 120–33.

Marx, K., F. Engels and V. Lenin (1972) *On Historical Materialism*, Moscow: Progress Publishers.

Mathias, P. (1970) "Living with the Neighbours: the Role of Economic History", in Harte (ed.) (1971), pp. 369–83.

Matthews, D. (1990) "Serendipity or Economics? Tin and the Theory of Mineral Discovery and Development, 1800–1920", *Business History*, vol XXXII, no 3, pp. 15–48.

Matthews, R. (1986) "The Economics of Institutions and the Sources of Growth", *Economic Journal*, vol 96, no 4, pp. 903–18.

McClelland, P. (1975) *Causal Explanation and Model Building in History, Economics, and the New Economic History*, Ithaca: Cornell University Press.

McCloskey, D. (1970) "Did Victorian Britain Fail?", *Economic History Review*, vol 23, no 3, pp. 446–59.

McCloskey, D. (1971) "International Differences in Productivity? Coal and Steel in America and Britain before World War 1", in McCloskey (ed.) (1971), pp. 285–310.

McCloskey, D. (1976) "Does the Past Have Useful Economics?", *Journal of Economic Literature*, vol 14, no 2, pp. 434–61.

McCloskey, D. (1978) "The Achievements of the Cliometric School", *Journal of Economic History*, vol 38, no 1, pp. 13–28.

McCloskey, D. (1981) "The Industrial Revolution, 1780–1860: a Survey", in Floud and McCloskey (eds) (1983), pp. 103–127.

McCloskey, D. (1986a) *The Rhetoric of Economics*, Brighton: Wheatsheaf.

McCloskey, D. (1986b) "Economics as Historical Science", in Parker (ed.) (1986), pp. 63–69.

McCloskey, D. (1987) *Econometric History*, London: Red Globe Press.

McCloskey, D. (1991) "History, Differential Equations, and the Problem of Narration", *History and Theory*, vol 30, no 1, pp. 21–36.

McCloskey, D. (2019) "Economic History as Humanomics", in Diebolt and Haupert (eds) (2019), pp. 109–22.

McCloskey, D. (ed.) (1971) *Essays on a Mature Economy: Britain after 1840*, Princeton: Princeton University Press.

McKendrick, N. (1959/60) "Josiah Wedgwood: an Eighteenth-Century Entrepreneur in Salesmanship and Marketing Techniques", *Economic History Review*, vol XII, no 3, pp. 408–33.

McKendrick, N. (1964) "Josiah Wedgwood and Thomas Bentley: an Inventor-Entrepreneur Partnership in the Industrial Revolution", *Transactions of the Royal Historical Society*, vol XIV, pp. 1–33.

McKendrick, N. (1973) "The Role of Science in the Industrial Revolution: a Study of Josiah Wedgwood as a Scientist and Industrial Chemist", in Teich and Young (eds) (1973), pp. 274–319.

McKendrick, N. (1982) "Commercialisation and the Economy", in McKendrick et al. (1982) Part I, pp. 9–196.

McKendrick, N. (1961) "Josiah Wedgwood and Factory Discipline", *Historical Journal*, vol IV, no 1, pp. 30–55.

McKendrick, N. (1970) "Josiah Wedgwood and Cost Accounting in the Industrial Revolution", *Economic History Review*, vol XXII, no 1, pp. 45–67.

McKendrick, N. (1974) "Home Demand and Economic Growth: a New View of the Role of Women and Children in the Industrial Revolution," in McKendrick (ed.) (1974), pp. 152–21.

McKendrick, N. (ed.) (1974) *Historical Perspectives: Studies in English Thought and Society in Honour of J. H. Plumb*, London: Europa Publications.

McKendrick, N., J. Brewer and J. Plumb (1982) *The Birth of a Consumer Society: the Commercialisation of Eighteenth Century England*, London: Europa.

McKenzie, R. (2000) *Trust on Trial: How the Microsoft Case Is Reframing the Rules of Competition*, Cambridge: Perseus.

McLean, J. and R. Haigh (1954) *The Growth of Integrated Oil Companies*, Norwood: Plimpton Press.

Merton, R. (1967) *Social Theory and Social Structure*, Toronto: Free Press, revised and enlarged from original of 1949.

Meyer, J. (1997) "Notes on Cliometrics' Fortieth", *American Economic Review*, vol 87, no 2, pp. 409–411.

Meyer, J. and A. Conrad (1957) "Economic Theory, Statistical Inference and Economic History", *Journal of Economic History*, vol 17, no 4, pp. 524–44.

Milgrom, P., Y. Qian and J. Roberts (1991) "Complementarities, Momentum, and the Evolution of Modern Manufacturing", *American Economic Review*, vol 81, no 2, pp. 84–88.

Miliband, R., L. Panitch and J. Saville (eds) (1987) *Conservatism in Britain and America: Rhetoric and Reality, Socialist Register*, 1987, London: Merlin Press.

Miller, B. (1981) *The Bon Marché: Bourgeois Culture and the Department Store, 1869–1920*, Princeton: Princeton University Press.

Miller, D. (ed.) (1995) *Acknowledging Consumption*, London: Routledge.

Mills, C. Wright (1959) *The Sociological Imagination*, New York: Oxford University Press.

Milonakis, D. (1993–4) "Prelude to the Genesis of Capitalism: the Dynamics of the Feudal Mode of Production", *Science and Society*, vol 57, no 4, pp. 390–419.

Milonakis, D. (1997) "The Dynamics of History: Structure and Agency in Historical Evolution", *Science and Society*, vol 61, no 3, pp. 303–329.

Milonakis, D. (2006) "Pioneers of Economic History", in Jomo and Fine (eds) (2006), pp. 269–292.

Milonakis, D. and B. Fine (2007) "Douglass North's Remaking of Economic History: a Critical Appraisal", *Review of Radical Political Economics*, vol 39, no 1, pp. 27–57. See Chapter 7.

Milonakis, D. and B. Fine (2009) *From Political Economy to Economics: Method, the Social and the Historical in the Evolution of Economic Theory*, London: Routledge.

Misa, T. (1999) "Comment", in Lamoreaux et al. (eds) (1999) within pp. 219–52.

Mitch, D. (2011) "Economic History in Departments of Economics: the Case of the University of Chicago, 1892 to the Present", *Social Science History*, vol 35, no 2, pp. 237–71.

Mokyr, J. (1977) "Demand vs Supply in the Industrial Revolution", *Journal of Economic History*, vol XXXVII, no 4, pp. 981–1008.

Mokyr, J. (1984) "Demand vs Supply in the Industrial Revolution: a Reply", *Journal of Economic History*, vol XLIV, no 3, pp. 806–9.

Mokyr, J. (1985) "The Industrial Revolution and the New Economic History", in Mokyr (ed.) (1985), pp. 1–52, but compare with updated version at https://faculty.wcas .northwestern.edu/jmokyr/monster.PDF.

Mokyr, J. (1993) "Editor's Introduction: the New Economic History and the Industrial Revolution", in Mokyr (ed.) (1993), pp. 1–131.

Mokyr, J. (2017) *Culture and Growth: the Origins of the Modern Economy*, Princeton: Princeton University Press.

Mokyr, J. (2021) "Attitudes, Aptitudes, and the Roots of the Great Enrichment", in Bisin and Federico (eds) (2021), pp. 773–94.

Mokyr, J. (ed.) (1985) *The Economics of the Industrial Revolution*, London: Routledge.

Mokyr, J. (ed.) (1993) *The British Industrial Revolution: an Economic Perspective*, Boulder: Westview Press.

Molho, A. and G. Wood (eds) (1998) *Imagined Histories: American Historians Interpret the Past*, Princeton: Princeton University Press.

Mowat, C. (1955) *Britain between the Wars, 1918–1940*, London: Methuen.

Murphy, G. (1965) "The 'New' History", *Explorations in Entrepreneurial History*, vol 2, no 2, pp. 132–46, reproduced in Andreano (ed.) (1970), pp. 1–16.

Musson, A. (ed.) (1972) *Science, Technology, and Economic Growth in the Eighteenth Century*, London: Routledge.

Myhrman, J. and B. Weingast (1994) "Douglass C. North's Contributions to Economics and Economic History", *Scandinavian Journal of Economics*, vol 96, no 2, pp. 185–193.

Nef, J. (1932) *The Rise of the British Coal Industry*, Volumes I and II, London: Routledge.

Nelson, R. (1997) "How New Is New Growth Theory", *Challenge*, Sept/Oct, pp. 29–58.

Neumann, A. (1934) *Economic Organisation of the British Coal Industry*, London: Routledge.

Newbury, C. (1989) *The Diamond Ring: Business, Politics, and Precious Stones in South Africa, 1867–1947*, Oxford: Clarendon Press.

Nicholas, S. (1982) "Total Factor Productivity Growth and the Revision of post-1870 British Economic History", *Economic History Review*, vol XXXV, no 1, pp. 85–98.

Nik-Khah, E. and R. Van Horn (2012) "Inland Empire: Economics Imperialism as an Imperative of Chicago Neoliberalism", *Journal of Economic Methodology*, vol 19, no 3, pp. 259–82.

Nilsson, E. (1993) "Review of Douglass North's *Institutions, Institutional Change and Economic Performance*", *Review of Radical Political Economics*, vol 25, no 3, p. 145.

Nore, P. and T. Turner (eds) (1980) *Oil and Class Struggle*, London: Zed Press.

North, D. (1963) "Quantitative Research in American Economic History", *American Economic Review*, vol 53, no 1, pp. 128–29.

North, D. (1965) "Economic History: Its Contribution to Economic Education, Research, and Policy", *American Economic Review*, vol 55, no 2, pp. 86–91.

North, D. (1974) "Beyond the New Economic History", *Journal of Economic History*, vol 34, no 1, pp. 1–7.

North, D. (1978) "Comment on McCloskey, Cohen, and Forster Papers", *Journal of Economic History*, vol 38, no 1 (The Tasks of Economic History), pp. 77–80.

North, D. (1981) *Structure and Change in Economic History*, New York: W. W. Norton.

North, D. (1989) "Institutions and Economic Growth: an Historical Introduction", *World Development*, vol 17, no 9, pp. 1319–32.

North, D. (1990) *Institutions, Institutional Change and Economic Performance*, Cambridge: Cambridge University Press.

North, D. (1992) "Privatization, Incentives, and Economic Performance", in Siebert (ed) (1992), pp. 1–13.

North, D. (1993a) "What Do We Mean by Rationality?", *Public Choice*, vol 77, no 1, pp. 159–62.

North, D. (1993b) "The Ultimate Sources of Economic Growth", in Szirmai et al. (eds) (1993), pp. 65–77.

North, D. (1994a) "Economic Performance through Time", *American Economic Review*, vol 84, no1, pp. 359–68.

North, D. (1994b) "The Historical Evolution of Polities", *International Review of Law and Economics*, vol 14, no 4, pp. 381–91.

North, D. (1995a) "Review of Bicchieri", *Journal of Economic Literature*, vol 33, no 2, pp. 821–2.

North, D. (1995b) "The New Institutional Economics and Third World Development", in Harriss et al. (eds) (1995), pp. 17–26.

North, D. (1997a) "Cliometrics – 40 Years Later", *American Economic Review*, vol 87, no 2, pp. 412–14.

North, D. (1997b) "The Contribution of the New Institutional Economics to an Understanding of the Transition Problem", WIDER Annual Lecture 1, March, Helsinki.

North, D. (1997c) "Prologue", in Drobak and Nye (eds) (1997), pp. 3–12.

North, D. (1999) *Understanding the Process of Economic Change*, London: Institute of Economic Affairs.

North, D. (2000) "Big-Bang Transformations of Economic Systems: an Introductory Note", *Journal of Institutional and Theoretical Economics*, vol 156, no 1, pp. 3–8.

North, D. and R. Thomas (1970) "An Economic Theory of the Growth of the Western World", *Economic History Review*, vol XXIII, no 1, pp. 1–17.

North, D. and R. Thomas (1973) *The Rise of the Western World: a New Economic History*, Cambridge: Cambridge University Press.

North, D. and B. Weingast (2000) "Introduction: Institutional Analysis and Economic History", *Journal of Economic History*, vol 60, no 2, pp. 414–417.

Nunn, N. (2021) "History as Evolution", in Bisin and Federico (eds) (2021), pp. 41–94.

Oliver, R. and G. Sanderson (eds) (1985) *The Cambridge History of Africa*, Volume 6, Cambridge: Cambridge University Press.

Parker, W. (1971) "From New to Old in Economic History", *Journal of Economic History*, vol 31, no 1, pp. 3–14.

Parker, W. (1986a) "An Historical Introduction", in Parker (ed.) (1986), pp. 1–12.

Parker, W. (1986b) "Afterword", in Parker (ed.) (1986), pp. 93–100.

Parker, W. (1989) "Review of Econometric History", *Journal of Economic History*, vol 49, no 2, p. 539–41.

Parker, W. (ed.) (1986) *Economic History and the Modern Economist*, Oxford: Basil Blackwell.

Patinkin, D. (1976) "Keynes and Econometrics: On the Interaction between the Macroeconomic Revolutions of the Interwar Period", *Econometrica*, vol 44, no 6, pp. 1091–123.

Paull, C. (1968) *Mechanisation in British and American Bituminous Coal Mines, 1890–1939*, unpublished MPhil thesis, University of London.

Persson, T. and G. Tabellini (2021) "Culture, Institutions, and Policy", in Bisin and Federico (eds) (2021), pp. 463–90.

Pitelis, C. (1998) "Transaction Costs and the Historical Evolution of the Capitalist Firm", *Journal of Economic Issues*, vol XXXII, no 4, pp. 999–1017.

Pitelis, C. (ed.) (1993) *Transaction Costs, Markets and Hierarchies*, Oxford: Basil Blackwell.

Plumb, J. (1982) "Commercialisation and Society, Part III", in McKendrick et al. (1982), pp. 265–334.

Pollard, S. (1964) "Economic History – A Science of Society?", *Past and Present*, no 30, pp. 3–22, reproduced in Harte (ed.) (1971), pp. 289–312.

Pollard, S. (1983) "Capitalism and Rationality: a Study of Measurements in British Coal Mining, circa 1750–1850", *Explorations in Economic History*, vol XX, no 1, pp. 110–29.

Postan, M. (1950) "Some Economic Evidence of Declining Population in the Later Middle Ages", *Economic History Review*, vol 2, no 3, pp. 221–46.

Postan, M. (1966) "England", in Postan (ed.) (1966), pp. 549–632.

Postan, M. (ed.) (1966) *Cambridge Economic History of Europe*, Volume 1, Cambridge: Cambridge University Press.

Press, E. and J. Washburn (2000) "The Kept University", *The Atlantic Monthly*, vol 285, no 3, pp. 39–54.

Primrose, D. (2022) "Behavioural Economics and Neuroeconomics", in Stilwell et al. (eds) (2022), pp. 390–410.

Puffert, D. (2019) "Path Dependence", in Diebolt and Haupert (2019), pp. 1583–1606.

Quittner, J. and S. Slatalla (1998) *Speeding the Net: the Inside Story of Netscape and How It Challenged Microsoft*, New York: Atlantic Monthly Press.

Raff, D. (1998) "Representative Firm Analysis and the Character of Competition: Glimpses from the Great Depression", *American Economic Review*, vol 88, no 2, pp. 57–61.

Rajan, R. and L. Zingales (1998) "Power in a Theory of the Firm", *Quarterly Journal of Economics*, vol CXIII, no 2, pp. 387–432.

Ransom, R., R. Sutch, and G. Walton (eds) (1982) *Explorations in the New Economic History: Essays in Honor of Douglass C. North*, New York: Academic Press.

Rashid, S. (1977) "Malthus' Model of General Gluts", *History of Political Economy*, vol XI, no 3, pp. 366–83, reproduced in Wood (ed.) (1986), Volume 3, pp. 224–38.

Redlich, F. (1965) "New and Traditional Approaches to Economic History and Their Interdependence", *Journal of Economic History*, vol XXV, no 4, pp. 480–95.

Redlich, F. (1968) "Potentialities and Pitfalls in Economic History", *Explorations in Entrepreneurial History*, vol 6, no 1, pp. 93–112, reproduced in Andreano (ed.) (1970), pp. 85–99.

Reports by the Board of Trade under Section 12 on the Working of Part I of the Mining Industry Act, 1926 (1928–39).

Reports of the Board of Trade under Section 7 of the Coal Mines Act 1930, on the Working of the Coal Selling Schemes under Part I of the Act (1931–38).

Rhodes, E. (1945) "Output, Labour and Machines in the Coalmining Industry in Great Britain", *Economica*, new series, vol 12, issue 46, pp. 101–10.

Ribeiro, A. (1984) *Dress in Eighteenth-Century Europe, 1715–1789*, Baltimore: Johns Hopkins University Press.

Robson, W. (ed.) (1937) *Public Enterprise: Developments in Social Ownership and Control in Great Britain*, London: George Allen & Unwin.

Roemer, J. (ed.) (1986) *Analytical Marxism*, Cambridge: Cambridge University Press.

Rohm, W. (1998) *The Microsoft File: the Secret Case against Bill Gates*, New York: Random House.

Roncaglia, A. (1985) *The International Oil Market*, London: MacMillan.

Rosenberg, N. (1968) "Adam Smith, Consumer Tastes, and Economic Growth", *Journal of Political Economy*, vol LXXVI, no 2, pp. 361–74, reproduced in Wood (ed.) (1984), Volume 3, pp. 222–33.

Rostow, W. (1957) "The Interrelation of Theory and Economic History", *Journal of Economic History*, vol 17, no 4, pp. 509–23.

Rostow, W. (1960/1990) *The Stages of Economic Growth: a Non-Communist Manifesto*, Cambridge: Cambridge University Press, third revised edition, 1990.

Rostow, W. (1986) "Professor Arrow on Economic Analysis and Economic History", in Parker (ed.) (1986), pp. 70–75.

Rutherford, M. (1994) *Institutions in Economics: the Old and the New Institutionalism*, Cambridge: Cambridge University Press.

Rutherford, M. (1995) "The Old and New Institutionalism: Can Bridges be Built?", *Journal of Economic Issues*, vol XXIX, no 2, pp. 443–451.

Sawyer, M. (1982) *Macroeconomics in Question*, London: Routledge.

Schabas, M. (1995) "Parmenides and the Cliometricians", within Little (ed.) (1995), pp. 183–209.

Schlesinger, A. (1962) "The Humanist Looks at Empirical Social Research", *American Sociological Review*, vol XXVII, no 6, pp. 768–71.

Schelling, T. (1990) "Thomas C. Schelling", in Swedberg (ed.) (1990), pp. 186–99.

Sen, A. (1961) "On Optimising the Rate of Saving", *Economic Journal*, vol 71, no 283, pp. 479–96.

Sen, A. (1969) "A Game Theoretical Analysis of Theories of Collectivism in Allocation", in Majumdar (ed.) (1969), pp. 1–17.

Sen, A. (1970) "The Impossibility of a Paretian Liberal", *Journal of Political Economy*, vol 78, no 1, pp. 152–57.

Shields, J. (ed.) (1989) *Conquering Unemployment: the Case for Economic Growth*, London: Palgrave Macmillan.

Shiller, R. (2019) *Narrative Economics: How Stories Go Viral and Drive Major Economic Events*, Princeton: Princeton University Press.

Siebert, H. (ed.) (1992) *Privatization: Symposium in Honor of Herbert Giersch*, Tübingen: Mohr.

Slater, G. and D. Spencer (2000) "The Uncertain Foundations of Transaction Costs Economics", *Journal of Economic Issues*, vol XXXIV, no 1, pp. 61–87.

Smith, R. (1961) *Sea-Coal for London*, London: Longmans.

Snooks, G. (1993a) "Preface", in Snooks (ed.) (1993), pp. XV–XVI.

Snooks, G. (1993b) "What Can Historical Analysis Contribute to the Science of Economics?", in Snooks (ed.) (1993), pp. 1–26.

Snooks, G. (1993c) "The Lost Dimension: Limitations of a Timeless Economics", in Snooks (ed.) (1993), pp. 41–66.

Snooks, G. (ed.) (1993) *Historical Analysis in Economics*, London: Routledge.

Solow, R. (1956) "A Contribution to the Theory of Economic Growth", *Quarterly Journal of Economics*, vol 70, no 1, pp. 65–94.

Solow, R. (1957) "Technical Change and the Aggregate Production Function", *Review of Economics and Statistics*, vol 39, no 3, pp. 312–20.

Solow, R. (1986) "Economic History and Economics", in Parker (ed.) (1986), pp. 21–29.

Sombart, W. (1967) *Luxury and Capitalism*, Ann Arbor: University of Michigan.

Sowell, T. (1963) "The General Glut Controversy Reconsidered", *Oxford Economic Papers*, vol xv, no 3, pp. 193–203, reproduced in Wood (ed.) (1986), Volume 3, pp. 131–41.

Stallabrass, J. (2002) "Digital Commons", *New Left Review*, no 15, May/June, pp. 141–6.

Stampp, K. (1976) "Introduction: a Humanistic Perspective", in David et al. (eds) (1976).

Stasavage, D. (2021) "Biogeography, Writing, and the Origins of the State", in Bisin and Federico (eds) (2021), pp. 881–902.

Stigler, G. and G. Becker (1977) "De Gustibus Non Est Disputandum", *American Economic Review*, vol 67, no 2, pp. 76–90.

Stiglitz, J. (1993) "Post Walrasian and Post Marxian Economics", *Journal of Economic Perspectives*, vol 7, no 1, pp. 109–14.

Stiglitz, J. (1998) "Sound Finance and Sustainable Development in Asia", Keynote Address to the Asia Development Forum, Manila, 12th March.

Stiglitz, J. (2002) "Information and the Change in the Paradigm in Economics", *American Economic Review*, vol 92, no 3, pp. 460–501.

Stilwell, F., D. Primrose and T. Thornton (eds) (2022) *Handbook of Alternative Theories of Political Economy*, Cheltenham: Edward Elgar.

Stock, J. and M. Watson (1988) "Variable Trends in Economic Time Series", *Journal of Economic Perspectives*, vol 2, no 3, pp. 147–74.

Supple, B. (1960) "Economic History and Economic Growth", *Journal of Economic History*, vol 20, no 4, pp. 548–56.

Supple, B. (1987) *The History of the British Coal Industry, Volume 4, 1913–46: the Political Economy of Decline*, Oxford: Clarendon.

Sutch, R. (1982) "Douglass North and the New Economic History", in Ransom et al. (eds) (1982), pp. 13–38.

Sutton, J. (1991) *Sunk Costs and Market Structure: Price Competition, Advertising, and the Evolution of Concentration*, Cambridge: MIT Press.

Sutton, J. (1995) "Comment", in Lamoreaux and Raff (eds) (1995), within pp. 55–100.

Swedberg, R. (ed.) (1990) *Economics and Sociology, Redefining Their Boundaries: Conversations with Economists and Sociologists*, Princeton: Princeton University Press.

Sweezy, P. (1938) *Monopoly and Competition in the English Coal Trade: 1550–1850*, Westport: Greenwood, 1972 reprint.

Szirmai, A., B. van Ark and D. Pilat (eds) (1993) *Explaining Economic Growth: Essays in Honour of Angus Maddison*, North-Holland: Elsevier.

Teich, M. and R. Young (eds) (1973) *Changing Perspectives in the History of Science: Essays in Honour of Joseph Needham*, London: Heinemann Educational.

Temin, P. (1991) "Introduction", in Temin (ed.) (1991), pp. 1–6.

Temin, P. (1995) "Comment", in Lamoreaux and Raff (eds) (1995), within pp. 257–322.

Temin, P. (1997) "Is It Kosher to Talk about Culture?", *Journal of Economic History*, vol 57, no 2, pp. 267–87.

Temin, P. (1998) "Commentary", *Review of the Federal Reserve Bank of St Louis*, vol 80, no 3, pp. 49–51.

Temin, P. (ed.) (1991) *Inside the Business Enterprise: Historical Perspectives on the Use of Information*, Chicago: Chicago University Press.

Thaler, R. (1987) "The Psychology and Economics Conference Handbook: Comments on Simon, on Einhorn and Hogarth, and on Tversky and Kahneman", in Hogarth and Reder (eds) (1987), pp. 95–100.

Therborn, G. (1976) *Science, Class and Society: On the Formation of Sociology and Historical Materialism*, London: New Left Books.

Thirsk, J. (1978) *Economic Policy and Projects: the Development of a Consumer Society in Early Modern England*, Oxford: Oxford University Press.

Thomas, I. (1937) "The Coal Mines Reorganisation Commission", in Robson (ed.) (1937), pp. 209–46.

Thrupp, S. (1957) "The Role of Comparison in the Development of Economic Theory", *Journal of Economic History*, vol 17, no 4, pp. 554–70.

Toye, J. (1995) "The New Institutional Economics and Its Implications for Development Theory", in Harriss et al. (eds) (1995), pp. 49–70.

Tozer, J. and S. Levitt (1983) *Fabric of Society: a Century of People and Their Clothes, 1770–1870*, London: L. Ashley.

Turrell, R. (1987) *Capital and Labour on the Kimberley Diamond Fields, 1871–1890*, Cambridge: Cambridge University Press.

Van Onselen, C. (1982a) *Studies in the Social and Economic History of the Witwatersrand, 1886–1914, vol 1, New Babylon*, Harlow: Longman.

Van Onselen, C. (1982b) *Studies in the Social and Economic History of the Witwatersrand, 1886–1914, vol 2, New Nineveh*, Harlow: Longman.

Vandenberg, P. (2002) "North's Institutionalism and the Prospect of Combining Theoretical Approaches", *Cambridge Journal of Economics*, vol 26, no 2, pp. 217–35.

Vatter, H. (1959) "The Malthusian Model of Income Determination and Its Contemporary Relevance", *Canadian Journal of Political Science*, vol xxv, no 1, pp. 60–4, reproduced in Wood (ed.) (1986), Volume 3, pp. 115–20.

Velthuis, O. (1999) "The Changing Relationship between Economic Sociology and Institutional Economics: from Talcott Parsons to Mark Granovetter", *American Journal of Economics and Sociology*, vol 58, no 4, pp. 629–49.

von Tunzelmann, N. (1978) *Steam Power and British Industrialisation to 1860*, Oxford: Oxford University Press.

Voth, H.-J. (2021), "Persistence – Myth and Mystery", in Bisin and Federico (eds) (2021), pp. 243–68.

Wallace, J. (1997) *Overdrive: Bill Gates and the Race to Control Cyberspace*, New York: John Wiley.

Weatherill, L. (1986) *The Growth of the Pottery Industry in England, 1660–1815*, New York: Garland Publishing.

Weatherill, L. (1988) *Consumer Behaviour and Material Culture in Britain, 1660–1760*, London: Routledge.

Whaples, R. (1991) "A Quantitative History of the Journal of Economic History and the Cliometric Revolution", *Journal of Economic History*, vol 51, no 2, pp. 289–301.

White, E. (1998) "Were Banks Special Intermediaries in Late Nineteenth-Century America", *Review of the Federal Reserve Bank of St Louis*, vol 80, no 3, pp. 13–32.

Williams, G. (1905) *The Diamond Mines of South Africa*, Vol 1, New York: B. F. Buck and Co.

Williams, S. (2002) *Free as in Freedom: Richard Stallman's Crusade for Free Software*, O'Reilly: Sebastopol, CA.

Williamson, H. and A. Daum (1959) *The American Petroleum Industry: the American Age of Illumination, 1859–1899*, Evanston: Northwestern University Press.

Williamson, H., R. Andreano, A. Daum and G. Klose (1963) *The American Petroleum Industry: the Age of Energy, 1899–1959*, Evanston: Northwestern University Press.

Williamson, O. (1975) *Markets and Hierarchies*, New York: Free Press.

Williamson, O. (1985) *The Economic Institutions of Capitalism*, New York: Free Press.

Winch, D. (1987) *Malthus*, Oxford: Oxford University Press.

World Bank (2002) *World Development Report: Institutions for Markets*, New York: Oxford University Press.

Wood, J. (ed.) (1984) *Adam Smith: Critical Assessments*, London: Routledge.

Wood, J. (ed.) (1986) *Thomas Robert Malthus: Critical Assessments*, Beckenham: Croom Helm.

Worger, W. (1987) *South Africa's City of Diamonds: Mine Workers and Monopoly Capitalism in Kimberley, 1867–1895*, New Haven: Yale University Press.

Yergin, D. (1991) *The Prize: the Epic Quest for Oil, Money and Power*, New York: Simon and Schuster.

Zafirovski, M. (2000) "The Rational Choice Generalization of Neoclassical Economics Reconsidered: Any Theoretical Legitimation for Economic Imperialism", *Sociological Theory*, vol 18, no 3, pp. 448–71.

Zollschan, G. and W. Hirsch (eds) (1964) *Explorations in Social Change*, Boston: Routledge and Kegan Paul.

Index

Acemoglu, D.   10, 10*n*13, 11, 15, 22, 22*n*22, 267
Aigner, E.   232*n*34, 267
Alston, L.   267, 274
amalgamations   84
American. *See also* USA   XI, 16, 105f.2, 120, 126, 130, 147, 204*n*41, 224, 232, 239*n*7
Americas   204*n*41, 224
analogy   21, 44, 45, 46, 86, 112, 193, 243, 259*n*40
analyses   10, 21, 26*n*28, 54, 73, 94, 100, 132, 171, 174, 235
analysis   9, 14, 23, 24*n*26, 29, 30, 36, 37, 38, 44, 46, 47, 48, 50, 51, 52, 70, 75, 76, 78, 81, 82, 92, 93, 94, 94*n*6, 96, 100, 103, 103*n*19, 114, 134, 136, 142, 146, 147, 148, 150, 151, 154, 161, 164, 166, 167, 173, 174, 176, 182, 185, 186, 188, 188*n*28, 189*n*29, 190, 192, 193, 194, 197, 198, 200, 202, 203, 210, 212, 216, 220, 225, 226*n*25, 229, 233, 234, 236*n*2, 241, 243, 243*n*14, 244, 247*n*23, 256, 257, 260
analytic   27, 211, 256, 257, 258
analytical   8, 37, 40, 41, 43, 51, 52, 74, 113, 125, 139, 144, 145, 148, 151, 152, 154, 155, 156, 157, 159, 160, 165, 168, 171, 172, 173, 175, 176, 182, 183, 193, 204, 205, 206, 212, 216, 220, 225, 233*n*36, 242, 245, 248*n*25, 250, 251, 254*n*32, 266
analytically   14, 38, 43, 50, 184*n*23, 197, 206, 213, 237, 247
Andreano, R.   267, 273, 280, 289, 292, 296
Anglo American   10, 109, 111, 229*n*30
Ankarloo, D.   170*n*4, 198, 200, 267
Annales School   231*n*33
anti-trust   108, 111, 254
Aoki, M.   229*n*30, 267, 282
applied economics   123
appropriation   21, 69, 72, 86, 87, 92, 93, 97, 98, 114, 123, 134, 141, 197, 246, 250
archives   15, 19, 29*n*31, 41, 81*n*11, 87*n*16, 226
Arestis, P.   267, 277
aristocracy   62, 194
Arrow, K.   13, 31, 239, 239*n*8, 267, 275, 279, 293
Arthur, W.   236*n*2, 237*n*2, 267
Ashman, S.   31*n*33, 267

Ashton, T.   135, 267
Asian   204*n*41, 229*n*30, 260, 260*n*41, 261, 261*n*42
asocial   32, 147, 166, 185, 219, 238
Assa, J.   26*n*27, 31*n*33, 267, 268
Assurance Game   33
Aston, T.   39, 268, 269
asymmetric   146, 174, 248*n*25, 262, 263, 265
asymmetries   3, 211, 231, 262, 263
asymmetry   44, 189
Atack, J.   146, 268
atheoretical   24, 231
Atkins, F.   94*n*5, 268
Atkinson, P.   268, 279, 282
atomised   52, 216
Auletta, K.   254*n*32, 254*n*34, 255, 256, 268
Auslander, L.   268
Australia   120
authoritarian   3, 32
axiomatic   40, 239
Aybar, S.   262*n*45, 268

Baffigi, A.   13*n*16, 268
Ball, M.   97, 98, 98*n*12, 268
banks and banking   184*n*23, 262, 262*n*44, 263, 264
Baran, P.   46*n*10, 268
barbarian   203
bargaining   155, 176*n*13, 180, 188*n*27, 194, 198, 216, 253
Barro, P.   25
Barro-type regressions   25
barter   53, 200
Bateman, M.   265*n*47, 268
Bates, R.   15, 148, 171*n*5, 256, 268
Bayliss, K.   2*n*4, 92*n*2, 164*n*8, 188*n*26, 268
BBI, bringing back in   4, 7, 8, 118, 235, 237
Becker, G.   3, 8, 11, 14, 118, 141, 142, 162, 206, 227*n*26, 230, 268, 294
behavior   130, 142, 152, 154, 155, 157, 166, 167, 210, 218, 226, 228, 236*n*2, 243, 248*n*25
behavioral   17, 133, 152, 155, 167
behaviour   43, 46, 49, 52, 57, 132, 133, 142, 153, 157, 164, 173, 174, 176, 182, 183, 183*n*22, 184*n*23, 185, 210, 211, 216, 237*n*3, 252, 253, 254*n*33

behavioural. *See also* neuroeconomics 4, 157, 171

beliefs 19, 26, 67, 69, 117, 143, 158, 159, 160*n*15, 161, 162, 164, 164*n*18, 165, 171, 183*n*20, 187, 218, 257

Ben-Schachar, A. 47*n*11, 268

bias 13*n*16, 24, 68*n*17, 76, 77, 78, 84*n*14, 88, 202, 211*n*11, 225

Bina, C. 97*n*9, 104*n*20, 111, 268

biological 21, 35, 141, 158, 162, 188, 242, 243, 247*n*23

Bisin, A. 9, 12, 20, 23, 267, 268, 269, 270, 280, 281, 285, 286, 289, 291, 294, 296

black box 156, 198, 210, 211, 246*n*21

blacks 59

Blankenburg, S. 268

Blaut, J. 204*n*41, 269

bombasines 60

Boniface, D. 148*n*9, 257, 269

boundaries 8, 12, 36, 51, 99, 116*n*2, 123, 146, 149, 198, 212, 221, 249, 258, 260, 266

bourgeoisie 62, 69, 112

Bowles, S. 22, 216, 218*n*16, 269

Boylan, T. 128, 269

Boyns, T. 74*n*5, 85, 269

brain 165*n*20, 171*n*7, 225*n*24

brand 153, 223, 253

Braudel, H. 42, 269

Breen, T. 44, 68*n*16, 269

Brenner, R. 38, 190, 192, 194, 195, 195*n*32, 268, 269

Brewer, J. 288

Briggs, A. 65, 66, 269

Brinkley, J. 255, 269

Britain 1, 67, 77, 99, 100, 120, 122, 122*n*7, 123, 239, 259*n*40

British 1, 25, 26, 43, 48, 67, 69, 71, 72, 73, 74, 85, 87, 91, 92, 99, 100, 103, 104, 107, 108, 113, 114, 120, 120*n*5, 122*n*9, 135*n*27, 208, 232*n*34, 259, 264

Broadberry, S. 25, 269

Bromley, S. 111, 269

Bruchey, S. 280

Bruland, K. 47*n*11, 270

Brunskill, I. 87*n*16, 99*n*14, 270

business history IX, 5, 17, 18, 27, 28, 52, 93, 94*n*6, 109*n*22, 206, 211, 212, 214, 214*n*13, 215, 218, 219, 222, 226*n*25, 229*n*31, 233, 237, 254*n*34

Buxton, N. 73, 74, 74*n*4, 75, 76, 78, 270

Caicedo, F. 23, 270

Cain, L. 270, 284

Callinicos, A. 160, 186, 187, 189*n*29, 270

Cambridge critique 211*n*11, 225*n*24

Cambridge economics 225*n*24

Campbell, C. 51*n*12, 270

Cannadine, D. 37, 39, 40, 41*n*5, 42, 69, 270

capacity, excess 45, 77, 88, 89*n*19

Cape Town 103

capital 1, 25, 47, 51, 61, 72, 73, 76, 77, 77*n*7, 77*n*8, 78, 84*n*14, 85, 88, 89, 90, 91, 93, 94, 95, 96, 97, 97*n*10, 98, 99, 100, 103, 106, 107, 108, 110, 112, 113, 114, 119, 146, 164, 168, 189, 197, 206, 211*n*11, 220, 221, 233, 238, 247, 247*n*22, 261, 261*n*43, 264, 265
   social 3, 3*n*7, 8, 119, 140, 206, 219*n*19, 229*n*30, 233*n*36, 248*n*24

capitalism 1, 30, 38, 58, 68, 70, 112, 113, 113*n*25, 114, 168, 179*n*18, 189, 196, 197, 220, 221, 224, 225, 233, 250

capitalist 45, 46, 53, 61, 67, 98, 103, 110, 113, 120, 191, 191*n*30, 194, 195, 197, 199, 220

Carrier, J. 140, 236, 270, 276

cartels 73, 74, 74*n*5, 75, 79, 81, 82, 83, 84, 88*n*17, 91, 92, 93, 94, 97, 104, 105, 106, 107, 108, 109, 110, 111, 112, 113, 114, 115

carts XI, 101, 106f.3

Cartwright, N. 23*n*25, 273

case studies IX, 1, 5, 6, 18, 21, 71, 91, 92, 114, 116, 125, 140, 204, 212, 215, 222, 233*n*36, 235, 235*n*1, 251, 261, 262

cast-offs 54, 60

catastrophe 163

categories 30, 53, 68, 126, 136, 147, 148, 167, 168, 189, 220, 221, 225, 229, 257

category 16, 189, 198, 219*n*19, 225

causation 18, 20, 21, 24, 29, 37, 41, 47*n*11, 50, 51, 52, 58, 68, 136, 137, 236*n*2

Cernat, A. 268

Chandler, A. 94*n*6, 135, 225, 270, 280

Chang, H.-J. 232*n*34, 261, 261*n*43, 270, 277, 283

chaos theory 163

chaotic 164, 188*n*26, 219

chemistry 165*n*20, 239

Chicago economics X, 8, 14, 15, 16, 16*n*18, 17, 18, 19, 117 children 57, 58, 60, 68, 74n4, 144, 253

China 120

Choi, J.-K. 269

choice

rational 140, 141, 142, 143, 166, 167, 168, 176, 177, 180, 182, 193, 199, 216, 221n20, 256, 257

choice. *See also* preferences and tastes 4n9, 22, 23, 32, 51, 60, 69, 132, 141, 142, 143, 150, 160, 161, 162, 166, 167, 168, 171n5, 173, 174, 176, 177, 178, 179, 182, 188n28, 193, 197, 199, 201, 214, 214n14, 218, 220, 236n2, 244, 249, 251, 252n31, 256

Christophers, B. 31n33, 270

Church, R. 3n6, 99, 113, 270

Cioni, M. 10, 10n12, 270

Clapham, J. 37, 116n2, 134

class 8, 22, 30, 41, 44, 45, 46, 52, 53n14, 54, 55, 57, 58, 59, 61, 62, 66, 67, 71, 96, 114, 135, 161, 184n23, 186, 187n25, 189, 189n29, 193, 194, 195, 212, 262

classes 26n27, 35, 48, 49, 53n13, 55, 58, 61, 62, 66, 67, 68, 69, 167, 183, 185, 186, 187n25, 188, 194

Classical Political Economy 53, 128n16, 207n3

climate 33n36, 46, 127n14, 140, 168, 247n23

cliometrics. *See* especially Chapters 1 and 5-9 and phases of, and new, newer and newest economic history 6, 7, 9, 10n14, 11, 12, 13, 13n6, 14, 15, 16, 17, 18, 20, 20n20, 24, 26n28, 27, 28, 29, 30, 31, 36, 37, 43, 50, 117, 118, 118n3, 119, 120, 121, 121n7, 122, 125, 126, 127, 127n14, 128, 129, 129n17, 132, 133, 134, 137, 138n30, 139, 143, 144, 144n6, 145, 147, 149, 150, 170, 171, 172, 207, 209, 209n7, 211n11, 219n18, 221, 221n20, 222, 223, 224, 225, 226, 227, 228n28, 231, 235n1, 238

clothes 55, 58, 59, 60, 61, 62, 63, 64, 65, 66, 67

clothing 38, 47, 54, 55, 56, 57, 60, 61, 63, 64, 65, 70, 92, 161

coal. *See* especially Chapters 3 and 4 2, 49, 71, 72, 73, 74, 74n4, 75, 77, 78, 79, 81, 82, 84, 85, 86, 91, 92, 93, 98n12, 99, 99n14, 100, 103, 104, 107, 108, 113, 114, 120, 120n5

Coase, R. 152, 173, 198, 210n8, 253, 270

Coats, A. 14, 121, 122, 122n9, 123, 124, 125, 126, 127, 128, 129, 232n34, 270, 271

coercion 180, 193, 257

cognition 161, 171, 242

cognitive 23, 164, 165, 168, 170, 171n7, 172, 183n20, 241

Cold War 33n36, 126

Cole, A. 50, 135, 271, 281

Cole, W. 50, 135, 271, 281

Coleman, D. 122, 122n9, 206, 271

collective 17, 22, 33, 34, 133, 142, 145, 146, 154, 157, 159, 161, 168, 183, 184, 184n23, 185, 186, 187, 187n25, 188, 188n28, 188n29, 205, 206, 208, 209, 229n30, 249, 253, 254, 256

colonial 11, 12n15, 179

commercial 53, 66, 107, 113, 180, 248, 252, 253, 255, 263

commercialisation 250, 250n27

commodities 53n14, 92, 97, 98, 113, 197

companies 81, 83, 84, 91, 99n14, 100n15, 102, 103, 107, 109, 109n22, 111, 254n34

comparative advantage 17, 20, 133

compensation, for coal royalty nationalisation 1938 72, 87n16, 99n14, 212

competition 4, 25, 37, 42, 47, 73, 79, 82, 85, 86, 88, 89, 90, 94, 95, 97, 101, 106, 108, 110, 113, 124, 130, 135, 145, 146, 149, 154, 158, 173, 175, 177, 178, 179, 192, 197, 210, 210n8, 214, 214n13, 219, 231, 236n2, 238, 246, 247n23, 250, 254n33, 255

concept 1, 31, 61, 67, 133, 140, 142, 147, 151, 154, 168, 174, 176, 176n14, 182, 185, 187, 188, 188n29, 193, 195, 196n35, 197, 198, 204n40, 205, 210, 225, 226, 238, 247

conceptual 24, 36, 134, 148, 158, 167, 188n29, 196, 197, 198, 211n11, 246n21, 247n23

conceptualisation 8, 10, 29, 43, 97, 108, 122n8, 185, 228

conflict 8, 22, 23, 33, 34, 35, 52, 53, 67, 86, 97, 98, 100, 106, 109, 114, 132, 138, 143, 148, 167, 168, 176n13, 179, 180, 182, 186, 188, 188n27, 192, 193, 194, 210, 216, 217, 219, 245n18

conquest 204n41, 257

Conrad, A. 125, 129, 129n17, 134, 137, 271, 280, 288

conservation 111

conservative 10, 52, 126, 204n40

consumer revolution 30, 37, 42, 48

consumer society   37, 40, 56, 58, 67, 68

consumerism   42, 68, 68*n*16

consumerist approach   37, 38, 39, 41, 42, 45,
    46, 47, 48, 50, 51, 53, 54, 68, 69

consumers   2, 2*n*4, 30, 37, 40, 42, 43, 44,
    45, 48, 54, 55, 57, 58, 64, 66, 67, 68, 69,
    69*n*17, 95, 210, 210*n*9, 244, 253, 259*n*39

consumption   2, 2*n*4, 2*n*5, 3*n*7, 30, 36, 37,
    38, 39, 40, 41, 44, 48, 49, 53*n*14, 56, 57,
    59, 61, 63, 64, 66, 67, 68, 68*n*16, 70, 91,
    92, 93, 95, 96, 111, 113, 113*n*24, 164*n*18,
    188*n*26, 192, 210*n*9, 220, 229*n*29, 233*n*36,
    252, 257

    conspicuous   68, 192

contemporary   X, 1, 23, 31, 37, 39, 40, 42, 45,
    53, 66, 68, 69, 73, 90, 92, 127*n*14, 128*n*16,
    135, 158, 171, 204, 205, 239*n*8, 246*n*19

context   IX, 1, 2*n*4, 7, 14, 23, 24, 25*n*27, 26*n*27,
    31*n*33, 36, 37, 38, 40, 41, 45, 49, 51, 54,
    55, 65, 67, 68, 72*n*2, 88, 90, 93, 94, 94*n*5,
    97, 100, 119, 125, 130, 135, 139, 147, 164,
    164*n*18, 165, 170*n*2, 185, 188*n*26, 189,
    197, 198, 203, 213, 218, 219, 219*n*19, 220,
    221, 226, 233*n*36, 236*n*2, 237, 241, 243,
    246*n*20, 246*n*21, 247, 247*n*22, 247*n*23,
    248, 248*n*24, 249*n*26, 252, 256, 257, 259,
    264, 265*n*47, 266

contingent   4, 72, 98, 112, 114, 155, 216, 237,
    244, 257

contracting   60, 102, 130, 153, 155, 193, 193*n*31,
    198, 201, 216, 217, 217*n*15, 218*n*16, 243,
    248*n*25, 250, 262

controversy   6, 17, 121, 124, 130, 133

conventional wisdom   10*n*14, 37, 72, 100, 120,
    124, 139, 205

core   4, 8, 23, 41, 122, 123, 153, 212, 234, 237,
    244, 246, 261

corporations. *See also* enterprises and
    firms   1, 33*n*36, 91, 110, 262

corporatism   12

corruption   261, 264, 265

cost   13*n*16, 29*n*31, 41*n*6, 48, 49, 60, 63, 65, 79,
    83, 84, 86, 101, 103, 103*n*19, 109, 111, 112,
    113, 150, 154, 162, 175, 181, 195, 198, 199,
    200, 201, 202, 202*n*39, 203, 203*n*40, 210,
    210*n*8, 210*n*9, 213, 230, 252

costs   49, 63, 79, 83, 84, 84*n*14, 86, 88, 95, 104,
    107, 108, 111, 115, 131, 152, 153, 154, 155,
    157, 161, 166, 174, 176, 179, 180, 181, 182,

    193, 197, 198, 199, 200, 201, 202, 203, 204,
    214*n*13, 223, 239, 240, 251

costs, transaction   26, 144, 146, 150, 151,
    152, 153, 154, 155, 156, 159, 166, 167, 174,
    177, 178, 179, 180, 181, 182, 193, 197, 198,
    199, 200, 201, 202, 203, 204, 204*n*41,
    218*n*16, 239

counterfactuals   17, 136, 136*n*28, 137,
    144, 221*n*20

court   62, 78, 250, 255, 258

Cowling, K.   46*n*10, 113*n*25, 271

Crafts, N.   50, 51, 54, 237, 258, 258*n*37, 259,
    259*n*39, 259*n*40, 260, 261, 263, 271,
    272, 285

credit   16*n*18, 98, 114, 215, 265*n*47

crime   14, 33

crisis   13, 26*n*27, 31, 40, 110, 120, 179, 180, 191,
    194, 260, 261, 261*n*42, 261*n*43

critical   X, 9, 13, 19, 29, 31*n*33, 34, 36, 38, 73,
    116, 119, 130, 131, 135, 141*n*3, 142, 145,
    145*n*8, 149, 157, 163, 165*n*20, 169, 170, 171,
    172, 174, 189, 195, 204, 206, 207, 208, 215,
    216, 221, 228, 229, 235, 241, 243*n*15, 246,
    247*n*23, 259*n*39

criticism   7, 23, 47, 51, 117, 129*n*17, 145, 169,
    193, 199, 200, 204

critics   X, 144, 145, 146, 207, 213, 221,
    226, 238

critique   2, 8, 19, 26*n*27, 28, 30, 43*n*7, 43*n*8,
    43*n*9, 46*n*10, 47*n*11, 54, 113*n*25, 117,
    120*n*5, 129*n*17, 132, 145, 156*n*13, 163, 165,
    172, 176*n*14, 177*n*17, 195*n*32, 197, 198,
    202*n*39, 211*n*11, 214*n*13, 218*n*16, 238*n*4,
    243, 243*n*15, 245*n*18, 246, 246*n*20,
    246*n*21, 248, 248*n*24, 249*n*26, 252,
    262, 265*n*47

cultural   4, 9, 26, 30, 69, 132, 138, 140, 167,
    219, 222, 228, 229, 229*n*31, 230, 233, 238,
    247*n*22, 249, 257, 258*n*37

culture   3, 8, 14, 22, 23, 26, 32, 33, 34, 35, 36,
    41, 52, 62, 69, 132, 142, 148, 160*n*16, 164,
    164*n*18, 165, 168, 185, 208, 210*n*9, 218, 219,
    222, 229, 229*n*30, 230, 233*n*36, 237, 238,
    239, 248*n*24, 256, 257, 265, 266

Cunnington, C.   62, 272

Cunnington, P.   62, 272

curriculum   227

customs   8, 66, 98, 142, 143, 145, 146, 147, 148,
    157, 160, 196*n*35, 221, 248*n*24

Dalle, J.-M. 273

Damodaran, S. 272, 278

Dasgupta, P. 95, 248, 248n24, 248n25, 272

data 10n14, 13, 13n16, 17, 20, 23, 24, 27, 28, 29, 29n31, 30, 74, 75, 76, 77, 79, 81n11, 87n16, 89, 99n14, 120, 124, 131, 144, 221n20, 226, 239n8, 254n34, 257

Daum, A. 104n20, 296

David, P. x, 6, 10, 11, 156, 156n13, 159, 221, 226, 234, 235, 236, 237, 238, 238n6, 239, 240, 241, 242, 243, 243n13, 244, 244n6, 245, 246, 246n21, 247, 248, 248n25, 249, 249n26, 250, 251, 253, 255, 256, 272, 273, 294

Davies, G. 43n8, 273

Davis, J. 128n16, 136, 147, 273

Davis, L. 128n16, 136, 147, 273

De Beers 91, 101, 102, 103, 103n19, 107, 109

de Grazia, V. 268, 273

de la Escosura, L. 13n16, 273

Deaton, A. 23, 23n25, 273

debates 2, 6, 7, 9, 12, 17, 18, 38, 40, 40n4, 57, 72n2, 74n4, 86n15, 88, 97, 98, 122, 122n8, 128, 134, 135, 136, 142, 144, 187n25, 225, 227, 237n2, 251, 259

decencies 56, 67

deconstruction 140, 141

Delamont, S. 268

demand 4, 8, 37, 38, 40, 41, 41n6, 42, 43, 44, 45, 46, 47, 48, 49, 50, 51, 51n12, 52, 53, 53n14, 54, 55, 56, 57, 58, 61, 63, 65, 66, 67, 68, 69, 69n17, 74n4, 77, 81, 82, 83, 84, 84n14, 89n19, 95, 95n8, 107, 109, 111, 128n15, 130, 145, 179, 246, 252, 258n37, 259n39, 259n39

effective 45, 50, 57, 59

democracy 22, 26n27, 62, 67, 103, 112

demography 14, 15, 17, 151, 159, 164, 183, 190, 192

determination 52, 113n24, 159, 186, 187

determined 22, 25, 32, 40, 43, 48, 72, 75, 82, 86, 93, 96, 141, 147, 148, 157, 159, 161, 162, 178, 185, 186, 188, 189n29, 190, 191, 192, 210, 220, 233, 253

determines 35, 46, 92, 174, 212n12

determining 18, 34, 53, 68, 83, 85, 87, 93, 148, 185, 246, 263

determinism 24, 132n20, 161, 165, 173, 243, 246

deterministic 4, 22, 28, 170, 205, 220, 229, 237, 240, 242, 246

development IX, 2, 3, 10n14, 11, 15, 18, 30, 31n33, 36, 38, 39, 41n5, 44, 48, 49, 55, 58, 61, 63, 66, 67, 72, 86, 91, 93, 94, 94n6, 95n8, 97, 97n10, 97n11, 105, 107, 108, 109, 112, 113n24, 114, 118n3, 122, 122n7, 133n23, 138n30, 141, 151, 152, 153, 168, 171n7, 172n8, 178, 180, 190, 191, 192, 194, 195, 196, 204n41, 206, 209n7, 211n10, 222, 225, 227n27, 238, 246, 247n23, 256, 258, 260, 261, 262, 263, 264

development economics. See also post Washington Consensus IX, 2, 39, 118n3, 141, 168, 206, 209n7, 227n27

development studies 2, 168, 227n27

Diamond Producers Association 109

diamonds 91, 92, 93, 94n4, 100, 100n16, 104, 105, 107, 108, 109, 110, 112, 113, 113n24, 114

dichotomy 42, 50, 134, 154

Diebolt, C. 9, 13, 18n19, 20n20, 25, 26n28, 29n31, 273, 274, 282, 284, 287, 292

diet 2n4, 59

Dietz, B. 49, 274

diffusion 10n14, 55, 56, 62, 65, 67, 244

diggers 103, 110n23

Dimakou, O. 25, 42, 278

diminishing returns 75, 89, 178, 179, 190, 191

Dintenfass, M. 74n5, 86, 274

disaggregated level 74, 84, 90, 219

disciplines. See individual fields IX, 3, 4, 7, 8, 9, 12, 13, 14, 19, 20, 21, 40, 83, 107, 119, 122, 123, 124, 127n14, 129, 131, 137, 141, 142, 214, 214n14, 218, 222, 223, 224, 225n24, 227, 231, 232n34, 240, 242n12

discourse 17, 18, 26, 130n18, 133, 148, 166, 197, 248n25

discrimination 14

distribution 25, 29, 44, 46, 47, 49, 52, 55, 57, 67, 91, 92, 96, 98, 108, 114, 179, 182, 190, 192, 197, 216, 219, 240, 255n36

Dobb, M. 38

domestic, market 38, 49, 50, 54, 58, 111, 112

domestics 57, 58, 59, 61, 64

Dorninger, C. 275

Douglas, M. 25, 88, 89, 116, 233n35, 274

dress 55, 58, 59, 60, 61, 62, 63, 64, 64n15, 65, 66

Drobak, J. 274, 280, 291

dualism 3, 4, 93n3, 126, 133, 140, 143, 168, 170n2, 175, 185, 231, 246n21
Duby, G. 196n33, 274
Dugger, W. 176m15, 274
durables, consumer. *See also* appliances 2, 2n4, 64
Durlauf, S. 245n17, 274
dynamics 1, 6, 22, 40, 47, 54, 55, 59, 61, 68, 70, 81, 93, 95, 96, 97, 147, 148, 151, 163, 172, 176, 197, 205, 237, 239n8, 240, 240m11, 242, 244, 246, 248n25

Easterbrook, W. 138n30, 274
Eatwell, J. 274, 286
econometrics 8, 9, 16, 24n26, 28, 29, 30, 52, 88, 123, 129, 137, 137n29, 219n18, 224, 227, 229, 232, 239n8
Economic History Association 211m10, 222, 232
economic history, old 17, 25, 28, 150
economics imperialism
   reverse 7, 9, 12
   watershed in x, 7, 9, 11, 12, 14, 17, 18, 19
Edquist, C. 245n18, 274
efficiency 4, 8, 35, 48, 72, 79, 87, 94, 97, 100, 101, 107, 108, 109, 114, 151, 154, 155, 156, 172n8, 175, 176m13, 178, 179, 180, 181, 195, 196, 197, 201, 202, 208, 236n2, 252n31
Eggertsson, T. 171n7, 267, 274
Egorov, G. 267
Egypt 179, 182, 192, 195
Eichengreen, B. 207n4, 274
eighteenth century 2, 13, 37, 38, 40, 42, 44, 48, 49, 50, 55, 56, 57, 58, 59, 60, 61, 62, 63, 64, 68, 68m16, 69, 259n39
Eisenach, J. 254n32, 274
eleventh century 196
Elizabethan age 104
Elton, G. 133, 274, 280
empirical 2n4, 2n5, 8, 12, 16, 17, 21, 23, 24n26, 25, 28, 29, 30, 31, 36, 37, 42, 43n9, 50, 51, 52, 54, 66, 79, 81, 83, 85, 89, 124, 127, 130, 133, 137, 155, 157, 190, 193, 200, 211m11, 213n13, 221, 227, 241, 251, 252, 254, 258, 260, 261, 262, 262n44
empiricism 177m17, 256
employer 55, 59, 60, 67
employment 25, 38, 43, 45, 48, 49, 50, 51, 58, 60, 66, 67, 68, 76, 77, 85, 259n39

emulation 44, 48, 49, 53m14, 54, 55, 56, 57, 59, 60, 61, 62, 63, 64, 67, 69
endogenous 25, 35, 95, 126, 136, 143, 146, 147, 148, 168, 187, 205, 209, 214n13, 217, 220, 238n6, 241, 249, 256, 257, 258, 259, 259n40, 260
endowments 4, 120, 146, 167
energy 40, 49, 92, 111, 124
enforcement 33, 34, 150, 151, 153, 154, 157, 160, 161, 171, 175, 175m12, 181, 197, 198, 199, 201, 202, 217
Engels, F. 198, 274, 287
Engerman, S. 120, 125n13, 129n17, 280
England 61, 66, 71, 120, 121, 180, 194
English 39, 41n6, 50, 116n2, 194, 259n39
enterprise. *See also* corporations and firms 81, 209, 211, 212
entrepreneurs 37, 41, 42, 47, 48, 52, 54, 68, 72, 85, 89, 120, 133n23, 158, 163, 177, 177m16, 186, 208, 222, 224, 225, 264
environment 9, 22, 31, 93n3, 143, 161, 165, 177, 190, 205, 212, 255, 263
epistemology 127, 128, 249, 249n26
equilibria 22, 34, 50, 147, 148, 163, 213, 220, 221, 237, 241, 244
equilibrium 4, 8, 21, 22, 25, 32, 35, 42, 46, 73, 89, 135, 146, 148, 158, 164, 171n5, 213, 223, 234, 241, 243, 248, 256, 257
equity 162
Erasmo, V. 31n34, 274
ESRC, Economic and Social Research Council 74n3, 81m11, 87m16, 92m1, 140m1, 206
Essletzbichler, J. 275
ethic 51m12, 53, 61, 152, 158, 160, 162
Europe 10, 41n6, 53, 67, 69, 73, 99, 100m15, 109, 120, 173, 180, 190, 194, 196n33, 199, 202, 204n41, 225, 232, 250
Evans, T. 74n3, 77, 77n8, 99, 275
Eversley, D. 64, 275
evolution 2n4, 7, 9, 10, 21, 26n28, 35, 37, 58, 61, 99, 103, 112, 127, 143, 144, 148, 158, 164, 165, 167, 171n6, 186, 187, 190, 192, 194, 203, 205, 207n3, 222, 224, 229, 229n31, 243, 245, 245m18, 247n23, 249
evolves 5, 6, 41, 101, 116, 139, 142, 149, 155, 158, 160, 160m15, 163, 164, 167, 172, 175, 177, 183n20, 194, 223, 234, 238, 242, 246n21, 255, 263, 266

exchange   53, 56, 57, 61, 68, 83, 131, 152, 153,
   153*n*11, 164, 174, 188*n*28, 189, 197, 198, 199,
   201, 202, 216, 257
exemplar   47, 125
exogenous   34, 35, 95, 126, 136, 143, 146, 148,
   159, 168, 182, 187, 190, 192, 220, 237*n*3,
   256, 257, 258, 259, 259*n*40, 260, 262
expectations   213, 241
exploitation   20, 33*n*36, 56, 67, 95, 105, 112,
   148, 155, 194, 197, 224, 225
exports   50, 51, 52, 83, 118, 202
externalities   3, 103, 236*n*2, 241, 246, 253, 256
extraction, mineral   86, 93, 95, 96, 99, 100,
   106, 107, 114

fabric   56, 61, 63, 64, 64*n*15, 65, 66, 99
failure, entrepreneurial   72, 85, 120, 208
falsification   127, 128, 145, 257
families   x, 14, 67, 70, 132, 162
fashion   38, 41*n*6, 45, 47, 48, 49, 54, 55, 56, 57,
   58, 59, 60, 61, 62, 63, 64, 64*n*15, 65, 66,
   67, 68, 69, 69*n*17, 117, 118, 125, 133, 141,
   176, 177, 178, 186, 218, 240, 264
Federico, A.   9, 12, 20, 267, 268, 269, 270, 280,
   281, 285, 286, 289, 291, 294, 296
female   2, 41*n*6, 59, 64, 68, 69*n*17
Fenoaltea, S.   13*n*16, 170*n*4, 193, 200, 268,
   273, 275
fertility   95, 97, 98, 121, 190, 191*n*30
feudalism   1, 53, 58, 180, 189, 190, 191, 192, 193,
   194, 196, 196*n*34, 197, 202, 203, 220, 250
Field, A.   21, 170*n*4, 190, 203, 222, 274, 275,
   281, 286
fields. *See also* individual fields   ix, 4, 7, 8,
   13*n*16, 15, 19, 20, 21, 24*n*26, 28, 44, 66, 119,
   120*n*4, 123, 139, 141, 143, 144, 146, 170, 179,
   211*n*11, 215
finance   1, 14, 31*n*33, 47, 74*n*5, 85, 86, 87, 94,
   95, 103, 107, 212, 237, 241, 261, 261*n*43,
   262, 263, 264, 265
financial   26*n*27, 31, 31*n*33, 79, 95, 120, 141,
   194, 255, 260, 261, 261*n*42, 261*n*43, 262,
   263, 264
financialisation   25*n*27, 31, 31*n*33, 92
firms. *See also* corporations and
   enterprises   43, 47, 133*n*23, 146, 198,
   199, 200, 210, 210*n*9, 211, 212, 212*n*12, 213,
   218, 219, 220, 229*n*30, 246, 252, 255, 264
Fischer, S.   203, 280

Fishlow, A.   133*n*23, 280
Flinn, M.   49, 280
Floud, R.   1*n*1, 121*n*7, 271, 280, 287
Fogel, R.   6, 7, 10*n*14, 15, 16, 17, 26*n*28, 120,
   125*n*13, 129*n*17, 133, 133*n*23, 135, 136,
   137*n*29, 170, 238, 272, 273, 274, 280
Fohlin, C.   264, 280
food   2, 2*n*4, 65, 92, 93*n*3, 217, 226*n*25, 249*n*26
Foray, D.   244, 273
forces, economic, social, productive, etc   38,
   43, 52, 53, 54, 103, 133, 191, 195, 196,
   205, 214
formal   4, 10, 10*n*14, 12, 54, 59, 75, 121, 123, 128,
   145, 148, 150, 153, 153*n*12, 155, 158, 163,
   168, 171, 174, 176*n*13, 213, 215, 222, 242*n*12,
   243, 244, 256
formalism   15, 70, 123, 137*n*29, 217, 230, 265
forms   1, 3, 11, 22, 24, 28, 36, 40, 49, 71, 74*n*4,
   78, 91, 107, 114, 115, 130, 145, 153, 166, 176,
   178, 180, 181, 183, 183*n*21, 186, 190, 196,
   197, 198, 200, 201, 211, 217, 218*n*16
Forty, A.   66, 104, 280, 281
foundations   43, 116*n*2, 143, 171*n*7, 224, 225,
   241, 248*n*25
Fourie, F.   198, 280
fourteenth century   179, 191
framework   14, 22, 37, 38, 40, 42, 43, 49, 51,
   55, 84, 124, 129*n*17, 131, 136, 147, 148,
   151, 155, 156, 160, 160*n*16, 163, 164, 165,
   166, 172, 175, 176, 177, 177*n*16, 182, 184,
   184*n*23, 185, 186, 187, 188, 193, 196, 198,
   199*n*37, 203, 204, 205, 220, 249, 251, 253,
   259, 260
framing   5, 8, 18, 92, 120, 125, 150
France   62, 120, 180, 194, 224
Frankema, E.   24, 280
free riders   166, 173, 175, 176, 186
freedom   3, 106, 131, 136*n*28, 194
freehold   194
Freeman, C.   280
Friedman, M.   14*n*17, 120, 280
frock-coat   62
functional   48, 126, 127*n*14, 141*n*4, 154,
   183, 204*n*40
fundamentals   9, 25, 79, 143, 152, 159, 164, 185,
   218, 220, 229
Furlough, E.   268, 273

Game, Assurance   33

games   15, 18, 22, 22n24, 32, 33n36, 34, 34n38,
     35, 146, 151, 157, 171n5, 171n7, 174, 213,
     213n13, 248n25, 257
game-theoretic   22, 157, 213n13
Gaski, J.   47n11, 281
Geary, F.   47n11, 281
General Strike   71, 85
Genoese   257
geographical   10, 232n34, 264
geography   141, 145n7, 246, 246n20, 246n21,
     247, 247n22
geological   72, 74n4, 76, 85, 100, 106
geology   76, 90, 115, 239
Gerdes, L   247n23, 275
Germany   203, 262
Gerschenkron, A.   129, 258, 260, 263, 264
Giddens, A.   159, 184, 184n23, 185, 188,
     188n29, 281
Gilboy, E.   44, 47n11, 281
Gintis, H.   216, 218n16, 269
global   23, 26n27, 31, 39, 112, 240, 247n23
globalisation   140
Goldin, C.   149, 281
Goodrich, C.   134n25, 281
goods   48, 53n14, 54, 55, 56, 57, 58, 59, 60, 62,
     63, 64, 65, 67, 96, 113n24, 148, 150, 179,
     192, 199, 200, 203, 233n35
Gordon, D.   128, 281
government   41, 65, 72, 85, 106, 109, 110, 111,
     123, 153, 155, 175n12, 180, 193, 202, 224,
     227, 237n2, 254, 258, 261, 262
Greasley, D.   73, 87, 88, 89, 90, 281
Great Depression   12, 14n17, 72, 81, 109, 120
Greece   179, 195
Greenwood, J.   23, 281, 294
Gregory, T.   100n16, 110, 110n23, 281
Greif, A.   15, 147, 148, 257, 268, 281
Groenewegen, J.   204, 281
groups   22, 57, 63, 65, 69, 92, 108, 109n22, 126,
     148, 151, 155, 157, 158, 166, 173, 184n23,
     188, 189n29, 212, 212n12, 225, 230, 261
growth theory, endogenous (new)   25,
     141, 145n7, 147, 211n11, 238n6, 258,
     258n37, 259n39
Guner, N.   281
Gupta, S.   272
Gutman, H.   273

Haigh, R.   108, 109n22, 288

Hancock, W.   135, 281
Hands, D.   165n20, 281
Hansen, G.   21, 281
Harley, S.   232n34, 285
Harris, L.   2, 43n8, 71, 91, 111, 278, 279
Harriss, J.   282, 290, 295
Hart, O.   217, 217n15, 282
Harte, N.   267, 271, 281, 282, 287, 291
Hartwell, R.   37, 122n7, 281, 282
Harvey, C.   93, 282
Haupert, M.   9, 13, 18n19, 20n20, 25, 26n28,
     29, 29n31, 273, 274, 282, 284, 287, 292
Hausmann, W.   49, 282
Hayami, Y.   229n30, 282
Hayek, F.   236
Heal, G.   95, 272
Heasman, M.   279
Heaton, H.   134n24, 232, 282
Hecht, J.   58, 59, 60, 282
Heckman, J.   15, 16, 245n17, 282
hegemony   15, 44
     US   5, 126, 224
Henley, A.   84, 84n14, 282
heterodoxy   IX, 16n18, 27, 28, 225n24, 232,
     232n34, 246
Hidy, M.   104n20, 108, 282
Hidy, R.   104n20, 108, 282
hierarchy   51, 67, 123, 164, 198, 201, 216
Higonnet, P.   272, 283
Hilton, R.   38, 193, 283
Hirsch, W.   286, 296
Hirshleifer, J.   251, 251n29, 252, 283
Hobsbawm, E.   1, 219n18, 221n20, 225n24, 283
Hodgson, G.   154, 184n23, 196n35, 203,
     232n34, 283
Hogarth, R.   283, 295
Holton, R.   193, 283
home   14, 57, 64, 65, 66, 69n17, 124, 181, 220
Homo economicus   120, 185
hostages   153n11, 189
Hounshell, D.   213n13, 283
households   54, 57, 58, 59, 60, 121, 141
housemaids   58, 60
housing   49, 58, 86, 92
Hughes, J.   122n7, 124, 124n11, 173n9, 282, 283
human   96, 119, 129n17, 132, 132n22, 146, 155,
     159, 164, 165, 166, 167, 171n7, 174, 183,
     183n22, 184n23, 185, 186, 187, 187n25,
     205, 210, 218, 219, 221, 228, 257

humanities   IX, 27, 220, 228
humanomics   27n29
Hunter, J.   282
Hyland, M.   283
hypotheses   3, 11, 27, 37, 40, 57, 66, 69, 74, 76,
      77, 78, 84, 96, 124, 130, 132n21, 167, 206,
      211, 221n20, 251, 252
hysteresis   237, 241, 244

IBM   240n10, 255
identities   2n5, 13, 141, 184n23, 187,
      187n25, 229n29
ideological   16n18, 39, 44, 45, 51n12, 68, 126,
      132, 141, 155, 158, 161, 162, 163, 168, 186,
      224, 225, 226, 230, 254
ideology   8, 26, 34, 53, 111, 126, 139, 143, 144,
      148, 149, 151, 154, 155, 157, 158, 159, 160,
      160n15, 161, 162, 163, 164, 165, 166, 167,
      168, 169, 171, 172n8, 173, 175, 176, 176n14,
      182, 183n20, 185, 187, 188n26, 189, 190,
      205, 227n27, 266
illiberal   31, 31n34, 32
imperialism   12n15, 103, 123
imports   103, 111, 112
incentives   27n29, 28, 33, 33n36, 34, 34n38,
      43, 79, 82, 83, 87, 97, 151, 155, 158, 163,
      169, 174, 175, 178, 180, 196n35, 197, 201,
      236n2, 249, 260, 265
incomes   26n27, 44, 46, 47, 49, 52, 53n13, 55,
      57, 58, 61, 63, 64, 65, 66, 67, 68, 154, 163,
      179, 192, 193
increasing returns   3, 25, 73, 77n7, 78,
      88, 214n13
India   120
individualism   8, 33, 34, 133, 168
individualistic   33, 35, 166, 170, 173, 176, 186,
      187, 188n27, 193, 206, 216, 229n30
individuals   4, 17, 22, 31, 32, 34n38, 52, 130,
      133, 141, 143, 146, 148, 151, 152, 155, 157,
      158, 159, 162, 174, 175, 176, 177, 180,
      182, 183, 184n23, 185, 186, 187n25, 188,
      188n28, 189, 197, 200, 208, 216, 219, 220,
      236, 257
induction   9, 12, 122n8, 134
industrial revolution   1, 15, 21, 25, 26, 36, 37,
      38, 39, 41, 42, 43, 44, 46, 47, 48, 49, 50,
      51, 52, 53, 54, 57, 66, 67, 70, 95, 178, 181,
      191, 195, 259, 259n39

industrialisation   41n5, 61, 263
industries. *See* particular sectors or
      aspects   26n27, 94, 95, 146, 212
inefficiency   48, 74, 79, 82, 85, 103, 104, 108,
      113, 151, 154, 155, 174, 175, 176, 176n13, 195,
      198, 201, 227, 236, 236n2, 243n13, 245,
      250, 251, 252, 253, 254, 255
inequality   2n5, 62, 67, 68, 226, 247n23
inflation   45
influence   3, 5, 6, 7, 10, 12, 15, 18, 27, 30, 37,
      39, 52, 56, 57, 58, 60, 61, 62, 93, 103,
      122, 126, 133, 135, 140, 142, 148, 151, 162,
      167, 170, 179, 182, 183, 186, 190, 204, 205,
      207n3, 216, 222, 223, 227, 231n33, 233,
      237, 241, 262
informal   54, 148, 149, 155, 158, 163, 164, 171,
      174, 217, 244, 245, 249, 265
information   23, 57, 143, 145, 146, 148, 149,
      156, 157, 163, 174, 188n28, 198, 206, 210,
      211, 212, 212n12, 214, 216, 217, 218, 219,
      220, 222, 223, 224, 227, 228, 228n28,
      229, 229n30, 230, 236n2, 238, 241, 248,
      248n25, 249, 249n26, 250, 253, 260, 262,
      263, 265, 266
informational   3, 5, 141, 143, 145, 148, 210n8,
      211, 212, 215, 216, 219, 220, 221, 231, 249,
      262, 263
information-theoretic   143, 145, 146,
      149, 212, 216, 217, 222, 223, 224, 228,
      228n28, 229, 229n30, 230, 238, 250, 262,
      265, 266
Ingham, G.   145n7, 283
Inkster, I.   47n11, 283
Innes, D.   100n16, 112, 283
innovation   27n29, 41n6, 42, 46, 47, 180, 181,
      232n34, 245, 247n23, 253, 260, 261
inputs   25, 37, 76, 78, 95, 96, 98, 148, 181, 200,
      220, 247, 260
insider lending   264
institutional   12, 15, 21, 22, 24n26, 26, 27n29,
      34, 70, 79, 143, 153, 155, 158, 159, 163,
      165, 168, 169, 171, 172, 173, 174, 175, 176,
      177n16, 178, 185, 196n35, 222, 225, 229n31,
      232n34, 253, 261, 261n42
institutionalised   127, 171n5, 192, 222, 223,
      233, 256
institutionalism   143, 172, 205
institutionally   123, 216, 231, 263

institutions   6, 7, 8, 11, 14, 15, 22, 23, 26,
    26n28, 32, 33, 34, 35, 69, 132n22, 138,
    139, 142, 143, 144, 145, 146, 148, 149, 151,
    152, 153n12, 154, 155, 158, 159, 160n6,
    161, 161n17, 162, 163, 164, 165, 166, 167,
    168, 169, 170, 171, 171n5, 172, 174, 175, 176,
    176n13, 179, 182, 185, 188, 188n28, 193,
    198, 201, 203, 204, 205, 208, 211n10, 217,
    220, 221, 223, 228, 232n34, 237, 245, 249,
    256, 257, 261, 263, 264, 265, 266
integration, horizontal and vertical   91, 92,
    94, 109, 109n22, 112, 113, 115, 181, 212
intellectual   3, 7, 31n32, 39, 44, 91, 117, 118,
    119, 122, 124, 125, 134, 138, 139, 140, 141,
    142, 143, 157, 159, 168, 170n2, 171, 173, 177,
    188, 205, 208n5, 211n11, 214, 214n14, 218,
    222, 223, 225, 227, 230, 231, 241, 242, 247,
    248n25, 249, 250
interdisciplinary   3, 8, 20, 24, 30, 36, 132n20,
    136, 147, 223
interest, in   1, 3, 11, 15, 21, 25n27, 28, 30,
    33, 33n36, 34, 42, 43, 55, 56, 65, 66,
    79, 98n12, 99, 99n14, 109, 124, 132n21,
    140, 141, 148, 152, 155, 165, 171, 172, 186,
    188n29, 226, 241, 242, 254, 261
international   112, 179, 224, 232, 241, 251
International Mining History Conference   93
internet   238n5, 254, 255n36
intervention   68, 71, 227, 260
intradisciplinary   7, 8, 9, 24, 212, 223
investment   45, 46, 50, 86, 87, 95, 96, 97,
    130, 148, 217, 259n39, 260, 260n41, 262,
    263, 264
iron   49, 120
irrationality   4, 9, 26, 130n18, 133, 136, 138,
    142, 143, 144, 145, 146, 149, 167, 168, 185,
    236n2, 239
Isherwood, B.   233n35, 274
Isolation Paradox   33, 34
Italy   120
Itaman, R.   31n33, 283
Itoh, M.   263n46, 283

Jabbar, H.   119, 283
Japan   120, 229n30, 262, 263
Javdani, M.   232n34, 283
Johannesburg   104n21
Johnson, B.   58, 267, 284
Johnson, S.   58, 267, 284

Jomo, K. S.   284, 289
Jones, E.   44, 275, 284

Kafka, A.   16, 284
Kaldor, N.   45
Kalecki, M.   46
Karwowski, E.   267
Kay, N.   237n2, 267, 284, 286
Keaney, M.   177n17, 204n41
Kerstholt, F.   281
Keynes, J. M.   29, 53, 122, 137n29, 147, 291
Keynesian   14, 15, 38, 42, 43, 43n8, 45, 52, 207
Kimberley   XI, 100, 102, 102f.1, 107, 109
Kindleberger, C.   239, 284
Kirby, M.   73, 74, 74n4, 75, 78, 79, 81, 82, 83,
    85, 113, 284
Klose, G.   296
knowledge   24n26, 151, 160, 164, 171n7, 178,
    200, 210, 214, 214n14, 218, 219, 226, 227,
    236, 239n8, 247, 248, 248n24, 248n25,
    249n26, 250, 262, 264
Knowles, R.   104, 284
Kopecky, K.   281
Korea   261n43, 263
Koshovets, O.   165n20, 284
Koxhoorn, N.   104n20, 111, 284
Koyama, M.   24n26, 284
Kozul-Wright, R.   268
Kreps, D.   271, 284
Krugman, P.   245n17, 246, 247, 252n30,
    273, 284
Kuhn, T.   124, 125, 125n12, 128
Kuhnian   124, 125, 128
Kuznets, S.   116n2, 129, 135, 137n29, 284

labor   131, 150, 178, 179, 181, 190, 199, 200, 202
labour   2, 3n7, 41n6, 46, 53, 54, 57, 58, 61,
    62, 63, 67, 68, 72, 75, 76, 77, 78, 84n14,
    85, 88, 89, 89n19, 90n20, 94, 94n4,
    95, 96, 98, 109, 112, 113n24, 114, 115, 141,
    145n7, 153, 167, 178, 179, 180, 187n25, 197,
    199, 200, 202, 203, 229n30, 238, 239,
    242, 247
laissez-faire   44, 251, 253
Lamoreaux, N.   5, 6, 121n7, 144n6, 146, 209,
    209n6, 210, 212, 212n12, 213, 214, 215, 217,
    218, 222, 222n22, 223, 224, 225, 226, 227,
    228, 228n28, 229, 230, 231, 232, 237, 261,
    264, 284, 285, 289, 294, 295

landed property 72, 85, 86, 91, 92, 93, 94, 96, 97, 98, 99, 99*n*14, 100, 111, 113, 114, 115
Landes, D. 225, 259, 283, 285
landlords 53, 53*n*14, 86, 93, 194, 220
landowners 72, 86, 91, 96, 99, 179
language 29, 142, 168, 252, 257
Lapavitsas, C. 262*n*45, 263, 263*n*46, 268, 279, 283, 285
law 27, 34, 53, 94*n*7, 96, 135, 174, 179, 194, 196, 239, 241, 242, 253
Lawson, T. 129, 243*n*15, 285
Lazear, E. 145, 285
Le Roy Ladurie, E. 190, 285
leases 40, 86, 98, 99, 194
Lee, F. 232*n*34, 285
legislation 100, 111, 148
legitimacy 4, 142, 200, 202, 247
leisure 67, 132
Lemire, B. 64*n*15, 285
Lenard, T. 254*n*32, 274
lenders 262, 263
Lenin, V. 38, 285, 287
Lenzen, G. 100*n*16, 285
Leopold, E. 36, 92, 93*n*3, 210*n*9, 249*n*26, 259*n*39, 279
Leverhulme Trust 37*n*1, 74*n*3
Levi, M. 268
Levine, D. 23, 285
Levitt, S. 56, 62, 64, 295
Lewis, C. 66, 269, 277, 282, 285
Lewis, P. 66, 269, 277, 282, 285
Leydesdorff, L. 273, 285
liberalism 31, 32, 141, 256
Liebowitz, S. 234, 236, 236*n*2, 246, 246*n*19, 251, 251*n*28, 252, 252*n*30, 252*n*31, 253, 254, 255, 256, 285, 286
life 38, 39, 40, 41, 44, 45, 49, 52, 59, 62, 64, 104*n*21, 135, 138, 173, 174, 185, 189, 213, 238, 257, 264
life-style 38, 41, 44, 45
linguistic turn 229
Liodakis, G. 276, 286
Lipartito, K. 219, 238*n*4, 286
literature 2, 6, 7, 9, 11, 17, 19, 31*n*32, 31*n*34, 39, 39*n*2, 40, 41, 50, 54, 94*n*7, 116*n*2, 117, 134, 136, 145, 147, 156, 160, 163, 164, 167, 171, 187, 200, 213, 214, 215, 225, 226, 229, 248*n*25
Little, D. 271, 280, 286, 293

Liverpool 61, 66
Lloyd, C. 183, 286
location theory 184*n*23, 241
lock in 236*n*2, 239, 245, 251
Lockwood, D. 159, 286
logic 21, 96, 103, 127*n*14, 137, 154, 201, 211*n*11
logical 11, 44, 50, 132, 199, 200, 211*n*11, 246*n*19, 249
logically 159, 167, 184, 184*n*23, 198, 199
Lohr, S. 255, 269
London 49, 58, 61, 63, 65, 66, 74*n*3, 104
long run 45, 48, 50, 222, 240*n*11, 243*n*14, 251, 259*n*39
lords 179, 180, 192, 193, 194, 197, 199, 200, 201, 202
Louçã, F. 127*n*14, 136, 280
Lucas, R. 15, 83, 286
luxuries 42, 48, 55, 56, 57, 61, 62, 63, 65, 67, 68, 69*n*17, 70, 192, 227

machinery 56, 61, 63, 65, 74*n*4, 77, 85, 88, 89, 90, 98, 112, 219, 221, 240
macroeconomics 14, 42, 43, 51, 123, 147, 182, 184, 228, 241, 247*n*23, 256, 258
Mader, P. 31*n*33, 286
maidservants 56, 60, 67
mainstream IX, X, 4, 5, 8, 21, 24, 26, 27*n*30, 28, 29, 30, 32, 33*n*36, 35, 36, 40, 41, 45, 54, 73, 117, 123, 125, 126, 128, 129, 130, 138, 139, 141, 143, 144, 146, 147, 148, 152, 156, 163, 167, 210*n*8, 215, 221*n*21, 227, 228, 229, 232, 232*n*34, 234, 237, 238*n*6, 242, 243, 243*n*14, 245, 247, 248, 249, 256, 261
Majumdar, T. 286, 293
male 33*n*37, 58, 59, 62, 65, 68, 104, 110, 120, 131, 132, 150, 264
Malthus, T. 39, 53, 53*n*14, 292, 296
management 107, 262
manifesto 17, 69, 117, 126, 132, 150, 259
mantua-maker 60, 64
manufacturing 46, 47, 56, 61, 63, 64, 106, 113*n*24, 254
marginal 48, 77, 85, 91, 102*n*18, 131, 136, 145, 156, 178, 210
marginalism 96, 122*n*8, 198
marginalist revolution IX, 5, 12, 28, 96, 118, 122*n*8, 207
Margo, R. 10, 10*n*12, 10*n*14, 21, 27, 29, 31*n*32, 286

Margolis, S.   234, 236, 236n2, 246, 246n19, 251, 252, 252n30, 252n31, 253, 254, 255, 256, 285, 286
market imperfections   IX, 3, 5, 7, 19, 20, 25, 26, 31, 43, 118, 138, 140, 142, 145, 146, 148, 149, 155, 157, 172, 206, 208, 209, 210n8, 211, 223, 231, 232, 235n1, 237, 238, 241, 242, 246, 246n19, 250, 256, 265
marketing   42, 47, 49, 68, 74n5, 79, 82, 86, 87, 94, 107, 108, 109, 114, 252
markets, perfect   3, 17, 18, 19, 117, 130n18, 140, 141, 149, 159, 207, 222, 234, 236, 266
Markov chain   244, 246n21
Marks, S.   100n16, 286
mark-up   84, 84n14
marriage   190, 191n30
Marshall, A.   43, 98n13, 116n2, 122, 147, 225n24
Marshallian   132n22, 241
Martin, R.   3n6, 74n3, 145n7, 246n21, 287
Marx, K.   1n3, 24, 38, 69, 72, 73, 96, 97, 97n9, 98, 98n12, 116n2, 128, 132, 132n20, 147, 159, 160, 160n16, 163, 187n25, 205, 223, 268, 275, 278, 287
Marxian   173, 205
Marxism   1, 53, 112, 132, 132n21, 165, 170, 173, 205
Marxist   IX, 1, 2, 44, 46, 53, 93, 96, 98, 133, 173n9, 187, 189
mass, production/consumption   38, 41n6, 48, 54, 55, 58, 61, 66
master   55, 58, 60, 66, 67, 68, 130
material culture   3, 5, 27, 35, 39, 42, 92, 140, 167, 168, 242
materials, raw   98, 99, 145, 218n17, 243
mathematical   2, 9, 10n14, 15, 28, 52, 135, 145, 213, 215, 222, 227, 230, 232, 243, 243n14, 244, 252, 265
mathematics   53, 147, 242n12, 244, 252, 256
Mathias, P.   135, 287
Matthews, D.   95n8, 202n39, 287
maximisation   4, 27n29, 128, 132, 152, 154, 155, 166, 167, 179, 182, 199, 199n37, 210
maximum   78, 130
McCarthyism   125, 127n14
McClelland, P.   137, 287
McCloskey, D.   1n1, 16, 16n18, 23, 26, 27n29, 45, 50, 51, 52, 54, 118, 119, 120, 120n5,

121n7, 127n14, 129, 136, 144, 147, 238n6, 239n9, 243, 266n48, 271, 272, 280, 282, 283, 284, 287, 290
McKendrick, N.   37, 41, 41n6, 42, 44, 47, 48, 55, 56, 57, 58, 59, 61, 62, 65, 66, 68, 69, 69n17, 287, 288, 291
McKenzie, R.   254n33, 288
McLean, J.   108, 109n22, 288
meaning   9, 27, 30, 35, 74n4, 82, 118n3, 125, 127, 136, 148, 150, 159, 161, 167, 187, 189, 216, 220, 229, 229n29, 236n2, 238, 247
mechanical   21, 156n13, 239, 240, 243
mechanisation   30, 73, 74, 74n4, 75, 76, 78, 84, 84n14, 85, 86, 87, 89, 90, 100, 113
mechanism   23, 24, 34, 42, 56, 59, 69, 108, 110, 113, 125, 153, 155, 159, 165, 171, 184, 214n13, 236n2, 241, 248n25
men   27, 44, 58, 64, 65, 68, 68n17, 71, 101, 132, 185n24, 192
Menashy, F.   119, 283
Mendes Loureiro, P.   2n5, 279
merger   20, 81, 81n11, 84
Mertens, D.   286
Merton, R.   160, 160n16, 161, 165, 288
method   2, 53, 63, 76, 77, 77n7, 107, 126, 136, 142, 144, 147, 207n3, 246, 255n36
methodenstreit   12, 122, 134
methodological   4, 36, 127, 128, 137, 143, 146, 158, 161, 165, 167, 168, 176, 183, 183n21, 184, 205, 211n11, 216, 217, 218, 221, 224, 229, 232, 238
    individualism   4, 143, 146, 158, 161, 165, 167, 168, 176, 182, 183, 183n21, 205, 216, 217, 218, 221, 229, 232, 233n35
methodological holism   183, 183n21
methodological structurism   183, 184
methodology   2n4, 8, 10, 10n14, 17, 20, 21, 23, 24, 28, 29, 30, 74, 79, 83, 89, 97, 100, 109, 120, 121, 122n8, 128, 129, 131, 133, 148, 168, 176, 209, 211, 218, 221, 228, 230, 230n32, 231, 232, 235, 243n15, 249, 252, 256
Meyer, J.   125, 129, 129n17, 134, 137, 271, 288
micro   43, 123, 143, 151, 182, 184, 255, 256, 258, 265, 265n47
microeconomics   5, 14, 42, 228, 241, 258, 263
microfoundations   239, 250
Microsoft   234, 246n19, 252, 254, 254n33, 254n34, 255

Middle Ages 179, 192
Midlands 61, 82
Milgate, M. 274
Milgrom, P. 245n17, 288
Miliband, R. 278, 288
military 111, 179, 180, 180n19, 192, 202
Miller, B. 66, 140, 236, 270, 276, 288
Miller, D. 66, 140, 236, 270, 276, 288
Mills, C. Wright 177n17, 288
Milonakis, D. 3, 5, 6, 6n10, 18, 116, 120n4, 140, 140n1, 149n10, 169, 170n2, 171, 176n14, 183, 193, 195n32, 207, 207n3, 208n5, 221, 228n28, 234, 279, 288, 289
mineowners 72, 73, 79, 82, 84, 85, 86, 87, 99, 100
minerals 72, 91, 92n1, 94, 94n7, 95, 95n8, 96, 97, 98, 99, 100, 100n15, 103n19, 105, 106, 107, 113, 115
minerals-energy
    complex 91, 92n1
miners 71, 72, 73, 85, 88, 103, 107
mines 49, 69n17, 72, 73, 74n4, 75, 76, 77, 78, 82, 83, 84, 86, 87, 87n16, 88, 89, 94, 94n5, 99, 100, 101, 102, 102n18, 103, 107, 109, 110, 206
Mingay, G. 275, 284
mining 30, 61, 72, 73, 76, 79, 81, 86n15, 91, 92, 93, 94, 94n4, 95, 95n8, 96, 98, 98n13, 99, 100n15, 101, 103, 110, 114, 115
Misa, T. 229n31, 289
Mitch, D. 15, 289
Mitra, S. 272
modelling 145, 148, 150, 156, 168, 215, 243, 243n14, 244
models 4, 8, 17, 21, 22, 23, 24n26, 26n28, 28, 29, 36, 45, 46, 50, 52, 54, 70, 75, 94, 112, 117, 125, 128, 133, 136, 137n29, 142, 145, 146, 147, 148, 149, 152, 153, 154, 156, 157, 158, 160, 161, 163, 165, 168, 171n5, 172n8, 182, 190, 209, 210, 210n8, 213, 213n13, 214, 215, 218n17, 219, 219n18, 220, 221, 224, 226, 227, 229, 230, 232, 237n2, 239, 239n8, 240, 240n11, 241, 243n14, 244, 245, 246, 246n21, 249, 252, 257, 258, 259, 261, 261n42
modern 1, 15, 21, 24n26, 26, 27, 29n31, 37, 40, 44, 48, 52, 56, 58, 70, 108, 114, 120, 126, 128n15, 130, 153, 163, 171n7, 175, 180, 192,

193, 194, 195, 197, 220, 242n12, 243n14, 249, 250, 258, 263, 264
modernisation 131
modernity 69
Modica, S. 23, 285
Mokyr, J. 26, 45, 47n11, 54, 211, 211n11, 245, 258n37, 259n40, 266n48, 289
Molho, A. 284, 289
monetarism 14, 43, 45, 227
monetary 14n17, 61, 120, 262, 263
money 14, 29n31, 41n6, 57, 59, 83n13, 199, 200, 224, 252, 263, 264, 265
monopoly 40, 46, 47, 48, 49, 79, 91, 93, 94, 96, 98, 101, 103, 103n19, 107, 108, 109n22, 110, 111, 112, 113, 113n25, 114, 225n24, 251, 252, 254, 255
Mont Pèlerin Society 16n18, 251n28
morals 44, 53, 146, 152, 158, 162, 264
Moro, A. 23, 269
motor
    of history 190, 205
    vehicles 251
Mowat, C. 71, 289
multiplier 45, 48, 51, 62
Munck, R. 283
Murfin, A. 40n4, 45, 46n10, 113n25, 279
Murphy, G. 128n15, 289
Musson, A. 47n11, 52, 289
Myhrman, J. 171n6, 289

Nagelkerke, A. 281
Naidoo, S. 269
narratives 16n18, 23, 26, 27, 27n30, 28, 38, 66, 171, 189, 203, 215, 231, 234, 237, 254n32, 256, 257, 258, 265, 266
National Bank Era 263
National Bureau of Economic
    Research 209
National Center for Supercomputing
    Applications (NCSA) 255n36
national system of innovation,
    NSI 245, 245n18
nationalisation 72, 73, 85, 87n16, 90, 92, 99n14, 100, 108
nation-states 146, 180, 193, 212, 212n12, 219
Nef, J. 49, 107, 289
Nelson, R. 145n7, 289
neo-Austrian 16n18, 256

neoclassical   13, 16n18, 17, 26n28, 40, 85, 86,
      91, 93, 95, 96, 102n18, 117, 121, 123, 127n14,
      129, 131, 132, 133, 134, 143, 144, 145, 147,
      149, 150, 151, 152, 154, 155, 157n14, 162,
      163, 164, 165, 166, 170, 172, 172n8, 173, 174,
      176, 177, 178, 181, 185, 186, 187, 198, 200,
      205, 209, 210, 210n8, 210n9, 211, 216, 217,
      218, 220, 222, 223, 224, 225, 228, 228n28,
      230, 231, 232, 237n2, 238, 238n6, 242,
      243n15, 258, 259
neoliberalism   IX, 3, 8, 16, 36, 71, 140, 141, 168,
      170n2, 231, 234, 246n19, 250, 251, 256
Netherlands   180
Netscape   254
networks   93n3, 241, 244, 251, 252, 254, 255
Neumann, A.   79, 289
neuroeconomics. See also behavioural   26,
      139, 165, 169
neuroscience   169, 266
New Classical Economics   15, 16, 43, 227
new economic history. See also
      cliometrics   IX, 5, 6, 10, 12, 13, 17, 18,
      19, 20, 25, 26, 30, 117, 118, 118n3, 119,
      121, 122n7, 125, 126, 128n15, 130, 131, 133,
      133n23, 134, 135, 138, 141, 145, 149, 150,
      162, 206, 207, 208, 209, 209n7, 211,
      211n11, 228, 231, 232, 237, 238, 259, 266
new institutional economics   6, 26n28, 141,
      145n7, 168, 172, 173
Newcastle   49, 91, 104
   Duke of   55
newer economic history. See also
      cliometrics   6, 19, 26, 118, 118n3, 143,
      144, 145, 145n8, 146, 148, 156, 168, 169,
      206, 208, 209, 211, 216, 222, 223, 229, 230,
      232, 233, 235n1, 237, 246n21, 265, 266
newest economic history. See also
      cliometrics   IX, 6, 10, 12, 18, 20, 26,
      118n3, 170, 207, 208, 232, 234, 235, 235n1,
      237, 241, 266
Newman, P.   274
Nicholas, S.   43n7, 290
Nilsson, E.   188, 188n28, 290
nineteenth century   42, 48, 56, 59, 61, 63, 65,
      72, 99, 100, 104, 105, 107, 120, 127n14,
      263, 264
Nobel Prize   6, 16, 33n36, 143, 170,
      217n15

non-market   3, 4, 64, 140, 145, 168, 172, 173,
      208, 211, 217, 221, 230, 231, 236, 237
Nore, P.   115, 290
normal science   124, 128
normative   158, 160, 163
norms   2n5, 4, 8, 37, 61, 103n19, 145, 146, 147,
      148, 152, 153, 153n12, 155, 157, 158, 160,
      161, 168, 174, 190, 229, 249
North, D.   6, 10n14, 11n14, 16, 17, 18, 26, 26n28,
      31, 116, 117, 118, 119, 121, 130, 131, 132n21,
      133n23, 137, 139, 140, 140n1, 142, 143,
      144, 148n9, 149, 149n10, 150, 151, 152,
      153, 153n11, 154, 155, 156, 157, 157n14, 158,
      159, 160, 160n15, 160n16, 161, 161n17, 162,
      163, 164, 164n18, 165, 165n19, 166, 167,
      168, 169, 170, 171, 171n5, 171n6, 171n7, 172,
      172n8, 173, 173n9, 174, 174n10, 175, 175n11,
      176, 176n13, 176n14, 177, 177n16, 178, 179,
      179n18, 180, 180n19, 181, 182, 183, 183n20,
      184, 186, 187, 188, 188n28, 189, 190, 191,
      192, 193, 193n31, 194, 195, 196, 197, 198,
      198n36, 199, 199n37, 200, 201, 201n38,
      202, 203, 204, 204n41, 205, 207, 208n5,
      221, 228n28, 245, 266, 267, 273, 274, 275,
      279, 280, 281, 289, 290, 291, 292, 294, 295
noughties   X, 6, 235n1
nouveau riche   44, 45
nuclear   33n36
Nuffield Foundation   74n3
Nunn, N.   21, 291
Nye, J.   274, 280, 291

obsolescence   59, 68, 180, 192
Ohanian, L.   281
oil   40, 91, 92, 93, 94, 97, 97n9, 99, 104,
      104n20, 105, 108, 109n22, 111, 112, 114, 115
Oliver, R.   286, 291
OPEC   40, 97
opportunism   27, 153, 155
optimising   3, 4, 4n9, 8, 22, 34, 35, 40, 52, 143,
      146, 148, 159, 162, 180, 192, 207, 208, 210,
      216, 217, 218, 219, 220, 224, 234, 236n2,
      248n25, 254, 262, 263, 265, 266
ore   15, 41, 93, 98n13, 101, 143, 229, 235, 254
organisations   70, 91, 101, 107, 108, 111, 153,
      158, 178, 179, 181, 188n28, 190, 191, 192,
      197, 198, 199, 201, 210, 211, 212, 213,
      213n13, 218, 220, 222, 241

orthodox 37, 38, 43, 44, 48, 50, 51, 73, 97*n*11, 103, 123, 134, 188, 188*n*28, 223, 254*n*32

orthodoxy 30, 31*n*33, 37, 41, 50, 54, 74, 95, 123

output 25, 41, 45, 46, 51, 52, 76, 77, 77*n*7, 79, 81, 82, 83, 83*n*12, 86, 88, 89, 90, 95, 96, 99, 101, 108, 109, 112, 113, 130, 131, 151, 154, 181, 182, 195, 197, 200, 210, 259*n*39

owners 71, 72, 87, 99, 104, 114, 131, 162, 196*n*35, 220

ownership XI, 2, 71, 72, 73, 74*n*4, 81, 86, 87*n*16, 91, 96, 97, 98, 99, 100, 100*n*15, 102f.1, 105, 107, 112, 113, 121*n*7, 131, 154, 171, 179, 189, 196, 197, 236*n*2

Ozturk, F. 281

Palermo, G. 198, 200, 267

pandemic 31

Panitch, L. 288

paradigm 16*n*18, 39, 124, 125, 128, 208, 247*n*23, 252*n*31

paradigms 252*n*31

parasitic 72, 145, 211*n*11, 229

Pareto 31, 32, 33, 155

Pareto, V. 31, 32, 33, 155

Park, H.-J. 270

Parker, W. 127*n*14, 130, 239, 239*n*7, 239*n*8, 267, 272, 284, 287, 291, 293, 294

Parsonian sociology 225, 231

Parsons, T. 136, 142, 177*n*17, 227*n*26, 230*n*32, 295

Passell, P. 146, 268

path dependence 6, 10, 11, 22, 31, 147, 155, 156, 156*n*13, 158, 159, 163, 168, 208, 220, 221, 221*n*21, 234, 235, 236, 236*n*2, 237, 237*n*2, 238, 239, 241, 243, 243*n*13, 244, 245, 246, 246*n*21, 247, 249, 250, 251, 253, 254, 256, 265

Patinkin, D. 137*n*29, 291

Paull, C. 85, 291

peasantry 179, 180, 191, 192, 193, 194, 197, 201

performance 26, 39, 41*n*5, 82, 84, 90, 91, 120, 131, 138, 151, 152, 153*n*12, 155, 156, 158, 159, 170, 172, 174, 175, 182, 189, 198, 204, 205, 212, 213, 229*n*30, 260, 262

period 80, 81

periodisation 39, 40, 41*n*5, 113*n*25, 189

periods X, 1, 12, 21, 31, 37, 40, 43, 47, 48, 49, 51, 54, 57, 58, 61, 62, 66, 68, 73, 75, 76, 77, 78, 79, 81, 82, 88, 89, 94, 99, 108, 111, 114, 121, 123, 126, 132*n*22, 134, 141, 161, 178, 189, 191, 192, 193, 196, 196*n*33, 198*n*36, 201, 203, 207, 208, 217, 224, 225, 225*n*24, 233, 246*n*21, 262

periphery 246

persistence 10, 11, 21, 24, 60, 63, 64, 65, 128, 175, 200, 235, 252*n*30, 253

Persistence Studies 10, 11, 24

Persson, T 22*n*23, 291

phases of economic history 18

Phases of economic history 11, 18, 19, 30, 134, 221, 237

phases of economics imperialism 18, 19, 30
   new (second) IX, 3, 5, 8, 18, 118, 118*n*3, 208, 223, 235*n*1, 239, 260, 262, 265
   newer (third) 3, 4, 5, 7, 8, 10, 19, 20, 23, 24, 28, 35, 83, 118*n*3, 139, 207, 209*n*7, 234, 235, 235*n*1, 237, 241
   old (first) IX, 3, 5, 12, 14, 15, 18, 19, 118*n*3, 169, 208, 209*n*7, 266

philosophical 125, 128, 226, 242*n*12

Philpin, C. 39, 268, 269

physical 75, 77, 96, 220, 239, 244

Pilat, D. 295

Pincus, J. 279

Pitelis, C. 198, 280, 291

players 34, 34*n*38, 35, 161, 213

Plumb, J. 67, 69, 288, 291

policy IX, 5, 9, 14*n*17, 16, 22, 26*n*27, 41*n*6, 43, 45, 48, 73, 85, 112, 123, 158, 172*n*8, 227*n*27, 254, 260, 261, 261*n*43, 262, 263

political IX, 1, 2, 5, 20, 22, 24, 24*n*26, 26*n*27, 27, 28, 30, 36, 39, 53, 53*n*14, 62, 73, 98, 103, 118, 121, 122, 125, 126, 128, 131, 135, 138, 141, 149, 156, 157, 158, 159, 164, 168, 172*n*8, 174, 175*n*12, 177*n*16, 179, 180, 183, 192, 197, 207, 218*n*16, 224, 233, 234, 245*n*18, 254, 260, 262, 264

political economy IX, 1, 5, 20, 22, 24, 24*n*26, 27, 28, 36, 39, 53, 73, 118, 138, 141, 207, 218*n*16, 224, 233, 234, 236, 254, 260

politics 41, 53, 71, 172*n*8, 188*n*28, 208, 257, 260

Pollard, S. 49, 135, 291, 292

poor 39, 69, 72, 84, 170

Popper, K. 125

Popperian 127

population   22, 41, 48, 49, 53, 53*n*14, 55, 58,
    61, 132*n*22, 177, 178, 179, 180, 182, 186, 190,
    191, 191*n*30, 192, 195, 244
positivism   127, 127*n*14, 128
possession   114, 192, 197
post Washington Consensus. *See also*
    World Bank and development
    economics   206
Postan, M.   190, 292
postmodern   3, 27, 30, 128, 140, 141, 148, 161,
    168, 170*n*2, 219, 228, 229, 229*n*29, 230,
    231, 233, 238
potter   41*n*6
Potteries   41*n*6, 49
pottery   3, 42, 47, 48, 49, 58, 68*n*16
poverty   24, 53*n*14
power   8, 22, 26*n*27, 27, 27*n*29, 30, 41*n*6, 55,
    56, 61, 69, 96, 98, 99, 110, 111, 112, 113*n*24,
    123, 132, 142, 143, 148, 153, 155, 167, 168,
    175*n*12, 176, 176*n*13, 177, 179, 180, 183,
    186, 187*n*25, 188, 188*n*27, 188*n*28, 192,
    193, 194, 197, 204*n*40, 216, 217, 218*n*16,
    225*n*24, 242, 245*n*18, 247*n*23, 262, 263
powerful   39, 52, 60, 124, 150, 155, 157, 171, 173,
    205, 257
powers   27*n*29, 78, 95, 110, 183, 186
practices   5, 8, 26, 28, 41, 59, 96, 97, 103*n*19,
    108, 115, 117, 122*n*8, 123, 133, 134, 172,
    184*n*23, 186, 208, 223, 231, 233*n*35, 251,
    255, 264, 265
practitioners   24*n*26, 119, 120, 124, 142, 144,
    165, 207, 211, 222, 225, 238
pragmatic   239*n*8
pragmatism   127
preference. *See also* choice and tastes   59,
    60, 92, 132*n*20, 243, 252*n*31
preferences. *See also* choice and tastes   4, 22,
    32, 54, 66, 95, 141, 146, 148, 156, 158, 159,
    162, 163, 167, 210, 244
pre-history   IX, X
Press, E.   250*n*27
Press, J.   93, 250*n*27, 292
Prevezer, M.   270, 279
price   25, 46, 48, 49, 60, 63, 77, 83, 86, 88,
    93, 95, 96, 97*n*10, 109, 112, 130, 155, 161,
    162, 171, 173, 173*n*9, 175, 179, 197, 198, 201,
    214*n*13, 230, 252, 252*n*31, 254, 256, 265

prices   41*n*6, 46, 47, 48, 49, 57, 60, 63, 79, 82,
    83, 84, 89, 107, 109, 110, 111, 150, 158, 162,
    163, 165, 174, 175, 176, 178, 188*n*28, 190,
    210, 217, 221, 243, 252, 255
pricing   79, 144, 162, 164, 165, 167, 168, 169, 171,
    177, 208*n*5, 252, 254
Primrose, D.   165*n*20, 292, 294
principle   8, 26, 28, 34, 43, 51, 75, 83, 95, 110,
    133, 134, 144, 149, 154, 155, 162, 163, 165,
    167, 168, 171, 177, 179, 182, 183, 192, 201,
    203, 204, 208, 208*n*5, 231, 233*n*35, 251,
    254, 255, 256
principles   3, 4, 8, 13, 14, 15, 17, 18, 21, 32, 95,
    135, 140, 161, 169, 207, 209, 213, 220,
    234, 261
private   44, 71, 72, 73, 100*n*15, 110, 178, 179, 180,
    197, 199, 224, 248, 248*n*25, 250, 254, 255,
    260, 261*n*43
problem   2*n*4, 29, 33, 34*n*38, 84, 84*n*14, 86,
    89, 90, 94, 95, 115, 132*n*21, 137*n*29, 150,
    152, 159, 166, 175, 176, 178, 186, 188*n*29,
    195, 197, 198, 202*n*39, 222, 230, 249, 257,
    258, 263
problems   15, 35, 40, 47, 51, 58, 81, 85, 87, 88,
    90, 94, 95, 99, 100, 103, 108, 112, 124, 125,
    137*n*29, 145, 146, 153, 154, 155, 159, 164,
    169, 175, 202, 203, 210, 211, 211*n*11, 212,
    213, 215, 217, 222, 228, 230, 240*n*11, 241,
    243*n*14, 248*n*25, 260, 262
process   22, 53, 55, 57, 63, 79, 86, 93*n*3, 98,
    101, 119, 137, 152, 159, 163, 174, 176, 177,
    179, 181, 182, 185, 187, 187*n*25, 188*n*27, 193,
    214*n*13, 232, 236*n*2, 240, 240*n*11, 241, 244,
    252, 258
processes   1, 92, 108, 112, 118, 127, 130, 134,
    147, 159, 161, 188, 195, 211*n*10, 212, 219,
    222, 228, 240, 240*n*11, 241, 244, 247*n*23,
    248, 254
producers   56, 63, 74, 76, 83, 85, 91, 107, 109,
    111, 112, 113, 114
production function   25, 35, 75, 76, 77, 78, 88,
    89, 89*n*19, 242
productive   50, 58, 73, 86, 94, 101, 107, 113, 114,
    130, 191, 195, 196, 259*n*39, 265
productivity   50, 63, 72, 75, 76, 77, 84, 87, 97,
    102*n*18, 130, 150, 152, 178, 181, 191, 191*n*30,
    195, 196, 196*n*33, 197, 259*n*39, 260

products   3, 38, 48, 50, 54, 56, 63, 65, 68, 77,
    85, 93, 107, 136, 145, 178, 181, 215, 216,
    236*n*2, 248, 251, 252, 254
profit   4, 45, 79, 86, 96, 97, 114, 125, 132, 197,
    210, 214, 220, 226, 236*n*2, 255
profitability   45, 46, 79, 84, 85, 86, 88, 93, 111,
    112, 113, 114, 179, 236*n*2
progress   25, 44, 73, 78, 121, 148, 167, 172*n*8,
    249, 249*n*26, 252, 260*n*41
    economic   38, 39, 44, 54, 67
    technical   25, 50, 52, 78, 241, 242, 258
proletarianisation   54, 58
properties   34, 95, 96, 99, 100, 108, 159, 184,
    184*n*23, 185, 187, 188*n*29, 189, 242, 262
property rights   103, 131, 143, 144, 151, 153, 154,
    155, 159, 165, 167, 173, 175, 175*n*12, 176,
    178, 179, 180, 181, 182, 190, 192, 193, 195,
    196, 196*n*35, 197, 199, 203, 204*n*41, 216,
    248*n*25, 249, 250, 253
protection   47, 108, 150, 151, 194, 230
provision   3, 63, 79, 82, 83, 91, 92, 93, 93*n*3,
    113, 217
    system of   2*n*4, 3
psychology   171*n*7
public   16, 17, 59, 72, 79, 100, 133, 248, 248*n*25,
    250, 254, 255, 255*n*36
Puffert, D.   236*n*2, 237*n*2, 292
puritan ethic   44, 62

Qian, Y.   288
qualitative   51, 52, 78, 129*n*17, 134*n*25, 195, 196,
    197, 242
quantitative   17, 21, 24, 49, 129, 129*n*17, 130,
    131, 133, 134*n*25, 149, 226, 243, 255
quantities   98, 100, 110, 227
Quittner, J.   254*n*34, 255*n*36, 292
quotas   79, 82, 83, 111
QWERTY   11, 156, 156*n*13, 234, 235, 240,
    240*n*10, 245, 246*n*19, 251, 252,
    252*n*30, 254

racism   123
Raff, D.   146, 209, 213, 215, 226*n*25, 285, 292,
    294, 295
railways   17, 43, 105, 238
Rajan, R.   217, 292
random   23, 28, 147, 162, 233, 236*n*2, 237,
    237*n*3, 244, 252*n*31

randomised control trials   23
Ransom, R.   292, 294
Rashid, S.   53*n*14, 292
rational   26, 130*n*18, 136, 138, 140, 141, 142, 143,
    144, 145, 146, 149, 154, 166, 167, 168, 176,
    177, 180, 182, 185, 186, 187, 193, 199, 208,
    210, 216, 221*n*20, 227, 236*n*2, 239, 251,
    256, 257
rationality   4, 9, 130, 133, 142, 149, 156, 157,
    161, 162, 163, 171*n*7, 173, 174, 174*n*10, 175,
    204*n*41, 218, 219, 224, 228, 252*n*31, 265
Reaganism   36
realism   4, 31, 40, 117, 123, 127*n*14, 133, 135,
    136, 138, 140, 151, 158, 161, 163, 210*n*8, 221,
    233, 240*n*11
recessions   107, 135
Reder, M.   283, 295
Redlich, F.   135*n*26, 211*n*10, 292
reductionism   4, 5, 8, 41, 51, 117, 118, 132, 135,
    143, 146, 165, 168, 216, 218, 220, 221, 235
reductionist   14, 19, 141, 145, 184, 230,
    242*n*12, 258
regional   61, 70, 82, 132, 179, 202, 247*n*23
regression   75, 137
regressions   25, 76, 209
regulation   43, 73, 81, 82, 261
relation   16*n*18, 38, 39, 52, 67, 75, 83, 97*n*10,
    98, 111, 112, 114, 182, 184*n*23, 187*n*25,
    188*n*29, 193, 193*n*31, 196*n*35, 197, 200,
    201, 206, 209, 236*n*2, 238, 247*n*23
relations   1, 4, 5, 12, 19, 22, 23, 26, 55, 58, 67,
    72, 87, 91, 103, 114, 124, 139, 157, 162, 171,
    183, 184*n*23, 186, 188, 191, 191*n*30, 193, 194,
    195, 196, 197, 205, 207, 207*n*2, 212, 213,
    217, 219, 224, 247*n*23
relationships   IX, 2, 3, 6, 7, 36, 58, 63, 66, 67,
    68, 88*n*18, 92, 99, 114, 116, 119, 130, 134,
    135, 137, 137*n*29, 139, 142, 149, 161*n*17,
    170, 176, 177, 182, 184, 189, 192, 193, 194,
    196*n*35, 197, 208, 214, 216, 234, 235*n*1, 247
relativist   140
religion   41, 157, 182
rent   40*n*4, 72, 72*n*2, 93, 95, 96, 97, 97*n*10,
    97*n*9, 98, 98*n*12, 100, 114, 192, 220,
    247*n*23, 261
    absolute   97, 97*n*10
reorganisation   78, 79, 85, 90, 100, 107
resource   40, 162, 164, 165, 178, 189, 242

resources   23, 40, 95, 99, 112, 113, 131, 135, 144, 152, 171, 177, 178, 180n19, 181, 182, 189, 190, 191, 197, 208, 238n5, 261
  exhaustible   40, 86, 95
restructuring   73, 79, 87, 91, 92, 131, 164, 263
revenues   82, 96, 97, 103, 109, 110, 155, 176, 179, 180, 193, 210
rhetoric   16n18, 26n27, 129, 137, 266n48
Rhodes, E.   77n7, 103, 103n19, 109, 195, 292
Ribeiro, A.   61, 63, 64, 292
Ricardian   91, 93, 95, 98, 100
Ricardo, D.   93, 96, 97, 223, 278
rich   37, 39, 44, 130, 170, 223
rigour   8, 10n14, 50, 51, 73, 137, 145
rival   42, 108, 154, 222, 250, 252, 252n31, 254
Robbins, L.   135
Roberts, J.   288
Robinson, J.   52, 267
Robson, W.   292, 295
Roemer, J.   269, 292
Rohm, W.   254n34, 292
Roman   195, 196, 197, 203
Roncaglia, A.   97, 293
Rosenberg, N.   53n13, 293
Rosentahl, J.-L.   268
Rosovsky, H.   283
Rostow, W.   69, 116n2, 123, 126, 131, 131n19, 132, 132n20, 132n22, 225, 239n8, 293
Rothman, H.   232n34, 283
royalties   40n4, 72, 72n2, 73, 75, 85, 86, 86n15, 87, 87n16, 96, 99n14, 100
rule   16, 17, 50, 129, 195, 232
rulers   154, 155, 175, 177, 179, 182, 186, 199, 201
rules   151, 152, 154, 155, 158, 161, 163, 166, 173, 174, 176, 176n13, 182, 183, 240n10, 257, 258n37
Russia   38, 120
Rustomjee, Z.   2, 91, 279
Rutherford, M.   159, 183n21, 204, 293

Sakshaug, J.   268
sales   55, 109, 110, 253
Sanderson, G.   286, 291
Saville, J.   288
savings   45, 242
Sawyer, M.   46n10, 267, 277, 293
scale, economies of   30, 46, 47, 73, 74, 75, 76, 77, 77n7, 78, 84, 87, 88, 88n18, 89, 90, 94n6, 103, 106, 240, 241

Scandinavia   120
scarcity   96, 173, 197, 227
Schabas, M.   121, 271, 293
Schelling, T.   171n7, 293
Schlesinger, A.   137, 293
Schmalensee, R.   255
Scholz-Wäckerle, M.   275
Schumpeter, J.   129, 147, 224, 260
Schumpeterian   260
Schwartz, A.   14n17, 120, 280
scientific   10n14, 17, 27, 27n29, 52, 124, 125, 127n14, 128, 131, 133, 242n12, 249, 249n26, 250
Scotland   82, 83, 87n16, 99n14
second-hand   60, 64
sector   31n33, 45, 48, 51, 54, 106, 112, 113, 151, 261n43, 263
sectors   25, 46, 48, 49, 93, 106, 113, 150
self-interest   33, 33n36, 34n38, 50, 53, 125, 126, 130, 142, 145, 155, 157, 167, 171
Sen, A.   31, 31n34, 31n35, 32, 33, 274, 279, 293
serfdom   179, 180, 190, 192, 193, 193n31, 194, 199, 200, 201, 202, 203, 220
servants   54, 55, 57, 58, 59, 60, 66, 67
services   31n33, 63, 131, 150, 154, 199, 200, 202, 203, 250
seventeenth century   180, 194, 249
sexism   123
Sharman, J.   148n9, 257, 269
Shields, J.   273, 293
Shiller, R.   27n30, 266n48, 293
shirking   153, 166, 173, 201
short run   42, 43, 50, 95n8, 240n11, 243n14, 251, 259n39
Siebert, H.   293
Simister, J   2n4, 280
Simon, H.   161, 163, 174n10, 295, 296
Sinha, D.   272
sixteenth century   202
sixth century   198
skills   15, 52, 66, 223, 226, 227, 240
Slatalla, S.   254n34, 255n36, 292
Slater, G.   198, 218n16, 293
slavery   6, 17, 120, 125, 129n17, 130, 136, 144, 145, 150, 162, 171, 178, 179, 180, 193, 200, 201, 202, 203, 220
Smith, Adam   24, 39, 46, 49, 53, 53n13, 58, 116n2, 128, 147, 223, 242, 242n12, 293, 296

Smith, R. 24, 39, 46, 49, 53, 53*n*13, 58, 116*n*2, 128, 147, 223, 242, 242*n*12, 293, 296

Snooks, G. 240*n*11, 242*n*12, 243*n*14, 272, 293, 294

SOAS, School of Oriental and African Studies 2, 141*n*4

social change 19, 37, 38, 52, 58, 69, 145, 193

social choice 2, 2*n*5, 31, 32

social practices 184*n*23, 187, 187*n*25

social relations 52, 57, 61, 66, 67, 68, 96, 100, 129*n*17, 191, 196, 216

social sciences IX, 3, 4, 5, 7, 8, 9, 12, 14, 15, 17, 18, 27, 30, 31, 40, 93, 119, 121, 131, 133, 136, 137, 140, 140*n*1, 141, 142, 143, 145, 147, 148, 159, 166, 167, 168, 170, 170*n*2, 171, 171*n*7, 187*n*25, 189*n*29, 206, 207*n*2, 209, 211*n*11, 216, 223, 224, 227, 230, 233, 235, 237, 241, 265

social structure 146, 183*n*22, 184*n*23, 186, 187*n*25, 191, 192, 197

social system 159, 184, 184*n*23, 185, 186, 187*n*25, 188, 189*n*29, 193

social systems 184*n*23, 185

social theory 4, 119, 148, 159, 168, 216, 217, 220, 227, 229, 230, 231

socio-economic 52, 138, 185, 189, 191, 263, 264

sociology 4*n*9, 20, 27, 30, 127*n*14, 128, 141, 142, 145*n*7, 160, 225, 227*n*26, 230*n*32, 248*n*25

software 30, 234, 246*n*19, 254, 254*n*34, 255, 255*n*36, 256

Solow, R. 13, 131, 239, 294

Sombart, W. 42, 294

Sonin, K. 267

South Africa IX, 1*n*2, 2, 31*n*33, 91, 92*n*1, 93, 94, 94*n*4, 100, 107, 109, 110, 115, 245*n*18, 262

south Wales 81, 82, 83, 85

sovereignty 106, 192, 197

Sowell, T. 53*n*14, 294

Spain 180

spatial 87, 94, 99, 100, 246*n*21, 249

specialisation 178, 181, 199, 217

Spencer, D. 198, 218*m*16, 293

Spindletop XI, 104, 105f.2, 106f.3

stability 83, 107, 108, 110, 112, 158, 159, 166, 167, 171*n*5, 173, 176, 179, 182, 202, 256, 262

stages 1, 1*m*1, 26, 53, 56, 69, 94, 104, 112, 113, 113*n*25, 114, 122*n*7, 127, 128, 131, 132, 139, 146, 152, 153*n*11, 167, 169, 171, 188, 189, 212, 220, 239, 262, 263, 264

stagnation 46, 96, 112, 113, 195

Stallabrass, J. 255*n*36, 294

Stampp, K. 131, 294

Standard Oil 108, 109*n*22, 111

Stasavage, D. 23, 294

state 1, 3, 8, 23, 25, 39, 45, 66, 67, 68, 71, 73, 74, 75, 79, 83, 84, 91, 92, 99, 108, 109, 110, 112, 113, 113*n*25, 133*n*23, 151, 153, 154, 157, 160, 166, 172*n*8, 173, 175, 176, 177, 178, 179, 180, 182, 186, 188, 189, 192, 194, 195, 196*n*35, 197, 199, 199*n*37, 205, 212, 217, 223, 236, 246, 250, 254, 257, 258, 260, 261*n*42, 263

   absolutist 194

   developmental 2, 247*n*23, 260, 261*n*42

   intervention 1, 3, 39, 45, 73, 91, 112, 236

   nation- 180, 193

statics 95, 151, 176

statistical 2, 9, 10*n*14, 12, 17, 20, 23, 26*n*27, 27, 29, 30, 36, 43, 54, 74, 74*n*3, 75, 76, 76*n*6, 78, 82, 121, 123, 124, 125, 129, 134, 137, 137*n*29, 142, 145, 147, 246, 265

steel 64*n*15, 120

Stigler, G. 14, 162, 294

Stiglitz, J. 3, 206, 210*n*8, 224, 224*n*23, 260*n*41, 294

Stilwell, F. 292, 294

stochastic 4, 21, 22, 147, 237, 243, 244, 246

Stock, J. 43*n*9

strategies 14, 16, 32, 34, 35, 47, 154, 211, 213, 237*n*3, 238, 249, 253, 261, 262

strike 71, 72

structural 4, 20, 79, 84, 87, 160, 177, 182, 183, 184*n*23, 185, 186, 187, 187*n*25, 188, 188*n*29, 192, 205, 213, 247*n*23

structuration 185

structure 41, 47, 52, 54, 61, 79, 87, 111, 112, 135, 151, 155, 158, 159, 160*n*15, 161, 164, 174, 178, 182, 183*n*20, 184, 184*n*23, 185, 187, 187*n*25, 189, 190, 191, 192, 194, 195, 205, 214*n*13, 217

structured 38, 52, 54, 165

structures 1, 51, 92, 145, 153, 158, 159, 183, 184, 184*n*23, 185, 186, 195, 216, 219, 242, 260

students 12, 119, 123, 232*n*34

subjective 131, 141, 148, 158, 159, 163, 183, 187, 188*n*29, 202, 257

Supple, B.   3*n*6, 74*n*5, 87, 113, 134, 294

supply   4, 8, 37, 38, 40, 42, 43, 44, 45, 46, 47,
48, 50, 51, 51*n*12, 52, 53, 54, 55, 66, 69, 70,
77, 94, 94*n*4, 95*n*8, 96, 97, 104, 108, 109,
130, 145, 226, 246, 258*n*37, 259*n*39

surplus   23, 72, 86, 92, 93, 97, 98, 112, 114, 192,
193, 194, 197

Sutch, R.   171*n*6, 273, 292, 294

Sutton, J.   213*n*13, 214*n*13, 294

Swedberg, R.   141, 268, 293, 294

Sweezy, P.   38, 46*n*10, 107, 112, 268, 276,
278, 294

symbolic   31, 40, 62, 122*n*8, 129

Szirmai, A.   290, 295

Tabellini, G.   22*n*23, 291

tailoring   63, 64, 66

tastes. *See also* choice and preferences   41*n*6,
53*n*13, 54, 55, 58, 59, 60, 61, 63, 65, 66,
67, 132*n*22, 241

tastes. *See also* choice, preferences and
tastes   68*n*16

taxes   49, 154, 180, 194

teaching   1, 2, 16, 121*n*7, 122, 129, 130

technical   2*n*5, 9, 10, 12, 14, 15, 20*n*20, 25, 26,
26*n*27, 28, 29, 34*n*38, 41, 50, 52, 63, 78,
94, 95, 98, 106, 113, 126, 156*n*13, 181, 190,
196*n*33, 215, 227, 239, 240, 241, 242, 245,
245*n*18, 246*n*21, 247*n*23, 249*n*26, 251,
252, 258, 258*n*37, 260, 260*n*41

techniques   15, 24*n*26, 27, 30, 41, 63, 75, 77*n*7,
78, 127*n*14, 128*n*15, 145, 161, 196, 227, 230,
232, 243, 244, 252*n*31

technology   4, 14, 15, 25, 29, 29*n*31, 43, 46, 54,
61, 89, 90, 115, 132*n*22, 146, 152, 156, 159,
164, 177, 180, 180*n*19, 181, 182, 183, 192,
220, 236*n*2, 239, 244, 245, 247, 248, 249,
249*n*26, 252, 252*n*31, 253

Teich, M   288, 295

Temin, P.   209, 210, 211, 212, 222, 229*n*30, 264,
273, 283, 285, 295

tendencies   41, 44, 52, 62, 96, 97, 108, 133, 154,
177, 191, 196*n*35, 216, 245

tenth century   199, 203

tenure, academic   2*n*5

Thaler, R.   142, 295

Thatcher, M.   71, 74*n*3

Thatcherism   36

theoretical   8, 17, 23, 29, 31, 36, 42, 43, 45, 46,
48, 52, 79, 85, 92, 94, 94*n*6, 97, 99, 100,
103*n*19, 113, 123, 144, 149*n*10, 151, 152,
166, 169, 171, 172, 175, 176, 177, 181, 182,
186, 188, 188*n*27, 190, 193, 198, 200, 201,
203, 204, 205, 211*n*11, 215, 224, 225, 229,
231, 237, 240, 240*n*11, 241, 250*n*27, 251,
258, 262

Therborn, G.   197, 295

Thirsk, J.   68*n*17, 295

thirteenth century   196, 196*n*33

Thomas, I.   78*n*10, 125, 175, 175*n*11, 178,
179, 180, 190, 192, 193, 199, 200, 201,
201*n*38, 202, 203, 272, 275, 287, 291, 293,
295, 296

Thomas, R.   78*n*10, 125, 175, 175*n*11, 178,
179, 180, 190, 192, 193, 199, 200, 201,
201*n*38, 202, 203, 272, 275, 287, 291, 293,
295, 296

Thornton, T.   294

Thrupp, S.   138*n*30, 295

tools, analytical   10*n*14, 131, 134, 146, 173, 176,
188*n*27, 258*n*37

total factor productivity   25, 29, 43, 43*n*7, 52,
84*n*14, 258, 260

total factor productivity, TFP   25, 29, 43,
43*n*7, 52, 84*n*14, 258, 260

Toye, J.   145*n*7, 198, 203*n*40, 295

Tozer, J.   56, 62, 64, 295

trade   12, 20, 50, 60, 61, 65, 66, 71, 95, 107, 109,
152, 163, 180, 202, 241, 251, 253

traditional   4, 8, 10*n*14, 12, 13, 15, 17, 18, 26,
26*n*28, 38, 40, 41, 46*n*10, 62, 68*n*17, 72,
74, 77, 103, 120, 121, 122, 126, 128, 130,
131, 133, 138, 142, 143, 145, 148, 167, 181,
190, 205, 209, 210, 210*n*8, 211, 216, 222,
223, 226*n*25, 228, 230, 231, 232, 239, 242,
242*n*12, 247, 255*n*36, 258*n*37

transformation   40, 50, 52, 54, 56, 57, 62, 67,
70, 194, 197, 263

transhistorical   177, 189, 220, 250

transition   1, 1*n*3, 53, 57, 135, 172*n*8, 203, 204,
212, 251

transport   49, 74*n*4, 90, 92, 95, 98, 98*n*13, 105

trends   12, 15, 43, 43*n*9, 62, 78, 135, 180, 190,
191, 239

trust   8, 33, 148, 168, 248*n*24, 254

Turner, T.   115, 290

Turrell, R.   100n16, 103, 103n19, 295
twentieth century   10, 13, 16, 45, 62, 65, 66,
        68n16, 72, 112, 263

uncertainty   74n4, 107, 142, 156, 174, 198, 212,
        241, 256
underconsumption   46, 112
underground   74n4, 90, 90n20, 99, 104, 111
unemployment   14, 43n7, 50, 85, 109, 255
uneven development   246, 247n23
United Kingdom   1n2, 10, 83n13, 90, 93,
        94, 94n6, 99n14, 121n7, 122, 123, 140n1,
        225n24, 232, 232n34, 262
United States. See also American   x, 5, 6,
        10, 12, 14, 17, 21, 21n21, 30, 33n36, 85, 93,
        94n6, 104, 108, 111, 112, 115, 118, 119, 120,
        121, 122, 123, 125, 126, 127, 149, 218n16,
        222, 224, 225, 225n24, 227, 232, 232n34,
        238, 254, 262, 263, 264
universal   7, 23, 25, 53, 69, 135, 147, 148, 167,
        168, 176, 189, 198, 212, 213, 220, 221, 230,
        239, 263, 264
University of Chicago   8, 14, 15, 16, 16n18, 17,
        18, 19, 117
urban   41, 62, 70
Uselding, P.   270, 284
utility   4, 27n29, 35, 63, 148, 152, 167, 210,
        210n9, 220, 234

value   1n3, 2, 16n18, 25, 29n31, 39n2, 48, 64,
        66, 69, 73, 79, 86, 92, 96, 97, 97n10, 98,
        112, 113n24, 123, 131, 132, 135, 148, 157, 159,
        160, 163, 164, 190, 197, 230, 242, 247n23,
        251, 256, 257, 264
van Ark, B.   295
van den Besselaar, P.   273, 285
Van der Zwan, N.   286
Van Onselen, C.   295
Vandenberg, P.   157n14, 176n15, 204, 295
variegated   4, 7, 8
Vasta, M.   270
Vatter, H.   53n14, 295
Veblen, T.   68n16
Velthuis, O.   142, 230n32, 295
Verdier, T.   23, 269
virtualism   140
von Tunzelmann, N.   40n3, 296
Voth, H.-J.   21, 296

voting   22, 157

wages   46, 54, 57, 58, 60, 61, 67, 84n14, 101,
        112, 150, 179, 179n18, 180, 194, 197, 200,
        220, 221
Wallace, J.   254n34, 255, 296
Wallis, K.   271, 284
Walton, G.   292
wants   31, 32, 53, 188n29, 211
wardrobe   59, 60, 62, 65
Washburn, J.   250n27
Watson, M.   43n9
wealthy   26n27, 38, 42, 57, 58, 59, 62, 63, 65,
        67, 152, 154, 155, 163, 175n12, 190, 191n30,
        199, 223
Weatherill, L.   44, 47, 48, 49, 296
Weber, M.   136, 159
Wedgwood, Sir Josiah   3, 41, 41n6, 42, 47, 48,
        68, 280, 287, 288
Weingast, B.   171n6, 268, 289
welfare   44, 107, 141, 175
Western   10, 130, 149, 152, 153, 156, 175, 190,
        196, 196n33, 196n34, 199, 242n12
Whaples, R.   120, 296
wholesale   68, 164
Wieland, H.-P.   275
Williams, R.   255n36, 268, 296
Williams, S.   255n36, 268, 296
Williamson, H.   104n20, 198, 245, 270, 296
Williamson, O.   104n20, 198, 245, 267,
        270, 296
Winch, D.   53, 53n14, 296
women   44, 57, 58, 60, 63, 64, 65, 66, 68,
        69n17, 74n4, 104, 162
Wood, G.   284, 289, 292, 293, 294, 295, 296
Wood, J.   284, 289, 292, 293, 294, 295, 296
workers   45, 46, 48, 57, 61, 66, 80, 81, 113, 194,
        220, 255
workforce   69n17, 109, 110, 114
working   3, 19, 21, 33, 34n38, 36, 53n14, 58, 59,
        61, 62, 65, 66, 77, 78, 84n14, 86, 98, 101,
        107, 114, 118, 119, 132n22, 138, 148, 161, 201,
        206, 207, 208, 210n8, 223, 224, 226, 235,
        238, 241, 263
World Bank. See also post Washington
        Consensus   204, 227n27, 246n20,
        264, 265
Wright, G.   177n17, 273, 279, 288

Wright, J.   177*n*17, 273, 279, 288

Yergin, D.   104*n*20, 296
Yoo, C.   270
Yorkshire   82, 85

Young, R.   223, 288, 295

Zafirovski, M.   142, 296
Zingales, L.   217, 292
Zollschan, G.   286, 296